Volume II: Since 1500

W9-BEC-202

DISCOVERING THE GLOBAL PAST

A Look at the Evidence

Merry E. Wiesner
University of Wisconsin—Milwaukee

William Bruce Wheeler
University of Tennessee, Knoxville

Franklin M. Doeringer
Lawrence University

Melvin E. Page
East Tennessee State University

HOUGHTON MIFFLIN COMPANY   Boston   New York

Senior Sponsoring Editor: Patricia A. Coryell
Assistant Editor: Jeanne Herring
Project Editor: Christina Horn
Senior Production/Design Coordinator: Jennifer Waddell
Manufacturing Manager: Florence Cadran

Cover Design: Len Massiglia
Cover Image: Opening of the First Railway in Japan (Shimbashi Station, Tokyo), 19th Century (print), Private Collection, The Bridgeman Art Library

Printed in the U.S.A.
Library of Congress Catalog Card Number: 96-76976
ISBN Student Text: 0-395-69987-8
ISBN Examination Copy: 0-395-84403-7
 3456789-QF-00 99 98

CONTENTS

CHAPTER FIVE
The "Discovery of Childhood" in England and America (1600–1800)   122

CHAPTER SIX
The Atlantic Slave Trade: Its Impact on West Africa (1600–1900)   162

CHAPTER NINE
Industrializing the Nation: Germany and Japan (1860–1900)

CHAPTER TEN
World War I: Global War (1914–1918)   286

CHAPTER FIFTEEN
Globalism and Tribalism: Challenges to the Contemporary Nation-State (1980s–1990s)   436

PREFACE

In 1919, Dean Harry Carman of Columbia University instituted a new course for undergraduates entitled Contemporary Civilization. Intended to broaden students' knowledge about the Western world as the United States emerged from its isolation to become a world leader, "C.C." (as the students quickly named it) spread to other colleges and universities and evolved into what became known as the introductory Western Civilization course, the staple of historical instruction for generations of college students.[1]

The Western Civilization course continues to be important in the shaping of student thought and in the imparting of valuable knowledge. From its inception, however, the course contained a number of inherent problems, chief among them its almost inevitable Eurocentrism—an implicit emphasis on the evolution and progress of the West and a corresponding overlooking or omission of the history of the rest of the globe. Attempting to correct this imbalance, a number of colleges and universities inaugurated courses in World History; in some cases this new course supplanted the Western Civilization course and in others stood side-by-side with it. Responding to the emergence of the "global village" and the increasing diversity of the United States's population, more and more colleges and universities have embraced this global perspective. As with its ancestor, Columbia's "C.C." course, the goal of World History is to provide students with an important introduction to the political, economic, social, and intellectual environment in which they live.

Students in World History courses are often overwhelmed by the amount of material presented, and we as instructors can lose sight of the fact that history is not simply something one learns about; it is something one does. One discovers the past, and what makes this pursuit exciting is not only the past that is discovered but the process of discovery itself. This process can be simultaneously exhilarating and frustrating, enlightening and confusing, but it is always challenging enough to convince those of us who are professional historians to spend our lives at it.

1. Ideas about such a course had been circulating in various American colleges and universities as early as the 1870s, but they got a special boost with the United States's entry into World War I. See Gilbert Allardyce, "The Rise and Fall of the Western Civilization Course," *American Historical Review*, 87 (June 1982), pp. 695–725; and Lawrence W. Levine, *The Opening of the American Mind: Canons, Culture, and History* (Boston: Beacon, 1996), especially pp. 54–74.

The primary goal of *Discovering the Global Past: A Look at the Evidence* is to allow students enrolled in world history courses to *do* history in the same way that we as historians do—to examine a group of original sources to answer questions about the past. The unique structure of this book clusters primary sources around a set of historical questions that students are asked to "solve." Unlike a source reader, this book prompts students to actually *analyze* a wide variety of authentic primary source material, to make inferences, and to draw conclusions in much the same way that historians do.

The evidence in this book is more varied than that in most source collections. We have included such visual evidence as coins, paintings, statues, literary illustrations, historical photographs, maps, cartoons, advertisements, and political posters. In choosing written evidence we again have tried to offer a broad sample—eulogies, wills, court records, oral testimonies, and statistical data all supplement letters, newspaper articles, speeches, memoirs, and other more traditional sources.

In order for students to learn history the way we as historians do, they must not only be confronted with the evidence, they must also learn how to use that evidence to arrive at a conclusion. In other words, they must learn historical methodology. Too often methodology (or even the notion that historians *have* a methodology) is reserved for upper-level majors or graduate students; beginning students are simply presented with historical facts and interpretations without being shown how these were unearthed or formulated. Students may learn that historians hold different interpretations of the significance of an event or individual or different ideas about causation, but they are not informed of how historians come to such conclusions.

Thus, along with evidence, we have provided explicit suggestions about how one might analyze that evidence, guiding students as they reach their own conclusions. As they work through the various chapters, students will discover not only that the sources of historical information are wide-ranging, but that the methodologies appropriate to understanding and using them are equally diverse. By doing history themselves, students will learn how intellectual historians handle philosophical treatises, economic historians quantitative data, social historians court records, and political and diplomatic historians theoretical treatises and memoirs. They will also be asked to consider the limitations of their evidence, to explore what historical questions it cannot answer as well as those it can. Instead of passive observers, students become active participants.

Each chapter is divided into six parts: The Problem, Background, The Method, The Evidence, Questions to Consider, and Epilogue. Each of the parts relates to or builds upon the others, creating a uniquely integrated chapter structure that helps guide the reader through the analytical process. "The Problem" section begins with a brief discussion of the central issues of the chapter and then states the questions students will explore. A "Background" section follows, designed to help students understand the historical context of the problem. The section called "The Method" gives students suggestions for studying and analyzing the evidence. "The Evidence" section is the heart of the chapter, providing a variety of primary source material on the particular historical event or issue described in the chapter's "Problem" section. The section called "Questions to Consider" focuses students' attention on specific evidence and on linkages among different evidence material. The "Epilogue" section gives the aftermath or the historical outcome of the evidence—what happened to the people involved, the results of a debate, and so on.

Within this framework, we have tried to present a series of historical issues and events of significance to the instructor as well as of interest to the student. We have also aimed to provide a balance among political, social, diplomatic, intellectual, and cultural history. In other words, we have attempted to create a kind of historical sampler that we believe will help students learn the methods and skills used by historians. Not only will these skills—analyzing arguments, developing hypotheses, comparing evidence, testing conclusions, and reevaluating material—enable students to master historical content; they will also provide the necessary foundation for critical thinking in other college courses and after college as well.

Because the amount of material in global history is so vast, we had to pick certain topics and geographic areas to highlight, though here too we have aimed at a balance. Some chapters are narrow in focus, providing students with an opportunity to delve deeply into a single case study, while others ask students to make comparisons among individuals, events, or developments in different cultures. We have included cultural comparisons that are frequently discussed in World History courses, such as classical Rome and Han China, as well as more unusual ones, such as peasant family life in early modern central Europe and Southeast Asia.

Discovering the Global Past is designed to accommodate any format of the World History course, from the small lecture/discussion class at a liberal arts or community college to the large lecture with discussions led by teaching assistants at a sizable university. The chapters may be used for individual assignments, team projects, class discussions, papers, and exams. Each is self-contained, so that any combination may be assigned. The book is not intended to replace a standard textbook, and it was written to accompany any World History text the instructor chooses. The Instructor's Resource Manual, written by the authors of the text, offers further suggestions for class discussion, as well as a variety of ways in which students' learning may be evaluated and annotated lists of recommendations for further reading.

A note on spellings: Many of the sources presented in this book were originally written in a language other than English, and often in an alphabet other than the Western (Roman) one. Over the centuries translators have devised various means of representing the sounds of other languages, and these conventions of translation have also changed over time. In general, we have used the most current spelling and orthographic conventions in our discussions and have left spellings as they appeared in the original translation in the sources. This means, for example, that Indian, Arabic, and Japanese words often have diacritical marks in the sources but not in our own material. For Chinese, in our own text we have used the pinyin system developed by the Chinese in the 1950s, with pinyin spellings indicated in brackets in the sources, most of which use the older Wade-Giles system.

We would like to thank the many students and instructors who have helped us in our efforts. We extend our gratitude to the following professors, who read and criticized the manuscript throughout its development:

Charles M. Barber, *Northeastern Illinois University*

Charlotte L. Beahan, *Murray State University*

Norman R. Bennett, *Boston University*

Matthew Ware Coulter, *Collin County Community College*

Linda T. Darling, *University of Arizona*

Steven C. Davidson, *Southwestern University*

L.T. Easley, *Campbell University*

Alexander Grab, *University of Maine*

Laird Jones, *Lock Haven University*

Carol Loats, *University of Southern Colorado*

Francisco A. Marmalejo, *Irvine Valley College*

Marilyn Morris, *University of North Texas*

Jim Rice, *Central Washington University*

Robert M. Seltzer, *Hunter College of the City University of New York*

Thomas C. Tirado, *Millersville University of Pennsylvania*

In addition to our colleagues across the United States, we would like to thank especially our colleagues at the University of Wisconsin—Milwaukee; the University of Tennessee, Knoxville; Lawrence University; and East Tennessee State University. Merry E. Wiesner wishes especially to thank Barbara Andaya, Judith Bennett, Mark Bradley, Holly Brewer, Martha Carlin, Jean Fleet, Marija Gajdardziska-Josifovska, Faye Getz, Michael Gordon, Abbas Hamdani, Anne Hansen, Jean Johnson, Jeffrey Merrick, Sheilagh Ogilvie, Jean Quataert, and Jane Waldbaum. Bruce Wheeler would like to thank Thomas Burman, Robert Bast, Todd Diacon, J. Daniel Bing, Owen Bradley, Palmira Brummett, W. Wayne Farris, Yen-ping Hao, and Vejas Liulevicius.

Franklin M. Doeringer wishes to thank all of his colleagues in the Lawrence University Department of History for their support and interest in this project. J. Michael Hittle and Edmund M. Kern deserve particular mention for reading over portions of manuscript and offering helpful comments. He also expresses his gratitude to Jane Parish Yang and Kuo-ming Sung in the Department of East Asian Languages and Cultures for their suggestions on material pertaining to China and East Asia. Finally, he extends special thanks to Peter J. Gilbert of the Lawrence library for his unflagging help in tracking down elusive sources and obscure references. Melvin E. Page would like to thank particularly the following colleagues and students: Steve Fritz, Jim Odom, Shannon Vance, Nancy Roy, Tim Carmichael, Julie Lind, Scott Bailey, and Grady Eades.

Finally, we would like to thank Jeanne Herring, Christina Horn, and the rest of the staff at Houghton Mifflin for their support.

M.E.W.

W.B.W.

F.M.D.

M.E.P.

CHAPTER ONE

CONCEPTUALIZING THE

MODERN WORLD (1500s)

A revolution in the way Europeans envisioned the world helped to launch the modern age of global interaction and interdependence. Renaissance scholarship, which altered so much of Western thought during the *Quattrocento,* or 1400s, changed the way in which Europeans understood and mapped the earth. They began to picture the earth on a new scale and to regard it as a global whole between whose parts long-distance maritime travel seemed not only conceivable but practical. Inspired by this vision, European captains like Columbus ventured out beyond familiar waters, exploring the entire globe and drawing its once separate regions and people into a single integrated world. More than anyone else, it was a Flemish mathematician and chart maker, Gerhardus Mercator (1512–1594), who helped express this new conception. In 1569 he won renown for a world map whose "projection," or way of translating the curved surface of the earth to a flat plane, solved a key

technical problem among cartographers and made a better map for navigators. First hailed as a practical navigational tool, Mercator's map later gained popularity among Europe's academic circles during the Scientific Revolution in the seventeenth century. With Europe's rise to global mastery, westernizing people everywhere adopted the map, making it the standard image of the modern world.

Though often associated with a modern, scientific point of view, the Mercator Projection Map does not provide an accurate picture of the earth's actual surface. In fact, it seriously distorts a number of features. For this reason, it has always drawn criticism of some sort. Recent critics, however, object to the perspective of the map, which they find highly ethnocentric. They argue that the map presents an image of the world shaped by Western values rather than scientific principles. Some opponents have even called upon international agencies to reject Mercator-style maps in favor of other depictions of the world. But the choice of alternatives creates fresh controversy because to one extent or another all world maps distort reality.

Of course professional map makers, or cartographers, have long been aware that mapping the globe inevitably entails distortion. More than anyone else, they realize that only on a sphere can the earth's curved surface accurately be duplicated: all efforts to depict it on a flat map require alteration of its shape. The logical solution would be to draw all maps on globes, but practical considerations make this difficult to do. Any large map of the world with a scale sufficient to show significant detail, particularly the kind of detail a navigator needs, would require a huge globe. Thus cartographers have always accepted the drawbacks in the nearly impossible task of projecting a spherical reality onto a flat plane to produce inexpensive and manageable maps.

In addition to this fundamental distortion, cartographers have often simplified or changed elements of their maps to help users find what they want to know more quickly or easily. The use of different-sized circles to show cities of varying population or the superimposition of colored lines to indicate elevations represent distortions of this sort. Besides these features, which result from conscious decisions, still other distortions may arise from unconscious choices. How a cartographer orients a map, frames it, and selects what to include in it, for example, may reflect prevailing beliefs of the time rather than specific cartographic needs. Maps thus cannot be viewed as simple depictions of geographic facts; often they reflect intellectual and cultural landscapes as well.

Accordingly this chapter looks at how maps present mental as well as geographic realities. It treats them like any other historical document and studies the way they reflect the values and outlook of their makers. Some of these reflections may be highly personal, but because map makers generally work in the context of established conventions, they more often project cultural rather than individual visions. Maps thus offer historians an important means of studying the perspectives of the past. And this chapter asks you to consider the Mercator Projection Map in this light. After reviewing the evidence, ask yourself, what cultural conventions helped shape the Mercator map? And what are the implications of such a culturally informed, scientific work? Doing so will not only show how cultural factors affect the way people see reality but offer insights into the way we have visualized the modern world.

BACKGROUND

The Mercator Projection Map derives from a long tradition of Western cartography, or map making. Begun in ancient Greece, it initially reflected an interest in cosmology or the nature of the universe rather than practical travel. Fascinated with ideal systems, the Greeks believed that a rational and harmonious order underlay the natural world, patterning it in perfect, geometric forms. This belief led the Pythagorean school of the fifth century B.C.E. to envision the world mathematically and to depict it as a sphere, the shape they deemed most nearly perfect. This vision reflected cosmological assumptions rather than empirical study. Greek thinkers believed the earth nestled at the core of a series of concentric, transparent orbs that rotated around it at varying rates, carrying with them the sun, moon, and planets. Calling this system the Celestial Sphere, they claimed its rhythmic motions gave visible proof of nature's harmony. Early Greek map makers thus looked to the sky and abstract mathematics when charting the Earth.

This approach led them to develop a gridwork-like system of imaginary lines to locate places on a map. One of the first Greek cartographers, Eratosthenes (276–195 B.C.E.), arbitrarily drew nine north-south lines, or *meridians*, through what he judged to be well-known or important cities. He located most of his east-west lines, or *parallels*, with equal arbitrariness but tried to relate them to celestial order by basing some of them on the *klimata*, imaginary lines associated with the sun's apparent seasonal movement, which we know as the equator and the tropics of Cancer and Capricorn. Unaware that the seasons resulted from a tilting of the earth's axis, the Greeks attributed them to an annual north-south shift of the sun across the globe. They thus named the paths that the sun appeared to trace across the sky at its most extreme summer and winter positions "tropics," meaning a "turning." Because the sun "turned" in its extreme summer path when the constellation

Cancer dominated the sky, the Greeks termed this path the tropic of Cancer. And they named its opposite path after the constellation Capricorn, which formed the backdrop for its winter "turning." Though visualized in the sky these paths could be mentally projected on the earth.

Hipparchus, an astronomer of the second century B.C.E., favored a more mathematically precise system with all parallels equally spaced and perpendicular to the meridians. The latter he envisioned as great circles, evenly located around the equator and convergent at the poles. His system appealed to Claudius Ptolemy, a Greek scholar of the second century C.E., who used it for a world map in his *Geographia*, a treatise on the nature of the earth. Ptolemy tried to align his gridwork even more closely with celestial order by deriving its measurement from the "equinoctial hour," or time of the equinoxes when the daylight and darkness are equal. Thus he laid out parallels so that each one marked a point where at the time of the equinox the length of the day would be fifteen minutes longer, obtaining regularly spaced lines that seemingly reflected cosmic intervals. He located meridians similarly, spacing them out evenly along the equator at intervals of "the third part of an equinoctial hour."

Ptolemy also grappled with the problem of distortion. Noting the need for a "certain adjustment" to allow a spherical surface to be depicted on a flat plane, he represented the meridians as straight lines at the equator but made them converge toward the poles and drew the parallels as arcs sharing a common center along the earth's axis. He claimed his approach succeeded in representing a curved surface on a flat plane. But as he openly admitted, this compromise was problematic, "since it is impossible for all of the parallels to keep the proportion that there is in a sphere."[1] His adjustment produced what modern cartographers term a conic projection, which distorts details in the polar regions but depicts mid-latitudes well. On this abstract grid, well-suited to a Mediterranean based map, Ptolemy laid out his conception of the world.

He put North at the top, a convention followed by modern Western cartography and one of its most obvious hallmarks. As he lacked information about the northern polar region and most of the southern hemisphere, he left out these areas, claiming that "the extent of our habitable earth from east to west all concede is much greater than its extent from the north pole to the south." His world map—to judge from surviving copies—included only twenty-one parallels north of the equator and one south of it. Like most Greeks of his time, he assumed that the equatorial zone must be uninhabitable due to its heat. He also ignored the Pacific side of the world about which he knew nothing, a factor that led him to inflate Eurasia while reducing the apparent diameter of the earth. Therefore, although called a world map, Ptolemy's work showed only a segment confined to Europe, North Africa, and parts of western and southern Asia.

Though Ptolemy's map became the standard world map during Roman times, it fell out of favor following the fall of Rome in the first centuries of the common era. As Rome declined, Hellenistic culture derived from Greek roots waned with it. Christianity, however, thrived, and around its beliefs a new mentality began to form. Christian thinkers deemed the natural world an imperfect reflection of a higher, divine reality. In their view, physical things merely obscured divine truth, which revealed itself directly to intellect through the spirit. Thus, they had little motive to study the natural world much less to model the earth with mathematical precision or to map its actual contours. More important to them was a symbolic map showing spiritual landmarks to divine grace. A new tradition of *mappæ mundi,* or world maps, thus evolved to meet this need in the sixth and seventh centuries. Though derived from diagrammatic Roman maps, they defined a new, medieval vision of the world quite unlike the older Hellenistic conception.

Because these maps show the earth as a perfect circle divided into three parts by a T-shaped confluence of waters, scholars today generally term them T-O maps. Its exact origin remains uncertain, but the T-O map had assumed its essential form by the seventh century. An early example appears in an encyclopedic work of that century, called the *Etymologies,* written by Isidore of Seville. Many subsequent variations survive. Highly influenced by passages in the Chris-

1. For Ptolemy's remarks, see *The Geography of Claudius Ptolemy,* trans. and ed. Edward L. Stevenson (New York, 1932), bk. I, chaps. XXI–XXIII, pp. 41–42.

tian Bible, all typically portray the world as a circle ("the circle of the earth" in Isaiah 40:22) surrounded by an encircling *Mare Oceanus,* or Ocean Sea. From this flow the waters that meet in the center to divide the land into the three continents of Asia, Africa, and Europe.

Unlike Ptolemy's map, T-O maps put the East at the top, giving prominence to paradise, which Genesis (2:8) located "eastward in Eden." This convention explains why *orientation,* or "eastward pointing," means taking correct bearings. Thus Asia appears above the other continents, separated from them by the rivers Tanais (the modern Don) on the left and the Nile on the right. The Mediterranean Sea, drawn as a simple perpendicular bisecting these two rivers and forming the stem of the T, occurs as a central feature partitioning Europe from Africa. Most maps also indicate a few important cities, particularly Jerusalem, which they symbolically place near the center of the map. Few actual geographic features appear, though these maps depict many sites of religious significance to Christians.

The medieval iconographical approach to cartography, like the Greek cosmological approach, produced maps for intellectual contemplation but of little practical value. Throughout ancient and medieval times in the West, however, travelers needed maps to help them find their way across land and sea. Hence a quite separate tradition of practical route maps developed to serve their needs. The Romans had a tradition of road maps that dated back at least to the time of Julius Caesar who ordered his son-in-law, Marcus Agrippa, to chart imperial highways. No actual Roman versions of this map, which was engraved on a marble slab in the Forum at Rome, remain, but its appearance may be duplicated in an eleventh- or twelfth-century copy of a late Roman road map of the empire known as the Peutinger Table (*Tabula Peutinger*). It shows highways together with sufficient schematic renditions of towns, rivers, and mountains to help a traveler maintain proper bearings. But it grossly distorts landforms, and the overall effect is that of a cartoon. Nonetheless, maps of this sort, like the Ebstorf map of Germany, continued in use during the European Middle Ages to illustrate routes of pilgrimage in guidebooks. Because texts provided most information, these maps merely showed towns, abbeys, crossroads, and so on as stylized icons.

European seafarers, however, needed more accurate maps. By late medieval times, they used two types, both of which were essential navigational aids. One was a partially blank map of open waters upon which navigators could lay out new courses; the other was a commercial chart of common coastal areas. The latter, sold in bound sets called *portolani* (Italian for "harbor books") in Mediterranean waters, provided navigators with detailed information on how to pilot ships using coastal landmarks. Devised for seamen, both represented an empirical approach to cartography unlike those used by earlier scholars whose world maps were tailored to suit abstract mathematical or theological principles. Most had a very limited focus. But an eight-panel work known as the Catalan Atlas, created by Abraham Cresques for King Charles V of France in 1375, shows the sea lanes from Britain and the Canary Islands in the west to the coast of India. Such *portolani* sets attest to a growing interest among Europeans in visualizing a larger world in more practical terms. The way navigators charted courses also began to reflect this interest.

Pilot maps gave landmarks from which a position might be taken by sight, but sailing charts used an abstract system of lines to help sailors keep their bearing when sailing out of view of land. This system had nothing to do with the old Greek gridwork of meridians and parallels. It was based instead on a web-like pattern of "lines of rhumb" (from the Spanish word *rhumba,* meaning a "ship's heading") upon which courses could be laid out. These lines indicated hypothetical bearings leading off to a number of abstract points, or "quarters," equally distributed around the world's edge—envisioned as an encircling Ocean Sea. The points to which the lines radiated were named after conventional "winds," or storm fronts, thought to originate near them. By the late Middle Ages, this device, which went back to Roman days, evolved into a system of eight primary points, four full and four half-winds, that could be expanded further by the addition of quarter- and eighth-winds. When all thirty-two such points were drawn, the resulting figure looked like a many petaled flower; and so it was called a "wind rose."

By drawing the points of the wind rose out into radiating lines of rhumb,

chart makers created a basic star-shaped design, which could be repeated regularly on a blank map to create an overlapping webwork of lines. Upon this webwork they then drew in coastlines and seas so that navigators could plot courses between landfalls parallel to the imaginary lines of rhumb. This system was so well established that Europeans adapted it for use with the compass when they obtained that device from the Arabs in the early 1300s, simply realigning the lines of rhumb to the cardinal compass points. By the 1500s, Flemish cartographers, then the leading chart makers of Europe, replaced the traditional names of the winds with the French terms for the compass points and used the fleur-de-lis, the French royal symbol, to mark North, the key point.

Like so many other aspects of European culture, map making changed with the fifteenth-century revival of classical Mediterranean learning. New interest in Greek thought rekindled speculation about the nature of the world and brought a shift in cartography. Ptolemy's world map, rediscovered in Byzantine copies, became popular again, as the development of the printing press in Germany allowed relatively inexpensive editions of his *Geographia* to circulate widely. Though underestimating the circumference of the earth and filled with errors, Ptolemy's map broadened European horizons. Unlike *portolani* and course-plotting charts, which remained too localized to inspire ventures into the unknown, the Ptolemaic map, as a theoretical construct, indicated uncharted areas as well as known regions. When redrawn with the system of rhumb line coordinates superimposed upon it, it offered mariners a global context in which to project new sailing routes. Thus the merger of the old, Greek cosmological style of cartography with medieval navigational conventions created a new, practical map of the world that promoted exploration.

Fifteenth-century Portuguese captains used updated versions of the Ptolemaic map to plot their voyages around Africa to India, and Columbus based his belief in the feasibility of sailing westward to Asia on them. Columbus's letters, in fact, clearly show that he obtained Ptolemaic-style charts from Paolo da Pozzo Toscanelli (1397–1482), a leading Florentine scholar and map maker who also advised King Alfonso of Portugal on sea routes around Africa. Though none remain, we know what Toscanelli's charts looked like because they were based on a world map that *has* survived. Known as the Martellus map after the name of its maker, Henricus Martellus, who drew it in 1489 on the eve of Europe's age of exploration, this map also inspired the Flemish chart maker Gerhardus Mercator.

Mercator's goal was not only to make an up-to-date world map but to create a better navigational tool for those sailing in unfamiliar waters far from Europe. Like most world maps of the mid-sixteenth century, it tried to show the Americas and Pacific Ocean in proper relationship to the Old World of Eurasia and Africa. But what really made it innovative was Mercator's effort to depict the earth's curved surface on a flat plane in a way that allowed mariners to plot

more accurate courses. As European sailors ventured on long voyages that eventually took them around the world, they found that plotting courses on a global map like Ptolemy's using conventional rhumb lines led to problems. The lines that appeared to be straight on the maps actually represented courses arching over the curved surface of the earth. On short voyages such as those in the Mediterranean, the discrepancy proved insignifcant. But on long voyages, ships on headings plotted as straight lines strayed far off course, and if sailing in uncharted regions without known landmarks by which to correct the error, they became hopelessly lost. True lines of rhumb, known as *loxodromes* (from the Greek words for "oblique running"), must take this curvature into account. But if drawn as curved lines on a flat map surface, they do not intersect meridians in the identical oblique angles that mariners needed to check their course bearings with a sextant.

Mercator wanted to solve this problem by making a world map that compensated for the curvature of the earth but allowed navigators to plot courses as straight lines intersecting meridians at constant angles. He did so, as he noted on the face of his 1569 map, by devising "a new proportion and a new arrangement of the meridians with reference to the parallels." His method was simple. It merely required drawing meridians parallel rather than convergent at the poles. Made this way, meridians and parallels coincided exactly with the north-south and east-west axes of the conventional wind rose pattern, and all the lines of rhumb radiating outward maintained constant angles with respect to them. Of course, this created another distortion, since true meridians form great circles around the earth that *do* converge at the poles.

This distortion, though barely noticeable at the equator where meridians almost parallel one another, becomes extreme near the poles. There, where they should converge, Mercator's meridians remain apart, grossly distorting all features. They make east-west distances near the poles appear much greater than they are and skew alignments out of proportion. To compensate, Mercator spaced the parallels or lines of longitude ever farther apart toward the poles so that their spacing increased in exact measure to the progressive spread of the meridians. By thus making a mile at the equator much shorter than a mile at the poles, Mercator minimized the way his projection contorted shapes near the poles. But this compensation makes landforms toward the polar regions appear much larger than they really are. Mercator, who was himself aware of this problem, found a partial solution by simply leaving the polar regions off of his map. Because nothing was

known about them in his time and most important sea lanes lay closer to the equator than the poles of the earth, gross polar distortion seemed a small price to pay for a very practical new kind of map.

Mercator's method of mapping caught on in Europe. Mercator himself won it acclaim through a three-volume set of maps that he and his son published from 1585 to 1595, coining the term *atlas* to designate a comprehensive cartographical survey of the world. But other Flemish map makers helped to popularize it. A fellow Fleming, Abrahim Ortel, used it to prepare maps for a book published in 1570 under the name *Theatrum Orbis Terrarum*. Soon others followed suit, most notably Jocondus Hondius who kept various versions of Mercator's map in print until 1637. Because of the high regard enjoyed by Flemish map makers at this time, European cartographers elsewhere followed their lead. Mercator's approach thus became the map on which explorers charted their findings and through which the image of the modern world first emerged. But, as recent critics charge, that image was far from objective.

THE METHOD

The task of determining the cultural perspective of the Mercator map, as you might guess, requires you to deal with cartographic materials. Therefore, maps make up the primary material presented in the Evidence section. Some illustrate the Western map-making tradition that formed the background of Mercator's work, whereas others depict alternate ways of portraying the globe. Comparisons between these materials and Mercator's map should help you detect the special features of the Mercator Projection Map and determine what elements it emphasizes at the expense of others.

Sources 1 and 2 show Mercator's original world map of 1569 and a standard modern map based on his projection. These are followed by reconstructions of two ancient maps from the classical Mediterranean world, Sources 3 and 4, illustrating the Greek tradition of cartography. Sources 5 through 7 present three examples of the diagrammatic and T-O shaped *mappæ mundi* produced in Europe during the Middle Ages. By way of contrast, Sources 8 through 10 display how differently people in some other cultures saw the world: Source 8 reproduces a twelfth-century Islamic map, and Sources 9 and 10 demonstrate the perspective of traditional Chinese cartographers. A fourteenth-century Catalan sea chart, Source 11, and a Florentine world map of 1489, Source 12, give some indication of the shift that came in Western map making with the Renaissance and created the immediate cartographic context in which Mercator worked. Finally, Source 13, a contemporary equal-area map, shows an alternate vision of the world advocated by those favoring a more global perspective.

An analysis of these different maps should allow you to uncover the conceptual framework of Mercator's map and recognize the cultural conventions reflected in it. Such an approach does not demand great expertise with the technical details of cartography. It does, however, ask you to consider the Mercator map as a cultural artifact and to approach it as a cultural historian would, view-ing it not so much as a device showing what the world actually looks like but as an abstraction reflecting the outlook of its creators. In other words, it requires you to "read" Mercator's map as a cultural document rather than a statement of geographic fact. To do so, you will have to look beyond its geographic details for clues to the values and assumptions that helped to shape it. Of course, to distinguish these elements in the first place, you need some awareness of the basic conventions of traditional map making.

Unfortunately, we do not have a lot of maps from which to reconstruct those conventions. Usually designed to be portable, most were made of lightweight, fragile materials that did not survive for very long. Until the start of the modern age of printing in the West during the fifteenth century, maps tended to be rare, handmade objects. Only a few, therefore, have come down to us from earlier times, particularly from the ancient world and distant cultures. And those that have are almost all handmade copies fraught with the errors and variants common to copies. So our understanding of old maps remains sketchy, and many questions plague efforts to study them. Nonetheless, enough survive for us to see that different cultures had unique ways of translating three-dimensional space and complex geography into visual conventions.

Without knowing these conventions, you often cannot make sense out of a map. As with any other document, you have to learn the "language" in which maps are written before you can read them. You will thus probably find some of the examples that follow totally confusing. Do not let this circumstance deter you. If nothing else, this bewilderment ought to convince you just how much conventions of this sort affect the way we envision reality. Our own maps today would seem just as confusing to people of other cultures as some of these do to you. Yet you can read them without trouble. With a little effort and some guidance, you will discover how to read the less familiar ones presented here, too, or at least how to interpret enough of their major features to make general comparisons possible. Moreover, in making the attempt you will, we hope, come to see familiar maps in a fresh light. For you will have learned to notice things you might otherwise take for granted.

Begin by simply looking carefully at each strange map and systematically noting what it shows. A threefold approach may help you search for clues to an understanding of its larger significance. First, note what devices, if any, each employs to orient the user and to locate points in relationship to each other. Most maps use a set of coordinates or some sort of framework from which an observer is expected to construe the reality represented. So look especially for signs of such devices. Often they involve explicit symbols like the compass points, grid lines, and mileage scales on modern maps that stand out clearly as unnatural features. Second, consider how each map frames a field of vision and thereby implies some coherence or unity to what it

shows. Ask yourself what the map defines or implies by this framing. What sort of entity does it visualize? Does it evoke a whole world, a specific region, a country, a community, or merely a network of connections like roads? This question leads to a related third and last consideration. What kinds of individual features appear on the map and how do they correlate to each other? Does it, for example, highlight some over others by making them larger or placing them in a prominent position?

Note, of course, that most of these components probably do not reproduce natural features. Lines of latitude, political boundaries, and "centers" exist in peoples' thoughts as abstractions rather than as elements of an actual landscape. They, like the maps that illustrate them, help us to visualize space and make sense of it in social terms so that we can talk about it coherently and direct one another around in it. For that very reason, of course, maps tend to reveal how we regard a space—that is, what we value most about it or want to do in it. Once you have identified the three types of information listed above for a given map, therefore, ask what this information tells you about the interests of the people who made and used it. How, for example, did they define or bound their world? What did they value enough to represent within it? And finally, what purpose or activity would the information presented serve?

In reaching some conclusion about these broad questions, you should begin to glimpse something of the overall "slant," or cultural perspective, that shapes a map. Using this insight, revisit the Mercator map with great care and try to detect elements that you might have otherwise ignored or that you might have considered too obvious to notate. Be just as systematic and ask the same questions of it as you did of the strange maps. What do your conclusions suggest about the way in which Europeans conceptualized the modern world and their place in it? Why might the perspective reflected in this map seem odd or even disturbing to some people, particularly now that European nations no longer dominate the world and we seem to be entering a new global age of interdependence?

THE EVIDENCE

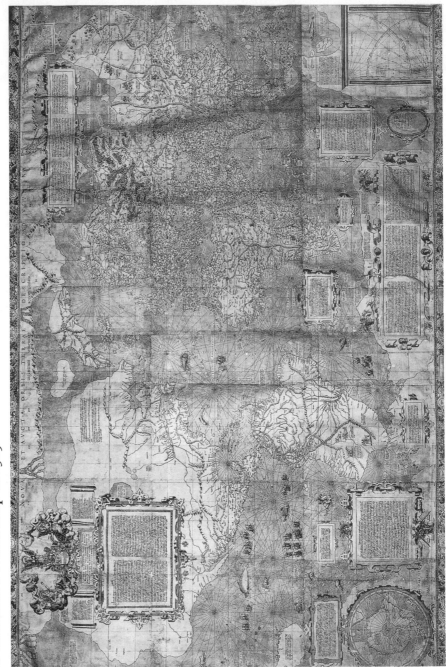

Source 1 from the Bibliothèque nationale de France.

1. Mercator's World Map of 1569

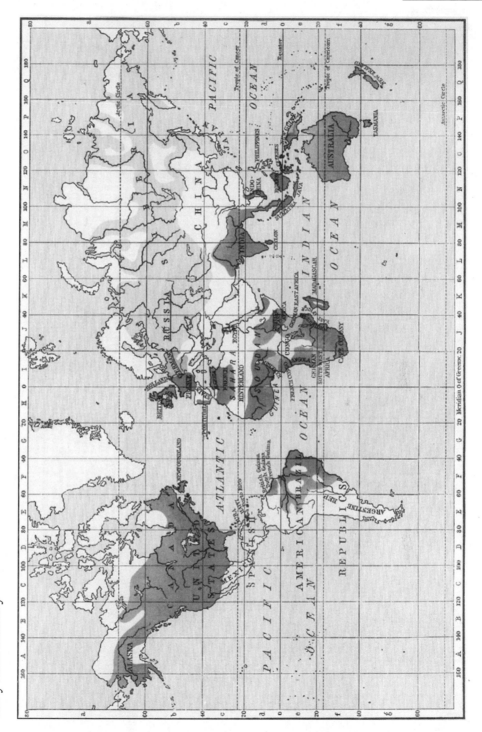

Source 2 from William R. Shepherd, Historical Atlas, 8th edition (New York: Barnes and Noble, 1956), p. 176.

2. Map of the World Based on Mercator Projection, early 20th century

Source 3 from John Onians, Art and Thought in the Hellenistic Age (Thames and Hudson, 1979). Reproduced by permission of Thames and Hudson.

3. A Modern Reconstruction of Eratosthenes' Map of the World, ca. 3rd century B.C.E.

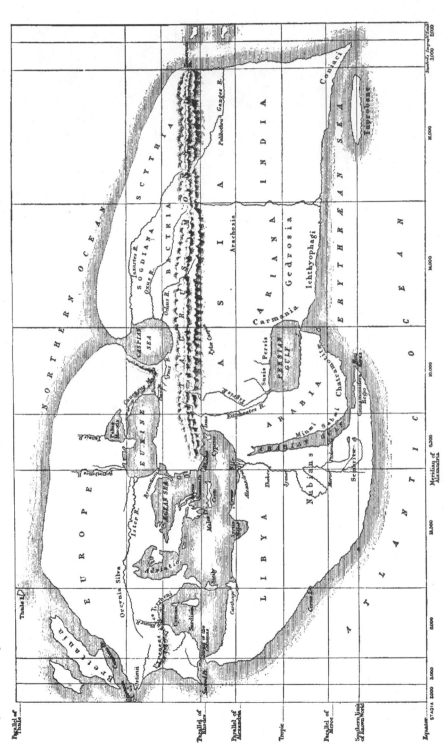

Source 4 from the British Library.

4. A Renaissance Reconstruction of Ptolemy's Map of the World

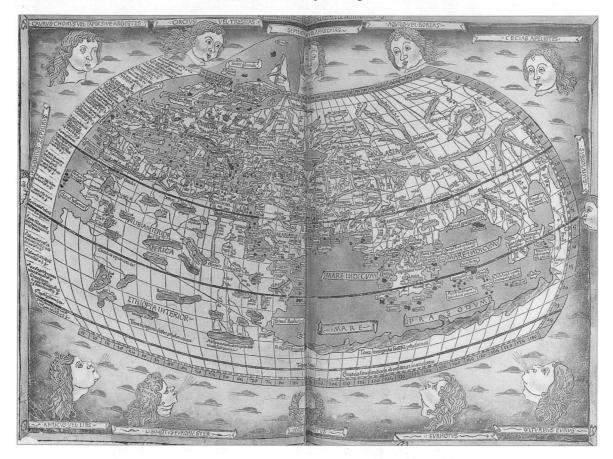

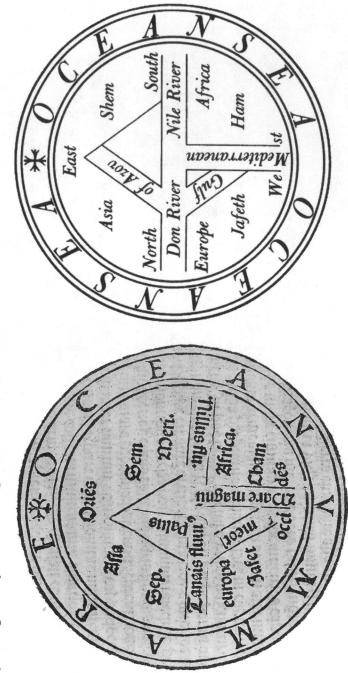

Source 5 from the Walters Art Gallery, Baltimore. Translation from Lloyd A. Brown, The Story of Maps (Boston: Little, Brown, 1950), opp. p. 103. Reproduced with permission.

5. Diagram by Isidore of Spain, 7th century, with translation

Source 6 from the British Library.

6. T-O Map by Beatus, 8th century

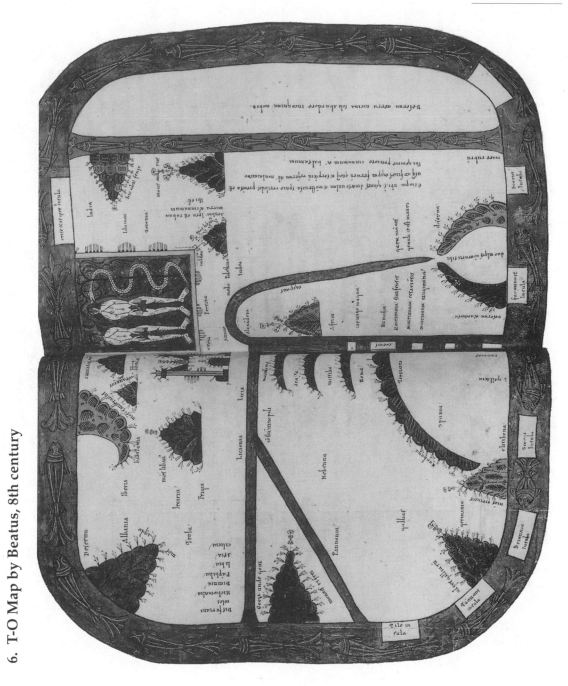

Source 7 from the Niedersächsische Landesbibliothek, Hanover.

7. Medieval Map of the World from Ebstorf, Germany

Source 8 from the Bibliothèque nationale de France.

8. The Islamic World Map of Al Idrisi, 12th century

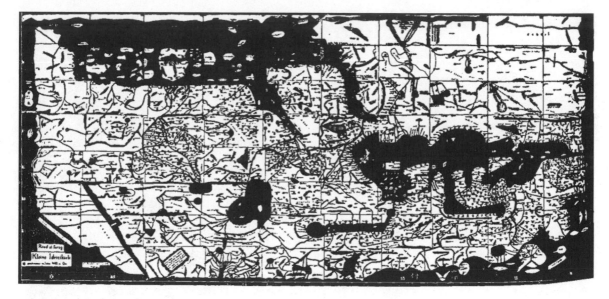

9. Korean Version of Chinese Cosmological Map, 17th century

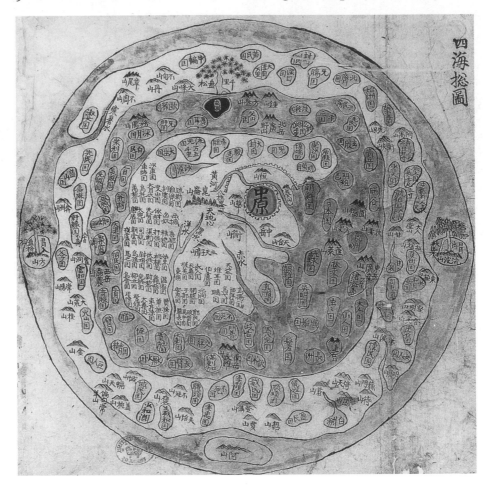

Source 10 from the Harvard-Yenching Library.

10. Ancient Chinese Mirror with TLV Cosmological Pattern, ca. 1600–1200 B.C.E.

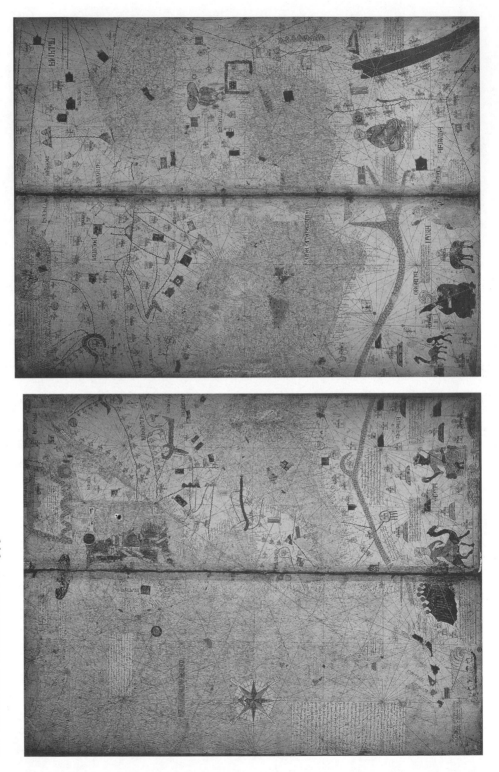

Source 11 from the Bibliothèque nationale de France.

11. From the Catalan Atlas, 1375

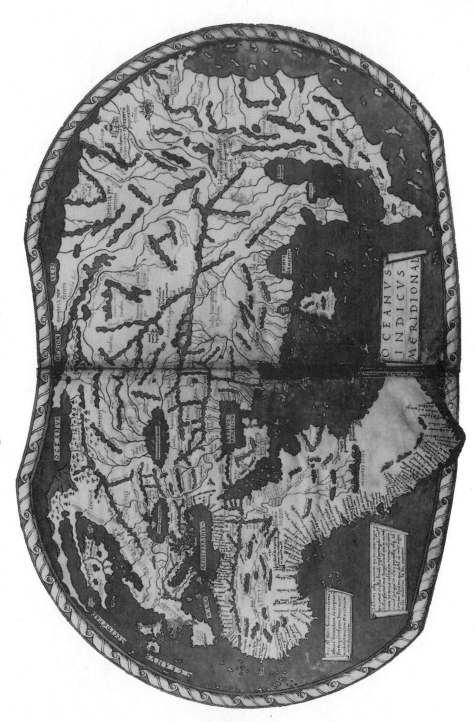

Source 12 from the British Library.

12. Henricus Martellus, Florentine Map of the World, 1489

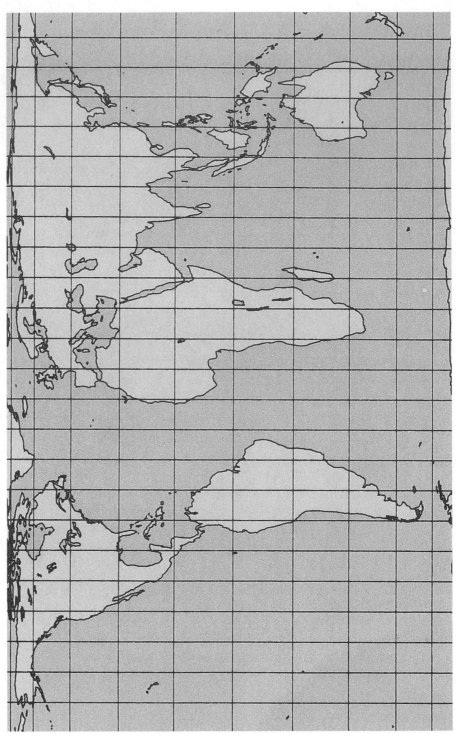

13. **Modern Equal-Area Map**

QUESTIONS TO CONSIDER

The obvious first step in any attempt to read the Mercator map as a cultural document reflecting the perspective of its time is to familiarize yourself with the map itself. Spend a few minutes, therefore, going over Source 1, the reproduction of Mercator's original world map of 1569. As you can see by comparing this reproduction with the more recent map in Source 2, standard modern world maps looked remarkably similar to Mercator's map, at least in their general outline and focus. Details, of course, vary a great deal, and at first glance you may find all the lines and drawings on the Mercator map more confusing than informative. Rather than trying to make sense of them now, turn to the reconstruction of the ancient Greek map of Eratosthenes that appears as Source 3. It offers an easier starting point for learning how to read maps. Like most ancient Greek maps, it is not only simpler but probably seems familiar, because so many modern Western maps share its conventions. Yet its details remain different enough that we have to observe them carefully to make sense of them.

Look, for example, at the way Eratosthenes framed and focused his "world" map. He clearly regarded the conjunction of western Asia, northern Africa (known to him as Libya), and Europe as the center of the world. Note how he laid out his map with North at the top and a strong horizontal axis running from the Mediterranean Sea to the Taurus Mountains on the Iranian plateau. This approach no doubt reflected an effort to depict the broader Greco-Persian world revealed through Alexander the Great's conquests. But look at the way he set up the abstract gridwork through which to locate places in relationship to one another. Both a key meridian and the midmost parallel run through the great Hellenistic city of Alexandria, making it the central point of reference. He also seems to have ignored the Southern Hemisphere, which he dismissed as too hot for human habitation, and let the edges of his map fade off into vague bodies of water. Though we cannot identify all the features included in his map, it apparently included mainly geographical elements—rivers, mountains, seas—as well as the location of important regions and cities. But could a traveler use this map to plan a journey?

Ptolemy adopted a similar focus and orientation in his famous world map. As you can see from one of the surviving copies reproduced as Source 4, he, too, centered it around the eastern end of the Mediterranean, a sea whose assumed centrality led the Romans of his day to give it its name, which means "middle of the earth." But Ptolemy considerably enlarged its scope, expanding the margins to include more of Asia and Africa and filling in more geographical details. He also clearly tried to show that the area depicted forms part of a much larger, and spherical, world. Despite his suggestion of a greater world, Ptolemy abandoned the old device of showing an encircling ocean to mask ignorance of unknown regions. Note, however, the curious land connection he posited between Africa and Asia. On the whole, his more regular gridwork of cosmologically determined meridians and parallels allowed him to locate places and natural features in fairly accurate relationships if not distances. As you can see, he made his map much more wide than tall, a fact that forced him to lay out eleven meridians of longitude but only nine parallels of latitude. Moreover, his use of icons for the twelve winds provided an additional frame of reference. Whom do you think would make use of such referents—and for what purpose? Current viewers often find Ptolemy's map remarkably "modern" in its focus and orientation despite its antiquity, and many deem it naturalistic in appearance. Why might this be so?

A comparison between these ancient Greek maps and medieval European T-O maps quickly shows the uniqueness of their features. Both focus on the eastern Mediterranean. But, as you can see from Source 5, a map attributed to a seventh-century Spanish bishop named Isidore of Spain, many medieval maps were so highly schematic that they seem to us more like diagrams. Note, for example, how Isidore abandoned efforts to suggest a spherical earth in favor of a flat, circular field. As even more diagrammatic versions show, this shape derived from the letter O and probably represented a symbolic rendering of the medieval concept of an *orbis mundi*, or "world orb." This schematic approach equally characterized the way medieval map makers treated geographic elements. As in the case of the encircling ocean sea, natural features were generally simplified into decorative details.

More significantly, T-O maps shifted the field of view of world maps. Look at Source 6, a more complex T-O map of the eighth century made by the Benedictine monk Beatus. Beatus put East rather than North at the top, making the Holy Land the central feature. This shift created an interesting hierarchical effect that had little to do with actual geography. For these maps usually located Eden, the Biblical paradise, eastward *above* Jerusalem, the holy city of Christianity. Both sites thus symbolically tower over the more worldly areas of early Christendom, which make up the bulk of the map. To allay any doubts about the spiritual symbolism of this orientation, most maps include an image of Christ at their apex. Look at this feature in Source 7, the Ebstorf German map of the world. Clearly East was uppermost here in more than a geographical sense. This scheme puts the Christian Holy Land in the place of honor at the top, with Europe relegated to a secondary spot in the lower left-hand quadrant on a par with Africa to its right. As all the pilgrimage sites and other iconographic details further show, these maps portray a distinctly Christian vision of the world.

The full implication of this reconfiguration may best be seen by comparing the T-O maps with the twelfth-century world map prepared by an Arabic cartographer, named Al Idrisi which appears as Source 8. Al Idrisi obviously still knew and followed the Ptolemaic tradition without any of the Christian changes, for his map incorporates both its framework and general outline. It, too, focuses on the eastern Mediterranean and uses

Ptolemy's system of meridians and parallels to locate places. But Al Idrisi reoriented his version so that South appears at the top, thereby giving North Africa more prominence and shifting Europe down into the lower right-hand corner. Consider the effect this change produced. It is also worth observing how this shift subtly made the Arabian peninsula and the Mesopotamian plain central features on his map. What city does this map highlight instead of Jerusalem?

An even clearer indication of the way in which cultural values affect the perspectives of maps may be seen by looking at examples from traditions not influenced by the Greeks. In such maps, few conventions will seem normal or natural enough to be decipherable on sight. Look, for example, at the seventeenth-century Korean copy of an old Chinese-style world map that appears as Source 9. Like the T-O maps of the medieval West, this work presents a highly schematic vision of the world. Here, too, the world appears as a disk encircled by the ocean. But within the world disk, shown with North at the top, a vast outer square of unknown land, marked with legendary sites, frames the Eurasian continent. Note how the latter appears as a rounded mass whose principle rivers all radiate out from a great central mountain, known as *Kunlun,* which supposedly stood under the palace of the god of Heaven and marked the axis of the earth. At either extreme to the right and left, two trees locate legendary sites where the sun and moon began and ended their daily course. What kind of landscape do these features evoke?

Some scholars think these maps duplicate a cosmological pattern found on implements associated with ancient Chinese cosmology, such as the mirror back depicted in Source 10. As you can see, both share a common design in which a circle encloses a square and a central boss. Thus an ancient cultural pattern, as symbolic in its own world as the T-O schema in the West, may have shaped this conception of the world. Yet the underlying paradigm did not prevent its makers from also recording actual geographic information. For lack of adequate information, they depicted western Asia as a vague realm filled only with the names of fantastic kingdoms, but they represented East Asia fairly well. The crenelated circle to the right of center marks the "Central" Plain of northern China, locked between the arms of the Yellow and Yangtze Rivers; like the Mediterranean in the West, this feature was deemed the center of the globe by the ancient Chinese, who thus called their homeland *Zhung-guo,* or the "Middle Land." To the north curves the Great Wall, which arcs toward the Korean peninsula and the Japanese archipelago lying just offshore. Nonetheless, a cultural image clearly underlies and shapes the geographic view.

Keep that possibility in mind as we turn back to the way in which Europeans began to map their expanding world on the eve of the modern period. Note how the makers of the Catalan Atlas, Source 11, rejected the usual medieval T-O scheme and revived the basic focus and orientation of the old Ptolemaic approach. The many diagonal lines of rhumb overlaid upon the segments of the Catalan Atlas, of course, provide clear indication of the new use for which such charts were intended. Yet the northward orientation and the wide but vertically flattened field focused on the eastern Mediterranean, equally demonstrate general familiarity with the perspective of old Ptolemaic maps. The Florentine Martellus world map, Source 12, shows how interest in this approach increased during the Renaissance as copies of Ptolemy's work began to circulate widely. Martellus expanded the edges of his map a bit, shifted its center to the Indian Ocean, and abandoned the land bridge between Africa and Asia, but the underlying image still reveals the Ptolemaic conception of the world. Here is graphic evidence of the impact of ancient thought on early modern Europe.

Now compare this early Renaissance vision of the world with the one presented in Source 1, the Mercator map of 1569. To incorporate the many new discoveries that explorers had reported back to Europe by his time, Mercator vastly expanded the scope and details of his map. For the moment, ignore the details and pay particular attention to the way in which he focused and framed his map. Although he continued to orient the field of his map to the north, note how he dramatically shifted its framework. The old Ptolemaic world image remained almost intact within his new map but scaled down and shifted off to the upper right-hand quadrant. Older European maps based on the Ptolemaic model generally position Eurasia so that western Europe and eastern Asia appear at

opposite ends of the earth. Mercator, however, edged Eurasia off to the right to make room for the Americas. In his new view, what now replaces the eastern Mediterranean as the center of the world? Note Asia's small overlap on the left near the North American coast and the implied size of the Pacific. What does this shift suggest about Mercator's viewpoint on the world?

After you have analyzed the framework of the map, look closer at the details. What system did Mercator use to locate places on his map? What do his choices intimate about his relationship with older cartographic traditions? And what do they imply about who he expected would use such a map? In this context, take time to locate the equator on Mercator's map and compare his treatment of this key coordinate with that in other maps. What factors might explain why Mercator did not center it between the top and bottom? Perhaps even more important, given the sliding scale of his projection, how did this skewing of the equator affect the appearance of other portions of the globe, particularly toward the poles? Compare the size of Africa and South America on his map with their counterparts on the equal-area map included as Source 13. Now reexamine the places and geographical features on Mercator's map. What natural features did he include? What regions, states, or cities seem to merit attention? Do these details provide any further clues about who would find his map useful and what they might do with it? Who would view the world from this perspective—and why?

EPILOGUE

In the centuries following Mercator's first publication of his map, Western cartographers devised many other ways to render the earth's surface on flat maps, including some that preserved equivalence of area. But because of the inherent problems involved in transposing a curved reality onto a flat representation, all such projections distorted some feature or another. Thus no alternate approach has ever proved fully satisfactory. More by default than design, therefore, the Mercator map retained its popularity in the West, often influencing the frame and focus of other maps if not always their method of projection. So it survived to attain the stature of a modern classic, conveying its image worldwide—until in recent decades it has come under increasing criticism for alleged ethnocentrism.

By this point you should have some insight into the reasons. To some it seems to incorporate vestiges of an old Mediterranean concept of a concentric world order in which a central region holds a superior position over the periphery. Certainly the vision it gives of the world is one centered around the North Atlantic region. Western Europe and North America dominate the field of view, and the rest of the globe seems marginalized, a position made worse by areal distortions. This pattern, of course, coincided with the actual international order created by Europeans during the heyday of their power. It also reflected a measure of truth during most of the twentieth century, when many people in the West talked about the dawn of a new Atlantic century in which the United States would join Western Europe in directing world affairs. And it offered a comforting picture of the democratic "West" throughout the Cold War era—despite its gross magnification of the Soviet "East." But to what extent does the image of the map symbolically convey a cultural hierarchy?

Non-Western people have always been chagrined by the way in which the map seems to depict their homelands as marginal places. During the period of decolonization following World War II, however, discontent with this vision mounted as Europe's patent decline called into question its centrality in world affairs. Representatives of newly emerging nations openly criticized its vision, particularly in the proceedings of the United Nations. Criticism of this sort has intensified recently as many of these nations now see themselves generically as a less-developed South in competition for scarce global resources with the more economically advanced countries of the North. In their eyes, the foreshortening of the Southern Hemisphere and the resulting diminishment of Africa and South America relative to northern landmasses have unpleasant, insulting connotations. How valid do *you* find these concerns? What might be a better image for the multicentered contemporary world?

CHAPTER TWO

FIRST ENCOUNTERS: THE CREATION

OF CULTURAL STEREOTYPES (1450–1650)

One of the most important aspects of world history involves the interactions of various peoples with one another. Centuries before what Europeans call their Age of Discovery, groups of people were aware that there were other human beings—some of them like themselves and others quite different—who inhabited other places; some made their homes in nearby valleys or plains or mountains and others were unimaginably far away.

How these groups of people chose to deal with one another—in harmony or hostility, in trade, warfare, intermarriage, and so on—depended to a great extent on how these peoples perceived one another. For it was often these perceptions, far more than realities, that tempered and even determined the types of relations they had.

Thus, as European explorers, traders, missionaries, and colonizers began to expand their horizons and influence beyond the Mediterranean in the fif-teenth and sixteenth centuries and embarked for what were for them the strange new lands of Africa, Asia, and the Americas, they inevitably carried with them a set of intellectual and cultural lenses through which they viewed the peoples they encountered. Moreover, they spread their own perceptions throughout Europe in the form of published letters, journals, memoirs, and observations, many of which were immensely popular. Indeed, it seems as if Europe could not get enough of these marvelous accounts of "new people" and "new worlds." For example, the great Dutch painter Rembrandt van Rijn was fascinated by non-Europeans who were brought, sometimes forcibly, to the Netherlands and painted portraits of many of them.[1]

1. On the popularity of explorers' accounts, Amerigo Vespucci's published letters were reprinted in sixty editions, Christopher Columbus's journal in twenty-two editions, and Hernando Cortés's in eighteen editions. See Fredi Chiappelli, et al., eds., *First Images of America: The Impact of the New World on the Old,* 2 vols. (Berkeley: University of California Press, 1976), vol. 2, p. 538.

Similarly, Africans, Americans, and Asians possessed their own cultures and saw Europeans through their own lenses. Ultimately, these perceptions—the Europeans' of non-Europeans and non-Europeans' of them—had an impact on how these different peoples treated and dealt with one another. Sometimes, the results were beneficial. Often, they were tragic.

In this chapter, you will be analyzing selected written accounts of first encounters between Europeans and sub-Saharan Africans, Native Americans, and Japanese. Your task in the chapter is twofold. First, by examining these accounts, determine the initial impressions that each side formed of the other. Then, use your historical imagination to reach some conclusions about how those impressions (whether accurate or inaccurate)

might have influenced how these peoples chose to deal with one another.

Before you begin, we want to emphasize the fact that these intellectual and cultural filters often prevented each side from understanding what the other was really like. The evidence presented in this chapter consists of *perceptions,* but not necessarily *reality.* And yet, as you might imagine, perceptions often are extremely powerful in influencing thought and actions. For example, Europeans dealt with non-Europeans not according to what those people were *really* like but rather what Europeans *perceived* them to be like. The same is true of non-Europeans' dealings with European explorers, traders, missionaries, and colonizers. This chapter addresses these perceptions (or misperceptions) and their consequences.

BACKGROUND

By the 1400s, Europeans were dramatically different from their ancestors of but a few centuries earlier, so different in fact that they were now prepared economically, scientifically, intellectually, and politically to embark upon their Age of Discovery (1450–1650).

Economically, the limited commerce of the era of the Crusades (1100s–1200s) had given way to burgeoning trade. The growth of trade had been made possible by increasing concentrations of wealth, which not only stimulated demand but also made possible new methods of investing and borrowing needed capi-

tal. The development of maritime insurance, first seen in Italian seaport cities but soon commonplace throughout Europe, made investors more willing to take risks. Finally, with the horrors of the Black Death buried, Europe's population slowly began to recover, thus generating increasing demand for goods and making possible the production of surpluses.

Intellectually and technologically, Europe was also prepared to undertake explorations. The Age of Discovery in Europe was also the age of Renaissance humanism, as Christopher Columbus, Amerigo Vespucci, Bartolomeu Dias, Leonardo da Vinci, Michelangelo, Erasmus, and William Shakespeare were roughly contem-

Chapter 2

First Encounters:

The Creation

of Cultural

Stereotypes

(1450–1650)

poraries. To such visionaries and others, old answers were pathetically insufficient, and a hunger for new knowledge prompted investigation and advances in astronomy, mathematics, geography, and physics as well as in literature, art, philosophy, and political theory. To improve navigation, Europeans were prepared to borrow from others: the magnetic compass from China via Muslims and the astrolabe (used to locate latitude) and the triangular ship's sail from the Arabs, among other innovations.

At the same time that Europe was becoming economically, intellectually, and technologically ready to expand its sway, the political institution of the nation-state was beginning to emerge, at first in Portugal and Spain and later in France, the Low Countries, and England. The monarchs of these evolving states groped toward a more permanent and stable government than mere dynastic rule. Such permanence and stability, these "enlightened" monarchs reasoned, could be achieved in part through the accumulation of great wealth by the central government. Looking to Italian port cities and Arab merchants as models, European monarchs saw that this wealth could be produced through trade.

But with Italian traders dominant in the Mediterranean and with the Turks' capture of Constantinople in 1453 sealing off land trade routes to the East, European monarchs and state-encouraged private merchants were forced into the Atlantic to find new trade routes. The European monarch who traditionally has been given credit for this vision is the Por-

tuguese Infante Dom Henrique, better known to us as Prince Henry the Navigator. Under Henry's sponsorship, Portuguese seamen inched down the western coast of Africa in attempts to find new sea routes to India and the Far East. Although Henry did not live to see his dream achieved (he died in 1460), his vision was taken up by his successors. In 1487, Bartolomeu Dias rounded the southern tip of Africa (Cape Agulhas),[2] and in May 1498 Vasco da Gama at last reached India.[3] By 1542, Portuguese explorers and traders had sailed to Japan.

With Portugal in control of the African sea routes to the East, rival monarchs of other emerging nations were forced to seek other trade lanes. Spain sponsored the voyages of Christopher Columbus, who convinced the Spanish throne that he could reach the riches of the East by sailing due west into the uncharted Atlantic. So also did France, the Netherlands, and England, slower starters in the frantic competition for trade routes because political unity and stability were achieved later in those nation-states. Indeed, in spite of the fact that explorers found two continents that had the potential to produce enormous wealth, the dream of finding a sea route to the East remained so

2. Cape Agulhas, not the Cape of Good Hope, is actually the southernmost point of Africa. Dias originally called the Cape of Good Hope the Cape of Storms, but the name was changed by King John II of Portugal.

3. Da Gama had the help of Indian navigator Ahmed ibn Majid, who came on board da Gama's ship at Malindi, a port on the east coast of Africa, in present-day Kenya, founded by the Portuguese in 1498.

strong that as late as 1638 French fur trader Jean Nicolet, encountering the Winnebago tribe of Native Americans on the western shore of Lake Michigan, donned a Chinese robe in anticipation of meeting the ruler of China.

The period in which Portuguese explorers and traders first began to probe the coastal areas of West Africa coincidentally was one of considerable instability in that region. Earlier, North African Berber and Arab traders had found organized kingdoms in West Africa and had carried on a brisk commerce in gold, silk and cotton cloth, dates, ivory, salt, and slaves.[4] By the year 1100, camel caravans regularly crossed the Sahara to reach the bustling trading centers of Timbuktu and Gao, bringing trade goods from the East as well as Islamic religion. Politically, the Kingdom of Ghana, a highly centralized military state, had been the dominant force in the region, but by 1200 it had declined, giving way to the Kingdom of Mali. North of Mali, the state of Songhai (also spelled Songhay and Songhi) by 1400 had declared its independence from Mali. At the time of the Portuguese encounters, population increases and invasions of Senegambia and Guinea in order to secure more gold for foreign trade had left West Africa politically and economically weakened and vulnerable to outside intrusion. By the 1500s, these political rivalries between West African states increased the number of slaves captured in battle, slaves

that Europeans were only too willing to purchase to work their new colonies in America.

By the time Europeans first encountered the various peoples they mistakenly but insistently called Indians, Native Americans had inhabited the Western Hemisphere for approximately 20,000 to 40,000 years. Although there is considerable disagreement about when these people first appeared in the Americas, it is virtually certain that they were not native to the Western Hemisphere, since no subhuman remains have ever been found. Probably they migrated from Asia sometime in the middle of the Pleistocene Age (75,000 to 8,000 B.C.E.). During that period, huge glaciers covered a large portion of North America, the ice cap extending southward to approximately the present United States–Canadian border. These glaciers, nearly 2 miles thick in some places, interrupted the water cycle because moisture falling as rain or snow was caught by the glaciers and frozen and thus was prevented from draining back into the seas or evaporating into the atmosphere. This process lowered ocean levels 250 to 300 feet, exposing a natural land bridge spanning the Bering Strait (between present-day Alaska and Russia)[5] across which people from Asia could easily migrate, probably in search of game. It is almost certain that various peoples from Asia did exactly that and then fol-

4. The Arabs called West Africa *Bilad al-Sudan,* or "Land of the Blacks."

5. Today the Bering Strait is only 180 feet deep; thus a lowering of ocean levels 250–300 feet would have exposed a considerable land bridge between Asia and North America.

Chapter 2

First Encounters:

The Creation

of Cultural

Stereotypes

(1450–1650)

lowed an ice-free corridor along the base of the Rocky Mountains southward into the more temperate areas of the American Southwest (which, because of the glaciers, were wetter and cooler than now and contained large lakes and forests) and then either eastward into other areas of North America or even farther southward into Central and South America. These migrations took thousands of years, and some peoples were still moving when European sails appeared on the horizon.

About 8000 B.C.E., the glacial cap began to retreat fairly rapidly, raising ocean levels to approximately their present-day levels, cutting off further migration from Asia and isolating America's first human inhabitants from other peoples for thousands of years (although some canoe travel was still possible). This isolation was almost surely the cause of the inhabitants' extraordinarily high susceptibility to the diseases that Europeans later brought with them, such as measles, tuberculosis, and smallpox, to which the populations of other continents had built up natural resistance. The glacial retreat also caused stretches of the American Southwest to become hot and arid, thus scattering Indian peoples in almost all directions. Nevertheless, for thousands of years a strong oral tradition enabled Native Americans to preserve stories of their origins and subsequent isolation. Almost all Native American peoples retained accounts of a long migration from the west and a flood.

The original inhabitants of the Western Hemisphere obtained their food principally by hunting and gathering, killing mammoths, huge bison, deer, elk, antelope, camels, horses, and other game with stone weapons and picking wild fruits and grasses. Beginning about 5000 B.C.E., however, people in present-day Mexico began practicing agriculture. By the time Europeans arrived, most Native Americans were domesticating plants and raising crops, although their levels of agricultural sophistication varied widely.

The development of agriculture (which occurred about the same time in Europe and the Americas) profoundly affected Native American life. Those peoples who adopted agriculture abandoned their nomadic ways and lived in settled villages (some of the Central American communities became magnificent cities). This more sedentary life permitted them to erect permanent housing, create and preserve pottery and art, and establish more complex political and social institutions. Agriculture also led to a gender-based division of labor, with women planting, raising, and harvesting crops and men hunting to supplement their villages' diets with game. With better food, and that in abundance, most likely Native American populations grew rapidly, thus prompting the onset of more complex political and social structures. The development of agriculture also affected these peoples' religious beliefs and ceremonies, increasing the homage to sun and rain gods who were thought to bring forth fruitful harvests. Contact with other Native American peoples led to trading, a practice with which Native

Americans were quite familiar by the time of European intrusion.

Those Native American cultures that made the transition from food gathering to food producing often attained an impressive degree of economic, political, social, and technological sophistication. In Central America, the Mayas of present-day Mexico and Guatemala built great cities, fashioned elaborate gold and silver jewelry, devised a form of writing, were proficient in mathematics and astronomy, and constructed a calendar that could predict solar eclipses and was more accurate than any system in use in Europe at the time. The conquerors of the Mayas, the Aztecs, built on the achievements of their predecessors, extending their political and economic power chiefly by subjugating other Native American peoples.[6] By the time Cortés and his army of four hundred men, sixteen horses, and a few cannon landed at Vera Cruz in 1519, the Aztecs had constructed the magnificent city of Tenochtitlán (the site of present-day Mexico City), which rivaled European cities in both size (approximately 300,000 people) and splendor.

Tenochtitlán contained monumental pyramids and public buildings, a fresh water supply brought to the city by complex engineering, causeways that connected the island city to other islands and the mainland, numerous skilled craftsmen, and even a compulsory education system for all male children. Raw materials and treasure flowed into Tenochtitlán as tribute from peoples under Aztec dominance, which stretched from the Pacific Ocean to the Gulf of Mexico and from central Mexico to present-day Guatemala. Little wonder that the conquistadors with Hernando Cortés were awed and enchanted when they saw it.

In the late thirteenth century, Kubilai Khan had attempted an invasion of Japan, thwarted when his fleet was destroyed by a typhoon, which the Japanese called *kamikaze* ("divine winds"). But, like the states of West Africa, in the sixteenth century Japan was suffering through an era of political instability when Portuguese explorers, traders, and missionaries first landed in the early 1540s. Wracked by almost constant civil war, the authority of the central government had been reduced to near-impotence. Similar to the feudal period in Western Europe in the tenth and eleventh centuries, Japan in the 1400s and 1500s was controlled by approximately 250 *daimyos* ("lords") who kept the islands in utter turmoil with their rivalries. Portuguese and, later, Dutch traders quickly moved in, as did Christian missionaries. In 1549, the Jesuit missionary Francis Xavier (later raised to sainthood) landed at Kagoshima. By 1600, approximately 300,000 Japanese people had been baptized Christians.

Beginning in 1568, Japan began a period of national consolidation. Under Oda Nobunaga, a samurai warrior, the daimyos gradually were

6. The Aztecs actually called themselves Mexica. Nor did Cortés ever use the word *Aztec*. The name Aztec was made popular in the eighteenth century by Jesuit scholar Francisco Javier Calavijero. Like the erroneous name "Indian," the name "Aztec" has persisted.

Chapter 2
First Encounters:
The Creation
of Cultural
Stereotypes
(1450–1650)

brought under central authority. Despite Nobunaga's assassination in 1582, the work of political centralization was continued under Nobunaga's principal general and successor Toyotomi Hideyoshi and, by 1598, was essentially complete.

The centralization of authority did not bode well for Europeans. Suspicious of Japanese Christians' conflicting loyalties and fearing that contact with European merchants was diluting the glories of Japanese culture, the Japanese government in 1635 began expelling Europeans, banning all things European (except firearms), and persecuting Japanese Christians (many of whom were crucified). Yet Dutch traders were al-lowed to remain on the tiny island of Deshima (in Nagasaki harbor) and Japanese people continued to be fascinated by western things. Many continued to engage in *rangaku* ("foreign studies").

To repeat, your task in this chapter is twofold. First, by examining several accounts of "first encounters," determine the initial impressions that each side created of the other. Once you have completed that analysis, then use your historical ingenuity to reach some conclusions about how these initial impressions might have influenced the ways Europeans and non-Europeans chose to deal with one another.

THE METHOD

To begin with, all of the accounts you will read, both by Europeans and by non-Europeans, pose some problems for historians. For one thing, each author is describing people of another culture through the lens of his own culture and experiences. Therefore, each observer may not have fully grasped what he actually was seeing. (For example, if you were to invite a person from another culture to accompany you to a college football game and then ask that person what he or she observed, you would expect the result to be a far cry from your daily sports page rundown.) In addition, each of the authors clearly hoped that his account would be read by other people. This invisible audi-ence too may have affected what and how he wrote. Nevertheless, because we are dealing with *perceptions* that various cultures had of one another at first contact, the accounts are not so flawed as they might at first appear. Moreover, nearly all the authors represented here actually were eyewitnesses to the events they describe; thus, for our purposes their evidence serves quite well.

As you read each account, pay special attention to reports of the following features (the fifth often will require you to indulge in historical speculation):

1. Physical appearance (bodies, hair, clothing, jewelry, and so on). Such descriptions can provide important clues about the authors' attitudes toward the peoples they are describ-

ing. Two particularly good examples are Columbus's description of the Arawaks (Source 4) and the anonymous Japanese author's description of the European (Source 13).

2. Nature or character (childlike, bellicose, honest, lazy, greedy, and so on). Be willing to read between the lines. For example, King Nzinga Mbemba of Kongo does not refer directly to Europeans and, in fact, on the surface seems to be more critical of his own people (Source 3). Is the king, however, implying something else?

3. Political, social, and religious traditions and practices (behavior of women, ceremonies, eating habits, government, sexual practices, and so on). These descriptions provide you with excellent material, as Europeans were often shocked by some of the practices of the peoples they encountered (Sources 2, 5, 11, and 12, for examples), as were non-Europeans of European practices (Sources 6, 13, 14, and 15 for examples). Remember that each narrator is looking through the lens of his own culture.

4. Overall impressions. Although these are rarely stated explicitly, each author certainly intended to give his readers a collective image of the peoples he encountered. Often you will have to infer that overall impression yourself from the bits of evidence in the accounts.

5. Advice. How should the people being described be dealt with? Here again, you may have to deduce this from each account. Just as often, however, you will have to be especially sensitive to what each author is *really* saying. For example, several European accounts reported that the peoples being described could be easily converted to Christianity (Sources 1 and 4, to name but two). Is the author implying that these peoples *should* be converted? Also, in Source 2 the anonymous reporter describes a brisk trade in West Africa in gold and slaves. Might one assume that this Portuguese seaman believes his country *should* engage in that profitable commerce? In the Native American account of Europeans, you will have to infer how they believed Europeans should be dealt with, since the account does not explicitly deal with that question. The African and Japanese accounts are somewhat more direct.

Be willing to read between the lines. Sometimes, for example, the author may tell a story about the people he is describing. What meaning is that story intended to convey? Also be sensitive to how the author's own culture has affected his perceptions (as, for example, when Mexia attempts to describe Japanese music in Source 12).

Finally, use the collective images you have found to predict how those views—often pervasive—might have affected the way these peoples chose to treat one another. That is, what behavior resulted from these attitudes?

Source 1 is an account of a 1593 shipwreck that took place off the coast of Africa. The author, not himself an eyewitness in this case, took the jour-

Chapter 2

First Encounters:

The Creation

of Cultural

Stereotypes

(1450–1650)

nal of the ship's pilot and interviewed several of the survivors before writing his account of the wreck of the *Santo Alberto* in 1597. Source 2 is a first-person account of encounters with Africans in Benin (in West Africa). The account was written sometime after 1535 and a popular Italian translation was published in 1550.

Nzinga Mbemba (Source 3) was the King of Kongo, the largest state in central West Africa. He came to the throne around 1506, succeeding his father, and in 1526 wrote three insistent letters to the king of Portugal. The Portuguese knew Nzinga Mbemba by his Christian name, Alfonso I.

Christopher Columbus kept a journal of his first voyage, which he presented to his patrons Ferdinand and Isabella upon his return. Both the journal and a duplicate copy have been lost forever. What we have in Source 4 is a reworked version of the original, done by Bartolome de las Casas in the 1530s. That document too was lost—for approximately 250 years—but was recovered in 1790 and now is preserved in the National Library in Madrid. Amerigo Vespucci's account (Source 5) of his 1497–1498 voyage was the most popular explorer account in Europe (can you guess why?), part of the reason why the New World became his namesake.

The Native American account of Cortés's invasion (Source 6) was rescued from destruction by Spanish priests and survived the *conquistadors* ("conquerors") attempts to obliterate all Native American records of what

they had done. The account was preserved for centuries in Roman Catholic monasteries and now resides in national museums or libraries both in Europe and in Mexico.

Torres, Xavier, Rodrigues, Valignano, and Mexia (Sources 8 through 12) all were Jesuit missionaries who spent years in Japan, China, and Macao attempting to convert the locals to Christianity. Indeed, all of these missionaries died in the East—Torres in Japan, Xavier and Mexia in China, and Rodrigues and Valignano in Macao. Girón (Source 7) was a merchant who traded in Japan.

Source 13, written by an anonymous author in 1639, is the initial chapter of a popular book entitled *Kirishitan [Christian] monogatari.* Suzuki Shosan wrote his attack on Christianity (Source 14) in Japan in 1642. He was an advocate of "ferocious Zen," a rather aggressive version of that philosophy. Tokugawa Iemitsu, author of the "Closed Country Edict of 1635," (Source 15), was *shogun* ("supreme military leader") from 1623 to 1651. The edict was written to the two *bugyo* ("commissioners") of Nagasaki, a center of Japanese Christianity.

Before you begin examining the evidence, let us offer a note of caution. Some of these accounts include strong ethnocentric, even racist, language and images. We included these accounts not to either shock or offend readers, but rather to accurately represent the kinds of descriptions individuals wrote after their "first encounters" with strangers.

THE EVIDENCE

AFRICA

European Accounts

Source 1 from C. R. Boxer, ed., The Tragic History of the Sea, 1589–1622: Narratives of the Shipwrecks of the Portuguese East Indiamen *(Cambridge: The Hakluyt Society, 1959), pp. 119–123.*

1. Joao Baptista Lavanha, 1597

It being now late, the chief of that region, who had heard from some of his Kaffirs that our people were there, came with about sixty Negroes to visit the Captain-major. When he drew near, Nuno Velho got up and went a few steps to receive him, and the Negro, after welcoming him by saying 'Nanhatá, Nanhatá,' as a sign of peace and friendship laid his hand on the Captain-major's beard and after stroking it kissed his own hand. All the other barbarians performed the same courtesy to our people, and ours to them. This Negro was called Luspance. He was fairly tall, well made, of a cheerful countenance, not very black, with a short beard, long moustaches, and appeared to be about forty-five years old. . . .

The dress of these Kaffirs was a mantle of calf-skins, with the hair on the outside, which they rub with grease to make soft. They are shod with two or three soles of raw hide fastened together in a round shape, secured to the foot with thongs and with this they run with great speed. They carry in their hand a thin stick to which is fastened the tail of an ape or of a fox, with which they clean themselves and shade their eyes when observing. This dress is used by nearly all the Negroes of this Kaffraria, and the kings and chiefs wear hanging from their left ear a little copper bell, without a clapper, which they make after their fashion.

These and all the other Kaffirs are herdsmen and husbandmen, by which means they subsist. Their husbandry is millet, which is white, about the size of a peppercorn, and forms the ear of a plant which resembles a reed in shape and size. From this millet, ground between two stones or in wooden mortars, they make flour, and of this they make cakes, which they bake under the embers. Of the same grain they make wine, mixing it with a lot of water, which after being fermented in a clay jar, cooled off, and turned sour, they drink with great gusto.

Their cattle are numerous, fat, tender, tasty, and large, the pastures being very fertile. Most of them are polled cows, in whose number and abundance their wealth consists. They also subsist on their milk and on the butter which they make from it.

Chapter 2

First Encounters:

The Creation

of Cultural

Stereotypes

(1450–1650)

They live together in small villages, in huts made of reed mats, which do not keep out the rain. These huts are round and low, and if any person dies in one of them, all the other huts and the whole village are pulled down, and they make others from the same material in another place, believing that in the village where their neighbour or relation died, everything will turn out unluckily. And thus, to save themselves this trouble, when anyone falls ill they carry him into the bush, so that if he dies it may be outside their huts. They surround their huts with a fence, within which they keep their cattle.

They sleep in skins of animals, on the earth, in a narrow pit measuring six or seven spans long and one or two deep. They use vessels of clay dried in the sun, and also of wood carved with some iron hatchets, which resemble a wedge set in a piece of wood, and they also use these for clearing the bush. In war they make use of assegais [slender spears]; and they have gelded whelps about the shape and size of our large curs.

They are very brutish and worship nothing, and thus they would receive our holy Christian faith very easily. They believe that the sky is another world like this one in which we live, inhabited by another kind of people, who cause the thunder by running and the rain by urinating. Most of the inhabitants of this land from latitude 29° southwards are circumcised. They are very sensual, and have as many wives as they can maintain, of whom they are jealous. They obey chiefs whom they call Ancosses.

The language is almost the same in the whole of Kaffraria, the difference between them resembling that between the languages of Italy, or between the ordinary ones of Spain. They seldom go far away from their villages, and thus they know and hear nothing except what concerns their neighbours. They are very covetous, and so long as they have not received payment they will serve, but if payment is made in advance no service is to be expected of them, for when they have received it they make off with it.

They value the most essential metals, such as iron and copper, and thus for very small pieces of either of these they will barter cattle, which is what they most prize, and with cattle they drive their trade and commerce, and cattle forms their treasure. Gold and silver have no value among them, nor does there appear to be either of these two metals in the country, for our people saw no signs of them in the regions through which they passed.

The above is all they noticed of the dress, customs, ceremonies, and laws of these Kaffirs, nor can there be more to take note of among so barbarous a people. . . .

Source 2 from John William Blake, ed. and trans., Europeans in West Africa, 1450–1560 *(London: The Hakluyt Society, 1942), vol. 1, pp. 145–153.*

2. Anonymous Portuguese
Pilot, ca. 1535

To understand the Negro traffic, one must know that over all the African coast facing west there are various countries and provinces, such as Guinea, the coast of Melegete, the kingdom of Benin, the kingdom of Kongo, six degrees from the equator and towards the south pole. There are many tribes and Negro kings here, and also communities which are partly Muslim and partly heathen. These are constantly making war among themselves. The kings are worshiped by their subjects, who believe that they come from heaven, and speak of them always with great reverence, at a distance and on bended knees. Great ceremony surrounds them, and many of these kings never allow themselves to be seen eating, so as not to destroy the belief of their subjects that they can live without food. They worship the sun, and believe that spirits are immortal, and that after death they go to the sun. Among others, there is in the kingdom of Benin an ancient custom, observed to the present day, that when the king dies, the people all assemble in a large field, in the center of which is a very deep well, wider at the bottom than at the mouth. They cast the body of the dead king into this well, and all his friends and servants gather round, and those who are judged to have been most dear to and favored by the king (this includes not a few, as all are anxious for the honor) voluntarily go down to keep him company. When they have done so, the people place a great stone over the mouth of the well, and remain by it day and night. On the second day, a few deputies remove the stone, and ask those below what they know, and if any of them have already gone to serve the king; and the reply is, No. On the third day, the same question is asked; and someone then replies that so-and-so, mentioning a name, has been the first to go, and so-and-so the second. It is considered highly praiseworthy to be the first, and he is spoken of with the greatest admiration by all the people, and considered happy and blessed. After four or five days all these unfortunate people die. When this is apparent to those above, since none reply to their questions, they inform their new king; who causes a great fire to be lit near the well, where numerous animals are roasted. These are given to the people to eat, and he with great ceremony is declared to be the true king, and takes the oath to govern well.

The Negroes of Guinea and Benin are very haphazard in their habits of eating. They have no set times for meals, and eat and drink four or five times a day, drinking water, or a wine which they distill from palms. They have no hair except for a few bristly strands on top of the head, and none grows; and the rest of the bodies are completely hairless. They live for the best part of 100 years, and are always vigorous, except at certain times of the year when they

Chapter 2

First Encounters:

The Creation

of Cultural

Stereotypes

(1450–1650)

become very weak, as if they had fever. They are then bled, and recover, having a great deal of blood in their system. Some of the Negroes in this country are so superstitious that they worship the first object they see on the day of recovery. A kind of plant called melegete, very like the sorgum of Italy, but in flavor like pepper, grows on this coast. . . .

African Account

Source 3 from Basil Davidson, trans., The African Past *(London: Curtis Brown, 1964), pp. 191–194.*

3. Nzinga Mbemba, 1526

Sir, Your Highness [King of Portugal] should know how our Kingdom is being lost in so many ways that it is convenient to provide for the necessary remedy, since this is caused by the excessive freedom given by your agents and officials to the men and merchants who are allowed to come to this Kingdom to set up shops with goods and many things which have been prohibited by us, and which they spread throughout our Kingdoms and Domains in such an abundance that many of our vassals, whom we had in obedience, do not comply because they have the things in greater abundance than we ourselves; and it was with these things that we had them content and subjected under our vassalage and jurisdiction, so it is doing a great harm not only to the service of God, but the security and peace of our Kingdoms and State as well.

And we cannot reckon how great the damage is, since the mentioned merchants are taking every day our natives, sons of the land and the sons of our noblemen and vassals and our relatives, because the thieves and men of bad conscience grab them wishing to have the things and wares of this Kingdom which they are ambitious of; they grab them and get them to be sold; and so great, Sir, is the corruption and licentiousness that our country is being completely depopulated, and Your Highness should not agree with this nor accept it as in your service. And to avoid it we need from those (your) Kingdoms no more than some priests and a few people to teach in schools, and no other goods except wine and flour for the holy sacrament. That is why we beg of Your Highness to help and assist us in this matter, commanding your factors that they should not send here either merchants or wares, because it is *our will that in these Kingdoms there should not be any trade of slaves nor outlet for them.* Concerning what is referred [to] above, again we beg of Your Highness to agree with it, since otherwise we cannot remedy such an obvious damage. Pray Our Lord in His mercy to have Your Highness under His guard and let you do forever the things of His service. . . .

Moreover, Sir, in our Kingdoms there is another great inconvenience which is of little service to God, and this is that many of our people, keenly desirous as they are of the wares and things of your Kingdoms, which are brought here by your people, and in order to satisfy their voracious appetite, seize many of our people, freed and exempt men, and very often it happens that they kidnap even noblemen and the sons of noblemen, and our relatives, and take them to be sold to the white men who are in our Kingdoms; and for this purpose they have concealed them; and others are brought during the night so that they might not be recognized.

And as soon as they are taken by the white men they are immediately ironed and branded with fire, and when they are carried to be embarked, if they are caught by our guards' men the whites allege that they have bought them but they cannot say from whom, so that it is our duty to do justice and to restore to the freemen their freedom, but it cannot be done if your subjects feel offended, as they claim to be.

And to avoid such a great evil we passed a law so that any white man living in our Kingdoms and wanting to purchase goods in any way should first inform three of our noblemen and officials of our court whom we rely upon in this matter, and these are Dom Pedro Manipanza and Dom Manuel Manissaba, our chief usher, and Gonçalo Pires our chief freighter, who should investigate if the mentioned goods are captives or free men, and if cleared by them there will be no further doubt nor embargo for them to be taken and embarked. But if the white men do not comply with it they will lose the aforementioned goods. And if we do them this favor and concession it is for the part Your Highness has in it, since we know that it is in your service too that these goods are taken from our Kingdom, otherwise we should not consent to this. . . .

AMERICA

European Accounts

Source 4 from Journal of the First Voyage to America, by Christopher Columbus *(New York: Albert Boni and Charles Boni, 1924), pp. 24–29.*

4. Christopher Columbus,
1530s

As I saw that they were very friendly to us, and perceived that they could be much more easily converted to our holy faith by gentle means than by force, I presented them with some red caps, and strings of beads to wear upon the neck, and many other trifles of small value, wherewith they were much delighted, and became wonderfully attached to us. Afterwards they came swimming to the boats, bringing parrots, balls of cotton thread, javelins and many other things which they exchanged for articles we gave them, such as glass beads, and hawk's bells; which trade was carried on with the utmost good will. But they seemed on the whole to me, to be a very poor people. They all

Chapter 2

First Encounters:

The Creation

of Cultural

Stereotypes

(1450–1650)

go completely naked, even the women, though I saw but one girl. All whom I saw were young, not above thirty years of age, well made, with fine shapes and faces; their hair short, and coarse like that of a horse's tail, combed toward the forehead, except a small portion which they suffer to hang down behind, and never cut. Some paint themselves with black, which makes them appear like those of the Canaries, neither black nor white; others with white, others with red, and others with such colours as they can find. Some paint the face, and some the whole body; others only the eyes, and others the nose. Weapons they have none, nor are acquainted with them, for I showed them swords which they grasped by the blades, and cut themselves through ignorance. They have no iron, their javelins being without it, and nothing more than sticks, though some have fish-bones or other things at the ends. They are all of a good size and stature, and handsomely formed. I saw some with scars of wounds upon their bodies, and demanded by signs the cause of them; they answered me in the same way, that there came people from other islands in the neighbourhood who endeavoured to make prisoners of them, and they defended themselves. I thought then, and still believe, that these were from the continent. It appears to me, that the people are ingenious, and would be good servants; and I am of opinion that they would very readily become Christians, as they appear to have no religion. They very quickly learn such words as are spoken to them. If it please our Lord, I intend at my return to carry home six of them to your Highnesses [Spain's monarchs, Ferdinand and Isabella] that they may learn our language. . . .

At daybreak great multitudes of men came to the shore, all young and of fine shapes, very handsome; their hair not curled but straight and coarse like horse-hair, and all with foreheads and heads much broader than any people I had hitherto seen; their eyes were large and very beautiful. . . .

They were straight-limbed without exception, and not with prominent bellies but handsomely shaped. They came to the ship in canoes, made of a single trunk of a tree, wrought in a wonderful manner considering the country; some of them large enough to contain forty or forty-five men, others of different sizes down to those fitted to hold but a single person. They rowed with an oar like a baker's peel, and wonderfully swift. . . .

Seeing some of them with little bits of this metal hanging at their noses, I gathered from them by signs that by going southward or steering round the island in that direction, there would be found a king who possessed large vessels of gold, and in great quantities. I endeavoured to procure them to lead the way thither, but found they were unacquainted with the route. . . .

The natives are an inoffensive people, and so desirous to possess any thing they saw with us, that they kept swimming off to the ships with whatever they could find, and readily bartered for any article we saw fit to give them in return, even such as broken platters and fragments of glass. . . .

I do not . . . see the necessity of fortifying the place, as the people here are simple in war-like matters, as your Highnesses will see by those seven which I have ordered to be taken and carried to Spain in order to learn our language and return, unless your Highnesses should choose to have them all transported to Castile, or held captive in the island. I could conquer the whole of them with fifty men, and govern them as I pleased. . . .

Source 5 from The Letters of Amerigo Vespucci, *trans. Clements R. Markham (London: The Hakluyt Society, 1894), pp. 6–21.*

5. Amerigo Vespucci, 1497–1498

What we knew of their life and customs was that they all go naked, as well the men as the women, without covering anything, no otherwise than as they come out of their mothers' wombs. They are of medium stature, and very well proportioned. The colour of their skins inclines to red, like the skin of a lion, and I believe that, if they were properly clothed, they would be white like ourselves. They have no hair whatever on their bodies, but they have very long black hair, especially the women, which beautifies them. They have not very beautiful faces, because they have long eyelids, which make them look like Tartars. They do not allow any hairs to grow on their eyebrows, nor eyelashes, nor in any other part except on the head, where it is rough and dishevelled. They are very agile in their persons, both in walking and running, as well the men as the women; and think nothing of running a league or two, as we often witnessed; and in this they have a very great advantage over us Christians. They swim wonderfully well, and the women better than the men; for we have found and seen them many times two leagues at sea, without any help whatever in swimming.

Their arms are bows and arrows, well made, except that they have no iron, nor any other kind of hard metal. Instead of iron they use teeth of animals or of fish, or a bit of wood well burnt at the point. They are sure shots, and where they aim they hit. In some places the women use these bows. They have other weapons like lances, hardened by fire, and clubs with the knobs very well carved. They wage war among themselves with people who do not speak their language, carrying it on with great cruelty, giving no quarter, if not inflicting greater punishment. . . .

They have no leader, nor do they march in any order, no one being captain. The cause of their wars is not the desire of rule nor to extend the limits of their dominions, but owing to some ancient feud that has arisen among them in former times. When asked why they made war, they have no other answer than that it is to avenge the death of their ancestors and their fathers. They have neither king nor lord, nor do they obey anyone, but live in freedom. Having moved themselves to wage war, when the enemy have killed or cap-

Chapter 2

First Encounters:

The Creation

of Cultural

Stereotypes

(1450–1650)

tured any of them, the oldest relation arises and goes preaching through the streets and calling upon his countrymen to come with him to avenge the death of his relation, and thus he moves them by compassion. They do not bring men to justice, nor punish a criminal. Neither the mother nor the father chastise their children, and it is wonderful that we never saw a quarrel among them. They show themselves simple in their talk, and are very sharp and cunning in securing their ends. They speak little, and in a low voice. . . .

Their mode of life is very barbarous, for they have no regular time for their meals, but they eat at any time that they have the wish, as often at night as in the day—indeed, they eat at all hours. They take their food on the ground, without napkin or any other cloth, eating out of earthen pots which they make, or out of half calabashes. They sleep in certain very large nets made of cotton, and suspended in the air. . . .

They are a people of cleanly habits as regards their bodies, and are constantly washing themselves. When they empty the stomach they do everything so as not to be seen, and in this they are clean and decent; but in making water they are dirty and without shame, for while talking with us they do such things without turning round, and without any shame. They do not practise matrimony among them, each man taking as many women as he likes, and when he is tired of a woman he repudiates her without either injury to himself or shame to the woman, for in this matter the woman has the same liberty as the man. They are not very jealous, but lascivious beyond measure, the women much more so than the men. I do not further refer to their contrivances for satisfying their inordinate desires, so that I may not offend against modesty. They are very prolific in bearing children, and in their pregnancy they are not excused any work whatever. The parturition is so easy, and accompanied by so little pain, that they are up and about the next day. They go to some river to wash, and presently are quite well, appearing on the water like fish. If they are angry with their husbands they easily cause abortion with certain poisonous herbs or roots, and destroy the child. Many infants perish in this way. . . .

They eat little flesh, unless it be human flesh, and your Magnificence must know that they are so inhuman as to transgress regarding this most bestial custom. For they eat all their enemies that they kill or take, as well females as males, with so much barbarity that it is a brutal thing to mention, how much more to see it, as has happened to me an infinite number of times. They were astonished at us when we told them that we did not eat our enemies. . . .

At a distance of three leagues from the beach we came to a village of few houses and many inhabitants, there not being more than nine habitations. Here we were received with so many barbarous ceremonies that the pen will not suffice to write them down. There were songs, dances, tears mingled with rejoicings, and plenty of food. We remained here for the night. Here they offered their wives to us, and we were unable to defend ourselves from them. We remained all night and half the next day. . . .

Next day we saw a great number of the people on shore, still with signs of war, sounding horns and various other instruments used by them for defiance, and all plumed and painted, so that it was a very strange thing to behold them. All the ships, therefore, consulted together, and it was concluded that these people desired hostility with us. It was then decided that we should do all in our power to make friends with them, and if they rejected our friendship we should treat them as enemies, and that we should make slaves of as many as we could take. Being armed as well as our means admitted, we returned to the shore. They did not oppose our landing, I believe from fear of the guns. Forty of our men landed in four detachments, each with a captain, and attacked them. After a long battle, many of them being killed, the rest were put to flight. We followed in pursuit until we came to a village, having taken nearly 250 prisoners. We burnt the village and returned to the ships with these 250 prisoners, leaving many killed and wounded. On our side no more than *one was killed, and twenty-two were wounded,* who all recovered. God be thanked! . . .

Native American Account

Source 6 from Miguel Leon-Portilla, ed., The Broken Spears: The Aztec Account of the Conquest of Mexico, *trans. Lysander Kemp (Boston: Beacon Press, 1962), pp. viii–ix, 30, 92–93, 128–144.*

6. Native American Account of Cortés's Conquest, ca. 1530

The envoys made sacrifices in front of the Captain.[7] At this, he grew very angry. When they offered him blood in an "eagle dish," he shouted at the man who offered it and struck him with his sword. The envoys departed at once. . . .

When the sacrifice was finished, the messengers reported to the king. They told him how they had made the journey, and what they had seen, and what food the strangers ate. Motecuhzoma[8] was astonished and terrified by their report, and the description of the strangers' food astonished him above all else.

He was also terrified to learn how the cannon roared, how its noise resounded, how it caused one to faint and grow deaf. The messengers told him: "A thing like a ball of stone comes out of its entrails: it comes out shooting sparks and raining fire. The smoke that comes out with it has a pestilent odor, like that of rotten mud. This odor penetrates even to the brain and causes the greatest discomfort. If the cannon is aimed against a mountain, the mountain

7. **the Captain:** Cortés.
8. **Motecuhzoma:** Montezuma.

Chapter 2

First Encounters:

The Creation

of Cultural

Stereotypes

(1450–1650)

splits and cracks open. If it is aimed against a tree, it shatters the tree into splinters. This is a most unnatural sight, as if the tree had exploded from within."

The messengers also said: "Their trappings and arms are all made of iron. They dress in iron and wear iron casques on their heads. Their swords are iron; their bows are iron; their shields are iron; their spears are iron. Their deer[9] carry them on their backs wherever they wish to go. These deer, our lord, are as tall as the roof of a house.

"The strangers' bodies are completely covered, so that only their faces can be seen. Their skin is white, as if it were made of lime. They have yellow hair, though some of them have black. Their beards are long and yellow, and their moustaches are also yellow. Their hair is curly, with very fine strands.

"As for their food, it is like human food. It is large and white, and not heavy.[10] It is something like straw, but with the taste of a cornstalk, of the pith of a cornstalk. It is a little sweet, as if it were flavored with honey; it tastes of honey, it is sweet-tasting food.

"Their dogs are enormous, with flat ears and long, dangling tongues. The color of their eyes is a burning yellow; their eyes flash fire and shoot off sparks. Their bellies are hollow, their flanks long and narrow. They are tireless and very powerful. They bound here and there, panting, with their tongues hanging out. And they are spotted like an ocelot."

When Motecuhzoma heard this report, he was filled with terror. It was as if his heart had fainted, as if it had shriveled. It was as if he were conquered by despair. . . .

Then the Captain marched to Tenochtitlan. He arrived here during the month called Bird, under the sign of the day 8-Wind. When he entered the city, we gave him chickens, eggs, corn, tortillas and drink. We also gave him firewood, and fodder for his deer. Some of these gifts were sent by the lord of Tenochtitlan, the rest by the lord of Tlatelolco.

Later the Captain marched back to the coast, leaving Don Pedro de Alvarado—The Sun—in command.

During this time, the people asked Motecuhzoma how they should celebrate their god's fiesta. He said: "Dress him in all his finery, in all his sacred ornaments.". . . They left their posts and went to dress him in his sacred finery: his ornaments and his paper clothing.

When this had been done, the celebrants began to sing their songs. That is how they celebrated the first day of the fiesta. On the second day they began to sing again, but without warning they were all put to death. . . . They [the Spanish soldiers] ran in among the dancers, forcing their way to the place

---

9. **deer:** horses.
10. **their food:** probably some form of pasta.

where the drums were played. They attacked the man who was drumming and cut off his arms. Then they cut off his head, and it rolled across the floor.

They attacked the celebrants, stabbing them, spearing them, striking them with their swords. They attacked some of them from behind, and these fell instantly to the ground with their entrails hanging out. Others they beheaded: they cut off their heads, or split their heads to pieces.

They struck others in the shoulders, and their arms were torn from their bodies. They wounded some in the thigh and some in the calf. They slashed others in the abdomen, and their entrails all spilled to the ground. Some attempted to run away, but their intestines dragged as they ran; they seemed to tangle their feet in their own entrails. No matter how they tried to save themselves, they could find no escape. . . .

The Sun treacherously murdered our people on the twentieth day after the Captain left for the coast. We allowed the Captain to return to the city in peace. But on the following day we attacked him with all our might, and that was the beginning of the war. . . .

JAPAN

European Accounts

Sources 7 through 12 from Michael Cooper, ed., They Came to Japan: An Anthology of European Reports on Japan, 1543–1640 *(Berkeley: University of California Press, 1965), pp. 39–41; p. 45; p. 46; p. 47; pp. 64–65; pp. 256–257.*

7. Bernardino de Avila Girón, 1590s

The women are white and usually of goodly appearance; many, indeed, are extremely comely and graceful. All the married women have their teeth stained black with the bark of a tree; maidens and widows do not stain their teeth in this way. None of them has fair hair or blue eyes, nor do they esteem such features. The women use neither perfume nor oil on their faces, neither do they use those filthy things which the women of our country are wont to employ. For indeed there are women who possess more bottles, phials and jugs of cosmetics than any apothecary, yet for all that do not have a better complexion than the Japanese woman who merely washes her face with water from any pond. But it is true that as a mark of honour married women are accustomed to putting on a little powder dissolved in water (although it is not really necessary) and a touch of colour on their lips to hide the dye which comes off on their lips when they stain their teeth. These days worldly women and those married to Chinese whiten their faces exceedingly.

They are of excellent character and as pious as their menfolk are cruel; they are very polite and have less defects than any other persons I have met. The

Chapter 2

First Encounters:

The Creation

of Cultural

Stereotypes

(1450–1650)

most infamous woman of all Japan will, at the very worst, be immodest; and for the most part this happens when they are widows and very rich, or when they have been weakened by poverty since childhood, or when their father, either because he was poor or because he was a knave, sold them, or when they allowed themselves to be abused, as happens amongst us at every hour. The worst possible woman is the one who drinks, but this happens only amongst the lowest women. Withal the women drink very little, although their menfolk are like Frenchmen. Once the women are married, they may be trusted completely for they are the most upright and faithful women in the whole world. And she who errs in this matter pays for it with her head.

8. Cosme de Torres, 1550s–1560s

These Japanese are better disposed to embrace our holy Faith than any other people in the world. They are as prudent as could be desired and are governed by reason just as much as, or even more than, Spaniards; they are more inquisitive than any other people I have met. No men in the wide world more like to hear sermons on how to serve their Creator and save their souls. Their conversation is so polite that they all seem to have been brought up in the palaces of great nobles; in fact, the compliments they pay each other are beyond description. They grumble but little about their neighbours and envy nobody. They do not gamble; just as theft is punished by death, so also gambling. As a pastime they practise with their weapons, at which they are extremely adept, or write couplets, just as the Romans composed poetry, and most of the gentry occupy themselves in this way. They are very brave and put much faith in their weapons; boys over the age of thirteen carry a sword and dagger, and never take them off. They have every kind of weapon, both offensive and defensive, and some are of great value; you may even find swords worth 1,500 *cruzados*. They do not have any kind of guns because they declare that they are for cowards alone. They are the best archers I have seen in this world. They look down on all other nations. . . .

9. Francis Xavier, 1549–1551

The Japanese have a high opinion of themselves because they think that no other nation can compare with them as regards weapons and valour, and so they look down on all foreigners. They greatly prize and value their arms, and prefer to have good weapons, decorated with gold and silver, more than anything else in the world. They carry a sword and dagger both inside and outside the house and lay them at their pillows when they sleep. Never in my life have I met people who rely so much on their arms. They are excellent archers and fight on foot, although there are horses in the country. They are very courteous to each other, but they do not show this courtesy to foreigners, whom they despise. They spend all their money on dress, weapons and servants, and do not possess any treasure. They are very warlike and are always involved in wars, and thus the ablest man becomes the greatest lord. They have but one king, although they have not obeyed him for more than 150 years, and for this reason these internal wars continue.

10. Joao Rodrigues, ca. 1620

[The Japanese] are so crafty in their hearts that nobody can understand them. Whence it is said that they have three hearts: a false one in their mouths for all the world to see, another within their breasts only for their friends, and the third in the depths of their hearts, reserved for themselves alone and never manifested to anybody. As a result all order decays here for everyone acts merely according to the present moment and speaks according to the circumstances and occasion. But they do not use this double dealing to cheat people in business matters, as do the Chinese in their transactions and thieving, for in this respect the Japanese are most exact; but they reserve their treachery for affairs of diplomacy and war in order not to be deceived themselves. And in particular when they wish to kill a person by treachery (a strategem often employed to avoid many deaths), they put on a great pretence by entertaining him with every sign of love and joy—and then in the middle of it all, off comes his head.

11. Alessandro Valignano, ca. 1583

[The] first bad quality [of the Japanese] is that they are much addicted to sensual vices and sins, a thing which has always been true of pagans. The men do not pay much attention to what their wives do in this respect because they trust them exceedingly, but both husbands and relatives may kill an adulterous wife and her partner at will. But even worse is their great dissipation in the sin that does not bear mentioning. This is regarded so lightly that both the boys and the men who consort with them brag and talk about it openly without trying to cover the matter up. This is because the bonzes teach that not only is it not a sin but that it is even something quite natural and virtuous and as such the bonzes to a certain extent reserve this practice for themselves. They are forbidden under grave penalties by ancient laws and customs to have the use of women and so they find a remedy for their disorderly appetites by preaching this pernicious doctrine to the blind pagans. They are certainly past masters in this teaching and so they are worse and more openly involved in it than other people. But their great influence over the people, coupled with the customs handed down by their forefathers, completely blinds the Japanese, who consequently do not realise how abominable and wicked is this sin, as reason itself plainly shows. . . .

Chapter 2

First Encounters:

The Creation

of Cultural

Stereotypes

(1450–1650)

They also have rites and ceremonies so different from those of all the other nations that it seems they deliberately try to be unlike any other people. The things which they do in this respect are beyond imagining and it may truly be said that Japan is a world the reverse of Europe; everything is so different and opposite that they are like us in practically nothing. So great is the difference in their food, clothing, honours, ceremonies, language, management of the household, in their way of negotiating, sitting, building, curing the wounded and sick, teaching and bringing up children, and in everything else, that it can be neither described nor understood. . . .

12. Lourenço Mexia, 1590s

Although [the Japanese] make use of pitch, neither going up nor down, their natural and artificial music is so dissonant and harsh to our ears that it is quite a trial to listen to it for a quarter of an hour; but to please the Japanese we are obliged to listen to it for many hours. They themselves like it so much that they do not think there is anything to equal it in the wide world, and although our music is melodious, it is regarded by them with repugnance. They put on many plays and dramas about various wholesome and joyful things during their festivals, but they are always accompanied by this music.

Sources 13 and 14 from George Elison, Deus Destroyed: The Image of Christianity in Early Modern Japan *(Cambridge: Harvard University Press, 1973), pp. 321–324; 377–378.*

13. Anonymous, *Kirishitan monogatari*, 1639

In the reign of Mikado Go-Nara no In, the hundred and eighth Emperor since the days of Jimmu, some time about the Kōji Period, a Southern Barbarian trading vessel came to our shores. From this ship for the first time emerged an unnamable creature, somewhat similar in shape to a human being, but looking rather more like a long-nosed goblin or the giant demon Mikoshi Nyūdō. Upon close interrogation it was discovered that this was a being called Bateren.

The length of his nose was the first thing which attracted attention: it was like a conch shell (though without its surface warts) attached by suction to his face. His eyes were as large as spectacles, and their insides were yellow. His head was small. On his hands and feet he had long claws. His height exceeded seven feet, and he was black all over; only his nose was red. His teeth were longer than the teeth of a horse. His hair was mouse-grey in color, and over his brow was a shaved spot in the outline of a winebowl turned over. What he said could not be understood at all: his voice was like the screech of an owl.

One and all rushed to see him, crowding all the roads in total lack of restraint. And all were agreed that this apparition was even more dreadful than the fiercest of goblins could ever be. His name was Urugan Bateren. Though at heart he planned to spread the Kirishitan [Christian] religion, he seemed intent first to survey the wisdom of the Japanese people. He brought with him all sort and manner of curious things from South Barbary.

In the Province of Tsu there lived at that time Takayama Lord Hida and his son Ukon Daibu. They extended reverence to this Bateren and became followers of his religion. Introducing him to the likes of Miyoshi Shūri no Daibu and Matsunaga Sōtai, they enabled him to remain in Japan. . . .

14. Suzuki Shosan, 1642

According to the Kirishitan teachings, the Great Buddha named Deus is the Lord of Heaven and Earth and is the One Buddha, self-sufficient in all things. He is the Creator of Heaven and Earth and of the myriad phenomena. This Buddha made his entry into the world one thousand six hundred years ago in South Barbary, saving all sentient beings. His name is Jesus Christus. That other lands do not know him, worshipping instead the worthless Amida and Shaka, is the depth of stupidity. Thus they claim, as I have heard.

To counter, I reply: If Deus is the Lord of Heaven and Earth, and if he created the terrestrial domain and the myriad phenomena, then why has this Deus until now left abandoned a boundless number of countries without making an appearance? Ever since heaven and earth were opened up, the Buddhas of the Three Worlds in alternating appearance have endeavored to save all sentient beings, for how many thousands and tens of thousands of years! But meanwhile, in the end Deus has not appeared in countries other than South Barbary; and what proof is there that he did make an appearance of late, in South Barbary alone? If Deus were truly the Lord of Heaven and Earth, then it has been great inattention on his part to permit mere attendant Buddhas to take over country upon country which he personally created, and allow them to spread their Law and endeavor to save all sentient beings, from the opening up of heaven and earth down to the present day. In truth, this Deus is a foolscap Buddha!

And then there is the story that Jesus Christus upon making his appearance was suspended upon a cross by unenlightened fools of this lower world. Is one to call this the Lord of Heaven and Earth? Is anything more bereft of reason? This Kirishitan sect will not recognize the existence of the One Buddha of Original Illumination and Thusness. They have falsely misappropriated one Buddha to venerate, and have come to this country to spread perniciousness and deviltry. They shall not escape Heaven's punishment for this offence! But many are the unenlightened who fail to see through their clumsy claims, who revere their teachings and even cast away their lives for them. Is this not a disgrace upon our country? Notorious even in foreign lands, lamentable indeed!

Chapter 2

First Encounters:

The Creation

of Cultural

Stereotypes

(1450–1650)

Source 14 from David John Lu, ed. and trans., Sources of Japanese History *(New York: Mc-Graw-Hill, 1974), vol. 1, pp. 207–208.*

15. Tokugawa Temitsu, "Closed Country Edict of 1635"

1. Japanese ships are strictly forbidden to leave for foreign countries.

2. No Japanese is permitted to go abroad. If there is anyone who attempts to do so secretly, he must be executed. The ship so involved must be impounded and its owner arrested, and the matter must be reported to the higher authority.

3. If any Japanese returns from overseas after residing there, he must be put to death.

4. If there is any place where the teachings of padres[11] is practiced, the two of you must order a thorough investigation.

5. Any informer revealing the whereabouts of the followers of padres must be rewarded accordingly. If anyone reveals the whereabouts of a high ranking padre, he must be given one hundred pieces of silver. For those of lower ranks, depending on the deed, the reward must be set accordingly.

6. If a foreign ship has an objection [to the measures adopted] and it becomes necessary to report the matter to Edo,[12] you may ask the Ōmura[13] domain to provide ships to guard the foreign ship. . . .

7. If there are any Southern Barbarians[14] who propagate the teachings of padres, or otherwise commit crimes, they may be incarcerated in the prison. . . .

8. All incoming ships must be carefully searched for the followers of padres. . . .

11. **padres:** fathers, or Roman Catholic priests.
12. **Edo:** Tokyo.
13. **Ōmura:** the area around Nagasaki.
14. **Southern Barbarians:** Europeans.

Now that you have read each account, paying special attention to the five items listed in the Method section of this chapter, you are ready to draw some inferences and conclusions from the evidence.

To begin, review each account and think of some adjectives (beautiful, ugly, honest, dishonest, and the like) that people reading the account at the time might have used to describe or characterize the people who are portrayed. List these adjectives for each account, arranging them according to the categories mentioned earlier: physical appearance, nature or character, traditions and practices, overall impressions, and advice on dealings. After you have done this for each account, use the adjectives to shape a collective image of the people being described. Do the same for the combined European accounts of Africans (or Native Americans or Japanese), and vice versa. Remember to be willing to "read between the lines."

The non-European accounts will require considerably more inference and guesswork on your part. In part this is because three of the four non-European accounts (Sources 3, 6, and 15) were not written specifically to describe European outsiders—only Suzuki Shosan's attack on Christianity (Source 14) could be said to have been so intended. Even so, close examination and analysis of these sources as well as a good deal of historical imagination will reap surprisingly good results.

EPILOGUE

In his introduction to an anthology of European accounts of Japan written between 1543 and 1640, historian Michael Cooper observes, "The Europeans had generally adopted the role of representatives of a superior race. . . . They had taken for granted that Europe was synonymous with the civilized world."[15] By viewing themselves as a superior people and consequently placing a badge of inferiority on every non-European they encountered, most Europeans could justify the sometimes shameful ways in which they dealt with non-European peoples. In Africa, the warring West African states offered Europeans slaves for the guns they were desperate to own. By 1730, approximately 180,000 guns annually were being brought to West Africa by European traders, a figure that increased to over 300,000 before 1800. In exchange, slave ships carried off an estimated 7.3 million people between 1600 and 1810, an average between 1700 and 1810 of approximately 54,500 per year. The destinations for most slaves were Brazil (which first instituted the plantation system in its most complete form),

15. Michael Cooper, ed., *They Came to Japan* (Berkeley: University of California Press, 1965), pp. xi–xii.

Chapter 2

First Encounters:

The Creation

of Cultural

Stereotypes

(1450–1650)

the sugar islands of the West Indies, and the British colonies of North America.

Yet Europeans generally avoided massive intrusion into West Africa until the late nineteenth century. Ironically, what gave Africans this respite was their native diseases. Would-be European colonizers fell prey to diseases like malaria, which had a 75 percent mortality rate at first contact among nonimmune people. Not until medical advances protected them could Europeans penetrate Africa to swallow up that continent in the late 1800s. Failing to use the respite for unification and preparation, the African states, still in disarray, fell quickly if violently.

The same trouble that gave West Africans some breathing room against European incursion nearly wiped out Native Americans: disease. Millions of Native Americans succumbed to the numerous diseases that Europeans unwittingly brought with them, especially smallpox and measles. Whole villages were wiped out, whole nations decimated, as (in the words of one Roman Catholic priest who traveled with Cortés) "they died in heaps." When the superiority of European military technology and the Native Americans' inability to unite against the invaders are added to the equation, their terrible vulnerability to European conquest is easy to understand.

Those Native Americans not subdued by disease, European force of arms, or lack of unity often undercut their own positions. As Native Americans came to desire the products of European mills and factories, they increasingly engaged in wholesale hunting and trapping of animals bearing the skins and furs prized in Europe, exchanging pelts for manufactured goods. Before the arrival of Europeans, Native Americans saw themselves as part of a complete ecosystem that could sustain all life as long as it was kept in balance. In contrast, Europeans saw the environment as a collection of commodities to be extracted and exploited, a perception that Native Americans who coveted European goods were forced to adopt. Thus not only did Native Americans lose their economic and cultural independence, but they also nearly annihilated certain animal species that had sustained them for so long. As warring West African states became dependent on European firearms and traded human beings in order to secure them, so many Native Americans bartered their ecosystem for ironware, weapons, and whiskey.

Japan's expulsion of most Europeans and European ideas (including Christianity) in 1635 and 1639 may have saved Japan from the fates that befell Africans and Native Americans. In 1720, when those prohibitions finally were relaxed, Japan was ready to embark on the ambitious task of economic modernization while at the same time attempting to preserve what they saw as a culture vastly superior to that of the European "barbarians." In 1854, the opening through which trade and ideas passed grew wider. By the late nineteenth century, Japan was the great economic power of Asia, a position it has continued to hold.

As the earth's peoples gradually began to encounter one another, they set in motion a biological "event" that would change many of their lives forever. This process involved the transplantation, sometimes accidentally, of various plants (sugar cane, rice, wheat, bananas, and so forth), animals (horses, pigs, cattle, sheep, cats), and diseases (smallpox, syphilis, and in our own time, AIDS). Indeed, almost five centuries later, that phenomenon is a universal fact of life. An Asian variety of gypsy moth is chewing its way through the forests of the Pacific Northwest. The zebra mussel, released by accident into the Great Lakes in ballast water from Eastern European ships, has spread into Illinois, Mississippi, Ohio, and Tennessee. In the Great Smoky Mountains of North Carolina and Tennessee, wild boars (imported from Germany for sportsmen in the nineteenth century) threaten the plants, grasses, and small animals of the region. A recent survey in Olympia National Park has identified 169 species of plants and animals not indigenous to the Western Hemisphere. In the southern United States, the kudzu vine (imported from Japan to combat erosion) was dubbed by the *Los Angeles Times* (July 21, 1992), "the national plant of Dixie" and is almost out of control in some areas. Whether purposeful or accidental, whether beneficial or detrimental, the environmental exchange continues.

Most of the Europeans who first encountered other people were celebrated as heroes in their native lands. Jesuit missionary to Japan Francis Xavier was elevated to sainthood in the Roman Catholic Church. Bartolomeu Dias and Vasco da Gama were honored in Portugal, as were Columbus, Cortés, and a host of conquistadors in Spain. Yet for some, fame was fleeting. Cortés returned to Spain in 1528 a fabulously wealthy man but over time lost most of his fortune in ill-fated expeditions and died in modest circumstances in 1547. In his will, he recognized the four children he had fathered by Native American women (Cortés was married at the time) and worried about the morality of what he had done. In 1562, his body was taken to Mexico to be reburied. In 1794, his remains were moved again, this time to the chapel of a Mexican hospital that he had endowed. In 1823, Cortés's remains disappeared for good, perhaps hidden to protect them from politically motivated grave robbers after Mexico declared its independence from Spain. (Rumors abound that the remains were secretly carried back across the Atlantic.) The ultimate, invincible conquistador has vanished, but his legacy lives on.

CHAPTER THREE

THE CONFUCIAN FAMILY (1600–1800)

In a novel called *Family,* Ba Jin, one of China's foremost modern writers, portrays the frustrations of Westernized youth in early twentieth-century China through the story of a single, well-to-do household. Stifled by familial conventions and the authority of their elders, the young people in this family crave the individual freedom associated with modern life. The boldest of them, goaded to the point of rebellion, finally cries out, "What a cursed life . . . ," and berates his brothers for their docility. "How much abuse can you take? You talk a lot about opposing the patriarchal family system, but actually you support it. Your ideas are new but your conduct is old. You're all spineless! You're full of contradictions!"[1]

To the generation of Ba Jin in the 1920s, the old-style family depicted

in this novel represented what was wrong with China and needed changing. They saw it as both a symbol and a source of China's backwardness because it embodied an outmoded Confucian doctrine of familialism known as *xiao* that hindered the growth of individualism. Often translated as "filiality" or "filial piety," this doctrine presumed that households, not individuals, formed the basis of society and that social health and stability depended on the vitality of a particular kind of patriarchal family. Consequently, it called upon people to seek esteem and identity through their family rather than through individual accomplishments and to set aside personal interests in deference to household leaders. Such values, twentieth-century reformers felt, stood in sharp contrast to those of the modern West where the individual was recognized as the basic unit of society and accorded legal rights and freedoms.

They argued that this familialism and the traditional family patterned upon it had to be destroyed before China could hope to adopt other

1. This passage comes from the Sidney Shapiro translation of *Family* (New York: Doubleday Anchor Books, 1972), pp. 94–95, a version originally published in China (Beijing: Foreign Languages Press, 1958).

modern Western institutions and values. Opposition to the Confucian family thus played a major role in Chinese reform movements from the first Cultural Revolution of 1916 down to the Great Proletarian Cultural Revolution of the 1960s. As a result, the Confucian family often served as a symbol of all the antiquated social and cultural values that reformers wished to change, continuing in a strange new way the old belief that society and family were intimately related. Rebellion against one clearly implied rebellion against the other.

Westernized reformers, however, were not the first Chinese to view the old family system with a critical eye. Already in the seventeenth and eighteenth centuries, a number of social observers had begun to show concern for what they viewed as its shortcomings, and a literary movement sprang up to expose some of its worst abuses. Unlike Westernized reformers of a later date, these premodern critics did not reject the Confucian family outright nor advocate a new set of social values. They accepted the idea that a healthy society depended on solid, traditional families. But they strongly objected to some of the practices that occurred within it, particularly the mistreatment of women and children. In their view, too many men took undue advantage of the household authority that the Confucian family system vested in them to victimize weaker members. Using novels and short stories to portray the most outrageous of these offenses, writers tried to bring about a more humane family—and society—by discrediting such abuse.

In doing so, in fact, these traditional critics reaffirmed what originally attracted Confucian thinkers to family life: the tendency of families to temper authority with compassion. Beginning with Confucius himself, who lived at the turn of the fifth century B.C.E., Confucians called for an ethical society in which people put principle above selfish desires. And because they felt that submission to authority helped people curb selfishness, they advocated hierarchical rather than equal social relations. Recognizing the problems created by overly rigid or overbearing authority, however, they cautioned people in positions of power to be humane as well as principled. No other institution, in their view, demonstrated how to balance these two qualities better than the patriarchal family, a seemingly "natural" group in which the affectionate authority of fathers elicited the loving respect of spouses and children. As they saw it, this family with its unique combination of compassion and power provided a model for society as a whole. For its patterns of leadership and deference assured humane rulers on one hand and respectful subjects on the other. For over two millennia, therefore, they argued that a just and stable society in China depended on the vitality of the Confucian family.

The strong and often conflicting opinions of the family held by these Chinese observers reflects a dilemma contemporary historians face in studying such institutions, particularly those that come out of non-Western traditions. They must consciously choose the cultural and ethical standpoint from which to approach their subjects. Such decisions are hard enough for those who want to view the past through non-Eurocentric eyes but remain culturally indebted to the West. But current ethical concerns complicate the matter further. Should contemporary historians, for example, try to set aside all current Western values and view the patriarchal family strictly from a traditional Confucian point of view? Or should they deal with it from an openly feminist stance, say, or perhaps as advocates of more traditional family standards? A globally minded historian, of course, must always be concerned with such perspectives. But dealing with an emotionally laden subject of this sort requires extra care in deciding how to treat the subject.

It should come as no surprise, then, that your task here is to decide how to approach the Confucian family. Should we, for example, treat it as a backward and oppressive institution that needs to be discredited—in order to foster a more individualistic, Western society in China, perhaps, or to counter abuses to women everywhere? Or should we present it as an important cultural legacy that may bring some balance to a contemporary world that has become supremely individualistic? Or yet again, in a related vein, maybe we should feature it as an institution with validity for East Asian societies, but not necessarily for the contemporary West. Other possibilities, too, will no doubt come to mind. But the question remains, how would *you* decide to approach an institution of this sort?

BACKGROUND

The family model envisioned by Confucian thinkers was always more of a social ideal than a widespread reality. In actual practice, the family, or *jia*, proved a rather flexible institution throughout Chinese history, assuming different forms and sizes to accommodate changing needs. By custom as well as imperial law, residential households, or *hu*, remained the basic family unit, but such households could and did vary a great deal in their composition as well as in their interaction with more distant

kin. In some situations, related households operated quite independently of each other, whereas in others they actively cooperated as branches of a common lineage. Variations frequently resulted from the different roles households played in traditional society.

Although primarily a social unit, providing companionship, nurture, and group support to its members, the household often also functioned as an economic institution. Farms, workshops, and businesses, for example, were often run as family enterprises in premodern China so that traditional households not only consumed goods in common but usually produced them in common as well. The family also served as a framework through which members could pool funds in order to undertake projects too expensive for individual members to afford and to provide social services for the young, the aged, and the needy. Households were religious units, too, and members regularly joined together in veneration of household gods and ancestral spirits. Belief in the continuing presence of deceased members who needed tending, of course, gave the living a unique sense of the family. As caretakers of past as well as future generations, they tended to regard the household patrimony not so much as their own property but a shared legacy that belonged as much to their forebears and progeny as to themselves.

By late traditional times, that is from the sixteenth through the nineteenth centuries, the most prevalent type of family found in China was the small *conjugal family* in which a married couple lived alone with their unwed children. This two-generational family well suited most of the population, who were farmers engaged in labor-intensive, subsistence agriculture, a form of farming in which people grew crops to feed their own households rather than for sale in a market. Because average farm holdings tended to be small, they could not support large numbers of dependents. Estimates vary, but probably something like two-thirds of all families in late traditional times were of this type and typically included no more than three

to six members. Most Chinese of the time thus grew up and lived out their lives in small households. Because farm families typically lived together in villages rather than on separate home sites scattered across the countryside, however, people regularly interacted in a larger social context.

Despite the fact that it was commonplace, the small, conjugal household was not the family that Confucians venerated. Their attention focused instead upon a less common version known as the *joint family*. In the joint family, male children remained with their parents after getting married, creating a large, multigenerational household whose adult members shared a common income along with domestic tasks. In its basic form, the joint family consisted of at least three generations: an original set of parents, their married sons and their wives, and all the grandchildren. But tradition held that up to five generations should remain together. Inasmuch as men could legally take more than one consort, even households with only the minimal number of generations could become very large indeed. And because most also employed large numbers of live-in porters, maids, cooks, and other domestic help, joint households often included dozens of people, and some became enormous establishments with a hundred or more residents.

A large income was generally necessary to support such large households, and so such joint families tended to be found only among wealthy strata of society. Affluent merchants and successful farmers who accumulated large acreage favored it, as did members of the official Mandarin elite, who by virtue of their success in the imperial examination system received special legal privileges and employment opportunities, including a near monopoly of government posts. Although elite households often maintained homes in the cities, most invested in farm land that could be rented out to increase their income. The need to supervise these investments as well as a tradition of genteel country living induced many to keep rural residences, too. And the ideal, if not always the reality, of upper-class life was a spacious, well-run country house overflowing with children and servants and surrounded by gardens and cultivated fields.

Even the wealthiest of the elite, however, found it difficult to maintain a large, multigenerational household over long periods of time. To do so, couples in each generation had to produce numerous sons who survived into adulthood to bear their offspring in turn. Moreover, the family had to avoid a break-up whenever the head of the household died. Because imperial law did not recognize primogeniture (inheritance by the eldest son), the death of the patriarch created a vulnerable situation for joint families. All sons could legally claim an equal portion of the estate, and any one of them might thus take his share of the family assets and move away, leaving the others that much poorer. This system of *partible* or equal inheritance tended to diminish a joint family's wealth and property over time and could ultimately

deprive remaining members of the resources necessary to sustain even a moderate household. It did, however, force new heads of the family to be considerate of siblings in order to attempt to forestall future splits.

To help offset this tendency toward fragmentation and to strengthen familialism, members of the elite, particularly in south China, often formed common descent groups called *zu*, or lineages. These were associations of families believed to have descended on the male side from a common ancestor. Viewing themselves as natural kinsmen, they promoted a corporate sense of identity by compiling genealogies and conducting family affairs in common. One of their most important functions was to assist with important family events like funerals and weddings and to conduct annual ancestral rites. But they also frequently ran schools for the children of members, loaned out capital within the group, and dispensed charity to needier branches. To finance these services, most invested funds collected from their membership in land or other revenue producing property. Such activities helped participating families survive difficult times and avoid their own disintegration.

Nonetheless, really large joint families remained relatively rare. Far more common was a smaller variant known as the *stem family*. In this version, only one married son, usually the eldest, remained at home with his parents. Since family descent was traced in a patrilinear fashion with the line from eldest son to eldest son viewed as its core, this combination of father and eldest son represented the main "stem" or trunk of the immediate family tree. Often the stem family resulted from the fragmentation of a bigger household or from the first efforts of a more prosperous couple to establish a joint family. It offered parents an important benefit: a live-in son and his wife could provide them with care in their old age. And because by custom such caretakers could enjoy full use of family property, it proved attractive to the younger generation, too, providing some protection from the claims of other siblings on the family patrimony.

Life in any of these elite households was far from casual. A strict hierarchy prevailed in all affairs, regulating who could do what and when. Status and authority depended upon the sex, age, and proximity of household members to the head of the family, who was usually the oldest adult male. Tradition firmly fixed the principles behind this hierarchy: females took second place to males, the young deferred to the old, and all obeyed the patriarch without question. Differences of age and relationship to the patriarch created distinctions within generations as well as between them. Although cousins, who usually grew up together within such families, were deemed a close-knit group and often given a common element in their names to emphasize their connection, they did not enjoy equal status. Boys, of course, outranked girls. But even among male children, those descended from the patriarch's principal wife rated higher than others, and the firstborn sons of all couples enjoyed greater favor than their siblings. These distinctions reflected a belief in patrilinear descent. Family lineage was reckoned only in terms of the male side and primarily through a main stem or family line engendered by the eldest son in every generation.

From this vantage point, women seemed to be only temporary adjuncts to the family rather than essential members—despite the fact that they were biologically as significant as the men to its continuity. Daughters, who would leave the paternal home to join other households at marriage and bear children elsewhere, seemed particularly superfluous. Though the birth of a girl as a firstborn child might occasionally be celebrated because it proved the fertility of the mother, female births were usually received with disappointment. The birth of a boy, however, was invariably a source of joy, representing renewal and continuity for the family and security for the mother. Only by producing a son could she really establish her position as a valuable member of her husband's family. Until she did so, in fact, she tended to be viewed as an outsider who could be sent away or replaced by another consort. A wife's sense of family, therefore, was probably very different from a husband's, since she had no acknowledged ties to ancestors nor any feeling of closeness to her spouse's relatives. Her immediate children, especially her sons, and their eventual male children, were the only relatives to whom she was securely bound. For that reason, a woman who failed to bear a son faced a life of great anxiety.

Because of their lower rank in the family, daughters were usually raised differently from sons. Elite families had no need to resort to female infanticide, as poor families sometimes did, but they generally lavished far more attention and affection upon sons who would remain in the household after they grew up than upon daughters who would be married off into other families. Both might enjoy considerable indulgence until about the age of six when serious training for later life usually began. Boys then began studying with male tutors who taught them to read and write so that they could go on to higher study outside the home. Girls, however, seldom received this kind of education. Instead, other women in the household taught them how to do needlework and perform household tasks.

Even more debilitating than denying girls education was the practice of tightly binding their feet. This painful custom was performed to keep their feet tiny, since the resulting "golden lotuses" were deemed highly erotic and an important allure in securing a husband. First adopted by professional entertainers in the fashionable quarters of commercial cities that sprang up in the Sung dynasty during the eleventh and twelfth centuries, this practice gradually gained popularity among the Mandarin elite. By the start of the Ming dynasty in the fourteenth century, it had become a prevalent status symbol for all who aspired to the upper reaches of the social world. Although the practice posed problems

for all women who had their feet bound, it proved particularly difficult for those who were not wealthy enough to afford many servants: it left them near-cripples with limited mobility and restricted them even more than their lack of education to a domestic life within the confines of the home.

Patrilineal considerations dominated marriage rites as much as child-rearing practices. Seen as a family rather than an individual matter, marriage was understood as a means of securing heirs to perpetuate the male line of descent. Romantic feelings, therefore, seldom received much consideration in marriages. Indeed, tradition held that the bride and groom should not be too emotionally involved at the start of a marriage because closeness might encourage them to side against the rest of the family. Ideally, both would be teenagers who only met face to face on their wedding night. For obvious reasons, then, marriages had to be arranged by older members of the family who relied on professional brokers, or "go-betweens," to find suitable partners for their offspring. A groom's family worried primarily about the health and character of a prospective bride, whereas a girl's family had to think about the status and security she would enjoy in the new home—and both weighed any advantages the alliance would bring their household.

Even after marriage, a couple seldom spent a lot of time together. Men had little to do with the day-to-day running of the household and were frequently out of the home. New brides, therefore, were left largely to the company of their mothers-in-law and other female relatives with whom they had to work closely in performing household tasks. The relationship between daughter-in-law and mother-in-law often proved more critical to the happiness of a family than the bond between husband and wife. A daughter-in-law, of course, posed a potential rival to a mother-in-law, because both depended on the same man to secure their status in the family. Tension between these two "outsiders" was proverbial. In the case of conflict, however, a daughter-in-law generally fared worse, because she was a newcomer and lower in generational status. Pleasing her mother-in-law thus became a bride's highest priority, but she also had to worry about pleasing her husband, if only to ensure that he fathered children who would enhance her value in the family.

Here, too, she was often at a disadvantage, for the standard of fidelity differed for men and women. Women were expected to remain absolutely faithful to their husbands, ostensibly to preserve their honor as well as to avoid bearing sons whose legitimacy might be questioned. Upper-class morals thus dictated that women stay within their homes as much as possible and keep to particular areas of the household where they would not encounter men other than their husbands and sons. Men, however, were under no such constraints. Although enjoined not to live dissolute lives, they were free to engage in occasional, discreet affairs with household maids or professional entertainers. They could also bring women into the household as concubines. Though not formal wives, concubines enjoyed a legal status in the family, particularly if they bore a son. In theory a man took a concubine only when his wife proved unable to bear an heir, and thus the practice could be justified as a means of perpetuating the family. But men of means often acquired concubines to gratify their own pleasure as much as to secure heirs. Generally purchased from poor families and thus considered a form of property, concubines had a more tenuous role in the patriarchal family than wives. Both wives and mothers-in-law had reason to resent concubines, and jealousy between these women was a frequent source of domestic strife in big, wealthy households.

However unpleasant life might become in a traditional household, wives seldom sought a divorce. Although legally available, it did not offer a very satisfactory solution, because "respectable" women had almost nowhere to turn once they left the marriage home. The stigma of divorce made second marriages difficult to arrange, and upper-class women could find almost no opportunities for acceptable employment outside the home. Moreover, the belief that daughters did not belong with their natal family made parents reluctant to welcome back a divorcee. As a result, unhappy wives usually remained with their husbands' families, trying to find solace in children, if they had any. In extreme cases, they escaped hopeless situations through suicide, finding in death a way to punish uncaring relatives with dishonor as well as to end their own suffering.

Difficult as the Confucian family may have proved for some of its individual members, it clearly did train people to think in group rather than personal terms. Children grew up not only with multiple siblings but often with many cousins. And from an early age, they became accustomed to recognizing and accommodating a vast array of older relatives. Precise names,

most without any Western equivalent, thus existed for all possible kinship relationships, and family members routinely defined themselves in terms of a complex household that instilled in them a keen sense of gender and age hierarchy. Peaks of authority regularly alternated with valleys of submission, forcing almost everyone to explore the nuances of group dynamics. Such experiences no doubt explain why group solidarity and harmony came to be so prized in the Confucian family.

THE METHOD

If you think about it, the question of how to view the Confucian family really has several facets. There is, of course, the matter of what the Confucian family may have been like in practice. This may seem a straightforward problem in social history, but a moment's reflection will remind you that what we today see of the past depends in no small part on what the people of the past have handed down to us. Thus it is important to know how the Chinese themselves have regarded the institution—both in traditional and modern terms—for their viewpoints have helped to determine how the institution has been remembered and represented. And underlying this consideration lurks still another: how do our contemporary attitudes affect what we choose to emphasize or show about a problematic institution of this sort?

In one way or another, therefore, you will have to come to grips with

each of these questions as you try to decide what position to take with regard to this institution. Doing so may not only give you some insight into how to regard the Confucian family in its historical context. We hope it will also make you aware of the problem all historians face in defining their relationship to a subject. That is, how does one approach something from another time or place? What is the proper degree of distance or involvement to take? In whose perspective, or in what context, should it be presented? These questions have no easy answers, particularly today, when new fields of history and new viewpoints are challenging longstanding assumptions almost daily.

Sources that bear directly on two of the considerations raised above appear in the Evidence section that follows. The first five represent documents that afford us some evidence of actual life in the Confucian family in late traditional times in China before the advent of modern Western ways. Source 1, a conventional elite family portrait from the sixteenth century, and Source 3, a painting of a typical upper-class rural compound from the same period, offer visual glimpses of such families and their homes. You can glean a more detailed sense of elite family life, however, from Source 2, part of a manual or set of practical instructions compiled in the late sixteenth century by one of the elders of the Miu lineage to help kinsmen run their member households. Gui Youguang's sixteenth-century essay entitled "A Sketch of My Mother," which appears as Source 4, reveals the personal side of such life in very moving and positive terms. On the other hand, Source 5, taken from a sixteenth-century village handbook, suggests a harsher side of family life, presenting sample contracts that detailed the legal terms for the sale of women and children.

The other five sources, though they do provide some additional information about family life, primarily illustrate different Chinese perspectives on the Confucian family. Sources 6 and 7 give orthodox Confucian views. Both come from texts written much earlier than the sixteenth century, but these two works, the *Classic of Filiality* of about the second century B.C.E. and Zhu Xi's twelfth-century *Family Rituals,* remained standard references on ideal family behavior throughout the late traditional period. Indeed, references to both appear in the first batch of documents. Sources 8 and 9 by way of contrast point out the abuses in the family system that began to trouble literary writers of the seventeenth and eighteenth centuries. Source 8, taken from Pu Sul-

ing's novel *The Bonds of Matrimony,* focuses on issues stemming from concubinage and divorce, while Source 9, a poem by Zheng Xie (Cheng Hsieh), deals with the problematic relationship between brides and their mothers-in-law. Finally, Source 10, part of a famous essay by the first head of the Chinese Communist Party and one of twentieth-century China's leading intellectuals, Chen Duxiu (Ch'en Tu-hsiu), expresses the disparaging view of the Confucian family adopted by westernizing reformers at the end of the traditional period.

A review of this documentary material should help to answer the first two questions posed at the start of this section—that is, what was the Confucian family like and how have the Chinese regarded it? But in dealing with the third problem, the way in which a current Westerner may see the Confucian family, you will have to think on your own about contemporary values and how they intrude to shape our perspective on the past. To help you in this process, you might take a moment at the start to jot down some key aspects of family life like romance, fidelity, divorce, child-rearing, gender, generational roles, and so on. Then as you go through the sources, take notes on how early Confucians, later critics, and eventual reformers viewed each of these. And finally, ask yourself how *you* view these same aspects. Do your views accord with any of the others? Why might that be so? Which views overall do you think should determine how we look back at the Confucian family? Why?

THE EVIDENCE

Source 1 from the Metropolitan Museum of Art. Anonymous gift, 1942 (42.190.1).

1. Ming Family Portrait, late 16th century

Source 2 from Patricia Buckley Ebrey, Chinese Civilization and Society: A Sourcebook *(New York: The Free Press, 1981), pp. 161–166.*

2. Family Instructions for the Miu Lineage, late 16th century

OBSERVE THE RITUALS AND PROPRIETIES

1. Capping and wedding ceremonies should be carried out according to one's means. Funerals and burials, being important matters, should be more elaborate, but one should still be mindful of financial considerations. Any other petty formalities not found in the *Book of Rites* should be abolished.

2. Marriage arrangements should not be made final by the presenting of betrothal gifts until the boy and girl have both reached thirteen; otherwise, time might bring about changes which cause regrets.

3. For the seasonal sacrifices, the ancestral temple should be prepared in advance and the ceremonies performed at dawn in accordance with [Chu Hsi's] *Family Rituals* and our own ancestral temple regulations. . . .

5. Sacrifices at the graves should be made on Tomb-Sweeping Day and at the Autumn Festival. Because the distances to different mountains vary, it is difficult to reach every grave on those days. Therefore, all branch families should be notified in advance of the order of priority: first, the founding father of our lineage; then ancestors earlier than great-great-grandfather; next, ancestors down to each person's grandfather. Established customs should be followed in deciding how much wine and meat should be used, how many different kinds of sacrificial offerings should be presented, and how much of the yearly budget should be spent on the sacrifices. All of these should be recorded in a special "sacrifice book" in order to set standards.

6. Not celebrating one's birthday has since ancient times been regarded as an exemplary virtue. An exception is the birthdays of those who are beyond their sixty-first year, which should be celebrated by their sons and grandsons drinking to their health. But under no circumstances should birthdays become pretexts for heavy drinking. If either of one's parents has died, it is an especially unfilial act to forget him or her and indulge in drinking and feasting. Furthermore, to drink until dead-drunk not only affects one's mind but also harms one's health. The numbers of people who have been ruined by drinking should serve as a warning.

7. On reaching five, a boy should be taught to recite the primers and not be allowed to show arrogance or laziness. On reaching six, a girl should be taught *Admonitions for Women* and not be allowed to venture out of her cham-

ber. If children are frequently given snacks and playfully entertained, their nature will be spoiled and they will grow up to be unruly and bad. This can be prevented if caught at an early age.

EXERCISE RESTRAINT

1. Our young people should know their place and observe correct manners. They are not permitted to gamble, to fight, to engage in lawsuits, or to deal in salt privately. Such unlawful acts will only lead to their own downfall.

2. If land or property is not obtained by righteous means, descendants will not be able to enjoy it. When the ancients invented characters, they put gold next to two spears to mean "money," indicating that the danger of plunder or robbery is associated with it. If money is not accumulated by good means, it will disperse like overflowing water; how could it be put to any good? The result is misfortune for oneself as well as for one's posterity. This is the meaning of the saying: "The way of Heaven detests fullness, and only the humble gain." Therefore, accumulation of great wealth inevitably leads to great loss. How true are the words of Lao Tzu!

A person's fortune and rank are predestined. One can only do one's best according to propriety and one's own ability; the rest is up to Heaven. If one is easily contented, then a diet of vegetables and soups provides a lifetime of joy. If one does not know one's limitations and tries to accumulate wealth by immoral and dishonest means, how can one avoid disaster? To be able to support oneself through life and not leave one's sons and grandsons in hunger and cold is enough; why should one toil so much?

3. Pride is a dangerous trait. Those who pride themselves on wealth, rank, or learning are inviting evil consequences. Even if one's accomplishments are indeed unique, there is no need to press them on anyone else. "The way of Heaven detests fullness, and only the humble gain." I have seen the truth of this saying many times.

4. Taking concubines in order to beget heirs should be a last resort, for the sons of the legal wife and the sons of the concubine are never of one mind, causing innumerable conflicts between half brothers. If the parents are in the least partial, problems will multiply, creating misfortune in later generations. Since families have been ruined because of this, it should not be taken lightly.

5. Just as diseases are caused by what goes into one's mouth, misfortunes are caused by what comes out of one's mouth. Those who are immoderate in eating and unrestrained in speaking have no one else to blame for their own ruin.

6. Most men lack resolve and listen to what their women say. As a result, blood relatives become estranged and competitiveness, suspicion, and distance arise between them. Therefore, when a wife first comes into a family, it should be made clear to her that such things are prohibited. "Start teaching one's son when he is a baby, start teaching one's daughter-in-law when she first arrives." That is to say, preventive measures should be taken early.

7. "A family's fortune can be foretold from whether its members are early risers" is a maxim of our ancient sages. Everyone, male and female, should rise before dawn and should not go to bed until after the first drum. Never should they indulge themselves in a false sense of security and leisure, for such behavior will eventually lead them to poverty.

8. Young family members who deliberately violate family regulations should be taken to the family temple, have their offenses reported to the ancestors, and be severely punished. They should then be taught to improve themselves. Those who do not accept punishment or persist in their wrongdoings will being harm to themselves.

9. As a preventive measure against the unpredictable, the gates should be closed at dusk, and no one should be allowed to go out. Even when there are visitors, dinner parties should end early, so that there will be no need for lighting lamps and candles. On very hot or very cold days, one should be especially considerate of the kitchen servants.

10. For generations this family has dwelt in the country, and everyone has had a set profession; therefore, our descendants should not be allowed to change their place of residence. After living in the city for three years, a person forgets everything about farming; after ten years, he does not even know his lineage. Extravagance and leisure transform people, and it is hard for anyone to remain unaffected. I once remarked that country living has all the advantages, and that the only legitimate excuse to live in a city temporarily is to flee from bandits.

11. The inner and outer rooms, halls, doorways, and furniture should be swept and dusted every morning at dawn. Dirty doorways and courtyards and haphazardly placed furniture are sure signs of a declining family. Therefore, a schedule should be followed for cleaning them, with no excuses allowed.

12. Those in charge of cooking and kitchen work should make sure that breakfast is served before nine o'clock in the morning and dinner before five o'clock in the afternoon. Every evening the iron wok and other utensils should be washed and put away, so that the next morning, after rising at dawn, one can expect tea and breakfast to be prepared immediately and served on time. In the kitchen no lamps are allowed in the morning or at

night. This is not only to save the expense, but also to avoid harmful contamination of food. Although this is a small matter, it has a great effect on health. Furthermore, since all members of the family have their regular work to do, letting them toil all day without giving them meals at regular hours is no way to provide comfort and relief for them. If these rules are deliberately violated, the person in charge will be punished as an example to the rest.

13. On the tenth and twenty-fifth days of every month, all the members of this branch, from the honored aged members to the youngsters, should gather at dusk for a meeting. Each will give an account of what he has learned, by either calling attention to examples of good and evil, or encouraging diligence, or expounding his obligations, or pointing out tasks to be completed. Each member will take turns presenting his own opinions and listening attentively to others. He should examine himself in the matters being discussed and make efforts to improve himself. The purpose of these meetings is to encourage one another in virtue and to correct each other's mistakes.

14. Women from lower-class families who stop at our houses tend to gossip, create conflicts, peek into the kitchens, or induce our women to believe in prayer and fortune-telling, thereby cheating them out of their money and possessions. Consequently, one should question these women often and punish those who come for no reason, so as to put a stop to the traffic.

15. Blood relatives are as close as the branches of a tree, yet their relationships can still be differentiated according to importance and priority: parents should be considered before brothers, and brothers should be considered before wives and children. Each person should fulfill his own duties and share with others profit and loss, joy and sorrow, life and death. In this way, the family will get along well and be blessed by Heaven. Should family members fight over property or end up treating each other like enemies, then when death or misfortune strikes they will be of even less use than strangers. If our ancestors have consciousness, they will not tolerate these unprincipled descendants who are but animals in man's clothing. Heaven responds to human vices with punishments as surely as an echo follows a sound. I hope my sons and grandsons take my words seriously.

16. To get along with patrilineal relatives, fellow villagers, and relatives through marriage, one should be gentle in speech and mild in manners. When one is opposed by others, one may remonstrate with them; but when others fall short because of their limitations, one should be tolerant. If one's youngsters or servants get into fights with others, one should look into oneself to find the blame. It is better to be wronged than to wrong others. Those who take affront and become enraged, who conceal their own shortcomings and seek to defeat others, are courting immediate misfortune. Even if the other party is unbearably unreasonable, one should contemplate the fact that the

ancient sages had to endure much more. If one remains tolerant and forgiving, one will be able to curb the other party's violence.

PRESERVE THE FAMILY PROPERTY

1. The houses, fields, and ponds that have been accumulated by the family should not be divided or sold. Violators of this rule will be severely admonished and barred from the ancestral temple.

2. Maps of the family graves should be printed. The graves are to be well taken care of and frequently repaired. The custodians of the graves should be treated well.

3. Books constitute the lifeline of a family. A record should be kept of their titles. They should be aired out at regular intervals, stored in a high chamber, and kept from being dispersed. In this way we can keep intact our ancestors' writings.

4. Paintings, maps, books, scrolls, and utensils should be stored in separate wooden cabinets. There should be a notebook in which all these are registered. Whenever an item is loaned to someone, a slip of paper with the description of the item should be temporarily pasted on the shelf. When the item is returned, it should be replaced in its original position.

5. There are many thieves in the country; therefore, one should be careful not to leave clothing and other objects about. Doors should be locked and carefully guarded. Be prepared! On noticing anything suspicious, look into it immediately and take preventive action, in order to achieve maximum security.

6. In order to cultivate the moral character of the young, one must severely punish those who are so unruly that they have no sense of righteousness or who so indulge their desires that they destroy their own health. One should also correct those who have improper hobbies, such as making too many friends and avoiding work, indulging in playing musical instruments and the game of Go, collecting art and valuables, composing music, singing, or dancing. All these hobbies destroy a person's ambition. Those who indulge in them may consider themselves free spirits; yet little do they know that these hobbies are their most harmful enemies.

7. If among patrilineal and affinal [by marriage] relatives and fellow villagers there are people who give importance to propriety and are respected for their learning and ability, one should frequently visit them to request advice and offer one's respects. Then, in case of emergencies in the family, one will be able to obtain help from them. Besides, receiving frequent advice is good in itself. By contrast, to make friends with the wrong sort of people and

join them in evil deeds is to set a trap for oneself. If one is jealous of upright gentlemen and avoids upright discourse, misfortune will strike, the family will be ruined, lives may even be lost. Then it will be too late for regrets.

8. Scholars, farmers, artisans, and merchants all hold respectable occupations. Scholarship ranks the highest; farming is next; and then craft and business. However, it should be up to the individual to measure his ability against his aspirations as well as to find the most suitable occupation for himself. In these family instructions, I have given first place to the profession of scholarship, but have also devoted a great deal of attention to the work of farmers, artisans, and merchants. These family instructions attempt to show the correct procedures to be followed in everyday life. If one truly understands them and fulfills the duties appropriate to his way of life; if one upholds public and private obligations; if one can in good conscience invite Heaven's favor, then misfortune will stay away and bliss will enter without conscious effort on one's part. In this way, a person can face his ancestors without shame and instruct his posterity; there are no other secrets to having good and capable descendants.

Source 3 from James Cahill, The Painter's Practice: How Artists Lived and Worked in Traditional China *(New York: Columbia University Press), p. 79. Reproduced by permission of the National Museum of China.*

3. Yüan Chiang, Section of "The East Garden" Handscroll, late 17th century

Source 4 from Poetry and Prose of the Ming and Qing (Beijing: Chinese Literature, Panda Books, 1986), pp. 40–42.

4. Gui Youguang, "A Sketch of My Mother," late 16th century

My mother, a daughter of the Zhou family, was born on the eleventh day of the second month of the first year of the Hong Zhi period [1488]. She came to our family at the age of sixteen and the next year gave birth to Shujing, my elder sister. The year after that I was born. The following year she had a girl who died at birth and a miscarriage a year later. The next year after a twelve-month pregnancy she was delivered of another son, Youshang. Shushun and Yougong were born in the two years following. Her health was better after Yougong's birth than when nursing the rest of us; but her mind was troubled and she confided to her maids that she felt such a brood of little ones a great burden. Then one old servant gave her two snails in a cup of water, saying, "Drink this, and you will have no more children." My mother drank the potion and subsequently lost her voice. On the twenty-third day of the fifth month of the eighth year of the Zheng De period [1513], she died. When we children saw our elders weep, we wept too, although we thought—poor fools!—that our mother was only sleeping. Then a portrait-painter was summoned to paint her portrait, and the family led out two of us, telling him: "For the upper half of the face, take Youguang as model; for the lower half, his elder sister." For we were the two who most resembled our mother.

My mother's own name was Gui. Her grandfather's name was Ming, her father's Xing, and he was a student of the Imperial College. Her mother's maiden name was He. Her family had lived for generations in Wujiaqiao, thirty li to the southeast of the county town. South of Qiandunpu, all the inhabitants from Zhiqiao to east of Xiaogang belong to the Zhou clan. Her father and three uncles were big merchants, but they were honest, simple folk, chatty as villagers and immensely attached to all their nephews and nieces. When my mother went back to Wujiaqiao she would work in the cotton fields, while during visits to town she would often weave by lamplight late into the night. Her father used to send men with gifts for us almost every other day; but though she had no worry about rice or salt, she worked as hard as if her next meal depended on it. In winter she got the maids to knead coal dust into coal-balls for the stove and lay them to dry by the steps. In her rooms was no waste, no idle hands in her house. While the bigger boys and girls clung to her clothes and the smallest sucked at her breast, her hands were still busy with sewing. Our home was spotless, the servants so kindly treated that even when she punished them they never complained. Every year when gifts of fish, crabs and sweetmeats came from her home, she would see that everybody had his share, and so the whole household rejoiced at the sight of messengers from Wujiaqiao. At seven I went to school with my cousin Yujia, and if the weather was bad, windy or drizzling, he stayed at home; but this was never allowed me, much as I longed for it. When my mother woke up in the night she made me recite whole passages from the *Book of Filial Piety,* pleased whenever I rattled them off without hestitating over a single word.

After my mother's death her own mother died. Indeed, an epidemic carried off thirty members of the Zhou family including her brother's wife and her fourth sister, who had married a man named Gu. Only her father and second brother survived. Eleven years after my mother's death, my eldest sister married Wang Sanjie—a match arranged by my mother. The year after that I started attending the prefectural school and four years later I married—another match she had arranged. In due course we had a daughter whom I loved dearly, for the little girl reminded us of my mother. In the middle of the night my wife and I would shed tears, because I could remember one or two trifles as if they had happened only yesterday, while all the rest was forgotten. Ah, Heaven have pity on those who have lost their mothers!

Source 5 from Patricia Buckley Ebrey, Chinese Civilization and Society: A Sourcebook *(New York: The Free Press, 1981), p. 139.*

5. Sample Contracts for Purchasing a Concubine and Selling a Son, 16th century

SAMPLE CONTRACT FOR THE PURCHASE OF A CONCUBINE

The undersigned, _____ , from _____ village, has agreed to give in marriage his own daughter _____ , aged _____ years, to the second party, _____ , as a concubine, through the mediator, _____ .

On this date the undersigned has received _____ amount as betrothal payment. He agrees to give his daughter away on the date selected by the second party. He will not dare to cause any difficulties or to extort more money from the second party. He also guarantees that the girl has not been previously betrothed, and that there is no question as to her origin. Should such questions arise, or should the girl run away, he will be held responsible. Should the girl die of unexpected circumstances, it is her fate, and not the responsibility of the second party.

This contract is drawn up as evidence of the agreement.

SAMPLE CONTRACT FOR THE SELLING OF A SON FOR ADOPTION

The undersigned, _____ , from _____ county, _____ village, is unable to raise his own son _____ , aged _____ years, because of poverty. After consulting his wife and relatives (uncle/brother _____ and _____ , etc.), he has decided to sell the child, through a mediator, to _____ as an adopted son.

On this date the undersigned received _____ amount of money from the second party, and the transaction was completed. The second party agrees to raise the child, who will be at his disposal for marriage, will be as obedient to him as a servant, and will not avoid labor or run away. This contract is signed out of the free will of both parties, there being no prior sales, and no questions as to the origin of the child; nor is the seller forced by a creditor to sell the child as payment for debts. From now on the child belongs to his new owner; alive, he shall never return to his original family; dead, he shall not be buried in the graveyard of his original family. Should he run away or be kidnapped, only the seller and the mediator are responsible; should the child die of unexpected cirumstances, it is his fate, and not the responsibility of his owner.

This contract, stamped with the palm prints of the child, is to be held by the owner as evidence of the transaction.

Source 6 from The Humanist Way in Ancient China: Essential Works of Confucianism, *ed. and trans. Ch'u Chai and Winberg Chai (New York: Bantam Books, 1965), pp. 326–334.*

6. From *Classic of Filiality,* or *Xiao Jing (Hsiao Ching),* ca. 2nd century B.C.E.

CHAPTER I: THE GENERAL THEME

The Master said: "Filial piety is the basis of virtue and the source of culture. Sit down again, and I will explain it to you. The body and the limbs, the hair and the skin, are given to one by one's parents, and to them no injury should come; this is where filial piety begins. To establish oneself and practice the *Tao* is to immortalize one's name and thereby to glorify one's parents; this is where filial piety ends. Thus, filial piety commences with service to parents; it proceeds with service to the sovereign; it is completed by the establishment of one's own personality.

"In the *Shih* it is said:

May you think of your ancestors,
And so cultivate their virtues!"

CHAPTER II: THE SON OF HEAVEN

The Master said: "One who loves one's parents does not dare to hate others. One who reveres one's parents does not dare to spurn others. When love and reverence are thus cherished in the service of one's parents, one's moral influence transforms the people, and one becomes a pattern to all within the four seas. This is the filial piety of the Son of Heaven.

"In the *Fu Code*, it is said:

When the One Man has blessings,
The millions of people rely on him."

CHAPTER VIII: GOVERNMENT BY FILIAL PIETY

The Master said: "Formerly the enlightened kings governed the world by filial piety. They did not dare to neglect the ministers of small states—to say nothing of the dukes, marquises, earls, viscounts, and barons! They thereby gained the good will of all the states to serve their early kings.

"Those who governed the states did not dare to ignore the widows and widowers—to say nothing of scholars and the people! They thereby gained the good will of all the subjects to serve their former princes.

"Those who regulated their families did not dare to mistreat their servants and concubines—to say nothing of their wives and children! They thereby gained the good will of others who served their parents.

CHAPTER XIV: ILLUSTRATION OF PERPETUATING THE NAME

The Master said: "The *chün-tzu* [gentleman] serves his parents with filial piety; thus his loyalty can be transferred to his sovereign. He serves his elder brother with brotherly deference; thus his respect can be transferred to his superiors. He orders his family well; thus his good order can be transferred to his public administration.

"Therefore, when one cultivates one's conduct within oneself, one's name will be perpetuated for future generations."

Source 7 from Chu Hsi's Family Rituals, trans. Patricia Ebrey (Princeton: Princeton University Press, 1991), pp. 28–32.

7. From Zhu Xi (Chu Hsi), *Family Rituals*, 12th century

In ancient times even prenatal instruction was practiced, not to mention postnatal education. From the time of a child's birth, even before he can understand, we familiarize him with the proprieties. How, then, can we ignore proper behavior when he is old enough to understand it? Confucius said that what is formed in childhood is like part of one's nature, what has been learned through practice becomes like instinct. The *Family Instructions of Mr. Yen* says, "Teach a bride when she first arrives; teach a child while it is still a baby." Therefore, from the time children begin to understand, they must be made to learn the distinctions of etiquette based on age and generation. In cases where they insult their parents or hit their elder brothers and sisters, if their parents laugh and praise them instead of scolding or punishing them, the children, not knowing right from wrong, will think such behavior is natural. By the time they are grown, their habits have been formed. Their parents now become angry and forbid them to do such things, but they find themselves unable to control them. As a result, the father will hate his son, and the son will resent his father. Cruelty and defiance of any sort can then occur, and all because the parents were short-sighted and failed to prevent the evil from the beginning; in other words, bad character is nourished by indulgence.

Source 8 from The Bonds of Matrimony/Hsing-shih Yin-yüan Chuan *(volume one)*, A Seventeenth Century Chinese Novel, *trans. Eve Alison Nyren (Lewiston, New York: The Edwin Mellen Press, 1995), pp. 117–120.*

8. From Pu Suling (P'u Su-ling), *The Bonds of Matrimony*, 17th century

Two types of people bring downfall to home and state
The home falls to concubines and favorites
The state crumbles before eunuchs
New friends divide old with their wiles
Strangers break up homes with a few little words
False tales might as well be true
When duty, goodness, flesh and blood
all turn to dust
Done to death and no regrets
Let the bystanders laugh until their jaws crack

Mrs. Kao talked Ms. Chi back into the house and with sweet words and sharp talked her out of her tantrum.

Ch'ao Yüan knew in his heart that there had been no priest. He knew that Chen ko had been conjuring up fake spectres and catching at the air. However, he didn't dare say anything that would put Chen ko in the wrong, and, also, now he had Ms. Chi where he wanted her he could divorce her on this pretext. With Ms. Chi out of the house, one of the goads to Chen ko's temper would be gone. That would make Chen ko happy, and then he could raise her to the position of his wife. He hadn't counted on old Chi and Chi Pa-la coming so fluently to Ms. Chi's defense.

Ms. Chi had a temper and couldn't be expected to stand for this injustice. Ch'ao Yüan had made the mistake of trying to split a rock with an iron spear and had ended up with his spear broken in two. Even though it looked as if he'd failed in his attempt to discredit her, was Ms. Chi content to be generous and let bygones be bygones? No, she was plotting how to peel off Chen ko's hide and reduce Chen ko to a bloody pulp. She was willing to pit her life against his in her quarrel with her husband.

However, she thought, "How could a mere weak women like me kill him? Even if I did succeed in it, it isn't any good for a woman to kill her husband, and if I did kill him but then failed in killing myself—I couldn't bear how people would treat me! But how else can I clear my name of his accusations that I keep priests?"

She thought it over and over and finally concluded, "I'm no match for him in a fight to the death. Why bother to go on like this? Even if I wait for my mother-in-law to come back, I don't suppose she'll protect me from the storm! No, after all, I'd be better off dead."

She was ninety-nine and then some percent decided when Old Mr. Chi and Chi Pa-la came to see her.

When they arrived at the front gate, Old Chi first sent in a message to Ch'ao Yüan asking, "Did you write that declaration of divorce? I'm here to take my innocent girl home."

Ch'ao Yüan evasively claimed to be sick in bed from all the stress of the quarrel and said he'd talk to them when he felt better.

Old Chi said, "We'd better get it over with. It won't stop with priests—next you'll be claiming she keeps actors." With that he went back to see Ms. Chi.

Ms. Chi asked her father, "Dad, is it true what Mrs. Kao told me, that you and Pa-la were across the street with Yü Mingwu when I came out screaming?"

Old Chi said, "Wasn't I just standing there talking about all this when out you came."

Ms. Chi asked, "What did Yü Ming-wu have to say?"

Old Chi replied, "Just after they left you, Hai-hui and the Nun Kuo ran into Yü Ming-wu, who was seeing some guests off. He asked them 'aren't you afraid of drying up under this wicked sun?' and he invited them to rest inside where it was cool. When you came out and stirred up such a fracas, those two were inside his house eating lunch."

Ms. Chi brought out a small package from an inside room.

"Here are fifty taels, two gold taels, and two pearls. My mother-in-law gave them all to me. Dad, you take these home and keep them for me until I come back home myself. These thirty taels of broken silver are what I've saved in the past few years, and this here is some jewelry I never wear—two bracelets, two pearl tiaras, and two gold hair ornaments—brother, you take these home for me. Take this length of blue satin and have a tailor sew it up quickly into a long sleeved robe for me, and have a half-coat made of this pink gauze. Have my sister-in-law make me some underthings with this floss, and keep the catty of floss that will be left over. Tomorrow, as soon as the clothes are made up, send them to me so I can go home dressed properly."

Old Chi asked, "Why do you want winter clothes like that now in the middle of the summer?"

"What's it to you?" she asked. "Don't ask such irritating questions. If you're going to hang around here telling me what to do, instead of getting those clothes made up for me, I guess I would be better off taking my case to court! I'm going to put a few other things of mine in a chest. Send a servant tomorrow to take the chest home. It's important to get those clothes made—I won't keep you to dinner."

She sent off her father and brother, and put everything in her room in order, just as if she really were planning to go home. She also took out a lot of clothes and gave them one by one to her maids and women.

One woman said, "Ma'am, it's silly to divide up all of your things like this. When the master said he was going to divorce you, he was just letting his mouth run away with him! You're his lawful wife, and he married you in a proper ceremony in front of his parents. How can he divorce you while his parents are absent? Ma'am, you shouldn't go home."

Ms. Chi said, "So according to you, I should wait until he drives me away with a stick?"

"Who would dare do that?" the woman said.

Ms. Chi also had them take some loose change from her bed and distribute it among the servants.

She said, "This is for you to remember me by."

Her maids said, "If you do go home for a while, you'd better lock up this room and take us with you to serve you there. It isn't as if there would be anything left for us to do here."

Ms. Chi said, "Of course you'll go, too, even if you don't come with me."

By now it was about eight in the morning, and nobody had sent them firewood for breakfast. With her own hands, Ms. Chi broke a couple of panels off her new sedan chair, heated up a pot and made breakfast.

One of the servants said, "What a shame! Wouldn't it be better to burn the old sedan chair and use the new one to travel in?"

Ms. Chi told her, "I'm going to be divorced and I won't be a member of the Ch'ao family any more. How can I use their sedan chair then?"

Ch'ao Yüan had found out that Ms. Chi was all packed up and ready to go home to her father. That fit in with his plans, but he didn't know when she would leave. In the morning of the eighth day of the sixth month, old Chi and Chi Pa-la had the clothes ready, and they took the clothes to Ms. Chi, in a package. They also had a few men go to pick up her trunk. Ms. Chi had only a cloth bundle left.

She said, "I decided this old furniture isn't worth more than a few cash and if I take it people will accuse me of being a thief, so who wants their things anyway."

"You're absolutely right," said Old Chi.

Ms. Chi said, "I haven't finished packing up, so I guess I'd better go back tomorrow, but you two don't have to come. The weather is hot, so I'll want to get into the house quickly. We can talk afterwards. If you have any use for the things I gave you yesterday, go ahead and use them. Don't sell them to give me money."

Old Chi said, "Listen to her talk! Aren't you being a little short-sighted? You'd better reconsider. Never mind that I'm no match for him, with his wealth and position. Even if I were, it isn't as if you could make him pay with his life. Listen to what I'm telling you."

For a while he tried to argue her out of her resolve to go through with the divorce.

They used wood from the new sedan chair to cook lunch.

Close to evening, Ms. Chi took a bath, lit some incense, and bound her hair up tight. She put many hair ornaments in her hair, and rings on her fingers. She wrapped her footbindings neatly. She put on new cinnabar-pink silk trousers with a moon-white damask under-garment next to her skin, then a sky blue short jacket with a cinnabar pink pongee jacket over it, a moon-white great robe and over it all her new blue satin wide-sleeved robe. Then she used a needle and thread to sew together all the layers of her clothes, so there wasn't the tiniest opening anywhere. She placed one gold and one silver piece in her mouth. Then she took a peach-red phoenix sash. Very quietly, she opened her door, walked out to the door of Ch'ao Yüan's rooms and hung herself on his door frame.

It all took less time than two cups of hot tea.

Etheral steps on air, the shade of a girl on a swing.

Source 9 from The Columbia Book of Later Chinese Poetry: Yüan, Ming, and Ch'ing Dynasties (1279–1911), *trans. and ed. Jonathan Chaves (New York: Columbia University Press, 1986), pp. 437–439.*

9. Zheng Xie (Cheng Hsieh), "Mother-in-law Is Cruel," 18th century

An old poem says, "'Mother-in-law is cruel?' 'Mother-in-law is cruel?' No, it's not that she's cruel, just that my fate is bad!" This can be said to be the height of loyalty, and it captures the traditional purport of the Three Hundred Poems. But the mothers-in-law do not appear to repent of their ways, so I have written this poem to describe in detail what the daughter-in-law's life is like, in the hope that it will act as an exhortation.

A young girl, only eleven,
leaves home to serve her in-laws.
How could she know how it feels to be a wife?
It's like calling her elder brother, "Husband."
The two young people feel bashful with each other;
they try to speak, but can only mumble.
Father-in-law sends her to the women's quarters
to embroider some new ornaments.
Mother-in-law gives her all kinds of awful jobs,
and sends her to the kitchen, knife in hand.
She tries dicing meat, but can't cut perfect cubes:
instead, she serves up ugly chunks on the tray.
She tries making soup, but gets the spicing wrong,
failing to distinguish "sour" and "hot."
Cutting firewood, she tears her soft hands;
tending the fires, the skin on her fingers wrinkles and dries.
Father-in-law says, "She's still young—
we must be patient in teaching her."
Mother-in-law says, "If she can't be taught when young,
who'll be able to handle her when she's grown up?
Haughty and proud, she'll take advantage of us when we're old and decrepit.
Arrogant and lewd, she'll drive our son to his knees!"
So today, she curses and scolds her,
and the next day has her whipped and beaten.
After five days of this, the girl has no untorn clothes to wear;
after ten days, even her skin is completely torn.
Facing the wall, she moans and weeps,
with sounds of sobbing and bitter sighs.
Mother-in-law says, "You're casting spells!
Bring the stick! Bring the knife and saw!
Your flesh can still be cut—
you're pretty chubby, not too skinny at all!
You still have hair on your head—
we'll pull it all out so your head looks like a gourd!
I can't live in the same life as you,
if you live, then my life is done!"
The old witch glares in anger
as if she's about to slaughter her.
And the husband?—He watches a while,
then joins in and shouts, "Have you no shame?"
Father-in-law tries to calm down his wife,

and gets yelled at himself: "You stupid old slave!"
The neighbors try to find out what's going on,
and they're yelled at too: "None of your business!"
Oh, this poor, poor girl from an impoverished family:
why doesn't she just jump into the river?
She can become a meal for the fish and turtles,
and escape this terrible suffering.
Oh, how cruel of heaven to allow this evil!
and to hear nothing of her cries.
A girl who becomes a young wife in this world
will suffer pain and unjust accusation.
Better to be a cow, a sheep or a pig:
you eat your fill—then one cut of the knife ends it all.
When her parents visit,
she wipes her tears and pretends that she is happy.
When her brothers visit,
she bears the pain, and says, "Mother-in-law is exhausted."
Her scars she covers with tattered clothes,
her bald head she explains as illness.
If she said a single word against mother-in-law
her life would end in a minute.

Source 10 from Sources of Chinese Tradition, *compiled by Wm. Theodore de Bary et al. (New York: Columbia University Press, 1960), pp. 815–818.*

10. From Chen Duxiu (Ch'en Tu-hsiu), "The Ways of Confucius and Modern Life," 1916

The pulse of modern life is economic and the fundamental principle of economic production is individual independence. Its effect has penetrated ethics. Consequently the independence of the individual in the ethical field and the independence of property in the economic field bear witness to each other, thus reaffirming the theory [of such interaction]. Because of this [interaction], social mores and material culture have taken a great step forward.

In China, the Confucianists have based their teachings on their ethical norms. Sons and wives possess neither personal individuality nor personal property. Fathers and elder brothers bring up their sons and younger brothers and are in turn supported by them. It is said in chapter thirty of the *Book of Rites* that "While parents are living, the son dares not regard his person or property as his own." [27:14] This is absolutely not the way to personal independence. . . .

In all modern constitutional states, whether monarchies or republics, there are political parties. Those who engage in party activities all express their spirit of independent conviction. They go their own way and need not agree with their fathers or husbands. When people are bound by the Confucian teachings of filial piety and obedience to the point of the son not deviating from the father's way even three years after his death and the woman obeying not only her father and husband but also her son, how can they form their own political party and make their own choice? The movement of women's participation in politics is also an aspect of women's life in modern civilization. When they are bound by the Confucian teaching that "To be a women means to submit," that "The wife's words should not travel beyond her own apartment," and that "A woman does not discuss affairs outside the home," would it not be unusual if they participated in politics?

In the West some widows choose to remain single because they are strongly attached to their late husbands and sometimes because they prefer a single life; they have nothing to do with what is called the chastity of widowhood. Widows who remarry are not despised by society at all. On the other hand, in the Chinese teaching of decorum, there is the doctrine of "no remarriage after the husband's death." It is considered to be extremely shameful and unchaste for a woman to serve two husbands or a man to serve two rulers. The *Book of Rites* also prohibits widows from wailing at night [27:21] and people from being friends with sons of widows. [9:21] For the sake of their family reputation, people have forced their daughters-in-law to remain widows. These women have had no freedom and have endured a most miserable life. Year after year these many promising young women have lived a physically and spiritually abnormal life. All this is the result of Confucian teachings of decorum [or rites].

In today's civilized society, social intercourse between men and women is a common practice. Some even say that because women have a tender nature and can temper the crudeness of man, they are necessary in public or private gatherings. It is not considered improper even for strangers to sit or dance together once they have been introduced by the host. In the way of Confucian teaching, however, "Men and women do not sit on the same mat," "Brothers- and sisters-in-law do not exchange inquiries about each other," "Married sisters do not sit on the same mat with brothers or eat from the same dish," "Men and women do not know each other's name except through a matchmaker and should have no social relations or show affection until after marriage presents have been exchanged," "Women must cover their faces when they go out," "Boys and girls seven years or older do not sit or eat together," "Men and women have no social relations except through a matchmaker and do not meet until after marriage presents have been exchanged," and "Except in religious sacrifices, men and women do not exchange wine cups." Such rules of decorum are not only inconsistent with the mode of life in Western society; they cannot even be observed in today's China.

[86]

Western women make their own living in various professions such as that of lawyer, physician, and store employee. But in the Confucian way, "In giving or receiving anything, a man or woman should not touch the other's hand," "A man does not talk about affairs inside [the household] and a woman does not talk about affairs outside [the household]," and "They do not exchange cups except in sacrificial rites and funerals." "A married woman is to obey" and the husband is the standard of the wife. Thus the wife is naturally supported by the husband and needs no independent livelihood.

A married woman is at first a stranger to her parents-in-law. She has only affection but no obligation toward them. In the West parents and children usually do not live together, and daughters-in-law, particularly, have no obligation to serve parents-in-law. But in the way of Confucius, a woman is to "revere and respect them and never to disobey day or night," "A woman obeys, that is, obeys her parents-in-law," "A woman serves her parent-in-law as she serves her own parents," she "never should disobey or be lazy in carrying out the orders of parents and parents-in-law." "If a man is very fond of his wife, but his parents do not like her, she should be divorced." (In ancient times there were many such cases, like that of Lu Yü [1125–1210].) "Unless told to retire to her own apartment, a woman does not do so, and if she has an errand to do, she must get permission from her parents-in-law." This is the reason why the tragedy of cruelty to daughters-in-law has never ceased in Chinese society.

According to Western customs, fathers do not discipline grown-up sons but leave them to the law of the country and the control of society. But in the way of Confucius, "When one's parents are angry and not pleased and beat him until he bleeds, he does not complain but instead arouses in himself the feelings of reverence and filial piety." This is the reason why in China there is the saying, "One has to die if his father wants him to, and the minister has to perish if his ruler wants him to.". . .

QUESTIONS TO CONSIDER

Breaking a complex problem down into smaller parts often helps to make it more manageable. Instead of addressing the larger issue of how to view the Confucian family all at once, therefore, try asking some more limited, specific questions about each of the sources in turn. As noted in the Method section, the first five offer glimpses into different aspects of family life in late traditional times. Collectively they provide a logical place to look for answers to the first question: What was the Confucian family like?

Source 1, the family portrait, provides a relatively realistic picture of an elite family toward the end of the Ming dynasty (1368–1644), in some ways a counterpart to the snapshots in our own family albums. But keep

[87]

in mind that ordinary people could not afford to commission such paintings in Ming China, and so such portraiture, far from seeking to reveal a casual moment in family life, served to call attention to the importance of the household in a very public and formal way. Note the posed, symmetrical arrangement of family members. What does the placement of different individuals suggest about relationships between members and their relative importance? Do some seem to stand out more than others? Why do you suppose no young children are shown? Compare this view with photographs you may have of your family. Would you want your family to be remembered this way?

The formality of the portrait reflects a great concern for careful, deliberate behavior that shows up in other documents as well. Source 2, the Miu family instructions, for example, painstakingly explains "the correct procedures to be followed in everyday life" as well as the particulars for formal family rituals. It repeatedly urges members to "exercise restraint" in all household affairs and observe a strict sense of propriety that rules out spontaneity and casual behavior. In this connection, look carefully at the final passage in the text, which purports to disclose the "secrets" of a successful family life. Would people today regard fulfillment of "duty" a measure of such success? What standard would you use to judge family success?

The need to reduce conflict in a large household may explain some of this concern for rules and restraint. What kinds of friction and fighting does Source 2 anticipate? The guide seems to attribute most such problems to unruly individual behavior. But the text singles out certain family members as most likely to be troublemakers. Who are they? What does this suggest about prevailing attitudes with regard to gender, age, and social level? How would you react to the "preventive measures" the texts prescribe as cure for such problems— particularly the seclusion of women or the household meetings called "to encourage one another in virtue and to correct each other's mistakes?" As you can see in this instance, family rules emphasized collective responsibility and group harmony. Individuality, however, was not totally ignored. For the text advises members to follow their own aspirations for occupations. Would this encouragement apply equally to all members?

The distaste of cities expressed in Source 2 reflects a deep-seated Confucian bias toward rural life. Upperclass Confucians believed that the simplicity and frugality of country living promoted a level of virtue difficult to sustain in urban environments. The text thus praises farming as second only to elite scholarship as an occupation and warns that the family's rural "houses, fields, and ponds" should never be divided or sold. As Source 3 shows, however, the country houses of the elite were hardly rustic cottages. Like urban residences, they were walled compounds with many interior halls and courtyards that could be assigned to different conjugal families and the many servants needed to maintain such an expansive household. Because the front halls served as public reception rooms and men's studies, women generally kept to the back parts. Outside its immediate walls spread park-like gardens, and farther beyond stretched farmland that was usually rented out to less fortunate families. Compare this kind of residence with contemporary suburban homes. What does architecture and setting in each case tell about the residents' interests and values?

Sources 4 and 5 offer two different glimpses into the lives of women and children in such big households. Source 4, "A Sketch of My Mother" shows the tender personal affections that often developed between men and women despite all the formality and ceremony that characterized life in the Confucian family. Notice which women in his family the author, Gui Youguang mentions—and whom he seems to have loved most. Because his father occupied a government post that kept him away from home for long periods, Gui's mother supervised his education and saw to his marriage on her own. Although she may have been as strict with him as any Confucian patriarch, he clearly felt close to her. Perhaps his regard for her explains his similar affection for his wife and daughter, and the fact that he makes nothing of his lack of a son. As Source 5, sample contracts for purchasing concubines and adoptive sons, indicates, many men in his situation did not accept an absence of male heirs so nonchalantly and resorted to these solutions. What do these documents tell you about the social and legal rights of women and children? Who seems to be in a

position to determine their fate? How do you react to the idea that some people could own others?

Confucians, who accepted adoption and concubinage, did so only as expedients to assure the continuity of the family. Here, as in most situations, they justified the sacrifice of individual satisfaction in the name of family benefit. The familialism underlying this attitude served as the subject of a much-quoted Confucian work known as the *Xiao Jing*, or *Classic of Filiality*, portions of which appear as Source 6. Notice how this work finds a larger social and political meaning in the subordination of individual needs to family benefit. To what higher purposes than family success does it say "filiality" leads? Do you think that such ends justify restraints on individualism? The importance of the home as the basic site for socialization and moral training continued to be a cherished Confucian idea, as you can see in Source 7. Taken from a work compiled by Zhu Xi, often ranked as the "Second Master" after Confucius, this passage affirms the Confucian belief that social order ultimately depends on family values and behavior. Note whom this text, too, identifies as most needing correction. Do you agree with its claim that in such cases "bad character is nourished by indulgence"?

Sources 8 and 9 provide sympathetic views of those who bore the brunt of punishment and sacrifice within the Confucian family. Source 8, taken from a seventeenth-century novel called *The Bonds of Matrimony* attributed to Pu Suling, presents the tragic end of an unhappy marriage.

In his youth, the ambitious husband, Chao Yuan (Ch'ao Yüan), agreed to marry the homely Ms. Qi (Chi) because of her family's prestige. Never very fond or considerate of her, he used her childlessness as an excuse to bring a concubine into the household. And when conflicts flared between the women, he threatened to divorce his wife on the pretext that she had an affair with a Buddhist priest who had come to counsel her. In the excerpt given here, she brings their marital crisis to a dramatic close. Why does she take this course? What do her reasons suggest about the options for unhappy women in the Confucian family?

The poem called "Mother-in-law Is Cruel," Source 9, looks at another kind of family crisis, the conflict between a new wife and her husband's mother. As you may have observed in some of the other sources, girls married at a young age in China, often at about thirteen, or at the onset of puberty. In this poem, the wife is even younger. Would such a marriage be legal, or even socially acceptable, in present-day Western society? Why not? Here again problems seem to stem from a conflict between two "women," although one is but a child. What explains the friction here? Inasmuch as a matriarch seems to be the source of misery in this case, could the author be implying that the nature of the Confucian family— rather than male domination—invites such abuse? For whom does he thus intend this exhortation?

In Source 10 Chen Duxiu offers a modern Western rationale for eliminating this archaic Chinese institu-tion altogether. For the most part he bases his argument on an appeal for greater individual freedom and equality. This argument, which typifies the modernizing trends that began to rock the world in the twentieth century, seemed extremely radical in China back in 1916. Would all Westerners have accepted it in 1916? For that matter, do you find all of it acceptable today? What do you think a staunch Confucian would have said in rebuttal to some of Chen's specific points, such as his claim that "the law of country and the control of society" should fully replace family authority? Would everyone in the West agree with that proposition now? Despite his scorn of tradition, Chen curiously perpetuates (in an inverted way) the Confucian insistence on an important link between family life and the state of society. For he says that open, conjugal families of the Western sort promote not only individualistic societies but economic development. In other words, national prosperity, as well as social health, depends on what goes on in the home. How reasonable does this claim seem to you? Would an erosion of family influence over individuals help or hinder a nation?

Having spent some time considering these separate questions, you should now be in a better position to deal with the larger issue posed as the central problem in this chapter. That is, what standpoint would *you* take in developing a history of the Confucian family? Before you give your final answer, think back over your replies to the various issues raised about individual sources in this section. Do you detect any clear pattern to your responses? What do they show about your own perspective on this institution? Is this a perspective you would consciously choose to adopt? Would you expect others to do the same? How would you defend or critique such a choice? What might be lost or gained by taking this approach?

EPILOGUE

Western reformers like Chen Duxiu eventually carried the day in China, following the initial turmoil unleashed by the collapse of the imperial monarchy in 1911 and decades of civil strife and foreign invasion. By 1949, the Chinese Communist Party, which Chen helped to found in 1921, took control over China and began a radical reform of the country. During the 1950s new reforms swept away the legal basis of the old patriarchal tradition, granting women and children full equality and protection under the law, while land redistribution and political modernization destroyed the elites with whom it had flourished. At the height of the Great Proletarian Cultural Revolution of the 1960s, Communist Party leader Mao Zedong lent his support to even more radical efforts, calling for the abolition of all family life in favor of collective living in giant communes. Although this extreme step failed, the last quarter of the twentieth century seemed to mark the end of the old Chinese tradition of familialism as well as of the patriarchal Confucian family.

Strangely enough, however, interest in this tradition began to revive during the 1980s, not in China but in the wealthier parts of East Asia where successful modernization had occurred. Indeed, some observers credit much of the contemporary success of countries like Japan, South Korea, and Taiwan to the survival of Confucian culture and family values that promote group interests over individual demands. They contend that the willingness of people in these areas to defer personal gains, obey authority, and uphold rules creates a stable and orderly society necessary for economic growth. Leaders in some East Asian countries have even begun to praise these traditional values and the Confucian family ethos as superior to once-coveted Western modernism. They point to sluggish economic growth and mounting social tensions in the West as symptoms of a social decline set in motion by excessive individualism and disregard for authority. It should come as no surprise, then, that attitudes toward the Confucian family may again change in East Asia, even in China where economic growth is accelerating. How might this eventuality affect the way future historians view the institution? Would it change the way you have decided to view the Confucian family?

CHAPTER FOUR

GENDER DIFFERENCES IN PEASANT

HOUSEHOLDS IN SOUTHEAST ASIA

AND CENTRAL EUROPE (1500–1850)

THE PROBLEM

For most of human history since the development of agriculture, the vast majority of the world's population have been peasants, living in small family units in villages and supporting themselves by farming. Roughly half of these peasants have been female, and their lives have been shaped by their gender, as have those of their male counterparts. One would think, then, that based on sheer numbers the historical experiences of peasants, male and female, would be easy to reconstruct. A glance at the catalog of academic journals held by many libraries would seem to confirm this, for there are journals devoted specifically to peasants—*Peasant Studies, The Journal of Peasant Studies*—and journals devoted specifically to women and gender—*The Journal of Women's History, Gender and History, Women's History Review*.

A closer examination, however, would reveal that most of the articles in the journals on peasants are explicitly or implicitly about male peasants, and most of the articles in the journals on women and gender are about individuals and groups that are not peasants. And in both types of journals, the preponderance of articles covers the modern period, that is, the nineteenth and twentieth centuries. Why is this? If you questioned the editors of both types of journals, or the authors of the articles in them, they would probably answer that the problem is a lack of sources. Despite their great numbers, peasant men and women have left little historical record. They were largely illiterate, and the groups that were literate in their societies—priests, scribes, government officials, chroniclers—were not interested in the day-to-day life of peasants as long as they supplied the necessary economic and military support for the rulers. Only during times of crisis—famines, natural disasters, war—might the lives of the peasantry be worthy of comment, and then often only as tallies of the dead or comments about unharvested crops. The lives of peasant women were particularly uninteresting to those recording "history," who were themselves usually upper- or middle-class males.

If you pushed the editors and authors a bit, however, they would probably admit that the same types of arguments were used about the paltry history of all peasants and all women until about twenty-five years ago. Both of these topics are quite new to the history arena—*Peasant Studies* began publication in 1976 and the *Journal of Women's History* in 1988—and both were at first somewhat controversial. In both of these fields, the answers made to those skeptical about the availability of sources was that we simply had to look harder. Information often came

in smaller doses than it did for more traditional subjects, but it was there. Not only were new types of sources discovered, but older sources were mined in ways that yielded information no one had realized was hidden below the surface.

That is just what you will be doing in this chapter: mining a very fresh claim, digging in a very new field to explore the history of peasant men and women in the premodern period. You will be investigating two parts of the world that have also been relatively understudied, central Europe and Southeast Asia, using several different types of sources to answer these questions: How did the experiences of men and women in early modern peasant households differ? How might these differences have been affected by economic change and how, in turn, might economic developments have been shaped by gender differences?

BACKGROUND

There are two ways to begin a new field of historical inquiry: the case study and the broad overview. The history of both peasants and women began with many case studies, in which the focus was on one individual, family, village, or small group, and in which the historian often emphasized what made the subject of the study unique or noteworthy. Along with such studies, however, some scholars wrote broad overviews, in which they gathered sources widely for a range of individuals and groups,

making generalizations that were then tested by further case studies and questioned in subsequent broad overviews. Case studies are usually the safer route, for broad overviews are open to criticism by specialists. Both methods are essential in a field's early development, however; case studies alone often make it difficult to see how developments are linked or why certain trends and patterns are important.

In this chapter we are beginning a broad overview, using sources from different centuries and from different countries in two widely separated parts of the world. The focus will be

Chapter 4

Gender

Differences

in Peasant

Households in

Southeast Asia

and Central

Europe

(1500–1850)

provided, not by chronology or geography, but by the specific questions we are asking. As with any scholars writing broad overviews, we must be somewhat selective in gathering and presenting the necessary background. Historians writing case studies generally read everything they can find about their area, immersing themselves in all topics touching local history. Those writing broad overviews must be more selective, sticking with materials that are directly relevant to their chosen topic.

In order to understand our sources, we need to know something about the rural economy, the setting for the peasant households we will be exploring. Though there are vast differences both between Southeast Asia and central Europe, and between countries and regions within these areas, there are also similarities. In both of these areas, the peasant household was generally small, made up of a nuclear family and perhaps a few other relatives, and occasionally some nonrelated individuals such as servants in central Europe and debt-slaves in Southeast Asia.[1] Though polygamy was tolerated in Southeast Asia, most men could only afford one

wife (a man paid bride-wealth to his wife or her family on marriage, the opposite of the European pattern of a bride or bride's family paying the groom a dowry). Divorce was easier there than it was in Christian central Europe, so unsatisfactory marriages could be readily ended; on the other hand, divorce was extremely rare in Europe. Because the death of a spouse was a frequent occurrence in both areas, families often included half-siblings and step-parents.

Both peasant economies revolved around grain-growing, with rice the predominant crop in the lowland areas of Southeast Asia and wheat and rye the main crops in central Europe. In both areas grain production was organized in a variety of ways: some agricultural work was subsistence (for the use of one's own family), some was for wages, and some was for discharging labor obligations to a landlord or lender. Peasants also raised other sorts of fruit and vegetable crops, maintained livestock, and gathered natural products. Their goods were not only for their own use and local trade and taxes, but also often part of the international trade that, beginning in the late fifteenth century, linked these parts of the world to each other and to the rest of the world. Pepper from Southeast Asia could be found on the tables of central Europe (perhaps not in peasant households, but certainly in those of their landlords), and Filipino converts to Christianity began to wear black veils and skirts woven in Germany. This international trading network was controlled by merchants of many nationalities—Dutch,

1. Debt-slavery or debt-bondage was a system in which one could exchange one's own labor or that of family members in order to repay debts or meet obligations. Sons-in-law could make themselves debt-bondsmen of their fathers-in-law in order to gain a wife; fathers could sell their children into bondage if their crops failed; individuals could sell themselves into bondage if business deals went bad. All members of a peasant family might become debt-bondsmen, though they continued to live together and worked some days of the week for themselves; debt-slaves did not necessarily live in the house of their master.

English, Chinese, Sumatran among others—and provided new opportunities for peasants, but also new dangers, as prices and demand were often determined by events half-way around the world and totally out of their control. In some parts of both regions, these new opportunities included work that was not strictly agricultural, such as spinning or weaving, but that was combined with farming or undertaken by some family members while others continued to devote most of their time to farming.

Along with these similarities and linkages, there were also significant differences between the two areas. Peasants in central Europe married much later than those in Southeast Asia (in their late twenties as compared to their late teens or early twenties) and a larger percentage of the population in Europe remained permanently unmarried. Thus, though in both areas the peasant household was normally made up of the married couple and their children, in Europe unmarried adult men and women also comprised a significant share of the population. In Europe the extended family played less of a role than in most of the societies of Southeast Asia. The harsher Euro-pean climate meant that houses had to be built more securely than they did in Southeast Asia, where the mild climate and frequent monsoons led to houses being built primarily of palm and bamboo. Such houses were easily destroyed, but quickly rebuilt. In central Europe houses were also built of perishable materials such as wood and mud, with thatch roofs, but with much thicker walls to with-stand snow and sleet. In neither area could most peasants afford many fur-nishings, though these were particu-larly sparse in Southeast Asia where eating was done on the floor and woven mats often served as beds.

In both areas peasants were fre-quently troubled by warfare, which destroyed crops and villages. Euro-pean armies by this period were largely paid professionals, either mercenaries who hired themselves out or standing armies paid by states; in Southeast Asia kings relied on their courtiers and great nobles to mobilize troops, though by the sev-enteenth century they began to use mercenaries as well, often Europeans or Japanese. Sometimes a source of employment opportunity for young peasant men, the army was more often a source of misery as soldiers lived off the lands they occupied.

THE METHOD

We will be using three basic types of sources for this chapter—legal docu-ments, travelers' reports, and visual depictions of peasant life. For each of these, we must take certain precau-tions and understand the context within which they were produced.

In general, legal documents, espe-cially law codes, are one of the ear-liest records we have from many of the world's societies and in some

Chapter 4

Gender

Differences

in Peasant

Households in

Southeast Asia

and Central

Europe

(1500–1850)

instances the only written record remaining. They have the benefit of being produced by a member of the society involved, not outsiders, and so they are generally viewed as reflecting local ideas and values, but in this chapter class and gender considerations complicate this advantage somewhat. The writers of legal codes and documents in both central Europe and Southeast Asia were educated men, men whose grandfathers may have been peasants but who were no longer part of that population themselves. They thus prescribe and describe aspects of peasant life such as land ownership and labor obligations, but they do not necessarily reflect peasant views or values. Even some of the practices they may describe as "traditional" may actually have been very new, with the legal writers simply calling them traditional to give them greater validity. (In both societies, peasants revered traditions as very important, closely approaching and in some areas of life exceeding written law in their strength and symbolism.) It is important to remember also that all law codes are prescriptive, that is, they are a description of how things *ought* to be, not how they are. We can thus use them to learn what the learned elite thought should be the case among peasants, but cannot use them as proof of living conditions and lifestyle.

In some ways our second type of source, travelers' reports, is the exact opposite of law codes. They were produced by outsiders, not insiders, and purported to be eyewitness descriptions of the traveler's observa-tions. One of the reasons for choosing these two geographic areas is that both were of great interest to visitors, and in particular to visitors who commented on rural life and gender roles. The Portuguese and the Spanish traded and conquered in Southeast Asia beginning in the sixteenth century, and later the Dutch and then the British and French absorbed parts of this area into their colonial empires, with merchants and government officials from all of these countries reporting on their experiences.

Though central Europe was not colonized by outsiders, it too was often regarded as "exotic" by travelers of a different sort, especially those young men and their tutors who embarked on what came to be known as the Grand Tour. Beginning in the eighteenth century, wealthy young men from Western Europe—England, France, and western Germany—began to view an extended circuit through all of the countries of Europe as essential to their education. The more inspired among them decided to write about their travels, often in multivolume works. Much of this travel literature discusses only cities, as the young men found the urban accommodations and entertainments much more to their liking than the countryside, but some of it also discusses rural life.

Like legal documents, travelers' reports must be used with caution. The authors may have been describing what they saw, but, of course, they saw things through the lens of their own culture and may have misunderstood the meaning of much of what was going on. Every author also set out with expectations about what he would find in the culture he was visiting, and these expectations inevitably shaped his impressions. Authors usually reported only what seemed unusual or different, so that things which were similar to their own culture went unnoted. Every author also often had a specific purpose in writing—colonists and government officials to convince a ruler to extend further support, merchants to explain and justify to their superiors any commercial difficulties, young men on tour to promote ideas of romantic nationalism current in late-eighteenth and early-nineteenth-century Europe or to praise or decry certain political systems or regimes. These reservations do not mean we should discount such reports as fiction, but instead keep in mind the background and intents of the authors when we do use them.

In some ways our third type of source—artistic depictions of peasants—might seem to be the most "objective," but here many of the same cautions apply. Most visual depictions of peasant life have not been done by peasants, male or female, but by trained artists, and some of the illustrations we rely on as evidence here were also made by men who were outsiders in terms of race as well as social class. Many times artistic depictions are not intended to describe reality, but, as with law codes, to describe the ideal or, as with travelers' reports, to voice a political critique.

You may at this point be thinking that the sources we will be using in this chapter are so limited by cautions and reservations that they can't possibly be very useful. Here the novelty of our questions, the fact that we are exploring a new field and pulling out bits of information from many sources, turns out to be helpful. Presenting gender differences in rural life was the main concern of none of our authors, so that they were probably more likely to be accurate in this than in other matters. The flip side of the question often put to historians by literary scholars, "How can you trust your sources?" is one that can guide us here: "Why would my sources mislead?" It is easy to see why colonists' reports of indigenous religious beliefs, or the sections in the king's law codes describing how the nobles had willingly given up their power might not be accurate, but why would an author misrepresent what men and women did in farm work? Thus, though we must be cautious, we need not simply discount our sources as fictitious.

Because our questions are so new, our methods in this chapter will be quite simple—careful reading and observation, followed by reflection and then devising a provisional answer to the central questions. You will be reading a great variety of sources, so you will find it imperative to keep notes on the aspects of men's and women's lives that you discover in order to answer the first question, and on the economic changes you see references to, in order to answer the second.

The first two sources are law codes from Southeast Asia. Source 1 is a selection from the Lê Code from Vietnam, a law code compiled during the Lê dynasty, which ruled Vietnam

Chapter 4

Gender

Differences

in Peasant

Households in

Southeast Asia

and Central

Europe

(1500–1850)

from 1428 to 1788. The oldest originals of the Lê Code are on woodblock prints. The founder of the Lê dynasty expelled the Ming Chinese from Vietnam where they had been ruling for twenty years, and many historians see a strong Chinese influence in this code; they comment that Vietnam was more influenced by China than the rest of Southeast Asia in attitudes toward the family, among other things. Therefore, we should be careful not to generalize from the Vietnamese situation to all of Southeast Asia. Experts also note, however, that in some situations, such as women's inheritance of property, the Lê Code departed from more restrictive Chinese legal practices. Source 2 is an extract from the Agama, a mid-sixteenth-century law text from Java. Read each of these sources and the explanatory notes that accompany them carefully. What gender differences do you see in terms of the property acquired by children in Vietnam? in terms of the value of ancestor worship by sons and daughters? How are the duties of husband and wife toward each other and the family different? What gender differences do you see in the value of debt-slaves in Java? Does marriage in Java immediately create an economic unit in terms of the property of husband and wife?

Sources 3 through 7 are legal records from central Europe, which again you should read carefully. Source 3 includes several articles from the law code of the territory of Salzburg, Austria, in 1526; Source 4 is an ordinance for vineyard workers from the south German duchy of Württemberg in

1550; Source 5 is an article from the law code of the duchy of Hohenlohe, Germany, in 1731; Source 6 is a part of the land register from the Silesian village of Zedlitz in 1790 describing the obligations of village residents toward their landlord (Silesia is now part of Poland and the Czech Republic); and Source 7 is the will of a rural weaver from the probate records of the village of Herrnhut in eastern Germany in 1856. How are the duties of husband and wife toward each other as described in the Salzburg law code different? What gender differences do you see in the inheritance practices in Salzburg? What restrictions characterize the legal rights of adult women in central Europe? What differences can you identify in the types of work done by men versus women, and in how these were paid if they were wage labor? According to the will reprinted in Source 7, what types of tools might a woman bring to a marriage or view as important for her own support? Does marriage appear to create a unification of property in central Europe?

In Sources 8 through 11, we turn back to Southeast Asia for the reports of colonists and merchants. Source 8 is from a report by Miguel de Loarca, one of the earliest conquerors and settlers in the Philippines, written in response to a royal decree in 1582; Source 9 consists of passages from a 1609 history of the Philippines written by Antonio de Morga, a Spanish lawyer and royal official; Source 10 is from a letter of Jeronimus Wonderaer, a Dutch merchant active in Vietnam, written in 1602; and Source 11 comes from a history of Sumatra first published in 1783, written by William Marsden, an English government official who had lived eight years in that colony. What differences mark the situation of female and male slaves? Do men who become debt-slaves enter into such a condition alone, or do their actions also make their wives slaves with them? What differences do you see in the types of work done by men and women in Philippine and Sumatran villages? between inheritance by male and female children? How did increased pepper production shape the types of work available for men and women?

Sources 12 through 14 are drawn from the reports of various travelers in central Europe: first, selections from a twelve-volume work by the German author Friedrich Nicolai describing his trips through Germany and Switzerland, published in 1783 (Source 12); next, a description of the island of Rügen, off the coast of eastern Germany in the Baltic Sea, by Johann Jacob Grümbke, a tutor and law student, published in 1805 (Source 13); and finally, an excerpt from a book on Hungary and Transylvania by the English traveler John Paget, published in 1839 (Source 14). What sorts of employments for rural men and women do the authors point out? How is labor rewarded, or how are laborers valued, by the authors and by the people they are describing? How is economic change affecting the employment of rural women and men?

You have already seen one visual illustration of rural life, in Paget's description, and our final sources for this chapter include four more. Source 15 is an illustration of Fil-ipinos working in the field from a 1734 map of the Philippines by Murillo Velarde; Source 16 is an illustration of a village house in Sumatra from Marsden's history of Sumatra; Source 17 is a woodcut of German peasants harvesting hay, produced in 1532 by an anonymous artist known as the Petrarch Master; Source 18 is an illustration and description of a woman dairy farmer that appeared in a book of costumes published in the German city of Nuremberg in 1766. Look carefully at each of these pictures. Which ideas about the division of labor suggested by the written sources do these illustrations support?

Now go back to your notes and begin piecing together your small, separate bits of information. Look first for information on gender differences that will allow you to answer the first of our questions. What differences have you discovered in the inheritance patterns of these two geographic areas? in the legal rights of men and women? in the types of work men and women usually do? in the way this work is valued and compensated? Do both men and women have the possibility of working independently, or do both work only for the household economy? Do both men and women have the right to own property or goods independently, and to make decisions about that property? What protection or legal recourse do women have if their husbands are not supporting them or if they are not happy with their husbands?

Now consider the indications of economic change you have discovered. What impact did pepper production have on at least some

Chapter 4

Gender

Differences

in Peasant

Households in

Southeast Asia

and Central

Europe

(1500–1850)

Southeast Asian women and men? What impact did increased cloth production have on rural women and men in both of these areas? Might this have been different if the cloth production was for local use as opposed to export? Why were peasants so easily absorbed into expanding cloth production? In what way did the existing gender division of labor contribute to this? Did women's opportunities for work independent of the household appear to increase or decrease with the economic changes documented here? Did this freedom depend at all on a woman's marital status?

Remember that we are attempting to sketch a broad overview in a very new field in this chapter, and therefore our answers will have to remain quite tentative. Though it is tempting also to compare the two geographic areas, the sketchiness of our sources doesn't really allow the type of direct comparison we have made in other chapters. In this chapter, we have taken sources from two widely separated areas, not to compare them, but to see if we can identify certain factors that are significant cross-culturally in shaping gender distinctions among peasants.

THE EVIDENCE

Source 1 from The Lê Code: Law in Traditional Vietnam, *Nguyen Ngoc Huy and Ta Van Tai with the cooperation of Tran Van Liem (Athens: University of Ohio Press, 1987), pp. 110, 111, 203, 204, 205.*

1. From the Lê Code, Vietnam, 16th–17th century

When a father and a mother have died intestate [leaving no will] and left land, the brothers and sisters who divide the property among themselves shall reserve one-twentieth of this property to constitute the *hương hỏa* [incense and fire] property[2] which shall be entrusted to the eldest brother. The remainder of the property shall be divided among them. Children of secondary wives or female serfs shall receive smaller parts [than children of the principal wife].

In the case in which the father and mother have left an oral will or a testament, the relevant regulations [concerning wills] shall apply. Heirs who violate this provision shall be deprived of their parts.

Whether in the families of high dignitaries, public servants, or ordinary people, old age or youth, or high or low social rank shall not be taken into ac-

2. *hương hỏa* **property:** a portion of the family property reserved to cover the expenses for sacrifices to the ancestors and for the maintenance of their tombs. The words *hương hỏa* actually mean incense and fire, which were kept burning on the ancestors' altar.

count when choosing descendants to perform ancestor worship: the normal rule is to entrust this task to the principal son; or, if this son has died, to the eldest grandson; or, there being no eldest grandson, to a younger son of the principal wife; or, the principal wife having no child, to the most virtuous among the children of the secondary wives.

In the case of the eldest son or eldest grandson being disabled or unworthy and thereby unable to assume responsibilities for ancestor worship, the family concerned shall inform the local authorities and select another descendant for the task. . . .

The management of the *hương hỏa* property shall be entrusted to the eldest son or, failing that, to the eldest daughter. Such property shall be one-twentieth of the total of the real property in the estate. . . .

If a son, although born of a man's former principal wife and already entrusted with the management of the *hương hỏa* property, has only a daughter, while another son, although born of a secondary wife or a serf of such a man or even chronically incapacitated, has a male offspring, the management of the *hương hỏa* property shall be entrusted to this grandson. This is to illustrate the principle that a family's name should never be left extinct [for lack of male worship heir]. . . .

When the eldest of two brothers in a family has only daughters while the younger has one son who has been already entrusted with the management of the *hương hỏa* property, if this son in turn has only daughters, such property shall be returned to the granddaughter of the eldest brother.

[*The following section of the Lê Code is
from the "47 Rules for Moral Education"
read to all villagers, including children,
on ritual feast days.*]

Article 4. Spouses must love and respect each other. Husbands must see to it that order and good conduct are the rules in their family and their character should be exemplary. Wives must serve and respect their parents-in-law. They shall not go against their husband's wishes and act jealously. Spouses must not leave each other out of frustration over being poor for a long time. . . .

Article 10. Wives must adhere to their primary obligation which is obeisance. They must serve their parents-in-law and live in harmony with their brothers-in-law. They must not pride themselves on their parents' wealth or social status to behave haughtily toward their husbands, or raise their voice, shout or indulge themselves in acts of jealousy, or request a divorce on the slightest reason. When in fault, they must follow the advice of their parents-in-law or husbands and modify their behavior. They shall not become angry with that and revile them or flee elsewhere or seek refuge in the neighborhood, thus gradually slipping toward debauchery. Violations of these obligations shall be reported by the ward, village or hamlet chiefs to the competent

Chapter 4

Gender

Differences

in Peasant

Households in

Southeast Asia

and Central

Europe

(1500–1850)

yamen [administrative and judicial bureaucrats who advised the magistrate] for punishment.

Source 2 from M. C. Hoadley and M. B. Hooker, An Introduction to Javanese Law: A Translation of and Commentary on the Agama *(Tucson: University of Arizona Press, 1981), p. 165, 192–193. Notes by Barbara Watson Andaya.*

2. From the Agama Law Code, Java, 16th century

A bondwoman[3] fleeing from her master and a bondman also fleeing from his master, if the two meet in their flight, marry, and live for a long time in another village, going so far as to have children, but are finally traced by their masters; then the children are divided: two parts go to the man's master, one part to the woman's master. If the husband dies first the master of the wife takes from the common household goods a head-load and the woman is restored to her master. If the wife dies first the man's master takes from the common household goods a shoulder-load[4] and the man is restored to his master. . . .

Concerning a person giving goods to children-in-law on the occasion of marriage; if then the new wife dies her possessions go to the husband, if the husband dies his possessions go to the wife. It is not permitted for the giver to take back the goods if there has occurred the "mixing of goods." The minimum time for this "mixing of goods" is twelve years.

Concerning a maiden given goods by her father out of love for her and later she marries but not long thereafter the girl dies; all the goods brought by her to the marriage are returned to the girl's father and mother because there has not yet occurred the "mixing of goods." In a like manner, all the goods of the husband if he dies shortly after the marriage are returned to his father.

If a person takes a dislike to his son-in-law, then the marriage of his daughter is dissolved; the bride price paid by the husband is repaid two-fold. In addition, the bridal gifts and all that given earlier, such as clothing, male sash, kain,[5] all of those things which were given, must be returned to the disliked former son-in-law.

3. **bondwoman:** slave or debt-slave.

4. **shoulder-load:** Indonesians, especially women, commonly carry goods on their heads. Although there was no precise standardization of weights, parties in any agreement would normally have a general idea of what such an amount might be. Unless a pole was used less could be carried on the shoulder than on the head.

5. **kain:** a sarong; cloth was always an important part of wedding gifts, representing the "female" side in contrast to money, knives, and other metal objects which were considered "masculine."

Concerning a newly married maiden who has not yet lain with her husband because she will not have him; the girl's bride price is returned two-fold. This is termed "scorned coitus."

Source 3 from Franz V. Spechtler and Rudolf Uminsky, eds., Die Salzburger Landesordnung von 1526, Göppinger Arbeiten zur Germanistik, Nr. 305 *(Göppingen, Kümmerle, 1981), pp. 119, 154, 197, 248–249. Translations by Merry E. Wiesner.*

3. From the Law Code of the Territory of Salzburg, Austria, 1526

It is to be accepted that both spouses have married themselves together from the time of the consummation of their marriage, body to body and goods to goods. . . .

The husband shall not spend away the dowry[6] or other goods of his wife unnecessarily with gambling or other useless frivolous pastimes, wasting and squandering it. Whoever does this is guilty of sending his wife into poverty. His wife, in order to secure her legacy and other goods she has brought to the marriage, may get an order requiring him to pledge and hold in trust for her some of his property. In the same way he is to act in a suitable manner in other things that pertain to their living together and act appropriately toward her. If there is no cause or she is not guilty of anything, he is not to hit her too hard, push her, throw her or carry out any other abuse. For her part, the wife should obey her husband in modesty and honorable fear, and be true and obedient to him. She should not provoke him with word or deed to disagreement or displeasure, through which he might be moved to strike her or punish her in unseemly ways. Also, without his knowledge and agreement she is not to do business [with any household goods] except those which she has brought to the marriage; if she does it will not be legally binding. . . .

The first and foremost heirs are the children who inherit from their parents. If a father and mother leave behind legitimate children out of their bodies, one or more sons or daughters, then these children inherit all paternal and maternal goods, landed property and movables, equally with each other. . . .

Women who do not have husbands, whether they are young or old, shall have a guardian and advisor in all matters of consequence and property, such as the selling of or other legal matters regarding landed property. Otherwise these transactions are not binding. In matters which do not involve court

---

6. **dowry:** an amount of goods, cash, and/or property that was brought by a wife to her husband on marriage; the husband could do with the dowry whatever he wished within the course of the marriage, though legally it continued to belong to his wife.

Chapter 4

Gender

Differences

in Peasant

Households in

Southeast Asia

and Central

Europe

(1500–1850)

actions and in other matters of little account they are not to be burdened with guardians against their will. . . .

Regarding wages for servants in the territory: Every builder's assistant who is skillful and capable should be given no more than 6 or 7 gulden per year and 5 pair of shoes. . . . A skillful and capable herdsman is to be given 3 gulden per year, one pair of cloth pants and 4 pair of shoes. A grown male servant or strong boy who is capable of doing a man's work is to be given 2 or 3 gulden and 4 pair of shoes and one pair of cloth pants. A female cook who can cook especially well and who has lots to cook in the houses of great lords or inns should be given 5 gulden and three pairs of shoes. A normal female cook who doesn't have to cook so much is to be given 3 or at the most 4 gulden and three pair of shoes. A strong adult dairy- or house-maid who is capable of doing all types of work is not to be given more than 2 gulden and 4 pair of shoes. A children's maid who is not capable of doing heavy work is not to be given more than 1 gulden as wages.

Source 4 from Stuttgart, Württembergisches Hauptstaatsarchiv, Generalreskripta, A38, Bü. 2, 1550. Translation by Merry E. Wiesner.

4. Regulations for Vineyard Workers in the Duchy of Württemberg, 1550

Men who work in the vineyards, doing work that is skilled, are to be paid 16 pence per day; in addition, they are to receive soup and wine to eat in the morning, at midday beer, vegetables, and meat, and in the evening soup, vegetables, and wine. Young boys are to be paid 10 pence per day. Women who work as haymakers are to be given 6 pence a day. If the employer wants to have them doing other work, he may make an agreement with them to pay them 7 or 8 pence. He may also give them soup and vegetables to eat in the morning—but no wine— milk and bread at midday, but nothing in the evening.

Source 5 from Karl Röslin, Abhandlung von besonderen weiblichen Rechten *(Mannheim, 1775), vol. 1, p. 94. Translation by Merry E. Weisner.*

5. From the Law Code of the Duchy of Hohenlohe, Germany, 1731

Women who have no husbands need to have an experienced man as their guardian when they are involved in legal processes, and also for significant business outside of the law courts, such as buying, selling, or trading landed property. In the same way they are not to be allowed to take part in legal cases without a guardian (except in criminal cases or cases pertaining to marriage). Thus those who do business with a woman without a guardian in matters outside of the law courts must be prepared that if this leads to a loss and they want to complain about it, the agreement will be annulled and everything will go back to the way it was before.

Source 6 from August Meitzen, Urkunden schlesicher Dörfer *(Breslau, 1863), pp. 334–335. Translation by Merry E. Wiesner.*

6. From the Land Register in the Silesian Village of Zedlitz, 1790

The eighteen households . . . are obliged to send as workers every day two people, that is the husband and also the wife, or instead of the latter, a qualified maid, to do whatever work is necessary. For the harvest they must bring a third person with them. The field workers begin harvest work at sunrise, stop from 6:30 to 7 for a half-hour breakfast, work again until 10, when they eat for an hour in the fields, and then work from 11 until 2. They eat an evening meal from 2 to 3, and then they work again without stopping until sunset. The wives of the field-workers begin work once they have taken care of the herds, work with the men and maids until 6:30, and then go from the fields back to the house to prepare the meal, which they bring to the men and maids in the fields at 10:00. They eat until 11, and then stay working in the fields until evening, although they do the same things between 2 and 3 with the evening meal. If a field-worker's wife has a baby during the harvest season, she is free from service for six weeks, but the maid must still come to work regardless of this. If she has a baby when it is not harvest-time, the maid is also free from service for fourteen days [and can help her].

Source 7 from Jean Quataert, transcriptions from Staatsarchiv Dresden, Aussenstelle Bautzen, Amtsgericht Hernnhut, Nr. 158, Nachlass des Johann Gottlieb Hänsch, 1856. Translation by Merry E. Wiesner.

7. Will of a Rural Weaver from the Village of Herrnhut in Eastern Germany, 1856

[Johann Gottlieb Hänsch] names as his heirs his wife; his children by his first marriage: Karl Gottlieb—now a weaver in Seifheim—and Ernestine Juliane—now married to a weaver in Eibau; and his children by his second marriage:

Chapter 4

Gender

Differences

in Peasant

Households in

Southeast Asia

and Central

Europe

(1500–1850)

Johann Gottlieb Hänsch [Jr.], and Johanna Rahele. . . . His wife is to have one-quarter of his estate and his son Karl Gottlieb is to have the part that is owed to him as required by the law; the rest is to be divided equally among his other children.

At the same time, he establishes the following bequests:

I. His wife Martha is to be given:

1. Free lodging for the rest of her life as long as she doesn't marry again in the inn which he owns in Neuberthelsdorf. This is to be in the main room of the inn. She is to have the right to have a chair there with her spooling reel and distaff, a place at the table and a stool by the window on one side, and the use of the fire in the porcelain stove to keep herself warm and for cooking, and also space for her shearing-frame.[7]

2. The use of one-quarter of the small room which is over the main room, specifically the place in this room which is directly over the stove.

3. A little place in the cellar for the storage of her potatoes, milk, and butter.

4. A place for the bleaching and drying of her wash.

5. A place to set out the things for her meals.

6. The freedom to do her wash in the house.

7. The freedom to use the innkeeper's latrine, though the dung remains the property of the innkeeper.[8]

8. A place in the attic for drying her wash.

9. Every year a bushel of edible potatoes.

10. Every year one-quarter of the fruit that grows on his property.

All of these things shall be reserved to his wife as soon as the inn in Neuberthelsdorf is sold, with the condition that she does not remarry.

He also bequeaths to his wife Martha a featherbed and a single bedstead.

II. Further he bequeaths to his son Johann all of his clothes, his newest work stool, a spinning-wheel, a bedstead, and a chest.

III. To his daughter [Ernestine Juliana] he bequeaths the following things which originally belonged to her mother:

1. A featherbed with 6 pillows.

2. A work stool with a spooling wheel and distaff.

---

7. **spooling reel, distaff, shearing-frame:** all tools for preparing thread for weaving or for finishing cloth once it has been woven.

8. Human dung was sometimes used along with animal droppings as fertilizer for fields.

3. A moderate-sized chest and a long chest.

4. A wardrobe for clothes, a bread box, and an arm-chair.

Immediately after his death his inn in Neuberthelsdorf is to be sold to Mr. Weisbieten, and his wife is to have back the 50 thalers that she brought to the marriage as a dowry.

Source 8 from Miguel de Loarca, Relation of the Filipinas Islands, *in* The Phillipine Islands 1493–1898, *vol. 5, ed. and trans. E. H. Blair and J. A. Robertson (Cleveland: Arthur H. Clark, 1902), pp. 143, 145.*

8. Report by Miguel de Loarca Describing the Philippines, 1582

Laws of slavery. No Indian in this country is made a slave or is put to death for any crime which he commits, even if it be theft, adultery, or murder—except that for each crime there is an established fine, which they have to pay in jewels or gold, and if the culprit is unable to pay the fine he will borrow the money, and pledge himself to the man from whom he borrows. As a result he becomes a slave, until he shall repay what was lent to him; after that, he is free again. Therefore, according to the crime committed, they are slaves; and there are three classes of slaves in these islands. The first, and the most thoroughly enslaved, is the bondman of him who is served in his own dwelling; such a slave they call *ayuey.* These slaves work three days for the master, and one for themselves.

Kinds of slavery. Another class of slaves are those called *tumaranpoc.* They live in their own houses, and are obliged to go to work for their master one day out of four, having the three days for themselves. . . .

There are other slaves, whom these people hold in most respect, who are called *tomatabans;* these work in the house of the master only when there is some banquet or revel. On such occasions they bring small gifts, and share in the drinking. But when one of these slaves dies, the property left by the slave is shared with his children by the master. During their lifetime, these slaves are bound to work for their master five days in a month. . . .

The ayuey women, like their husbands, work in the houses of chiefs. The tumaranpoque women, if they have children, serve half of the month in spinning and weaving cotton, which their masters supply; and during the other half of the month they work for themselves. The tomataban women spin only one hank of cotton each month for their masters, who furnish to them the cotton in the boll. Only the ayueys receive food and clothing from their masters; to the others the masters give nothing.

Chapter 4

Gender

Differences

in Peasant

Households in

Southeast Asia

and Central

Europe

(1500–1850)

Source 9 from Antonio de Morga, History of the Phillipine Islands, *ed. and trans. E. H. Blair and J. A. Robertson (Cleveland: Arthur H. Clark, 1907), vol. 2, pp. 79, 125–127.*

9. From Antonio de Morga, *History of the Philippine Islands*, 1609

The women have needlework as their employment and occupation, and they are very clever at it, and at all kinds of sewing. They weave cloth and spin cotton, and serve in the houses of their husbands and fathers. They pound the rice for eating, and prepare the other food. They raise fowls and swine, and keep the houses, while the men are engaged in the labors of the field, and in their fishing, navigation, and trading. . . .

The dowry was furnished by the man, being given by his parents. The wife furnished nothing for the marriage, until she had inherited it from her parents. The solemnity of the marriage consisted in nothing more than the agreement between the parents and relatives of the contracting parties, the payment of the dowry agreed upon to the father of the bride, and the assembling at the wife's parents' house of all the relatives to eat and drink until they would fall down. . . .

In inheritances all the legitimate children inherited equally from their parents whatever property they had acquired. If there were any movable or landed property which they had received from their parents, such went to the nearest relatives and the collateral side of that stock, if there were no legitimate children. . . .

If any chief was lord of a barangai,[9] then in that case, the eldest son of an ynasaba[10] succeeded him. If he died, the second son succeeded. If there were no sons, then the daughters succeeded in the same order. If there were no legitimate successors, the succession went to the nearest relative belonging to the lineage and relationship of the chief who had been the last possessor of it.

Source 10 from Li Tana and Anthony Reid, eds., Southern Vietnam under the Nguyen: Documents on the Economic History of Cochinchina (Dang Trong), 1602–1777 *(Pasir Panjang, Singapore: Institute of Southeast Asian Studies, 1993), pp. 17–19.*

10. From a Letter of Jeronimus Wonderaer, 1602

I had intended to stay over another day, in the hope that I could still make some additions because I was told that a merchant from Senoa[11] with ten or

9. **barangai:** the followers of a particular chief.

10. **ynasaba:** principal wife, whose children were considered legitimate.

11. **Senoa:** the province of Thuân Hóa in central Vietnam.

twelve bags. Coming about evening time, it was a man and a woman, and the woman did the talking while the man listened and agreed. When they came to our house, I was told that an important merchant woman of Senoa was here, so I went to see her. She said that she had come here at the king's desire with some bags of pepper as a small sample, and if we could come to an agreement she was able to deliver a large quantity at once. Altogether they were two sisters and one brother who were able to deliver a good quantity. I answered that if we could come to an agreement, I would take what they had brought along with whatever quantity they could deliver, on the condition that I liked it, and [also] that rather than deal with many I preferred to deal with one person—if that person was found to be fair—and when I had received everything I would pay cash, or if tradegoods pleased them more then tradegoods would be delivered. Thereupon she said that she had come from the uplands with a small sample in order to find out what I would offer her, and on hearing that it would suffice then she would bring down a good quantity, so could I please say what I would want to give for it. I demanded to know if that was the way to negotiate in her country, explaining that our way of doing things was not so, and that I doubted if she were so ignorant as to imagine that if I wanted to sell her several lakens[12] or other wares, she would tell me what she would give for them before I had told her the selling price. [I went on] that we should not try to catch the other asleep, she had come to sell and I had come to buy; that I would have thought we had both reached the same age, I with grey hair and she too; and so if she knew how to play her role in the negotiations, I permitted myself the luxury of thinking I knew a little too because I had also seen the world in my time. She looked at me, the man was completely silent without saying one word; at last she made a long speech which in the end came to the point that other nations bought for ten *tael*,[13] but since it was wares and tradegoods which she received as payment in these cases, she was willing—since I would give her cash—to deliver for eight *tael* even though the wares she had accepted were as good for her as cash.

I asked her if that was her last price and she said yes; I answered her that I thought she was playing games with me or took me for a fool, that I could play that game with her too, yet I respected her for her age and her person. And even though I looked simple in her eyes and not all pomp and pride like the Portuguese, with whom she had traded many times, I hoped to satisfy her and everyone with whom I traded so that nobody would have any complaints. And although I thanked her for the trouble she had taken to come here, at that price her goods were not for me; nor did I think that my money was for her as long as she kept on babbling. Thus we took leave from each other, for she did not want to change her tune, and I did not want to make an offer lest they keep thinking we were cornered into taking the pepper, which

12. **lakens:** European woolen cloth.
13. *tael:* a certain weight of gold or silver, usually 37.8 grams.

[109]

Chapter 4
Gender
Differences
in Peasant
Households in
Southeast Asia
and Central
Europe
(1500–1850)

is what they had made her and others believe. So I kept my cool, and it was enough to know that there was still much old pepper in the country.

On the morning of 5th ditto the merchant woman from Senoa came to me again and, after many words, at least came to the point that I should make her a bid; even if it was only two *tael* she would not mind. This I did after explaining that I did not want to make fun of her, but would make her a bid as a merchant should who has decided to buy, indeed as much or more than the price was before we arrived. I offered her three and a half *tael*, adding that if she would raise it to four she would have to await my response, and that they had no right to try and catch us napping. Not long afterwards the Portuguese woman came to me, telling me that the king had summoned her and sent her to ask me whether this was my final decision or would I be prepared to go up to five *tael*; for even though he had spoken to the merchant woman from Senoa, it could not be done for four *tael*. I answered that I regretted it deeply that his majesty had taken so much trouble for my sake, and thanked him for all the good deeds he had shown us; that I realized the sale was not to take place because I did not intend to give more, as indeed I had already said to his majesty on an earlier occasion. She has passed this on to the king but I have not received an answer yet. She said that the merchant woman had already returned to her home. I answered that it was good, I also hoped to leave soon for my home, the ships, once I had paid his majesty. The woman from Senoa had explained that among other [reasons for leaving] she had two large houses full of pepper which she had had to leave unattended. It was satisfying to hear from her the same thing I had heard from the barber. To offer more, Sir, I did not think wise.

Source 11 from William Marsden, The History of Sumatra, *reprint of the 3rd ed. (Kuala Lumpur: Oxford University Press, 1966), pp. 71, 137, 382.*

11. From William Marsden,
The History of Sumatra, 1783

When the periodical rains begin to fall, which takes place gradually about October, the planter assembles his neighbours (whom he assists in turn), and with the aid of his whole family proceeds to sow his ground, endeavouring to complete the task in the course of one day. In order to ensure success, he fixes, by the priest's assistance, on a lucky day, and vows the sacrifice of a kid, if his crop should prove favourable; the performance of which is sacredly observed, and is the occasion of a feast in every family after harvest. The manner of sowing is this. Two or three men enter the plantation, as it is usual to call the *padi*-field, holding in each hand sticks about five feet long and two inches diameter, bluntly pointed, with which, striking them into the ground as they advance, they make small, shallow holes, at the distance of about five inches from each other. These are followed by the women and elder children with small baskets containing the seed-grain (saved with care from the choicest of the preceding crop) of which they drop four or five grains into every hole, and passing on, are followed by the younger children, who with their feet (in the use of which the natives are nearly as expert as with their hands) cover them lightly from the adjacent earth, that the seed may not be too much exposed to the birds, which, as might be expected, often prove destructive foes. . . .

[On pepper-harvesting.]   As soon as any of the berries or corns redden, the bunch is reckoned fit for gathering, the remainder being then generally full-grown, although green; nor would it answer to wait for the whole to change colour, as the most mature would drop off. It is collected in small baskets slung over the shoulder, and with the assistance of the women and children conveyed to a smooth, level spot of clean, hard ground, near the garden or the village, where it is spread, sometimes upon mats, to dry in the sun; but exposed at the same time to the vicissitudes of the weather, which are not much regarded, nor thought to injure it. In this situation it becomes black and shrivelled, as we see it in Europe, and as it dries is hand-rubbed occasionally to separate the grains from the stalk. . . .

[On marriage.]   The parents of the girl always receive a valuable consideration (in buffaloes or horses) from the person to whom she is given in marriage; which is returned when a divorce takes place against the man's inclination. The daughters, as elsewhere, are looked upon as the riches of the fathers.

The condition of the women appears to be no other than that of slaves, the husbands having the power of selling their wives and children. They alone, beside the domestic duties, work in the rice plantations. These are prepared in the same mode as in the rest of the island; except that in the central parts, the country being clearer, the plough and harrow, drawn by buffaloes, are more used. The men, when not engaged in war, their favourite occupation, commonly lead an idle, inactive life, passing the day in playing on a kind of flute, crowned with garlands of flowers; among which the *globe-amaranthus,* a native of the country, mostly prevails. They are said, however, to hunt deer on horseback, and to be attached to the diversion of horse-racing. They ride boldly without a saddle or stirrups, frequently throwing their hands upwards whilst pushing their horse to full speed. The bit of the bridle is of iron, and has several joints; the head-stall and reins of rattan; in some parts the reins, or halter rather, is of *iju,* and the bit of wood. They are, like the rest of the Sumatrans, much addicted to gaming, and the practice is under no kind of restraint, until it destroys itself by the ruin of one of the parties. When a man loses more money than he is able to pay, he is confined and sold as a slave; being the most usual mode by which they become such.

Chapter 4

Gender

Differences

in Peasant

Households in

Southeast Asia

and Central

Europe

(1500–1850)

Source 12 from Friedrich Nicolai, Beschreibung einer Reise durch Deutschland und die Schweiz im Jahre 1781 *(Berlin and Stettin, 1793), vol. 11, pp. 169–170; vol. 8, p. 26. Translation by Merry E. Wiesner.*

12. Friedrich Nicolai's Descriptions of Weaving in South Germany, 1781

There are two principal people who make this type of woolen cloth in Tübingen, namely Abraham Koch's widow and Johann Wilhelm Elsenhaus's widow. In the year 1795 each of them kept eight looms occupied in her house and eight outside of her house, which provided work through spinning for all of the nearby villages. . . .

In Augsburg I visited the cotton manufactory of Herr von Schule. . . . I have rarely seen an establishment of this type which gave me such pleasure. Everything gave evidence of order, cleanliness, comfort, and beneficial, purposeful arrangements. About 350 people worked there, including many women and children who had come from nearby villages. In summer the workers came every day at 6 and worked until 8 in the evening, though they were not paid hourly wages, but by the piece. We were shown young girls who could only earn 8 kreutzer a day, and on the other hand a fabric-printer who was reputed to have earned up to 2 gold Louis per week, which seemed almost impossible to me.[14]

Source 13 from Johann Jacob Grümbke, Streifzüge durch das Rügenland, *ed. Albert Burckhardt (Leipzig: F. A. Brockhaus, 1805), p. 182.*

13. Johann Jacob Grümbke's Description of Harvesting Grain in Rügen, 1805

The harvest begins around the middle of August and is ended in the first half of September, although it is often extended because of bad thunderstorms. With rye one uses only a scythe, which the landowner's officials on large estates own and for which they receive a certain payment. Sickles are not at all common, for on large fields their use is too tiresome and time-consuming. It is an entertaining view when one sees a row of 12, 16, or 20 strong men swinging scythes according to the beat that the front reaper sets. . . . The cut grain normally lays for a short time in rows, before it is put in sheaves, though care is taken to bind the rye as quickly as possible after it has been cut with the

14. Though it is difficult to make an exact comparison, the printer appears to have been making about fifty times what the little girls were: a kreutzer was a small coin worth one-quarter of a penny; a gold Louis was a large gold coin.

scythe. The sheaves are piled against one another in heaps, and each heap is about six or seven rows apart. The number of sheaves in each pile is arbitrary. Binding, piling into heaps, and loading the grain is normally done by women, who appear throughout the fields in white clothing.

Source 14 from John Paget, Hungary and Transylvania *(New York: The Arno Press, 1971; reprint of London: Bentley, 1839), vol. 1, p. 367; vol. 2, pp. 133–134, 138, 140, 146–147, 270–271. Photograph courtesy of Harvard College Library.*

14. From John Paget, *Hungary and Transylvania,* 1839

That the Wallack[15] is idle and drunken it would be very difficult to deny. Even in the midst of harvest you will see him lying in the sun sleeping all the more comfortably because he knows he ought to be working. His corn is always the last cut, and it is very often left to shell on the ground for want of timely gathering. . . .

Another cause for laziness may be found in the paucity of the Wallack's wants, and in the ease with which they are supplied. The earth, almost spontaneously, affords him maize for his *polenta,*[16]—or *mamaliga,* as he calls it,—and his wife manufactures from the wool and hemp of his little farm all that is required for his household use and personal clothing. . . .

The only occupation in which the Wallack shows any peculiar talent, is that of a carpenter; here, I believe, he is allowed to excel. His house frequently bears proof of his taste in this particular in the wooden ornaments about the gates, windows, and roof; and it is rarely the church and cross are not adorned with the rude carvings of the Wallack's knife. Domestic manufactures, too, assume an importance unknown amongst more civilized people. The Wallack grows his own flax, his wife spins it into yarn, weaves it into cloth, dyes it of various colours, cuts it out, and works it up into clothes for her family. The wool goes through nearly the same processes; and is made to serve for leg-wrappings, aprons, jackets, and cloaks. The sheepskin cap and sandals are mostly of home fabrication, so that this ignorant peasant has more knowledge of the ways and means of procuring for himself what is necessary for his existence and happiness than half the wise men of Europe: that he should not, however, be a perfect master of so many trades is scarcely wonderful. . . .

The Wallack woman is never by any chance seen idle. As she returns from market it is her breast that is bulged out with the purchases of the day; it is her head that bears the water from the village well; she dyes the wool or flax, spins the thread, weaves the web, and makes the dresses of her family. In harvest she joins the men in cutting the corn, and though less strong, she is more

15. **Wallack:** Rumanian.
16. *polenta:* cornmeal mush.

Chapter 4

Gender

Differences

in Peasant

Households in

Southeast Asia

and Central

Europe

(1500–1850)

active and willing at the task. She uses the spindle and distaff[17] as the princesses of Homer did, and as they are still used in the Campagna of Rome, and they are scarcely ever out of her hand. You may see her at the market suckling her child, higgling for her eggs and butter, and twirling her spindle at the same time, with a dexterity really astonishing. As far as cleanliness goes, however, she is a bad housewife; nor does her labour produce great effects. Among the German settlers it is a proverb, "to be as busy as a Wallack woman, and do as little.". . .

In our drive up the valley we observed a new style of nursing, which necessity—ever fruitful mother—had taught the women to have recourse to when engaged in the business of the harvest. Three strong poles are planted into the

ground, and made to meet at the top; and from these is slung a kind of hammock, in which the child lies; while a blanket is thrown over the whole to protect the little nestling from the sun. . . .

It is difficult to find for the uneducated peasant-woman an occupation more befitting her powers of mind and body, more consistent with her duties of mother and housekeeper, than is afforded by the simple processes of spinning and weaving. If this is taken away, and the means of applying herself to higher and more difficult objects are not afforded, she has little left but idleness, or the coarse degrading labours of the field. . . . What a pity it is, that all these beautiful costumes,[18] and the honest pride and self-esteem they give rise to, must disappear, as soon as the cheap wares of Manchester, or some other cotton capital, gain entrance to these valleys, and drive household manufactures from the field! If real civilization, founded on improved institutions and an enlightened system of education, do not accompany the introduction of luxuries produced by machinery, they may become a curse instead of a blessing to a people.

17. **spindle and distaff:** implements for spinning thread from wool or flax.

18. Paget refers to the exquisitely embroidered outfits made and worn by peasant women for festivals and compares them to the cheap cotton cloth produced in Manchester, England, one of the early centers of large-scale cloth production.

Source 15 from Anthony Reid, Southeast Asia in the Age of Commerce, *vol. 1:* The Lands Below the Winds *(New Haven: Yale University Press, 1988), p. 23. Reproduced courtesy of the Harvard-Yenching Library.*

15. Illustration from a Map of the Philippines, 1734

1.Cayman,ô Cocodrilo de que eftan llenos los rios de eftasYslas. 2. Saua Culebra mui grande. 3.Indio enbaIaque arando con vn Carabao, ô Bufalo. 4. Luzon, en que fepila el arroz, y ádonde fe llamò fuzon eftaYsla.

Source 16 from William Marsden, The History of Sumatra *(Kuala Lumpur: Oxford University Press, 1966 [reprint of the third edition]), plate 19. Reproduced with permission of Oxford University Press, Malaysia.*

16. A Village Scene in Sumatra, 1783

Source 17 from W. Scheidig, Die Holzschnitte des Petrarca-Meisters *(Berlin, 1955), p. 255.*

17. Hay-making in Germany, 1532

Chapter 4

Gender

Differences

in Peasant

Households in

Southeast Asia

and Central

Europe

(1500–1850)

Source 18 from Deutliche Vorstellung der Nürnbergischen Trachten *(Nürnberg, 1766). Translation by Merry E. Wiesner.*

18. A Female Dairy Farmer in Nuremberg, Germany, 1766

Beneath her picture in this book of costumes was a description:

She comes every day from the country to the city, or she stays several days during the week, and sells the products of her animals and things that she has made. She belongs to the people who shout [in the streets], of which there are many in Nuremberg. Here is her call: "Good milk, you housewives! Eggs and lard! Good butter! Good buttermilk!" Connected with these cries are a certain Nuremberg peasant dialect and a certain tone, that one can recognize immediately once one has heard it. Sometimes she also calls out: "Sauerkraut! White cabbage! Cream!" and other things. Some of these women do not call out, but go silently through the streets and have their own houses where they always unload their wares and where people wait for them, or at least wait for their milk and butter for their morning coffee. The cleaner each dairy-farmer is, the more customers and buyers she has. There are also those who arrange themselves and their baskets, cloths, and copper jugs in such an attractive way that their wares easily meet with approval.

QUESTIONS TO CONSIDER

The Method section of this chapter asks a number of questions that relate to specific sources and suggests ways to compare information gained from these sources. Before you prepare your answers to the chapter's central questions, it might be worthwhile to reflect on some of the cautions regarding the sources that are also noted in that section. All of our sources, whether from Southeast Asia or central Europe, come from the pens of educated men, and you may have found some surprising similarities among them in terms of their attitudes toward peasant men and women.

For example, several of the travelers' reports describe the women as busy and industrious, but the men as lazy. In Source 11, William Marsden comments that in Sumatra, "The men, when not engaged in war, their favorite occupation, commonly lead an idle, inactive life." The illustration for his book (Source 16) reinforces this remark, for the women are depicted as busy taking care of children and pounding rice, while the men are simply standing or sitting around. In Source 14, John Paget notes that the Wallack man is "idle and drunken," but "the Wallack woman is never by any chance seen idle." Why do you think this was a common observation? (It is repeated in many other reports by explorers, missionaries, and travelers from throughout the world.) Why might it become a stereotype for cultures regarded as inferior or backward?

As you have discovered, this stereotype did not affect the wages of men and women, for men were invariably paid more for work at a similar skill level than women. What attitudes or assumptions might account for this difference? From reading Source 4, you know that male and female agricultural workers were sometimes given different amounts and types of food. How might this in turn affect their ability to perform various agricultural tasks?

According to Sources 3 and 5, European women were prohibited from carrying out business or acting legally without the approval of their husbands or guardians. Do these restrictions help explain why the European merchant Jeronimus Wonderaer (Source 10) comments twice that though both a male and female pepper merchant came to see him, she did the talking while he was completely silent? What other evidence do you see in the European comments about Southeast Asia (Sources 8–11) of the cultural background of the authors shaping their reports?

Another issue is that of cleanliness, which emerges in Sources 12 (the cotton manufactory is clean and orderly), 13 (the women wear white clothing in the fields), 14 (the Wallack women are "bad housewives"), and 18 (the cleaner dairy farmers are more prosperous). Why would largely middle-class male authors have thought such distinctions important enough to note? How might cleanliness (or its absence) also become a stereotype?

Because stereotypes about women and about other cultures often shape

Chapter 4

Gender

Differences

in Peasant

Households in

Southeast Asia

and Central

Europe

(1500–1850)

the way economic decisions are made, they are particularly important to keep in mind when you are considering the issue of how gender differences might have shaped economic development. In Source 14, John Paget, for example, describes the Wallack women as "less strong [though] more active and willing at the task," and notes that no occupation is more fitting for a peasant woman nor "more consistent with her duties of mother and housekeeper" than spinning and weaving. How might attitudes such as this have affected the hiring practices of early large-scale cloth manufacturers?

Though the sources we have used do reflect cultural biases, they also supply enough information to answer the central questions for this chapter: How did the experiences of men and women in early modern peasant households differ? How might these differences have been affected by economic change and how, in turn, might economic developments have been shaped by gender differences?

EPILOGUE

As we have frequently noted, none of the evidence in this chapter was actually produced by peasant men or women themselves. This lack is one of the problems that has plagued research into the history of both peasants and women: all of the readily available information comes from people who were somehow outsiders, different from the peasants in terms of social class, race, religion, level of education, place of residence, and, for female peasants, gender. For some cultures, and particularly for those in the premodern era, we will probably never find any original sources that come directly from peasants, but sometimes intensive digging can yield gratifying results. For example, more work has been done to date on peasants and particularly peasant women in India than in Southeast Asia or central Europe; these efforts have led to the discovery of new sources, such as this poem by the Indian peasant woman Ratanbai, active sometime during the twelfth to the fourteenth century:

[My spinning wheel is dear to me, my sister]

My spinning wheel is dear to me, my sister;
My household depends on it.
My husband married me and departed;
He went abroad to earn a living.

After twelve years he returned
With a copper coin and a half;
He went to bathe in the Ganga,
Dropped the copper coin and a half.

Mother, father, father-in-law, mother-in-law,
One and all rejected us;
The spinning wheel was our savior,
To it we clung.

I paid off all my husband's debts
And over and above

[120]

Tying coin after coin in the corner of my
   sari
I earned a whole rupee.[19]

Given what you have read in this chapter about the activities of rural women in spinning and cloth-making, the sentiments of this Indian woman probably do not surprise you. However, that she had time to write such a poem and that it survived—these facts are surprising, but the search for sources has yielded many surprising treasures.

Another avenue for discovering the ideas and sentiments of peasant women and men themselves has been to use oral interviews with contemporary village residents, and then extrapolate backward. Thus anthropological accounts are used to flesh out historical studies, yielding a much livelier story. This must be done with caution, however, for often notions that are described as "traditional" really go back only a few generations. This same reservation applies to using statistical studies begun in the twentieth century. In one of these, for example, government observers in East Java in the 1920s recorded the number of working hours for men, women, and children in rice production, discovering that two-thirds of the time spent on the production of rice was

women's.[20] Because the women were observed doing the same tasks in rice production that early modern women did—planting, weeding, and harvesting—we might be tempted to conclude that this same proportion applied in earlier centuries as well, especially because the methods of rice production have not changed dramatically. We can't be sure of this, however, because other economic changes—such as the availability of work outside the village—may have upset the gender and age balance of the work force engaged in rice production. This sort of regressive method can thus be somewhat helpful as support for conclusions gained from historical evidence, but such projections can't be used alone as proof of developments in earlier centuries.

The search for sources goes on, however, and many of the questions we can now answer with some certainty regarding peasant men and women in many parts of the world were considered unanswerable just a short time ago. The answers to many questions continue to elude us, but now that peasants have irrevocably joined more elite groups as people with a history, their stories may disappear at a slower rate.

19. Susie Tharu and K. Lalita, *Women Writing in India, 600 B.C. to the Present* (New York: The Feminist Press, 1991), vol. 1, pp. 89–90. Translated by Nita Ramaiya.

20. Elsbeth Locher-Scholten, "Female Labour in Twentieth Century Java," in *Indonesian Women in Focus: Past and Present Notions*, edited by Elsbeth Locher-Scholten and Anke Niehof (Dordrecht, Holland: Foris Publications, 1987), pp. 82–83.

CHAPTER FIVE

THE "DISCOVERY OF CHILDHOOD"

IN ENGLAND AND AMERICA

(1600–1800)

Dramatic changes swept Europe from the fifteenth through the seventeenth centuries, among them the development of capitalism, the intellectual changes of the Renaissance and Scientific Revolution, the religious upheaval of the Protestant Reformation, the growth of centralized nation-states, and the burgeoning of overseas empires. In fact, this period has often been termed "the beginning of the modern world," or referred to as the "early modern period," which implies the same pivotal significance. As historians over the last twenty-five years have turned their attention from political and intellectual developments to more detailed investigation of the lives of ordinary people, they have often tried to fit changes in everyday life into the periodization based on political and intellectual history. Thus many of them have been interested in

finding the "birth of the modern family" to parallel the "birth of the modern state," and have searched for signs in the early modern period.

As you might expect, there is much debate about exactly what makes a certain type of family "modern," but some of the key elements identified by many historians are that children in modern families are seen as intrinsically different from adults, appreciated for this difference, and treated in special ways. Modern parents recognize childhood as a separate stage in life, a time for moral as well as vocational training. Proper training could take a long time, so passage to adulthood needs to be postponed; wealthy boys in England could at fourteen serve on juries until 1695 and marry until 1753, an age subsequently regarded as far too young for such adult responsibilities.

The idea that a modern notion of childhood emerged in the early modern period was stated most forcefully first by the French historian Philippe Ariès, who saw it developing among educational reformers and middle-class parents in the sixteenth century, then spreading to the upper classes by the eighteenth century and to the lower by the nineteenth century. This "discovery of childhood" also resulted in parents treating their children better, according to many historians, who found gruesome examples of indifference or cruelty to children in earlier centuries.

This theory has been criticized for a number of reasons. Medieval historians have found counterexamples of great kindness toward children and concern for their well-being long before the seventeenth century, and discovered many statements indicating that people regarded childhood as a distinct stage in life. Scholars of the eighteenth and nineteenth centuries have pointed out that though people may have been told to treat children lovingly and nurture them, the way most children were actually treated bore little resemblance to tenderness. Family historians of the early modern period itself have discovered wide variation both in attitudes toward children and in the behavior that resulted from those attitudes.

Your task in this chapter is to analyze some of the evidence that has been used (often by all sides) in this debate and develop your own theory of early modern childhood. What attitudes about children and childhood emerge in descriptions of children, both real and fictional, and in the words of children themselves? How did these change during the seventeenth and eighteenth centuries, and in what ways might these attitudes be termed "modern"?

BACKGROUND

Attitudes toward children in England and America in the seventeenth and eighteenth centuries were shaped by a number of factors, which various historians have weighted differently in their search for the roots of the discovery of childhood.

For many historians, religious developments are the most important factor. With the division of western Christianity into various denominations in the sixteenth century, both Protestants and Catholics felt it necessary to compete for the religious allegiance of young people. Both camps proposed plans for schools, and the Protestants in particular emphasized home Bible reading as an important way to develop children's morality and piety.

The English Puritans carried this concern further, writing the first books specifically designed for children, as well as a number of books that attempted to teach parents how to raise their children. Puritans in both England and the American colonies generally accepted the religious doctrine of Original Sin, which holds that children are born sinful because the first people, Adam and Eve, sinned by disobeying God, and everyone since Eden has inherited this

Chapter 5
The "Discovery
of Childhood"
in England
and America
(1600–1800)

tendency to sin. The effects of this doctrine on the actual treatment of children have been disputed, however, with some historians maintaining that it led Puritans to attempt to beat the sin out of their children and teach them early on about their unworthiness, whereas others assert that it led to better care and education because parents felt children could not develop properly on their own. They note that viewing children as innocent could actually be *more* repressive as it led to attempts to shield children and young people from all "adult" concerns, including social problems and sexuality, which left them ill-prepared for later life.

The Puritans who settled in Massachusetts and other parts of the American colonies brought their ideas about childhood with them, and added to these their sense of mission in a New World and the importance of young people in this calling. They also mixed with other religious groups in the colonies and were confronted with new challenges as they built towns and expanded the frontier. Some historians have suggested that, particularly in the colonies, it is wrong to speak of a uniform attitude toward children or a single line of development in this attitude. Instead, they argue that parenting modes varied—often within the same town—from authoritarian, stressing shame and guilt, to affectionate, stressing sociability and gentility.

Some authors emphasize intellectual developments outside religion as the most important factors in changing attitudes toward children. Ariès and others find the first signs of a new view of childhood among Italian humanists in the fifteenth century, as they stressed the importance of a long period of education devoted to developing the moral and intellectual character of those boys who would grow to be political and intellectual leaders. (The humanists were much more ambivalent about the importance of extended education for girls.) This new idea of childhood carried over into Renaissance art, for small children were again depicted with realistic proportions—as they had been in classical antiquity—instead of simply as miniature adults.

The rediscovery of the classical world in Renaissance Europe included not simply art but also philosophy and literature, with the opinions of Greek thinkers serving as the basis for many philosophical movements. Among those who were particularly concerned with children and education was a group of neo-Platonists at Cambridge University in the 1680s. These philosophers, building on Plato's notion that children are born with certain concepts already in their minds, asserted that children have not only innate knowledge, but also innate goodness. This innate goodness forms the basis for a person's conscience and sympathy to others, an idea that stands in sharp contrast to that of Original Sin. The Quakers, one of the new religious sects that emerged in England in the seventeenth century, held similar views on the goodness of children.

The English philosopher John Locke (1632–1704) directly refuted this idea in *An Essay Concerning Human Understanding,* published in

1690, in which he attempted to demonstrate that all human ideas come from experience. To Locke, the mind at birth was a blank slate, a *tabula rasa*, that was then shaped by the experience of the five senses and by reflection on those experiences. Locke applied his proposition to the rearing and training of children in *Some Thoughts Concerning Education* (1693), which was translated into six other languages and became the most popular book on education in the early modern period.

In addition to Locke's treatise on education, the writings of the French-Swiss philosopher Jean-Jacques Rousseau (1712–1778) were extremely influential in shaping early modern attitudes toward childhood. Rousseau's ideas are stated most clearly in *Emile* (1762), the story of a boy and his tutor, which opens with this sentence: "The Author of Nature makes all things good; man meddles with them and they become evil." As this sentence demonstrates, Rousseau saw nature as the source of all good and human institutions as the source of all evil; consequently, his program of education was one in which Emile's tutor attempted to let him develop naturally, learning about the world as he became interested in it. The boy's formal education did not begin until he was twelve, and then it was driven solely by his curiosity. Rousseau believed that qualities such as morality and charity would develop easily if children were taught by example rather than precept, and he portrays Emile as ready to begin a life of public leadership at twenty-five. At the end of *Emile* is a section called "So-phie, or Woman," in which Rousseau sets out his ideas for girls' education. Sophie's education is aimed at making her the perfect companion for Emile, so she is to be trained primarily to learn what other people will want her to do. Reading is not a necessary skill, nor is anything else that might encourage or enable her to think for herself. Though Rousseau made no attempt to put the ideas of *Emile* into practice, educational reformers in many parts of Europe did, and his notion of the superiority of the natural over the civilized or artificial became an important theme in much literature for and about children.

While many authors point to changes in religious and philosophical ideas, others point to material factors as significant shapers of attitudes toward and treatment of children. The production of toys and books specifically for children is generally seen as key evidence of the recognition that childhood was distinctive. Such playthings and pastimes were not possible until the development of the printing press in the mid-fifteenth century, which made books affordable for those who were not wealthy, and the growth at about the same time of specialized handicrafts and a market for consumer goods. The first professional toy makers established themselves in Italian and German cities in the fifteenth century, and toys were exported from there all over Europe and to the American colonies. The first specialized toy shops opened in London in about 1750, and the first jigsaw puzzle—of a map—was made in 1762 by a tutor who used it to teach geography.

Chapter 5
The "Discovery
of Childhood"
in England
and America
(1600–1800)

Children's literature developed slightly later, beginning with Charles Perrault's publication of *Tales of Past Time* in France in 1697. This collection of fairy tales, with a title page showing an older woman identified as "Mother Goose," became popular first with adults at the French court, and was soon translated into English. Puritans and others debated whether the stories it contained were suitable for children, but it sparked many imitations, including many by religious writers attempting to produce something that *was* suitable in their eyes, such as Isaac Watts's *Divine and Moral Songs for Children* (1715). This volume was extremely popular, with more editions published in America before 1800 than the Bible. Less serious children's literature also flourished, with the first book of English nursery rhymes published in 1744, and adventure books written for adults such as *Robinson Crusoe* adapted for children. One of the earliest publishers of children's books in England was a follower of Locke who noted in the 1740s that he was following Locke's advice in producing materials specifically for the young. At the same time, special copy books with alternating blank pages began to appear, with sayings and poems for children to copy as they learned to write.

The effects on children of the development of commercial capitalism was not all fun and fairy tales, however, but also, according to some analysts, a strong sense that children needed to be trained from an early age to be satisfied with their position in life. For poor children, this meant ingraining habits of labor and guarding against idleness. Beginning in the sixteenth century in England, poor children over the age of six were supposed to be set to work (Locke advised three as the youngest age to begin this), either in workhouses or as craft apprentices. Throughout the eighteenth century workhouses and their affiliated charity schools were established in England, though only rarely were these financially viable, as the children usually could not earn enough to pay for their keep.

Charity schools and apprenticeship could never handle all of the poor children of England, and beginning in the seventeenth century, children who were orphaned or whose parents could not support them could be sent to the North American colonies as indentured servants. They were bound by their indenture to serve a number of years or until they reached a certain age, usually twenty-one. Colonial children were also bound out as indentured servants by their parents or guardians or, if they were poor, taken from their parents and indentured by the government, with the agreement sealed by a contract. These contracts often stipulated that the master was to provide education and training along with room and board, and colonial governments interfered when they felt parents or masters were not instilling the proper moral values in the children under their control.

No such provisions were made, of course, for the African children who entered the North American colonies as slaves. Though in the seventeenth century there was some disagreement among slave traders about whether it was profitable to transport young children, by the eighteenth century children and young people were favored. Slave families in North America were frequently split up, though sometimes courts attempted to keep very young children with their mothers. By the eighteenth century in some colonies, such as New Jersey, owners were ordered to teach their slaves to read, whereas in others, such as South Carolina, teaching slaves to read and write was forbidden.

THE METHOD

To answer the central questions in this chapter, you will be using six types of sources: diaries, letters, published essays, official records, portraits, and literature written for children. Because one of the questions asks you to assess change over time, the evidence is presented roughly in chronological order. Each type of source must be approached in a slightly different way, for they differ in their intended audience and purpose, and in how directly they discuss children and childhood. For all the evidence, however, the most important method is careful reading and observation.

Sources 1, 7, 11, and 22 are diary entries: 1, 7, and 22 come from the diaries of parents; Source 11 from a daughter. Though we usually think of diaries as private documents recording our thoughts and emotions, early modern people regarded diaries primarily as a place to record their spiritual development, and often expected to share their insights with others. More prominent individuals knew that their diaries might later be published, so shaped their entries accordingly. We cannot read them, thus, as necessarily revealing the writer's "true" emotions, but they are excellent sources about what feelings and opinions were acceptable to share with others. The diarists represent a range of status. Source 1 is from the diary of Lady Anne Clifford (1590–1676), an English noblewoman who was married at nineteen and had the first of her five children, a daughter (whom she refers to in the diary as "the Child") several years later; a portrait of this daughter accompanies the diary. One of the most extensive colonial diaries was that of Cotton Mather (1663–1728) (Source 7), an extremely influential Puritan clergyman and writer, who was married several times and had a large number of children. Source 11 draws from the diary of a young girl, Anna Winslow (1760–1779), who was sent by her parents in Nova Scotia to Boston to be "finished" at Boston schools; she began her diary when she was about twelve in order to practice writing and to describe her life in Boston for her parents. Her portrait also accompanies the diary. The final diary evidence (Source 22) was written by Susan Huntington (1791–1823), the daughter of a Connecticut minister and the mother of several children, whose diaries and

Chapter 5

The "Discovery
of Childhood"
in England
and America
(1600–1800)

letters were published after her death by a pastor who had been her friend.

Letters from any period of history, including those reprinted here, range from the official to the personal; thus they vary widely in style, even while generally following certain conventions. (This continues today, of course, for we address people in letters as "dear" whom we would never otherwise address that way, and close letters with "truly" or "sincerely" when we may not feel that way at all.) Effective letters both follow conventions so as not to offend the addressee and clearly communicate the purpose or request of the writer. Sources 2 and 3 are letters from the mid-seventeenth century referring to the transportation of children from London to the colonies as indentured servants; Source 2 was sent by an official of the Virginia Company and Source 3 by a private citizen.

Sources 15 and 16 are letters from former slaves. A group who had gained their freedom by joining the British forces in the American War of Independence and had been transported first to Nova Scotia and then to Sierra Leone in 1792 under the auspices of an English company establishing a settlement there write to complain of broken promises in Source 15. A former slave still in the United States asks that her children be released in Source 16.

Sometimes letters closely resemble official documents and reports in that their prime purpose is to convey information rather than beg a favor. Such letters and official reports, such as Sources 4 and 5 on indentured servants, 12 on children in early factories, and 13 and 14 on the slave trade, are often our best source for what was actually happening to children. They are also likely to reveal people's true attitudes, for their authors were less self-conscious than those writing diaries or supplicatory letters, and less bound to shape their words to please readers.

In these diaries and letters, you will be interpreting references to children and childhood in documents designed primarily for other purposes. However, a large number of essays were published in Europe and America during the seventeenth and eighteenth century in which children were discussed directly. (Indeed, the sheer number and popularity of these is one of the key pieces of evidence for those arguing in favor of a "discovery of childhood.") Sources 6 and 21 are extracts from two of the best-known of these: Source 6 from Locke's *Some Thoughts Concerning Education* (1693) and Source 21 from Mary Wollstonecraft's *Thoughts on the Education of Daughters* (1787). Wollstonecraft (1759–1797) was an English writer and feminist, and incidentally the mother of *Frankenstein*'s creator, Mary Shelley. In both essays, the authors state their ideas clearly, so your investigation is more straightforward than with diaries and letters.

The last type of sources we will be using for this chapter are books written for children. Sources 8 through 10 come from the first quarter of the eighteenth century, the time of the earliest published children's literature, and Sources 17 and 18 from the end of the eighteenth century, after the publication of Rousseau's *Emile*. Unlike other types of literature, children's literature must appeal to two markets—children themselves and the adults who will buy the books and perhaps read them to children. All of the examples reprinted here went through many printings, sometimes into the twentieth century, so they obviously appealed to the adults who bought books. We can thus trust them as good indicators of what adults *thought* children should be reading, as well as adult attitudes toward children, because they were, of course, written by adults. As you read them, then, you need to think about why adults might have given children these particular stories.

Learning what children actually enjoyed reading is more difficult to discover than learning what books adults bought, and can best be seen in references to childhood reading in other sources. The final two pieces of evidence are references to reading from the late eighteenth century. In Source 19 the rural nature poet John Clare (1793–1864), whose formal education was minimal, tells of his early delight in reading, and in Source 20, Irish novelist Maria Edgeworth (1767–1849), who herself wrote many stories for children, judges the value of reading adventures.

Because we are using so many different types of sources in this chapter, each of which has its own peculiarities of interpretation, it might be best to make a brief summary of the attitudes you see expressed in each selection immediately after reading it, and a note as to exactly what phrases or words conveyed these attitudes. For example, with the diarists who are parents, how do they talk about their own children? about childhood in general? How do they see their duties as parents? Or for the children's literature, consider how the children are portrayed. Are they innocent? foolish? wicked? Which children are portrayed positively and which negatively? What characteristics in either children or adults are described positively or negatively? Is there an attempt to shield children from the world? What does it appear that the authors hope children will learn from hearing or reading this? These summaries will not only help you trace change (or the lack of it) over time but will also keep your conclusions tied to your sources. Sticking to the evidence in one's sources is an important quality in all historical scholarship, of course, and one that each side in the "discovery of childhood" debate accuses the other of neglecting.

Chapter 5
The "Discovery
of Childhood"
in England
and America
(1600–1800)

THE EVIDENCE

Source 1 from The Diary of the Lady Anne Clifford, *ed. Vita Sackville-West (London: William Heinemann, 1924), pp. 51–52, 54, 55, 62, 66, 67. Portrait by permission of Lord Sackville, Knole Estates. Photographer: Lime Tree Photographic Studios.*

1. From the Diary of Lady Anne Clifford, 1617

*Lady Margaret Sackville, daughter of Richard Sackville,
3rd Earl of Dorset and Lady Anne Clifford*
"The Child"

[January]

Upon the 22nd the Child had her 6th fit of the ague[1] in the morning. Mr *Smith*[2] went up in the coach to *London* to my Lord[3] to whom I wrote a letter to let him know in what case the Child was. . . .

The same day my Lord came down to *Knole*[4] to see the Child.

Upon the 23rd my Lord went up betimes to London again. The same day the Child put on her red baize coats.

Upon the 25th I spent most of my time in working and in going up and down to see the Child. About 5 or 6 o'clock the fit took her, which lasted 6 or 7 hours. . . .

[February]

Upon the 12th the Child had a bitter fit of her ague again, insomuch I was fearful of her that I could hardly sleep all night, so I beseeched GOD Almighty to be merciful to me and spare her life. . . .

After supper the Child's nose bled which I think was the chief cause she was rid of her ague. . . .

Upon the 21st the Child had an extreme fit of the ague and the Doctor set by her all the afternoon and gave her a salt powder to put in her beer. . . .

[April]

Upon the 6th after supper because my Lord was sullen and not willing to go into the nursery I made *Mary* bring the Child to him into my chamber, which was the 1st time she stirred abroad since she was sick.

[May]

Upon the 1st I cut the Child's strings[5] off from her coats and made her use togs[6] alone, so as she had two or three falls at first but had no hurt with them.

The 2nd the Child put on her first coat that was laced with lace, being of red baize. . . .

The 8th I spent this day in working, the time being very tedious unto me as having neither comfort nor company, only the Child. . . .

After supper I went with the Child who rode the piebald nag that came out of *Westmoreland* to M^rs————. The 14th the Child came to lie with me, which was the first time that ever she lay all night in a bed with me since she was born.

1. **ague:** a malaria-like fever.
2. **Mr. Smith:** one of Lady Anne's servants.
3. **my Lord:** Lady Anne's husband, Richard Sackville.
4. **Knole:** the estate where Lady Anne lived.
5. **strings:** long laces attached to a very young child learning to walk, held by an adult to keep the child from falling.
6. **togs:** heavy outer garments.

Chapter 5
The "Discovery
of Childhood"
in England
and America
(1600–1800)

Source 2 from Susan M. Kingsbury, ed., The Records of the Virginia Company of London: The Court Book, from the Manuscript in the Library of Congress, *III (Washington, 1933), p. 259.*

2. Letter from Sir Edwin Sandys of the Virginia Company Requesting Authority to Coerce Children to Go to Virginia, 1620

Right Honorable [Sir Robert Naughton of the King's Privy Council]:

Being unable to give my personal attendance upon the Lords [the Privy Council], I have presumed to address my suit in these few lines unto your Honor. The City of London have by act of their Common Council, appointed one hundred children out of their superfluous multitude to be transported to Virginia; there to be bound apprentices for certain years, and afterward with very beneficial conditions for the children. And have granted moreover a levy of five hundred pounds among themselves for the appareling of those children, and toward their charges of transportation. Now it falleth out that among those children, sundry being ill disposed, and fitter for any remote place than for this City, declare their unwillingness to go to Virginia, of whom the City is especially desirious to be disburdened, and in Virginia under severe masters they may be brought to goodness. But this City wanting authority to deliver, and the Virginia Company to transport, these persons against their wills, the burden is laid upon me, by humble suit unto the Lords to procure higher authority for the warranting thereof. May it please your Honor therefore, to vouchsafe unto us of the Company here, and to the whole plantation in Virginia, that noble favor, as to be a means unto their Lordships out of their accustomed goodness, and by their higher authority, to discharge both the City and our Company of this difficulty, as their Lordships and your Honors in your wisdom shall find most expedient. For whose health and prosperity our Company will always pray. . . .

Source 3 from London, Public Record Office, CO 1/22. no. 56, quoted in Robert H. Bremner, Children and Youth in America: A Documentary History, *Volume 1: 1600–1865 (Cambridge: Harvard University Press, 1970), p. 12.*

3. Letter from George C. to Sir Anthony Ashley Cooper of the House of Commons, 1668

I have inquired after the child that was lost, and have spoken with the parents. His name was John Brookes. The last night he was after much trouble and charge freed again, and he relates that there are divers other children in the ship crying, that were enticed away from their parents, that are kept and detained in the ship. The name of the ship is the Seven Brothers and as I hear bound for Virginia; and she is now fallen down to Gravesend, and, if a speedy course be not taken to stop her she will be gone. I heard of two other ships in the river that are at the same work, although the parents of the children see their children in the ship, yet without money they will not let them have them. The woman and child will wait on you, where you approach and when to give you this relation and 'tis believed there are divers people and others carried away that are strangers come from other parts, so that it were good to get the ships searched, and to see who are against their wills carried away. Pray you move it in the House to have a law to make it death.[7] I am confident your mercy to these innocent children will ground a blessing on yourself your own. Pray let not your great affairs put this good work out of your head to stop the ships and discharge the children.

> Your most humble servant
> George [last name torn away]

Source 4 from Laws and Liberties of Massachusetts, *p. 38, quoted in Robert H. Bremner,* Children and Youth in America: A Documentary History, *volume 1: 1600–1865 (Cambridge: Harvard University Press, 1970), p. 115.*

4. Massachusetts Law Regarding Runaway Servants, 1648

It is also ordered that when any servants shall run from their masters or any other inhabitants shall privily go away with suspicion of ill intentions, it shall be lawful for the next magistrate, or the constable and two of the chief inhabitants where no magistrate is, to press men and boats or pinnaces at the public charge to pursue such persons by sea or land and bring them back by force of arms.

Source 5 from "Boston Records, 1600–1701," in Seventh Report of the Boston Record Commissioners *(Boston, 1881), p. 67.*

5. Boston Case Regarding Poor Children, 1672

It was ordered that notice be given to the several persons under-written that they, within one month after the date hereof, dispose of their several Children

---

7. Although such a bill was introduced and debated in Parliament in 1670/71, it was not passed.

Chapter 5
The "Discovery
of Childhood"
in England
and America
(1600–1800)

(herein nominated or mentioned) abroad for servants, to serve by Indentures for some term of years, according to their ages and capacities, which if they refuse or neglect to do the Magistrates and Selectmen [city officials] will take their said children from them, and place them with such masters as they shall provide according as the law directs. And that they that do according to this order dispose of their children do make return of the names of Masters and children so put out to service, with their Indentures to the Selectmen at their next monthly Meeting being the last Monday in April next.

John Glovers daughter about twelve years of age.

Bryan Morphews daughter-in-law Martha Dorman about twelve years.

John Bohamans daughter Mary about fourteen years.

Robert Peggs daughter Alice above twelve years.

John Griffens daughter about ten years.

William Spowells daughter about twenty years.

William Brownes daughter about fifteen years unless she can excuse the service of a Nurse attending upon her weak Mother.

Widow Crocums three daughters.

William Hambeltons daughter about twelve years.

Edward Golds son about twenty years.

John Dawes his son about seventeen years.

Thomas Williams his son Charles about eight years.

Source 6 from James Axtell, ed., The Educational Writings of John Locke *(Cambridge: Cambridge University Press, 1968), pp. 156–157, 172–173, 181, 182, 183, 187–188.*

6. From John Locke,
Some Thoughts Concerning
Education, **1693**

But if a right Course be taken with Children, there will not be so much need of the Application of the common Rewards and Punishments as we imagine, and as the general Practice has established. For all their innocent Folly, Playing, and *Childish Actions, are to be left perfectly free and unrestrained,* as far as they can consist with the Respect due to those that are present; and that with the greatest Allowance. If these Faults of their Age, rather than of the Children themselves, were, as they should be, left only to Time and Imitation, and riper Years to cure, Children would escape a great deal of mis-applied and useless Correction; which either fails to over-power the Natural Disposition of their Childhood, and so, by an ineffectual Familiarity, makes Correction in other necessary Cases of less use; or else, if it be of Force to restrain the natural Gaiety of that Age, it serves only to spoil the Temper both of Body and Mind. If the Noise and Bustle of their Play prove at any Time inconvenient, or un-suitable to the Place or Company they are in, (which can only be where their Parents are) a Look or a Word from the Father or Mother, if they have established the Authority they should, will be enough either to remove, or quiet them for that Time. But this Gamesome Humour, which is wisely adapted by Nature to their Age and Temper, should rather be encouraged, to keep up their Spirits, and improve their Strength and Health than curbed or restrained: And the chief Art is to make all that they have to do, Sport and Play too.

And here give me Leave to take Notice of one thing I think a Fault in the or-dinary Method of Education; and that is, The Charging of Children's Memo-ries, upon all Occasions, with *Rules* and Precepts, which they often do not un-derstand, and constantly as soon forget as given. . . .

None of the Things they are to learn should ever be made a Burthen to them, or imposed on them as a *Task*. Whatever is so proposed presently be-comes irksome: The Mind takes an Aversion to it, though before it were a Thing of Delight or Indifferency. Let a Child be but ordered to whip his Top at a certain Time every Day, whether he has, or has not a Mind to it; let this be but required of him as a Duty, wherein he must spend so many Hours Morn-ing and Afternoon, and see whether he will not soon be weary of any Play at this Rate. Is it not so with grown Men? What they do chearfully of themselves, do they not presently grow sick of, and can no more endure, as soon as they find it is expected of them, as a Duty? Children have as much a Mind to shew that they are free, that their own good Actions come from themselves, that they are absolute and independent, as any of the proudest of you grown Men, think of them as you please. . . .

It will perhaps be wondered that I mention *Reasoning* with Children: And yet I cannot but think that the true Way of Dealing with them. They understand it as early as they do Language; and, if I mis-observe not, they love to be treated as Rational Creatures sooner than is imagined. 'Tis a Pride should be cherished in them, and as much as can be, made the greatest instrument to turn them by. . . .

But of all the Ways whereby Children are to be instructed, and their Man-ners formed, the plainest, easiest, and most efficacious, is, to set before their Eyes the *Examples* of those Things you would have them do, or avoid. Which, when they are pointed out to them, in the Practice of Persons within their Knowledge, with some Reflections on their Beauty or Unbecomingness, are of more force to draw or deterr their Imitation, than any Discourses which can be made to them. . . .

But, as I said before, *Beating* is the worst, and therefore the last Means to be used in the Correction of Children; and that only in Cases of Extremity, after all gentler Ways have been tried, and proved unsuccessful: Which, if well ob-served, there will be very seldom any need of Blows. . . .

Chapter 5

The "Discovery

of Childhood"

in England

and America

(1600–1800)

Children should from their first beginning to talk, have some *Discreet, Sober,* nay, *Wise* Person about, whose Care it should be to Fashion them aright, and keep them from all ill, especially the infection of bad Company. I think this Province requires great *Sobriety, Temperance, Tenderness, Diligence,* and *Discretion;* Qualities hardly to be found united in Persons, that are to be had for ordinary Salaries; nor easily to be found any where. As to the Charge of it, I think it will be the Money best laid out, that can be, about our Children; and therefore though it may be Expensive more than is ordinary, yet it cannot be thought dear. He that at any Rate procures his Child a good Mind, well Principled, temper'd to Vertue and Usefulness, and adorned with Civility and good Breeding, makes a better purchase for him, than if he laid out the Money for an Addition of more Earth to his former Acres. Spare it in Toys and Play-Games, in Silk and Ribbons, Laces and other useless Expences, as much as you please; but be not sparing in so necessary a Part as this. 'Tis not good Husbandry to make his Fortune rich, and his Mind poor. I have often with great Admiration seen People lavish it profusely in tricking up their Children in fine Clothes, Lodging and Feeding them Sumptuously, allowing them more than enough of useless Servants, and yet at the same time starve their Minds, and not take sufficient Care to cover that, which is the most Shameful Nakedness, *viz.* their natural wrong Inclinations and Ignorance. This I can look on as no other than a Sacrificing to their own Vanity; it shewing more their Pride, than true Care of the good of their Children.

Source 7 from Diary of Cotton Mather, *vol. 1: 1681–1709. (New York: Frederick Ungar, n.d.), pp. 348, 366, 367, 369, 445, 447, 454–455.*

7. From the Diary of Cotton Mather, 1700–1703

[May 20, 1700]

The terrible *Convulsions,* which threaten the Life of my little, and lovely *Son,* do now grow to that Extremity, as to render his Cure little short of desperate: all Means, and Hopes do fail. But when I am carrying and resigning the Child unto the Lord, I have it strangely assured me from Heaven, *that the Child shall recover.* The good Angel of the Lord has told me so!

[October 5]

My charming little Daughter *Nanny,* was yesterday taken with a violent, and a threatening Feavour, which began with a terrible Convulsion, whereof the Spectators feared that she never would recover.

Seeing the *Angel of Death,* to stand thus, with a drawn Sword, over my Family, I sett apart this Day, for Prayer, with Fasting, on that Occasion. When I was resigning the Child unto the Lord, and professing that if shee might not live to be a Servant of the Lord Jesus Christ, I did not ask for her Life, I received an astonishing Assurance from Heaven, *that the Child should recover.*

[October 8]

The Lord this Week mercifully grants a Recovery to my sick Daughter; yea, and a more speedy One, than the Child has had, from her two such Feavours, in the two former Years. Thus has this Child, been strangely several Times given me from the Dead!

My Son also is recovered of his Fitts, diverse Months ago, and more than so, is become an healthy and an hearty Child.

[October 28]

About this Time, our Booksellers reprinting the Excellent *Janewayes Token for Children,*[8] I was willing to charm the Children of *New England* unto the Fear of God, with the Exemples of some *Children* that were exemplary for it, in this Countrey, and being furnished with six or seven remarkable Narratives, I putt them into shape, and gave the little Book unto the Booksellers. 'Tis Entituled, *A Token for the Children of New England.*[9]

This Evening, my Family received an extraordinary Deliverance. My lovely Daughter *Nibby,* was alone, and while she was thus alone, the Candle some how sett her Head-gear on a light Fire. The Child was neither able to help herself, nor to cry out for Help; the Flame consumed all before it and was just come as far as her Head. In one Quarter of a Minute more, the Child had been destroy'd; but a Person accidentally then passing by the Window, just in the Nick of Time, saw thro' the Window an unusual Blaze; and running in most happily, not only was the Child's Life saved, but also she gott no manner of Hurt.

What shall I render to the Lord, for such a wonderful Salvation? Truly, I will study and contrive some special Return of Gratitude, unto the Saviour of my Child.

[October 30, 1702]

On this Day, my little Daughter *Nibby,* began to fall sick of the Small-pox. The dreadful Disease, which is raging in the Neighbourhood, is now gott into my poor Family. God prepare me, God prepare me, for what is coming upon me!

The Child, was favourably visited, in comparison of what many are.

[November 24]

My Daughter *Nanny* was taken Sick. She proved full and blind, and very sore of the Distemper.[10]

---

8. Mather refers to an English book written for children by the clergyman James Janeway and published in 1671, relating stories of children who showed great religious faith.

9. Printed in Boston in 1700.

10. **distemper:** here, smallpox.

Chapter 5

The "Discovery

of Childhood"

in England

and America

(1600–1800)

My Son *Increase,* was taken sick. He also proved pretty full and blind, and sore; tho' not so bad as his Sister.

The little Creatures keep calling for me so often to pray with them, that I can scarce do it less than ten or a dozen times in a day; besides what I do with my Neighbours.

[January 3, 1703]

My pretty little *Nanny* fell into a violent and malignant *Fever.* It proceeded unto such a Degree, as to throw the Child into horrible Convulsions. Her Agonies were so very great, that I could even have been glad, that she might have been by Death Released out of them. I sett apart, Wednesday for Prayer with Fasting before the Lord, on purpose to humble myself, and resign my Child, and obtain an easy and speedy Death, and everlasting Life, rather than a Continuance of Life in this world, for her; for she lay speechless, and I had no more Hope of her being restored unto me, than of the Five, that now ly in the Tomb with their lovely Mother.[11]. . .

Tho' the Child lay speechless all Day, in the Evening she recovered so much Speech, as to surprise all about her, with saying; *I heard my Father give me away to Day; but I shall not dy this Time, for all that!* So she fell speechless again; and lay two Dayes more in the perfect Jawes of Death. But after all, unto the Astonishment of us all, the Child recovered.

Source 8 from A Little Book for Little Children, *by T. W. (London, ca. 1703).*

8. "A was an Archer," from *A Little Book for Little Children,* 1703

THE ALPHABET

A was an Archer, and shot at a Frog;
B was a Blind-man, and led by a Dog:
C was a Cutpurse, and liv'd in disgrace;
D was a Drunkard, and had a red Face:
E was an Eater, a Glutton was he;
F was a fighter, and fought with a Flea:
G was a Gyant, and pul'd down a House;
H was a Hunter, and hunted a Mouse.
I was an ill Man, and hated by all;
K was a Knave, and he rob'd great and small.

11. **their lovely Mother:** Mather's first wife, who had died a month earlier. Mather's second wife died in a measles epidemic ten years later, along with three of his children; only two of his fifteen children survived him.

L was a Liar, and told many Lies;
M was a Madman, and beat out his Eyes.
N was a Nobleman, nobly born;
O was an Ostler, and stole Horses Corn.
P was a Pedlar, and sold many Pins;
Q was a Quarreller, and broke both his Shins.
R was a Rogue, and run about Town;
S was a Sailor, a Man of Renown.
T was a Taylor, and Knavishly bent;
U was a Userer took Ten *per Cent.*
W was a Writer, and Money he earn'd;
X was one *Xenophon*, prudent and learn'd.
Y was a Yeoman, and work'd for his Bread;
Z was one *Zeno* the Great, but he's dead.

Source 9 from Isaac Watts, Divine Songs Attempted in Easy Language for the Use of Children *(Derby: Henry Mozley and Sons, 1715), pp. 38–39, 43–44.*

9. From Isaac Watts, *Divine Songs . . . for the Use of Children*, 1715

SONG XX.
AGAINST IDLENESS AND MISCHIEF.

How doth the little busy bee
  Improve each shining hour,
And gather honey all the day
  From every opening flower.

How skilfully she builds her cell!
  How neat she spreads the wax!

Chapter 5
The "Discovery
of Childhood"
in England
and America
(1600–1800)

And labours hard to store it well
　　With the sweet food she makes.

In works of labour or of skill,
　　I would be busy too;
For Satan finds some mischief still
　　For idle hands to do.

In books, or works, or healthful play,
　　Let my first years be past;
That I may give for every day
　　Some good account at last.

SONG XXIII.
OBEDIENCE TO PARENTS.

Let children that would fear the Lord
　　Hear what their teachers say;
With reverence meet their parents' word,
　　And with delight obey.

Have you not heard what dreadful plagues
　　Are threaten'd by the Lord,
To him that breaks his father's law,
　　Or mocks his mother's word?

What heavy guilt upon him lies!
　　How cursed is his name!
The ravens shall pick out his eyes,
　　And eagles eat the same.

But those who worship God, and give
   Their parents honour due,
Here on this earth they long shall live,
   And live hereafter too.

Source 10 from Charles Perrault, Histories or Tales of Past Times: Classics of Children's
Literature *(Garland: New York and London, 1977; reprint of 1729 ed. printed for J. Pote and
R. Montagu, London), pp. 1–8. Illustration reproduced with permission of Garland Press.*

10. Charles Perrault, "The Little Red Riding-Hood," 1729

TALE I.

There was once upon a time a little country girl, born in a village, the prettiest
little creature that ever was seen. Her mother was beyond reason excessively
fond of her, and her grandmother yet much more. This good woman caused
to be made for her a little red Riding-Hood; which made her look so very
pretty, that every body call'd her, *The little red Riding-Hood.*

One day, her mother having made some custards, said to her, Go my little
Biddy, for her christian name was *Biddy,* go and see how your grandmother
does, for I hear she has been very ill, carry her a custard, and this little pot of
butter. *The little red Riding-Hood* sets out immediately to go to her grandmother, who lived in another village. As she was going through the wood, she
met with *Gossop Wolfe,* who had a good mind to eat her up, but he did not
dare, because of some faggot-makers[12] that were in the forest.

He asked of her whither she was going: The poor child, who did not know
how dangerous a thing it is to stay and hear a Wolfe talk, said to him, I am
going to see my grandmamma, and carry her a custard pye, and a little pot of
butter my mamma sends her. Does she live far off? said the Wolfe. Oh! ay, said

12. **faggot-makers:** wood-cutters.

Chapter 5

The "Discovery

of Childhood"

in England

and America

(1600–1800)

the little red Riding-Hood, on the other side of the mill below yonder, at the first house in the village. Well, said the Wolfe, and I'll go and see her too; I'll go this way, and go you that, and we shall see who will be there soonest.

The Wolfe began to run as fast as he was able, the shortest way; and the little girl went the longest, diverting her self in gathering nuts, running after butterflies, and making nose-gays of all the little flowers she met with. The Wolfe was not long before he came to the grandmother's house; he knocked at the door *toc toc.* Who's there? Your grand-daughter, *The little red Riding-Hood,* said the Wolfe, counterfeiting her voice, who has brought you a custard pye, and a little pot of butter mamma sends you.

The good grandmother, who was in bed, because she found herself some-what ill, cried out, Pull the bobbin, and the latch will go up. The Wolfe pull'd the bobbin, and the door open'd; upon which he fell upon the good woman, and eat her up in the tenth part of a moment; for he had eaten nothing for above three days before. After that, he shut the door, and went into the grand-mother's bed, expecting *the little red Riding-Hood,* who came some time after-wards, and knock'd at the door *toc toc, Who's there?* The *little red Riding-Hood,* who hearing the big voice of the Wolfe, was at first afraid; but believing her grandmother had got a cold, and was grown hoarse, said, it is your grand-daughter, *The little red Riding-Hood,* who has brought you a custard pye, and a little pot of butter mamma sends you. The Wolfe cried out to her, softening his voice as much as he could, Pull the bobbin, and the latch will go up. The *little red Riding-Hood* pull'd the bobbin, and the door opened.

The Wolfe seeing her come in, said to her, hiding himself under the clothes. Put the custard, and the little pot of butter upon the stool, and come into bed to me. *The little red Riding-Hood* undressed herself, and went into bed, where she was very much astonished to see how her grandmother looked in her night-cloaths: So she said to her, *Grandmamma, what great arms you have got!* It is better to embrace thee my pretty child. *Grandmamma, what great legs you have got!* it is to run the better my child. *Grandmamma, what great ears you have got!* It is to hear the better my child. *Grandmamma, what great eyes you have got!* It is to see the better my child. *Grandmamma, what great teeth you have got!* It is to eat thee up. And upon saying these words, this wicked Wolfe fell upon *the little Red Riding-Hood,* and eat her up.

THE MORAL.

From this short story easy we discern
What conduct all young people ought to learn.
But above all, the growing ladies fair,
Whose orient rosy Blooms begin t'appear:
Who, Beauties in the fragrant spring of age!
With pretty airs young hearts are apt t'engage.

Ill do they listen to all sorts of tongues,
Since some enchant and lure like Syrens songs.[13]
No wonder therefore 'tis if overpowr'd,
So many of them has the Wolfe devour'd.
The Wolfe, I say, for Wolves too sure there are
Of every sort, and every character.
Some of them mild and gentle-humour'd be
Of noise and gall, and rancour wholly free;
Who tame, familiar, full of complaisance;
Ogle and leer, languish, cajole and glance;
With luring tongues, and language wondrous sweet,
Follow young ladies as they walk the street,
Ev'n to their very houses and bed-side,
And though their true designs they artful hide,
Yet ah! these simp'ring Wolves, who does not see
Most dang'rous of all Wolves in fact to be?

13. **Syrens songs:** the Sirens were, in Greek mythology, women who lured sailors to their deaths by singing entrancing songs.

Chapter 5

The "Discovery

of Childhood"

in England

and America

(1600–1800)

Source 11 from Alice Morse Earle, ed., Diary of Anna Green Winslow: A Boston School Girl of 1771 *(Boston: Houghton Mifflin, 1896), pp. 5–6, 18, 47, 56–57. Portrait reproduced with permission of the publisher and by courtesy of the Arthur and Elizabeth Schlesinger Library on the History of Women in America.*

11. From the Diary of Anna Green Winslow, 1771–1772

Anna Green Winslow

November the 29th.—My aunt Deming gives her love to you[14] and says it is this morning 12 years since she had the pleasure of congratulating papa and you on the birth of your scribling daughter. She hopes if I live 12 years longer that I shall write and do everything better than can be expected in the *past* 12.

BOSTON January 25 1772.

Hon'd Mamma, My Hon'd Papa has never signified to me his approbation[15] of my journals, from whence I infer, that he either never reads them, or does

14. Winslow is addressing her mother here.
15. **approbation:** approval.

not give himself the trouble to remember any of their contents, tho' some part has been address'd to him, so, for the future, I shall trouble only you with this part of my scribble—

[March 10]

I believe unless something remarkable should happen, such as a *warm day,* my mamma will consent that I dedicate a few of my next essays to papa. I think the second thing I said to aunt this morning was, that I intended to be *very good all day.* To make this out,

"Next unto *God,* dear Parents I address
 Myself to you in humble Thankfulness,
"For all your Care & Charge on me bestow'd;
"The means of Learning unto me allow'd,
"Go on I pray, & let me still pursue
"Those Golden Arts the Vulgar never knew."
     Yr Dutifull Daughter
         Anna Green Winslow.

The poetry I transcrib'd from my Copy Book.

Yesterday afternoon I visited Miss Polly Deming & took her with me to Mr Rogers' in the evening where Mr Hunt discours'd upon the 7th question of the catechism viz what are the decrees of God? I remember a good many of his observations, which I have got set down on a loose paper. But my aunt says that a Miss of 12 year's old cant possibly do justice to the nicest subject in Divinity, & therefore had better not attempt a repetition of perticulars, that she finds lie (as may be easily concluded) somewhat confused in my young mind. She also says, that in her poor judgment, Mr Hunt discours'd soundly as well as ingeniously upon the subject, & very much to her instruction & satisfaction. My Papa inform'd me in his last letter that he had done me the honor to read my journals & that he approv'd of some part of them, I suppose he means that he likes some parts better than other, indeed it would be wonderful, as aunt says, if a gentleman of papa's understanding & judgment cou'd be highly entertain'd with *every little* saying or observation that came from a girl of my years & that I ought to esteem it a great favour that he notices any of my simple matter with his *approbation.*

Chapter 5

The "Discovery

of Childhood"

in England

and America

(1600–1800)

Source 12 from John Fitzpatrick, ed., The Diaries of George Washington, 1748–1799, *(Boston, 1925), vol. 4, pp. 37–38.*

12. George Washington Reports on a Boston Cloth Factory, 1789

Went after an early breakfast, to visit the duck[16] manufacture, which appeared to be carrying on with spirit, and is in a prosperous way. They have manufactured 32 pieces of duck of 30 or 40 yds. each in a week; and expect in a short time to increase it to [   ]. They have 28 looms at work, and 14 girls spinning with both hands (the flax being fastened to their [waist]). Children (girls) turn the wheels for them, and with this assistance each spinner can turn out 14 lbs. of thread per day when they stick to it, but as they are paid by the piece, or work they do, there is no other restraint upon them but to come at 8 o'clock in the morning, and return at 6 in the evening. They are the daughters of decayed families,[17] and are girls of character—none others are admitted. The number of hands now employed in the different parts of the work is [   ] but the managers expect to increase them to [   ]. This is a work of public utility and private advantage.

Sources 13 and 14 from Elizabeth Donnan, ed., Documents Illustrative of the History of the Slave Trade to America *(Washington: Carnegie Institution of Washington, 1930–1935), vol. 2, pp. 138–139; pp. 571–572.*

13. Letter from William Ellery, a Rhode Island Merchant, 1746

[To Captain Pollipus Hammond:]

You being Master of our Sloop *Anstis* and ready to Sail, our orders are that you imbrace the first opportunity and make the best of your way for the Coast of Africa when please God you arrive there dispose of our Cargoe to the best advantage, make us returns in Negroes, Gold Dust and whatever you think will answer. If you have a good Trade for Negroes may purchase forty or Fifty Negroes. Get most of them mere Boys and Girl, some Men, let them be Young, No very small Children. Make all possable Dispatch, take care of your Vessells

---

16. **duck:** a type of heavy cloth.
17. **decayed families:** honorable, hard-working families who had fallen on hard times.

Bottom. If you meet with disapointment in your Trade and cannot get home some time in October next may go to Barbados and Dispose of your Negroes, reserving Eight likely boyes to bring home.

14. Thomas Clarkson Reports on Child Stealing on the African Coast, 1789

Inquiring today of a Negro lad, how he came into the situation of a slave, he informed me that he had been stolen from his parents in the interior country above Cape Rouge; that the inhabitants of the shore usually came up in bodies for this purpose, and that they unfortunately met with him, and brought him to Goree in company with others, whom they had taken in the same manner. . . .

Since our arrival here, the king of Barbasin has twice sent out his military to attack his own villages in the night. They have been very unsuccessful, having taken but three children. They had no better fortune last night, having brought in but one girl.

Source 15 from Christopher Fyfe, ed., "Our Children Free and Happy": Letters from Black Settlers in Africa in the 1790s (Edinburgh: Edinburgh University Press, 1991), pp. 37, 38.

15. Settlers' Letter and Petition to the Directors of the Sierra Leone Company, London, 1793

We have not the Education which White Men have yet we have feeling the same as other Human Beings and would wish to do every thing we can for to make our Children free and happy after us but as we feel our selves much put upon & distressed by your Council here we are afraid if such conduct continues we shall be unhappy while we live and our Children may be in bondage after us. . . . There is no Store here but the Company's and the extortionate Price we are obliged to pay for every thing we have out of it keeps us always behind hand so that we have nothing to lay out for a Rainy Day or for our Children after us. . . .

Mr Dawes[18] seems to wish to rule us just as bad as if we were all Slaves which we cannot bear but we do not wish to make any disturbance in the Colony but would chuse that every thing should go on quietly till we hear

---

18. **Mr. Dawes:** the governor of the colony, appointed by the company.

Chapter 5
The "Discovery
of Childhood"
in England
and America
(1600–1800)

from you as we are sure we will then have justice shown us for we have a great deal of Confidence in you and we have never known since we came here what footing we are on but are afraid concerning the happiness of our Children for as we have not Justice shewn us we do not expect our Children after us will unless your Honrs will look into the matter. . . .

We are afraid these things are not told to your Honrs as they are here and we are doubtful about our Fate and the Fate of our Children as the Promises made us has not been perfom'd.

Source 16 from John Blassingame, Slave Testimony: Two Centuries of Letters, Speeches, Interviews, and Autobiographies *(Baton Rouge: Louisiana State University Press, 1977), pp. 7–8.*

16. Letter from Judith Cocks, a Former Slave, to James Hillhouse, her Former Owner, 1795

Sir

I have been so unhappy at Mrs. Woodbridges that I was obliged to leeve thare by the consent of Mrs. Woodbridge who gave up my Indentures and has offen said that had she known that I was so sickly and expencieve she would not have brought me to this Country   but all this is the least of my trouble and I can truly say sir had I nothing else or no one but myself I am sure I should not make any complaint to you   But my Little son Jupiter who is now with Mrs. Woodbridge is my greatest care and from what she says and from the useage he meets with there is so trying to me that I am all most distracted   therefore if you will be so kind as to write me how Long Jupiter is to remain with them as she tells me he is to live with her until he is twenty five years of age   this is something that I had no idea of   I all ways thought that he was to return with me to new england or at Longest only ten years   these are matters I must beg of you sir to let me know as quick as you can make it convenient   I hope you will excuse me of troub Ling you wich I think you will do when you think that I am here in A strange country without one Friend to advise me   Mrs. Woodbridge setts out for connecticut and I make no doubt but she will apply to buy Jupiter's time which I beg you will be so good as not to sell to her   I had much reather he wold return and Live with you as she allows all her sons to thump and beat him the same as if he was a Dog   Mrs. Woodbridge may tell you that I have behaved bad but I call on all the nabours to know wheather I have not behaved well and wheather I was so much to blame   She has called me A theif and I denie   I have don my duty as well as I could to her and all her family as well as my Strength wold allow of   I have not ronged her nor her family   the nabours advised me to rite you for the childs sake   I went to the Gentlemen of the town for these advise   thay told me I could get back without any difficulty   I entend to return

remember me to all your family if you please   I thank you for sending me word my dauter was well   this is my hand writing remain the greatest humility[,] you Humble servant

Judith Cocks

please [dont?] show this to Mrs. Woodbridge

Source 17 from John Newbery, The History of Little Goody Two-Shoes *(New York and London: Garland, 1977; reprint of 1765 ed. printed for J. Newbery, London), pp. 4–5, 17–21, 24–28, 36, 38–39. Illustrations reproduced with permission of Garland Press.*

17. **From John Newbery,** *Goody Two-Shoes,* **1765**

All the World must allow, that *Two Shoes* was not her real Name. No; her Father's Name was *Meanwell;* and he was for many Years a considerable Farmer in the Parish where *Margery* was born; but by the Misfortunes which he met with in Business, and the wicked Persecutions of Sir *Timothy Gripe,* and an overgrown Farmer called *Graspall,* he was effectually ruined. . . .

Care and Discontent shortened the Days of Little *Margery's* Father.—He was forced from his Family, and seized with a violent Fever in a Place where Dr. *James's* Powder was not to be had, and where he died miserably. *Margery's* poor Mother survived the Loss of her Husband but a few Days, and died of a broken Heart, leaving *Margery* and her little Brother to the wide World. . . .

Chapter 5

The "Discovery

of Childhood"

in England

and America

(1600–1800)

They were both very ragged, and *Tommy* had two Shoes, but *Margery* had but one. They had nothing, poor Things, to support them (not being in their own Parish) but what they picked from the Hedges, or got from the poor People, and they lay every Night in a Barn. Their Relations took no Notice of them; no, they were rich and ashamed to own such a poor little ragged Girl as *Margery*, and such a dirty little curl-pated Boy as *Tommy*. . . .

> [*Margery and Tommy meet a kindly*
> *clergyman, Mr. Smith, who arranges for*
> *Tommy to go to London and be taken on as*
> *a sailor; and he provides shoes for*
> *Margery.*]

Nothing could have supported Little *Margery* under the Affliction she was in for the Loss of her Brother but the Pleasure she took in her *two Shoes*. She ran out to Mrs. *Smith* as soon as they were put on, and stroking down her ragged Apron thus,

cried out, *Two Shoes, Mame, see two Shoes*. And so she behaved to all the People she met, and by that Means obtained the Name of *Goody Two Shoes*, though her Playmates called her *Old Goody Two Shoes*.

CHAP. IV.
HOW LITTLE MARGERY LEARNED TO READ, AND BY DEGREES TAUGHT OTHERS.

Little *Margery* saw how good, and how wise Mr. *Smith* was, and concluded, that this was owing to his great Learning, therefore she wanted of all Things to learn to read. For this Purpose she used to meet the little Boys and Girls as they came from School, borrow their Books, and sit down and read till they returned;

By this Means she soon got more Learning than any of her Playmates, and laid the following Scheme for instructing those who were more ignorant than her-self. She found, that only the following Letters were required to spell all the Words in the World; but as some of these Letters are large and some small, she with her Knife cut out of several Pieces of Wood ten Setts of each of these:

a b c d e f g h i j k l m n o
p q r s t u v w x y z.

And six Setts of these:

A B C D E F G H I K L M N
O P Q R S T U V W X Y Z.

And having got an old Spelling-Book, she made her Companions set up all the Words they wanted to spell, and after that she taught them to compose Sentences. You know what a Sentence is, my Dear, *I will be good,* is a Sentence; and is made up, as you see, of several Words. . . .

The Letters being brought upon the Table, one of the little ones set up the following Sentence. . . .

I pray GOD *to bless this whole Company, and all our Friends, and all our Enemies.*

To this last *Polly Sullen* objected, and said, truly, she did not know why she should pray for her Enemies? Not pray for your Enemies, says Little *Margery;* yes, you must, you are no Christian, if you don't forgive your Enemies, and do Good for Evil. *Polly* still pouted, upon which Little *Margery* said, though she was poor, and obliged to lie in a Barn, she would not keep Company with such a naughty, proud, perverse Girl as *Polly;* and was going away; however the Difference was made up.

Chapter 5
The "Discovery
of Childhood"
in England
and America
(1600–1800)

Source 18 from Thomas Day, The History of Sandford and Merton *(New York and London: Garland, 1977; reprint of 1793 edition printed for J. Stockdale, London), pp. 1–2, 3–4, 5–6, 10–11, 12–13, 15, 16.*

18. From Arthur Day, *The History of Sandford and Merton*, 1793

In the western part of England lived a gentleman of great fortune, whose name was Merton. He had a large estate in the island of Jamaica, where he had past the greater part of his life, and was master of many servants, who cultivated sugar and other valuable things for his advantage. He had only one son, of whom he was excessively fond; and to educate this child properly was the reason of his determining to stay some years in England. Tommy Merton, who, at the time he came from Jamaica, was only six years old, was naturally a very good-natured boy, but unfortunately had been spoiled by too much indulgence. While he lived in Jamaica, he had several black servants to wait upon him, who were forbidden upon any account to contradict him. If he walked, there always went two negroes with him, one of whom carried a large umbrella to keep the sun from him, and the other was to carry him in his arms, whenever he was tired. Besides this, he was always dressed in silk or laced cloaths, and had a fine gilded carriage, which was borne upon men's shoulders, in which he made visits to his play-fellows. His mother was so excessively fond of him, that she gave him every thing he cried for, and would never let him learn to read, because he complained that it made his head ach.

The consequence of this was, that, though Master Merton had every thing he wanted, he became very fretful and unhappy. . . .

By this kind of education, when Master Merton came over to England, he could neither write, nor read, nor cypher; he could use none of his limbs with ease, nor bear any degree of fatigue; but he was very proud, fretful, and impatient.

Very near to Mr. Merton's seat lived a plain honest farmer, whose name was Sandford. This man had, like Mr. Merton, an only son, about six years old, whose name was Harry. Harry, as he had been always accustomed to run about in the fields, to follow the labourers while they were ploughing, and to drive the sheep to their pasture, was active, strong, hardy, and fresh-coloured. He was neither so fair, nor so delicately shaped as Master Merton; but he had an honest, good-natured countenance, which made every body love him; was never out of humour, and took the greatest pleasure in obliging every body. If little Harry saw a poor wretch who wanted victuals, while he was eating his dinner, he was sure to give him half, and sometimes the whole: nay, so very good-natured was he to every thing, that he would never go into the fields to take the eggs of poor birds, or their young ones, nor practice any other kind of sport which gave pain to poor animals, who are as capable of feeling as we ourselves, though they have no words to express their sufferings. . . . Even toads and frogs, and spiders, and such kind of disagreeable animals, which most people destroy whereever they find them, were perfectly safe with Harry: he used to say they had a right to live as well as we, and that it was cruel and unjust to kill creatures only because we did not like them.

These sentiments made little Harry a great favourite with every body, particularly with the clergyman of the parish, who became so fond of him, that he taught him to read and write, and had him almost always with him. . . .

[*Tommy and Harry meet when Harry pulls
a snake off Tommy's leg; Harry is then
invited to the manor-house for dinner.*]

After dinner, Mrs. Merton filled a large glass with wine, and, giving it to Harry, bid him drink it up; but he thanked her, and said he was not dry. But, my dear, says she, this is very sweet and pleasant, and, as you are a good boy, you may drink it up. Aye! but, madam, Mr. Barlow says, that we must only eat when we are hungry, and drink when we are dry; and that we must only eat and drink such things as are easily met with, otherwise we shall grow peevish and vexed when we can't get them. And this was the way that the apostles did, who were all very good men. And they never minded what they eat or drank, but lived upon dry bread and water; and when any body offered them money, they would not take it, but told him to be good, and give it to the poor and the sick; and so they made the world a great deal better—and therefore it is not fit to mind what we live upon, but we should take what we can get and be contented; just as the beasts and birds do, who lodge in the open air, and live upon herbs, and drink nothing but water, and yet they are strong, and active, and healthy.

Upon my word, says Mr. Merton, this little man is a great philosopher, and we should be much obliged to Mr. Barlow, if he would take our Tommy under his care, for he grows a great boy, and it is time that he should know something. What say you, Tommy, should you like to be a philosopher? Indeed, papa, I don't know what a philosopher is, but I should like to be a king; because he's finer and richer than any body else, and has nothing to do, and every body waits upon him, and is afraid of him. Well said, my dear, says Mrs. Merton, and rose and kissed him, and a king you deserve to be with such a spirit, and here's a glass of wine for you for making such a pretty answer. And should not you like to be a king too, little Harry? Indeed, madam, I don't know what that is; but I hope I shall soon be big enough to go to plough, and get my own living, and then I shall want nobody to wait upon me. What a difference there is between the children of farmers and gentlemen! whispered Mrs. Merton to her husband, looking rather contemptuously upon Harry. I am not sure, said Mr. Merton, that for this time the advantage is on the side of

Chapter 5

The "Discovery

of Childhood"

in England

and America

(1600–1800)

our son. But should not you like to be rich, my dear, says he to Harry? No indeed, sir. No, simpleton, says Mrs. Merton, and why not? Because the only rich man I ever saw is squire Chace, who lives hard by, and he rides among people's corn, and breaks down their hedges, and shoots their poultry, and kills their dogs, and lames their cattle, and abuses the poor, and they say he does all this because he's rich; but every body hates him, though they dare not tell him so to his face—and I would not be hated for any thing in the world. . . .

But at the mansion-house, much of the conversation in the mean time was employed in examining the merits of little Harry. Mrs. Merton acknowledged his bravery and openness of temper; she was also struck with the general good-nature and benevolence of his character; but she contended there were a certain grossness and indelicacy in his ideas which distinguish the children of the lower and middling classes of people from those of persons of fashion. Mr. Merton, on the contrary, contended that he had never before seen a child whose sentiments and dispositions would do so much honour even to the most elevated situations. . . .

Source 19 from E. Robinson and Geoffrey Summerfield, eds., Selected Poems and Prose of John Clare *(London: Oxford University Press, 1978), p. 100.*

19. John Clare Reports on his Childhood Reading, 1790s

I was fond of books before I began to write poetry. These were such that chance came at—6py [six-penny] Pamphlets that are in the possession of every door-calling hawker, and found on every bookstall at fairs and markets, whose titles are as familiar with every one as his own name. Shall I repeat some of them—"Little Red Riding Hood," "Valentine and Orson," "Jack and the Jiant" . . . "The Seven Sleepers," "Tom Hickathrift," "Johnny Armstrong" . . . and many others. Shall I go on? No, these have memorys as common as Prayer Books and Psalters with the peasantry. Such were the books that delighted me and I saved all the pence I got to buy them for they were the whole world of literature to me and I knew of no other. I carried them in my pocket and read them at my leisure and they was the ever weary food of winter evenings, ere Milton Shakespeare and Thomson had ever existed in my memory, and I feel a love for them still. Nay, I cannot help fancying now that Cock Robin, Babes in the Wood, Mother Hubbard and her Cat, etc., etc., are real poetry in all its native simplicity and as it should be. I know I am foolish enough to have fancys different from others and childhood is a strong spell over my feelings but I think so on and cannot help it.

Source 20 from R. L. and Maria Edgeworth, Practical Education *(London: J. Johnson, 1798), vol. 1, pp. 335–338.*

20. Maria Edgeworth
Discusses Children's Reading,
1798

There is a class of books which amuses the imagination of children without acting upon their feelings. We do not allude to fairy-tales, for we apprehend that these are not now much read, but we mean voyages and travels; these interest young people universally. Robinson Crusoe, Gulliver, and the Three Russian Sailors, who were cast away upon the coast of Norway, are general favourites. No child can ever read an account of a shipwreck, or even a storm, without pleasure. A desert island is a delightful place. . . . Savages, especially if they happen to be cannibals, are sure to be admired, and the more hair-breadth escapes the hero of the tale has survived, and the more marvellous his adventures, the more sympathy he excites.

Will it be thought to proceed from a spirit of contradiction if we remark, that these species of reading should not early be chosen for boys of an enterprising temper, unless they are intended for a seafaring life, or for the army? The taste for adventure is absolutely incompatible with sober perseverance necessary to success in any other liberal professions. To girls this species of reading cannot be as dangerous as it is to boys; girl must very soon perceive the impossibility of their rambling about the world in quest of adventures; and where there appears an obvious impossibility in gratifying any wish, it is not likely to become, or at least to continue, a torment to the imagination. When a young man deliberates upon what course of life he shall follow, the patient drudgery of a trade, the laborious mental exertions requisite to prepare him for a profession, must appear to him in a formidable light, compared with the alluring prospects presented by an adventuring imagination. The histories of realities written in an entertaining manner appear not only better suited to the purposes of education, but also more agreeable to young people than improbable fiction.

Chapter 5

The "Discovery
of Childhood"
in England
and America
(1600–1800)

Source 21 from Mary Wollstonecraft, Thoughts on the Education of Daughters *(Oxford and New York: Woodstock Books, 1994; reprint of 1797 edition publihed for J. Johnson in London), pp. 12, 16–22.*

21. From Mary Wollstonecraft, *Thoughts on the Education of Daughters,* 1798

How then are the tender minds of children to be cultivated?—

Children should be permitted to enter into conversation; but it requires great discernment to find out such subjects as will gradually improve them. Animals are the first objects which catch their attention; and I think little stories about them would not only amuse but instruct at the same time, and have the best effect in forming the temper and cultivating the good dispositions of the heart. There are many little books which have this tendency. One in particular I recollect: The Perambulations of a Mouse. I cannot here help mentioning a book of hymns, in measured prose, written by the ingenious author of many other proper lessons for children. These hymns, I imagine, would contribute to fill the heart with religious sentiments and affections; and, if I may be allowed the expression, make the Deity obvious to the senses. The understanding, however, should not be overloaded any more than the stomach. Intellectual improvements, like the growth and formation of the body, must be gradual—yet there is no reason why the mind should lie fallow, while its "frail tenement" is imperceptibly fitting itself for a more reasonable inhabitant. It will not lie fallow; promiscuous seeds will be sown by accident, and they will shoot up with the wheat, and perhaps never be eradicated.

Whenever a child asks a question, it should always have a reasonable answer given it. Its little passions should be engaged. They are mostly fond of stories, and proper ones would improve them even while they are amused. Instead of these, their heads are filled with improbable tales, and superstitious accounts of invisible beings, which breed strange prejudices and vain fears in their minds.

The riot too of the kitchen, or any other place where children are left only with servants, makes the decent restraint of the parlour irksome. A girl, who has vivacity, soon grows a romp; and if there are male servants, they go out a walking with them, and will frequently take little freedoms with Miss, the bearing with which gives a forwardness to her air, and makes her pert. The becoming modesty, which being accustomed to converse with superiors, will give a girl, is entirely done away. I must own, I am quite charmed when I see a sweet young creature, shrinking as it were from observation, and listening rather than talking. It is possible a girl may have this manner without having a very good understanding. If it should be so, this dissidence prevents her from being troublesome. . . .

The first things, then, that children ought to be encouraged to observe, are a strict adherence to truth; a proper submission to superiors; and condescension to inferiors.

Source 22 from Benjamin B. Wisner, Memoirs of the Late Mrs. Susan Huntington *(Boston: Crocker and Brewster, 1833), pp. 79, 89–90, 131–132.*

22. From the Diary of Susan Huntington, 1812–1815

May 21, 1812. Deeply impressed with a sense of the vast importance of a mother's duties, and the lasting effect of youthful impressions, I this day resolve to endeavor, at all times, by my precepts and by my example, to inspire my children with just notions of right and wrong, of what is to be avoided and what pursued, of what is sacredly to be desired, and what unreservedly deprecated. . . .

February 7, [1813]. There is scarcely any subject concerning which I feel more anxiety, than the proper education of my children. It is a difficult and delicate subject, and the more I reflect on my duty to them, the more I feel how much is to be learnt by myself. The person who undertakes to form the infant mind, to cut off the distorted shoots, and direct and fashion those which may, in due time, become fruitful and lovely branches, ought to possess a deep and accurate knowledge of human nature. . . .

[April 4, 1815]. The truth is, no one can govern a family of children well without much reflection and, what the world calls, trouble. There must be an accurate judgment formed respecting the character of each child, and a *regular* and *consistent* method, adapted to each pursued. And what is more difficult still, the parent must uniformly govern herself. This, certainly, is not easy; it calls for the unremitted exertion of several most eminent and rare christian graces.

QUESTIONS TO CONSIDER

The first question for this chapter asks you to assess attitudes toward children, which, as we have discussed, are expressed directly in some sources and indirectly in others. Look again at Source 1. Why do you think Lady Clifford continually refers to her daughter as "the Child"? Does she seem concerned with her

Chapter 5

The "Discovery

of Childhood"

in England

and America

(1600–1800)

welfare? Her daughter was about two years old at the time of these diary entries; do you find any evidence that Lady Clifford saw children as having needs different than adults? How would you describe the way her daughter, Lady Margaret, appears in the portrait?

Sources 2 through 5 all refer to indentured servants in the American colonies during the seventeenth century. What attitudes toward children emerge from these? Do you find unanimity or a range of opinion?

In Source 6, what does Locke suggest is the best way to teach children? What attributes occur naturally in them? What are parents' most important responsibilities? In what ways are children similar to, and different from, adults? In Source 7, how does Cotton Mather deal with the frequent illnesses of his children? Those who argue that people were cold or unfeeling toward their children in earlier centuries point to the high rates of child mortality as a reason for this aloofness; they contend that people chose not to get too emotionally involved with their children because so many died so young. Does Mather's diary support or contradict this argument?

Sources 8, 9, and 10 come from some of the first literature designed for children published in English. What lessons or morals are explicitly stated? What underlying attitudes toward children emerge from the rhymes in "A was an Archer," or the contrast between good and bad children in "Obedience to Parents"? What special lessons are girls to take away from "The Little Red Riding-Hood"?

In Source 11, how does Anna Winslow relate to the adults around her, such as her aunt? to her distant mother and father? How does she view her own ability to understand adult subjects, such as theology? What sorts of materials has she been given to copy in order to learn handwriting? How would you describe the way she is portrayed in the miniature? In Source 12, George Washington describes girls about the same age as Anna Winslow working in a cloth factory. What does he find noteworthy about these girls and their work?

Sources 13 and 14 are drawn from letters or essays discussing the slave trade. What do these reveal about the treatment of African children? Sources 15 and 16 are letters in which ex-slaves make reference to their children. Why might the petitioning settlers of Source 15 mention their children so frequently in reporting that they have not received what had been promised? What is Judith Cocks requesting? How does she describe her feelings toward her children?

Sources 17 through 20 take us back again to the world of children's literature, beginning with two best-sellers from the late eighteenth century. What characteristics of the main characters in *Goody Two-Shoes* and *Sandford and Merton* are held up for emulation? What moral lessons do the authors want to be sure children learn? What practical suggestions emerge in *Goody Two-Shoes* for the education of children? What does the discussion by John Clare (Source 19) reveal about what children *wanted* to read? How does Maria Edgeworth (Source 20) view this type of reading? Does it give children the moral lessons she thinks they need? Judging by Clare's comments, is she being realistic in her assessment of what children actually liked to read?

The final two sources offer comments on children's education from the late eighteenth and early nineteenth centuries. What advice do Wollstonecraft and Huntington offer about the best ways to train young children? What does their advice imply (or state) about children's natures?

You should now have some rather extensive notes about attitudes toward children, and can begin to form your answer for the first question in this chapter: What attitudes about children and childhood emerge in descriptions of children, both real and fictional, and in the words of children themselves? As you do, think about the possible reasons for any contradictions that strike you. Along with differences of opinion among authors, have you found that attitudes toward children are shaped by the children's race and class? Do you find differences in the way poor versus rich children are viewed? in assumptions about education and proper reading for boys versus girls? How would you compare the way African and African-American children were treated in American culture with the way their parents viewed them? Do people express different attitudes toward their own children as compared with the children of other people, that is, does there seem to be a dis-

tinction between their opinions about children they know and childhood in general? Do you find contradictions in ideas about children within the writings of a single author? What might account for this?

The second question, in part, asks you to address the issue of change over time. What differences do you find between the seventeenth and early eighteenth century sources and those of the later eighteenth century? What continuities? What differences do you see in the two groups of children's literature (Sources 8–10 from the early eighteenth century and Sources 17 and 18 from the later eighteenth century)? Do you find traces of Locke's or Rousseau's ideas in them?

The second question then asks you to assess whether any new attitudes you have found might be termed "modern." In order to address this issue, you have to determine first what you mean by the word *modern.* To do that, ask yourself what attitudes toward or ways of treating children—whether you approve of them or not—seem familiar. Which seem particularly foreign? Do those that seem familiar appear more often in the later sources than the earlier?

You are now ready to answer the central questions for this chapter: What attitudes about children and childhood emerge in descriptions of children, both real and fictional, and in the words of children themselves? How did these change during the seventeenth and eighteenth centuries, and in what ways might these attitudes be termed "modern"?

Chapter 5
The "Discovery
of Childhood"
in England
and America
(1600–1800)

EPILOGUE

Though certain historical developments are clearly unique—there was only one American Revolution, only one Ming dynasty—when we are investigating broad intellectual changes such as those in ideas about childhood, it is important to step back from the time and place in question to get the benefit of a larger framework. Before you make your final judgment about whether there was a so-called discovery of childhood during the early modern period, then, you may want to think back to what you might have learned about childhood in earlier periods of Western history, or think forward to what you know about childhood today. Rather than one "discovery of childhood," could attitudes toward children be cyclical? The Roman educator Quintilian (ca. 35–95 C.E.) wrote in his *On the Early Education of the Citizen-Orator:* "It is the disposition of the pupil, and the care taken of him, that make the whole difference. . . . Let his instruction be an amusement to him; let him be questioned and praised. . . . Application to learning depends on the will, which cannot be forced. But that boys should suffer corporal punishment, though it be an accepted custom, I by no means approve. . . . No man should be allowed too much authority over an age so weak and so unable to resist ill treatment."[19] How does this opinion fit with the recommendations of Locke or Wollstonecraft? Does Quintilian's statement alter your conclusions at all? How do the sentiments of the authors you read in this chapter fit with contemporary discussions in the media about children and education?

In addition to taking a longer view chronologically, it is also useful when testing theories of historical change to take a broader view geographically. Does the dating of the "discovery of childhood" make sense only in the Western world? Was there a similar intellectual change in other cultures, and if so, when? If there was, what were the contributing intellectual, economic, and social factors? If not, why not? Were attitudes toward children significantly different in cultures which were not Christian? Al-Ghazâlî (1058–1111), the Islamic theologian, philosopher, and mystic, wrote in *O Disciple*: "Parents are responsible for looking after their children properly. To their hands the innocent child is confided with his pure conscience and stainless soul. His heart, resembling a mirror, is ready to reflect anything put before it and he imitates carefully whatever he watches. He may be an ideal citizen if he is educated well and he may be a harmful person if he is ill trained or neglected. His parents, relations, as well as teachers, will share with him his happiness or suffer from his being evil. So it is the duty of the parents or guardian to pay full attention to the child; teach him good behavior, edify him and keep him away from bad company. He must be accustomed to rough and hard life and not luxury.

19. Quintilian, *On the Early Education of the Citizen-Orator,* trans. James J. Murphy (Indianapolis: Library of Liberal Arts, 1965), pp. 15, 19–20, 26, 27.

Self-respect, modesty, and sincerity must be among his outstanding qualities. He should not be encouraged to be fond of money or material things as this is the first step towards useless quarrels."[20] Does this sound familiar? Might Thomas Day, the author of *Sandford and Merton*, have drawn the same conclusions from reading al-Ghazâlî that he drew from reading Rousseau?

It is, of course, dangerous to use only two other authors when putting a historical issue into a broader framework, for these two may profess ideas completely atypical of their own cultures and so give readers a wrong impression. Should you wish to explore the issue of attitudes toward children further, and test your conclusions for this chapter against those of other scholars, the best place to turn would be two journals, one that focuses directly on childhood, and one that includes this among other areas: *The History of Childhood Quarterly*, which began publication in 1973, and *The Journal of Family History*, which began publication in 1976.

20. Quoted in Baldoon Dhingra, ed., *Asia Through Asian Eyes* (Rutland, Vermont: Charles E. Tuttle, 1959), p. 183.

CHAPTER SIX

THE ATLANTIC SLAVE TRADE:

ITS IMPACT ON WEST AFRICA

(1600–1900)

THE PROBLEM

In the mid-seventeenth century, opposition to the Atlantic slave trade began to surface in Britain and elsewhere. Much of this opposition had religious and humanitarian origins, focusing primarily on the harsh conditions and lack of freedom to which slaves were doomed in the New World. In response, a number of pro-slavery arguments were advanced defending the capture, enslavement, and transport of Africans to the Americas. An early, and typical, example of such views was set out in an anonymous letter to the *London Magazine* in 1740:

> The Inhabitants of Guinea [in West Africa] are indeed in a most deplorable . . . and more wretched . . . State of Slavery, under the arbitrary Powers of their [local] Princes both as to Life and Property. . . . All that can be done in such a Case is, to communicate as

much Liberty, and Happiness, as such circumstances will admit, and . . . this is certainly by the Guinea Trade [in slaves]. For, by purchasing, or rather ransoming the Negroes from their national Tyrants, and transplanting them under the benign Influences of the Law, and Gospel, they are advanced to much greater degrees.[1]

Similar arguments were made in the United States a century later in support of the nation's slave economy. By insisting that slavery was, in fact, beneficial to Africans themselves, defenders of slavery and the Atlantic slave trade sought to justify their activities. Since then, apologists for the slave trade—even for discrimination against the descendants of slaves—have expressed comparable opinions.[2] Defenders of European

1. "The African Slave Trade Defended," *London Magazine* 9 (1740): 493–494.

2. For example, the classic defense of slavery in the United States is George Fitzhugh, *Cannibals All! or, Slaves Without Masters* (Richmond, 1857).

imperialism have, as well, used similar reasoning in making the case for colonial domination of Africa and other areas of the world.

Yet while scholars have for many years analyzed the effect of the slave trade on the societies of the Americas, only relatively recently have historians begun to consider the impact of the Atlantic slave trade on Africa itself. The most serious efforts followed the publication of Professor Philip Curtin's important book, *The Atlantic Slave Trade: A Census,* in 1969. Curtin's estimates of the volume of the slave trade were much lower than some figures in popular circulation, in some cases five times lower. If he were correct, one implication might be that the exportation of African slaves was not a large drain on the population of the continent. Some of Curtin's critics worried that this might leave the impression that the slave trade was not so bad after all.

Of course, there is a moral argument as well, one that all will recognize. A single African, one captive transported against her will across the Atlantic, was both a personal tragedy and a social evil. Yet what was the effect of the Atlantic slave trade on those who remained behind, on African societies themselves? Did any Africans benefit in any way from this trade in human beings? Or did the traffic in slaves have a uniformly negative effect on Africans?

In this chapter you will examine a variety of evidence, including narrative accounts, contemporary drawings, and demographic data, as well as statistical tables, charts, and graphs drawn from them. You may find considerable variability in the data. How many people left the western coast of Africa as slaves? Over what period of time? Did the numbers, and time periods, vary by regions? You will also find narratives of participants in the Atlantic slave trade, both African and European. Taking both the observations and the numbers together, were any benefits derived by Africans? And, conversely, what were the costs of the slave trade, both to individual Africans and to their societies? Overall, what was the net effect of the Atlantic slave trade on the people and societies of West Africa?

BACKGROUND

Slavery is an old institution, but not quite as old as the human population itself. Only with the rise of complex societies in which there were clear divisions of labor, and accompanying social classes, did slavery emerge as a part of many social systems. Evidence exists of slavery in Ur, perhaps the earliest Mesopotamian city-state. In Egypt, too, slaves were a vital source of much-needed labor; some of them were no doubt Africans from the lands south of Egypt along the upper reaches of the Nile Valley.

Also prominent in the ancient world, of course, were slaves in Greece and Rome. Greek slaves were

Chapter 6

The Atlantic

Slave Trade:

Its Impact on

West Africa

(1600–1900)

for the most part associated with the principal city-states, and many were skilled in various crafts. This was also true in the city of Rome itself, but as the metropolis expanded into an empire, its slaves increasingly were used as agricultural laborers in the highly productive *latifundia* (large estates) in central Italy; by the second century B.C.E. perhaps more than 30 percent of the inhabitants of Italy itself were slaves.

There is also clear evidence of various types of slavery in India, China, Southeast Asia, Arabia, the Americas, and yes, Africa as well, by the time of European expansion in the fifteenth century. In Europe, however, slavery gradually gave way to serfdom, although among some Europeans—such as the Vikings—the use of slaves continued well after the collapse of the Roman Empire. With the expansion of Islam out of Arabia into Persia, North Africa, and beyond, slavery was also extended as an Islamic institution.

Yet it was in the eastern Mediterranean that a significant development occurred that centuries later would help to shape the patterns of slave labor in the Atlantic slave trade. There, European Crusaders, accustomed to patterns of both Christian and Islamic slavery during the Crusades, adapted the institution to the production of sugar. First in the Crusader domains in Syria and Palestine, then on to Cyprus and Malta, slaves were used in the arduous and unpleasant work of planting cane and producing sugar from it. Few, if any, humans were willing to labor in the cane fields; only the coercion associated with slavery made the plantations profitable.

With the beginning of fifteenth-century Atlantic voyages, especially from Portugal, the sugar estates were extended into the Atlantic, on the Canary and Madeira Islands. Perhaps more significantly, by late in the century sugar plantations were begun on Sao Thomé, just off the western coast of Africa in the Bight of Biafra. From as early as the 1440s, the Portuguese began purchasing and taking African slaves to Portugal itself and to the Atlantic islands, adding these newcomers to their large numbers of Muslim slaves from Arabia, North Africa, and the Iberian peninsula itself; all became part of an undifferentiated labor force.

By about this same time a clear pattern of slavery had developed in Africa as well. Many African societies, both large and small, were organized around systems of extended kinship. Family and clan groups formed the basis of not only social and political, but also economic life. Both wealth and power were frequently determined—and even measured—by the extent of the kinship group. More people meant greater wealth and power; the larger the population, the greater both the prestige and productive capacity of the group. Thus, the expansion of a group to include fictive as well as biological kin often was an attractive avenue to greater status for the group itself and especially for its leaders.

In this context, slavery became a part of some African societies. As a judicial punishment (in the absence of prisons) and as a means of dealing with occasional war captives, slaves increased the population of many kinship groups. For some individuals and families, impoverished by economic or social circumstances, the sale of selected people—even close relatives—into slave status provided a significant economic boost. Given the social importance of these African slaves, they were treated as a significant part of society, valued for the increased size and status they brought to the group as well as for their productive capacity. Seldom, however, were they treated simply as interchangeable units of labor. Some were given positions of trust; others married into the kinship group and their children were no longer considered slaves. Not infrequently many of them returned to the status of free human beings—fictive kin—among the people whom they had served as slaves.

Nonetheless, there can be little doubt that in 1500 Africans were a decided minority among the world's slaves, although in a few places such as Sao Thomé they were probably the majority. Within two centuries, with the rise of the Atlantic trade in slaves from Africa to the Americas, the situation reversed. Africans and their descendants were, by 1700, clearly a majority of all the world's slaves. Yet in the Americas most were not valued members of society but merely chattel, little more than units of labor, one to be replaced by another, treated more like cattle than human beings.

These changes were the result of European expectations that their newly conquered lands yield a rapid economic return for those who had opened them to exploitation. There was gold and silver to be mined and, before long, sugar to be produced to satisfy a growing demand in Europe. Of course the early European settlers had no intention of doing such unpleasant work themselves. At first Native American captives were put to these tasks, but the results were most unsatisfactory. Diseases brought by the Europeans to the New World—influenza and smallpox chief among them—took an extraordinary toll on local peoples who had no immunities to them. Their plight was exacerbated by the frequently harsh conditions under which they were forced to labor.

Although larger and larger numbers of Native Americans might be used for such tasks, it soon became clear that another source of labor for the distasteful tasks necessary to European mines and plantations in the New World needed to be found. In addition, some religious leaders, perhaps foremost among them Bartolme de las Casas, considered it more humane to find slaves who they believed would not so readily succumb under the dire conditions of working for the Europeans. An obvious solution was Africans. They had successfully labored in sugar plantations on the Atlantic islands. They did not seem so vulnerable to disease; their immune systems had centuries of exposure to the diseases of the Mediterranean world. Most were accustomed to tropical climates. And over half a century of European experience on the west coast of Africa suggested that ample supplies of African slaves were readily available.

Chapter 6

The Atlantic

Slave Trade:

Its Impact on

West Africa

(1600–1900)

Indeed, Europeans soon began to seek more and more slaves from the Africans with whom they dealt along the western coast of the continent. European merchants found results to be very satisfying, as Africans proved willing to meet the greater demand. In many circumstances African merchants and rulers saw the trade as an opportunity to make gains for themselves. Frequently, Europeans were expected to provide political and even military alliances, in addition to particular trade goods (including firearms). Other African societies that balked at meeting the increasing demand for slaves soon found that their commercial and diplomatic contacts with Europeans on the coast were dependent upon their willingness to sell human beings into bondage.

Beginning early in the seventeenth century, then, Africans were transported in ever-increasing numbers to the islands of the Caribbean and the mainlands of the Americas. First Portugal and Spain, then Great Britain and the Netherlands, and ultimately France, Sweden and virtually every European maritime nation became involved in the Atlantic slave trade. Ships from colonial North America (later the United States) also carried human cargoes across the Atlantic. These ventures were certainly profitable, even more so as special ships were designed to better accommodate increasing numbers of chained slaves. That many African captives died in the cramped quarters as the slave ships traversed the Atlantic was seen as little more than one of the costs of doing business.

Although humanitarian concerns about the slave trade had begun in the middle of the seventeenth century, such objections to the traffic grew both louder and more insistent near the end of the following century. None doubt the importance of that effort, but some historians have concluded the humanitarians were aided immeasurably in their cause by the rising tide of industrialism and its economic preference for wage—not slave—labor. This is not surprising as antislavery campaigns gained greatest currency in Great Britain and the new United States. Early in the nineteenth century, and following Denmark's lead (1804), Great Britain in 1807 prohibited its citizens and subjects from engaging in the trade in human beings. And the U.S. Constitution, ratified in 1791, specified an end to the slave trade by 1808.

Some nations were reluctant to follow suit. Other merchant sailors were willing to continue transporting slaves across the Atlantic, even though they were legally forbidden from doing so. As a result, British warships (and for a time United States naval vessels as well) patrolled the waters off the west African coast attempting to stop the traffic. As other European nations came to support such actions, the slave trade greatly reduced in volume, except to Brazil where it remained legal until the 1850s.

Frequently slave vessels were captured on the high seas. Rather than trying to return slaves to their lands of origin, naval commanders disembarked the human cargoes at humanitarian settlements on the west coast of Africa, most notably the British colony of Freetown in Sierra Leone. There, and at other similar stations (such as Libreville and Monrovia), missionaries and a few government officials assisted the transplanted Africans in making new lives for themselves, frequently joined by former slaves transported back to Africa from the Americas.

In a sense, this development brought the Atlantic slave trade full circle, back to Africa itself. Although the slave commerce lingered until the abolition of slavery itself in Brazil late in the nineteenth century, it had already been in decline for more than fifty years. There can be little doubt that over its four centuries the Atlantic slave trade had an important impact on world history. Yet the return of some former slaves to the continent of their heritage or birth did little to alter the changes that the slave trade had brought to Africa and Africans themselves.

THE METHOD

It appears clear to all concerned with the subject that the Atlantic slave trade involved the removal of millions of Africans from the continent of their birth. Therefore, a starting point in analyzing the impact of that trade upon Africa must be an attempt to estimate that figure as best we can. In Source 1 you will find such an estimate, based on the research of many historians into shipping and commercial records, as well as complicated mathematical calculations from census data. Although not all historians would fully agree with this estimate, it is a reasonably accurate assessment, drawn from currently available data, and well within the range accepted by most scholars in Africa, Europe, and the Americas.

Obviously, these simple continent-wide statistics cannot, by themselves, offer much information to help you assess the costs (or any benefits) of the slave trade for Africa. You will need to use other data based on similar statistics, developed by historians using complex demographic models to assess population patterns and changes over time. Source 2 is a simple world population projection, broken down by continents and regions. Compare Africa's population growth with that of other world areas; then consider this along with the data of African slave exports you have already seen.

Comparing African population trends—including slave trade export statistics—within a larger context is just one way to view questions of the impact of the slave trade on Africa. However, since Africa is a large continent (over three times the size of the United States), it may also be useful to look at population and slave export figures for particular regions. The next group of sources will allow you to do so. The map that sets the stage (Source 3) indicates the western coastal regions of the continent and their hinter-

Chapter 6

The Atlantic

Slave Trade:

Its Impact on

West Africa

(1600–1900)

lands, where a majority of the slaves in the Atlantic trade originated.

Source 4 consists of graphs of both slave exports and population trends for each of those regions during the two most active centuries of the Atlantic trade, from 1700 to 1900. Well-developed mathematical formulas, using carefully researched yet necessarily incomplete statistics, provided regional projections of the volume of slave exports (in thousands of persons) shown in solid lines. In addition, similar models were used to calculate total population figures for each area; the dashed lines indicate a conservative estimate of total population (in millions of persons) for each region during the same time.

Even a quick look at these graphs reveals wide variations in slave exports from the different coastal areas; the variations are significant enough to warrant a more careful examination. Consider, for example, when each region was at its peak as a provider of slaves, and when its total population rose and declined. See if you can determine any correlations between the two graphed lines. When slave exports increase, does population decrease? Remember that correlations (apparent connections between two sets of data) do not by themselves prove that one trend caused the other. The correlations may only suggest that possibility, which needs to be explored and verified by means of other sources.

Source 5 may help you begin to do this. These are demographic models of typical African societies for the periods (a) before, (b) during, and (c) shortly after their involvement with the slave trade. As you will observe, some societies lost people to enslavement during the period of the Atlantic trade, and others gained people during the same time. For sets (b) and (c), the population of slaves exported is shown by a third graph. Each graph represents the distribution of population by age and gender in such societies. The first set of these bar graphs (a) presents normal age and gender distributions in West African societies prior to involvement with the slave trade. Notice the relative comparability of those distributions for both societies that will lose and societies that will gain people in slave transactions.

The next set of graphs (b) represents typical age and gender distributions after an initial intense period of enslavement and export; of course, such periods came at different times in various parts of each of the regions. Compare the changes the slave trade brought, not just in exported slaves and loss of people by some societies to the trade, but also the gains in population for some through involvement in the slave trade. The final set of these graphs (c) projects what frequently happens to the gender and age distribution of the population in each of those societies (and among the exported slave population) after an interval of fifteen years of diminished slave trade.

These demographic models are very useful in trying to see how the slave trade might have affected total population size in various parts of Africa. Remember that total population in any society is affected not just by people who leave or join the group, but also by normal births and deaths. The models here do not measure any of these exactly, but they do give some indication of the effect of newcomers to each type of society, as well as the capacity of each to grow through births. Might the gender and age distributions have an effect on the birthrate? Thinking about these models may help you to reach some conclusions about the correlations you observed earlier between slave exports and population.

Sources 6 and 7 are woodcut drawings, from contemporary descriptions, of Dutch trade along the western coast of Africa (although not precisely the same place). They represent institutions and patterns of trade at the beginning (Source 6) and near the middle (Source 7) of the seventeenth century. Compare the two to see if you can detect any changes in the patterns and institutions of trade—which was at least partially trade in slaves—over the first half of the century. Who seems to dominate the trade in each case? How?

Two European accounts of trading for slaves along the West African coast follow the drawings. Source 8 is a very early English account; Source 9 is a Dutch narrative written over a century and a quarter later. Both not only characterize their own actions and those of their countrymen, but also paint a picture of African involvement with them in the slave trade. Try to discern what those African actions are and, if you can, what these sources suggest about the nature of African interest in supplying slaves for export. You should also consider if there were any changes in those actions and interests over time and in different regions.

Sources 10 and 11 are accounts by Africans of their capture, enslavement, and embarkation for the New World. These narratives come from a seventy-five-year period in the late eighteenth and early nineteenth centuries when the Atlantic slave trade peaked in volume. Both were written by men taken into slavery in the interior of Africa not far from the Gulf of Guinea. Read these accounts first as personal stories, seeing how the lives and experiences of the two men were both similar and different.

Then glance through the two narratives again. This time look for clues to the impact of slave trade on the societies from which these men came. What were the costs to each of the societies? Did anyone benefit from this trade? Compare these two African narratives with Source 12, Rev. H. M. Waddell's account of how abolition of the trade changed African societies at his mission station. Does Waddell's description suggest other potential costs or benefits from the slave trade?

The view of King Osei Bonsu of Ashanti, which follows in Source 13, is especially interesting, as it purports to reflect the views of Africans in the Gold Coast hinterland to the abolition of the Atlantic slave trade. While we cannot be certain that Osei Bonsu was quoted precisely by Joseph Dupuis, historians have generally accepted that this is a relatively accurate portrayal of at least some African opinion. Do you find any similarities between these statements

Chapter 6

The Atlantic

Slave Trade:

Its Impact on

West Africa

(1600–1900)

and the previous accounts, both European and African, of how the slave trade operated among the peoples of the continent?

The last narrative was written by an African who was rescued from a slave vessel on the high seas not long after leaving his mother continent. The centerpiece of this account by Bishop Samuel Crowther (Source 14) is the dramatic story of his release and return to Africa, but not back to his home. His experience of return to Africa was not uncommon, but was duplicated many times by Africans taken to Libreville, Gabon, by French warships, or to Monrovia, Liberia, by vessels of the U.S. Navy West Africa Squadron, which was charged with helping to end the Atlantic trade in slaves.

How does Crowther seem to feel about being set free? about being returned to Africa? Does he seem excited, or merely resigned, to living in a new home on the old continent? His tale may give you a window through which you might glimpse an additional aspect of the slave trade in Africa itself. Once you consider this, and the other evidence presented, you should be able to enlarge, and focus, your vision of the Atlantic slave trade. Then you will be in a better position to answer the key questions posed at the beginning of this chapter: What were the costs of the slave trade to West Africa? Were there any benefits? And what was the overall effect of the Atlantic slave trade on the peoples and societies of West Africa?

THE EVIDENCE

Source 1 from Paul E. Lovejoy, "The Volume of the Atlantic Slave Trade: A Consensus," Journal of African History *22 (1982): 494.*

1. Volume of the Atlantic Slave Trade from Africa, 1450–1900

Slave Exports from Africa: The Atlantic Trade

Period	Volume	Percent
1450–1600	367,000	3.1%
1601–1700	1,868,000	16.0
1701–1800	6,133,000	52.4
1801–1900	3,330,000	28.5
Total	11,698,000	100.0

Source 2 from E. A. Wrigley, Population and History *(New York: McGraw-Hill, 1969), p. 207.*

2. Estimated World Population Trends, 1750–2000

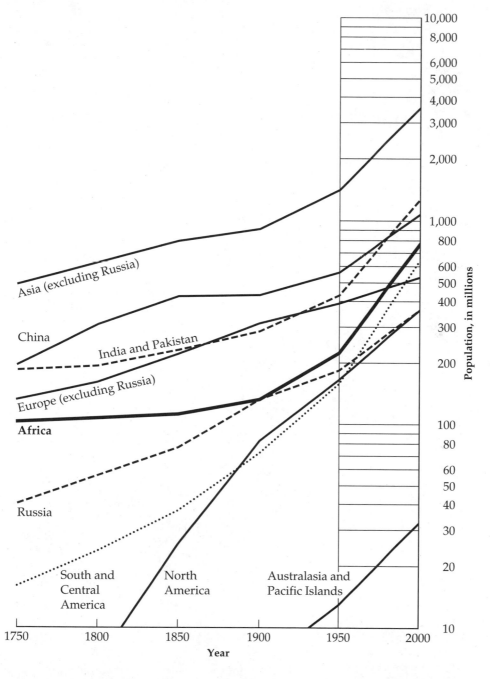

Sources 3 through 5 adapted from Patrick Manning, Slavery and African Life *(Cambridge: Cambridge University Press, 1990), pp. 10; p. 43; pp. 63–72.*

3. Principal Regions of African Slave Exports to the Atlantic Slave Trade, 1700–1900

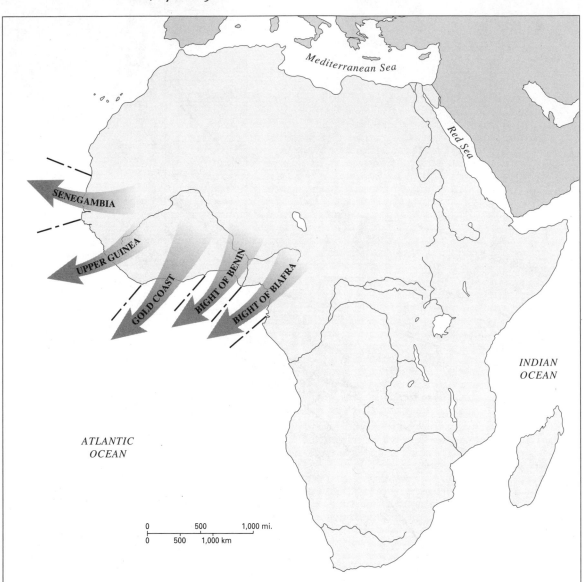

4. Total Population and Slave Exports from West Africa, by Region, 1700–1900

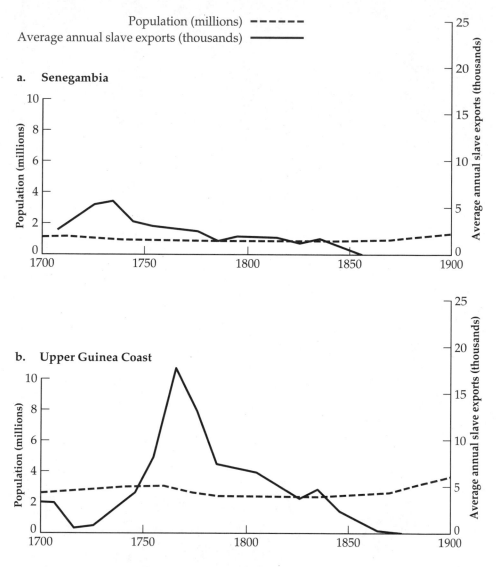

Population (millions) – – – – – –
Average annual slave exports (thousands) ————

a.   Senegambia

b.   Upper Guinea Coast

Chapter 6

The Atlantic

Slave Trade:

Its Impact on

West Africa

(1600–1900)

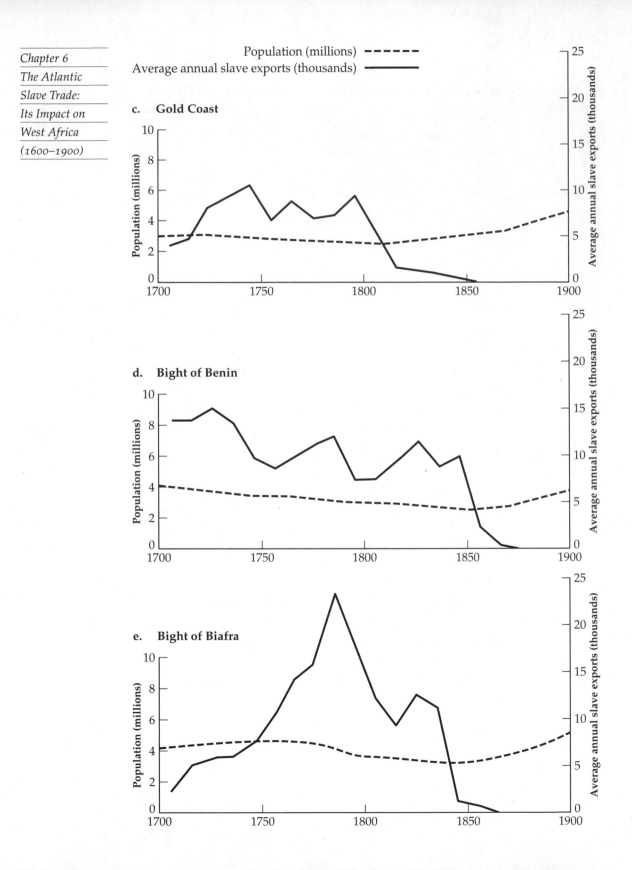

Population (millions) - - - - -
Average annual slave exports (thousands) ——————

c. **Gold Coast**

d. **Bight of Benin**

e. **Bight of Biafra**

5. Demographics in West African Societies Before, During, and After Enslavements for the Atlantic Slave Trade

a. Gender and Age Distribution Before Enslavement

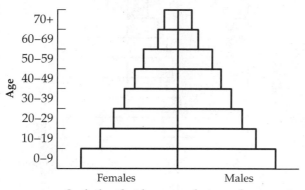

Societies that lose people to enslavement

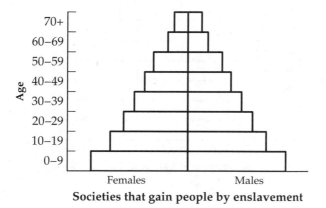

Societies that gain people by enslavement

Chapter 6

The Atlantic

Slave Trade:

Its Impact on

West Africa

(1600–1900)

**b. Gender and Age Distribution During Period
of Enslavement**

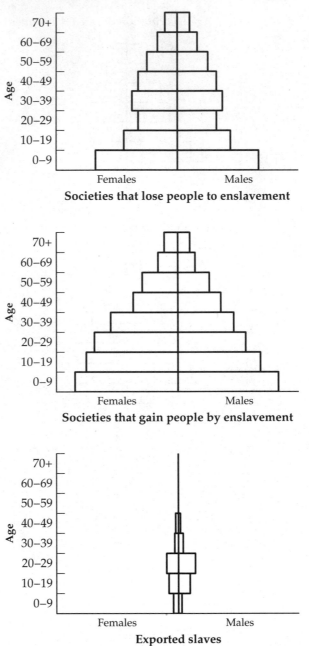

Societies that lose people to enslavement

Societies that gain people by enslavement

Exported slaves

c. **Gender and Age Distribution Fifteen Years After the End of Enslavement**

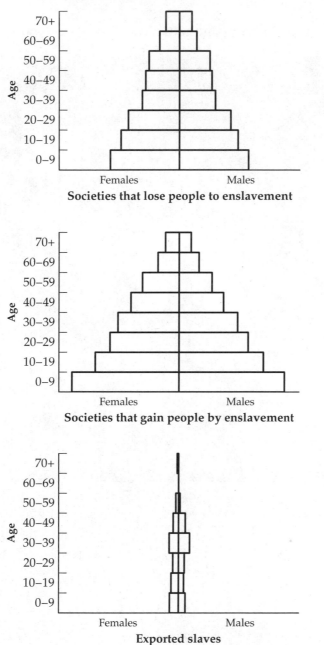

Societies that lose people to enslavement

Societies that gain people by enslavement

Exported slaves

Source 6 from DeBry, Voyages, *1601; reprinted in George Francis Dow,* Slave Ships and Slaving *(Salem, Mass.: Marine Research Society, 1927), facing p. 26. Courtesy Harvard College Library.*

6. Dutch Ships Trading on the Guinea Coast, ca. 1600

(A) Ship. (B) African merchants. (C) How goods are passed from the canoes to the shore. (D) Where the merchants have to pay a tax to the chief. (E) Canoe being carried up the beach.

Source 7 from Ogilby, Africa, *1670; reprinted in George Francis Dow,* Slave Ships and Slaving *(Salem, Mass.: Marine Research Society, 1927), facing p. 54. Courtesy Harvard College Library.*

7. Dutch Trading Castle (Fortified Commercial Station) *Cormantine* on the Gold Coast, 1600s

Chapter 6

The Atlantic

Slave Trade:

Its Impact on

West Africa

(1600–1900)

Source 8 from The Hawkins Voyages *(London: The Hakluyt Society, 1878), first series, no. 57, pp. 71–72.*

8. Sir John Hawkins Describes a Slave Trading Voyage, 1568

. . . We passed the time upon the coast of Guinea, searching with all diligence, the Rivers from Rio grande, unto Sierra Leona, till the twelfth of Januarie, in which time wee had not gotten together a hundredth and fiftie Negroes: yet notwithstanding the sickness of our men, and the late time of the yeere commanded us away, and thus having nothing wherewith to seeke the coast of the West Indies, I was with the rest of our Companie in consultation to goe to the coast of the Myne, hoping therto have obtained some golde for our wares, and thereby to have defraied our charge. But even in that present instant, there came to us a Negroe, sent from a King, oppressed by other Kings his neighbours, desiring our aide, with promise, that as many Negroes as by these wares might be obtained, as well of his part, as of ours, should be at our pleasure: whereupon we concluded to give aide, and sent 120 of our men, which the fifteenth of Januarie, assaulted a towne of the Negroes of our Allies adversaries, which had in it 8000 Inhabitants, and very strongly impaled and fenced, after their manner, but it was so well defended, that our men prevailed not but lost six men, and 40 hurt, so that our men sent forthwith to me for more helpe: whereupon considering that the good successe of this enterprise might highly further the commodotie of our voyage, I went myselfe, and with the helpe of the King of our side, assaulted the towne both by land and sea, and very hardly with fire, (their houses being covered with dry Palme leaves) obtained the towne, and put the Inhabitants to flight, where we tooke 250 persons, men, women, and children, and by our friend the King of our side, there was taken 600 prisoners, whereof we hoped to have had our choice: but the Negro (in which nation is seldome or never found truth) meant nothing lesse: for that night he removed his campe, and prisoners, so that we were faine to content us with those fewe which we had gotten our selves. Now had we obtained between 400 and 500 Negroes, wherewith we thought it somewhat reasonable to seeke the coast of the West Indies, and there, for our Negroes, and other our merchandize, we hoped to obtaine, whereof to countervaile our charges with some gaines, whereunto we proceeded with all diligence, furnished our watring, took fuell, and departed the coast of Guinea the third of Februarie.

Source 9 from William Bosman, A New Narrative and Accurate Description of the Coast of Guinea, *2nd ed., translated from the Dutch (London, 1721), reprinted in David Northrup,* The Atlantic Slave Trade *(Lexington, Mass.: D. C. Heath, 1994), pp. 71–72.*

9. William Bosman, Slave Trading at Whydah on the Bight of Benin, ca. 1700

The first business of one of our factors [agents] when he comes to Fida [Whydah], is to satisfy the customs of the king and the great men, which amounts to about a hundred pounds in Guinea value, as the goods must yield there. After which we have free license to trade, which is published throughout the whole land by the crier.

But yet before we can deal with any person, we are obliged to buy the king's whole stock of slaves at a set price, which is commonly one third or one fourth higher than ordinary; after which, we obtain free leave to deal with all his subjects, of what rank soever. But if there happen to be no stock of slaves, the factor must then resolve to run the risk of trusting the inhabitants with goods to the value of one or two hundred slaves; which commodities they send into the inland country, in order to buy with them slaves at all markets, and that sometimes two hundred miles deep in the country. For you ought to be informed, that markets of men are here kept in the same manner as those of beasts with us.

Not a few in our country fondly imagine that parents here sell their children, men their wives, and one brother the other. But those who think so, do deceive themselves; for this never happens on any other account but that of necessity, or some great crime; but most of the slaves that are offered to us, are prisoners of war, which are sold by the victors as their booty.

When these slaves come to Fida, they are put in prison all together; and when we treat concerning buying them, they are all brought out together in a large plain; where, by our surgeons, whose province it is, they are thoroughly examined, even to the smallest member, and that naked both men and women, without the least distinction or modesty. Those that are approved as good, are set on one side; and the lame or faulty are set by as invalids, which are here called *mackrons:* these are such as are above five and thirty years old, or are maimed in the arms, legs or feet; have lost a tooth, are grey-haired, or have films over their eyes; as well as all those which are affected with any venereal distemper, or several other diseases.

The invalids and the maimed being thrown out, as I have told you, the remainder are numbered, and it is entered who delivered them. In the meanwhile, a burning iron, with the arms or name of the companies, lies in the fire, with which ours are marked on the breast. This is done that we may distinguish them from the slaves of the English, French, or others (which are also

Chapter 6

The Atlantic

Slave Trade:

Its Impact on

West Africa

(1600–1900)

marked with their mark), and to prevent the Negroes exchanging them for worse, at which they have a good hand. I doubt not but this trade seems very barbarous to you, but since it is followed by mere necessity, it must go on; but we yet take all possible care that they are not burned too hard, especially the women, who are more tender than the men.

We are seldom long detained in the buying of these slaves, because their price is established, the women being one fourth or fifth part cheaper than the men. The disputes which we generally have with the owners of these slaves are, that we will not give them such goods as they ask for them, especially the *boesies* [cowry shells] (as I have told you, the money of this country) of which they are very fond, though we generally make a division on this head, in order to make one part of the goods help off another; because those slaves which are paid for in *boesies*, cost the company one half more than those bought with other goods. . . .

Source 10 from Olaudah Equiano, The Interesting Narrative of the Life of Olaudah Equiano, *ed. Robert J. Allison (New York, 1791; rpt. Boston, Bedford Books, 1995), pp. 38, 47–48, 50–54.*

10. Olaudah Equiano's Account of His Capture and Enslavement in Iboland, near the Bight of Biafra, 1756

As we live[d] in a country where nature is prodigal of her favors, our wants are few and easily supplied; of course we have . . . markets, at which I have been frequently with my mother. These are sometimes visited by stout mahogany-colored men [Africans] from the south-west of us. . . . They generally bring us fire-arms, gun-powder, hats, beads, and dried fish. . . . They always carry slaves through our land; but the strictest account is exacted of their manner of procuring them before they are suffered to pass.

Sometimes, indeed, we sold slaves to them, but they were only prisoners of war, or such among us as had been convicted of kidnapping, or adultery, and some other crimes, which we esteemed heinous. This practice of kidnapping induces me to think, that, notwithstanding all our strictness, their principal business among us was to trepan [trick] our people. . . .

One day, when all our people were gone out to their works as usual, and only I and my dear sister were left to mind the house, two men and a woman got over our walls, and in a moment seized us both, and, without giving us time to cry out, or make resistance, they stopped our mouths, and ran off with us into the nearest wood. Here they tied our hands, and continued to carry us as far as they could, till night came on. . . . The next morning we left the house, and continued travelling all the day. For a long time we had kept the woods, but at last we came into a road which I believed I knew . . . we had advanced but a little way before I discovered some people at a distance, on which I began to cry out for their assistance; but my cries had no other effect than to make them tie me faster and stop my mouth, and then they put me into a large sack. . . .

The next day proved a day of greater sorrow than I had yet experienced; for my sister and I were then separated, while we lay clasped in each other's arms. It was in vain that we besought them not to part us; she was torn from me, and immediately carried away. . . . At length, after many days' travelling, during which I had often changed masters, I got into the hands of a chieftain, in a very pleasant country. . . . Although I was a great many days' journey from my father's house, yet these people spoke exactly the same language with us. . . .

I was there I suppose about a month . . . [and then] I was again sold. I was now carried to the left of the sun's rising, through many dreary wastes and dismal woods, amidst the hideous roarings of wild beasts. . . .

I was again sold, and carried through a number of places, till after travelling a considerable time, I came to a town called Tinmah, in the most beautiful country I had yet seen in Africa. . . . Their money consisted of little white [cowrie] shells, the size of the finger nail. I was sold here for one hundred and seventy-two of them, by a merchant who lived and brought me there.

I had been about two or three days at his house, . . . [and then] I was bought of the merchant, and went home with them. . . . The next day I was washed and perfumed, and when meal time came, I was led into the presence of my mistress, and ate and drank before her with her son. . . . In this resemblance to my former happy state, I passed about two months. . . . One morning early, while my dear master and companion was still asleep, I was awakened out of my reverie to fresh sorrow, and hurried away even amongst the uncircumcised. . . .

At last I came to the banks of a large river which was covered with canoes, in which the people appeared to live with their household utensils, and provisions of all kinds. I was beyond measure astonished at this, as I had never before seen any water larger than a pond or a rivulet; and my surprise was mingled with no small fear when I was put into one of these canoes, and we began to paddle and move along the river. . . .

Thus I continued to travel, sometimes by land, sometimes by water, through different countries and various nations, till, at the end of six or seven months after I had been kidnapped, I arrived at the sea coast.

The first object which saluted my eyes when I arrived on the coast, was the sea, and a slave ship, which was then riding at anchor, and waiting for its cargo. These filled me with astonishment, which was soon converted into terror, when I was carried on board. I was immediately handled, and tossed up to see if I were sound. . . .

Chapter 6

The Atlantic

Slave Trade:

Its Impact on

West Africa

(1600–1900)

I was soon put down under the decks, and there I received such a salutation in my nostrils as I had never experienced in my life: so that, with the loathsomeness of the stench, and crying together, I became so sick and low that I was not able to eat, nor had I the least desire to taste anything. . . .

Source 11 from Joseph Wright, "Description of a Slave War," in John Beecham, Ashantee and the Gold Coast *(London: John Mason, 1841), pp. 349–356.*

11. Joseph Wright Tells of His Capture and Enslavement in Egbaland, North of the Bight of Benin, mid-1820s

I was born of respectable parents . . . we were all boys except one girl—and we all were with our parents until this last tumultuous war which was the cause of our separations. . . . All the time we heard of that war in a far distant land, we confidently thought they will not come to us. Alas . . . to our surprise, they came and besieged us round about.

. . . [S]even months after the war had besieged us, all the mighty men of war consulted together to go to another Country in order to buy us some food to preserve us children of the land. . . . At the time they left me and all my brethren, they knew not that they would never see us again in the flesh. . . .

The city was in danger of being taken every day, because there remained but women and young men and boys in the town. . . .

[*A short time later the city was overrun.*]

. . . The enemies had fully taken the city. When I saw none of them pass by my father's house to take us for slaves, I then took my brethren with me. We came out in the street, and when we walked about 50 fathoms from our house, we saw the city on fire, and before us the enemies coming in the street. We met with them, and they caught us separately.

. . . [T]he man who took me in the city took me and made a present to the chief man of war who commanded the band which he belonged to; for the custom was when any of their company went with bands of war, if he catch slaves, half of the slaves he would give to his Captain. I was with them in the camp about ten days, during which time they used to send me for fire wood.

. . . [T]he person who I then belonged to sent me home to his wife for sale, and I was with his wife one day and a half. She sent for a trade man to examine me. They stripped me naked. The man examined me all over. They went aside from me to make a bargain. In a few hours after that, the man came again. My mistress told me to go with the man and fetch some rum. Just as I went out of her sight, the man stripped me of my clothes and sent it to my mistress. Then I knew that they only deceived me by saying go with the man to fetch me some rum.

Then I went along with this man who had bought me from my mistress. The man tried to feed me and make me clean as possible for the next market day: for one day out of six is general market day. . . . Early in the morning we came to the market. Many hundreds of slaves, we were put in rows, so that we all could be seen at one view by the buyers; and in about five hours another trade man came and bought me . . . and we sailed for his home directly. We arrived about twelve o'clock in the night. The town where we had just arrived, by name of Ikko [Lagos], is the place where the Portuguese traded. Early in the morning we were brought to a white Portuguese for sale. After strict examination, the white man put me and some others aside. After that, they then made a bargain, how much he would take for each one of us. After they were well agreed, the white man sent us to the slave fold. When we entered into the slave fold, the slaves shouted for joy for having seen another of their countrymen in the fold. These are the articles the Portuguese paid for slaves: tobacco, rum, clothes, powder, gun, cutlasses, brass, iron rods, and jackey [jaki] which is our country money. . . .

I was there in the fold for about two months, with a rope on my neck. All the young boys had ropes on their necks in a row, and all the men with chains in a long row, for about fifty persons in a row, so that no one could escape without the others. At one time, the town took fire, and about fifty slaves were consumed because the entry was crowded—so that these slaves were burnt. . . .

Next day, early in the morning, we were all brought down close to salt water to be put in canoes. We all were heavy and sorrowful in heart, because we were going to leave our land for another which we never knew; and not only so, but when we saw the waves of the salt water on which we were just to enter, it discouraged us the more, for we had heard that the Portuguese were going to eat us when we got to their country.

Source 12 from Hope Masterton Waddell, Twenty-Nine Years in the West Indies and Central Africa *(London, 1863), p. 321.*

12. Hope Masterton Waddell, Slave Trading Practices at Old Calabar on the Bight of Biafra, 1847

While the foreign slave trade prevailed, the masters easily got quit of their troublesome people, and the fear of it had a deterring effect on the rest. Often

Chapter 6

The Atlantic

Slave Trade:

Its Impact on

West Africa

(1600–1900)

therefore was the wish expressed that it could be resumed, if only to the extent of one ship in the year, to let them sell off their bad people. But the effect would probably have been, if conceded, to multiply the bad people in order to sell them. It is easy for a master to make his people bad, when he wants an excuse for disposing of them. The insincerity of the parties, who wished to get rid of their "bad people" in that way, soon appeared, when I offered to take such and send them away once a year without putting them to any expense. No, no, they must have their price first.

The constant influx of new people, during the slave trade, used to keep the country in continual alarm. The masters were cruelly severe in order to break the spirit of the slaves, the latter were often desperate, sometimes ferocious. Since the trade ceased a change has appeared; and more consideration and forbearance on the one part has produced more contentment and real submission and respect on the other. No longer afraid of being sold over the great waters, or eaten at sea, as they used to believe, they are more disposed to settle in their new country, and make the best of their condition, as others have done before them.

Source 13 from Joseph Dupuis, Journal of a Residence in Ashantee *(London: Henry Colburn, 1824), pp. 162–164.*

13. King Osei Bonsu, An Ashanti View of the Slave Trade, 1820

"Now," said the king, after a pause, "I have another palaver [issue for discussion], and you must help me to talk it. A long time ago the great king [of England] liked plenty of trade, more than now; then many ships came, and they bought ivory, gold, and slaves; but now he will not let the ships come as before, and the people buy gold and ivory only. This is what I have in my head, so now tell me truly, like a friend, why does the king do so?"

"His majesty's question," I replied, "was connected with a great palaver, which my instructions did not authorise me to discuss. I had nothing to say regarding the slave trade."

"I know that too," retorted the king; "because, if my master [a diplomatic reference to the King of England] liked that trade, you would have told me so before. I only want to hear what you think as a friend: this is not like the other palavers." I was confessedly at a loss for an argument that might pass as a satisfactory reason, and the sequel proved that my doubts were not groundless. The king did not deem it plausible, that this obnoxious traffic should have been abolished from motive of humanity alone;

neither would he admit that it lessened the number either of domestic or foreign wars.

Taking up one of my observations, he remarked, "The white men who go to council with your master, and pray to the great God for him, do not understand my country, or they would not say the slave trade was bad. But if they think it bad now, why did they think it good before. Is not your law an old law, the same as the Crammo [Muslim] law? Do you not both serve the same God, only you have different fashions and customs? Crammos are strong people in fetische [powers of belief], and they say the law is good, because the great God made the book; so they buy slaves, and teach them good things, which they knew not before. This makes every body love the Crammos, and they go every where up and down, and the people give them food when they want it. Then these men come all the way from the great water [the river Niger], and from Manding, and Dagomba, and Killinga; they stop and trade for slaves, and then go home. If the great king would like to restore this trade, it would be good for the white men and for me too, because Ashantee is a country for war, and the people are strong; so if you talk that palaver for me properly, in the white country, if you go there, I will give you plenty of gold, and I will make you richer than all the white men."

I urged the impossibility of the king's request, promising, however, to record his sentiments faithfully. "Well then," said the king, "you must put down in my master's book all I shall say, and then he will look to it, now he is my friend. And when he sees what is true, he will surely restore that trade. I cannot make war to catch slaves in the bush, like a thief. My ancestors never did so. But if I fight a king, and kill him when he is insolent, then certainly I must have his gold, and his slaves, and the people are mine too. Do not the white kings act like this? Because I hear the old men say, that before I conquered Fantee and killed the Braffoes and the kings, that white men came in great ships, and fought and killed many people; and then they took the gold and slaves to the white country: and sometimes they fought together. This is all the same as these black countries. The great God and the fetische made war for strong men every where, because then they can pay plenty of gold and proper sacrifice. When I fought Gaman, I did not make war for slaves, but because Dinkera [the king] sent me an arrogant message and killed my people, and refused to pay me gold as his father did. Then my fetische made me strong like my ancestors, and I killed Dinkera, and took his gold, and brought more than 20,000 slaves to Coomassy. Some of these people being bad men, I washed my stool in their blood for the fetische. But then some were good people, and these I sold or gave to my captains: many, moreover, died, because this country does not grow too much corn like Sarem, and what can I do? Unless I kill or sell them, they will grow strong and kill my people. Now you must tell my master that these slaves can work for him, and if he wants 10,000 he can have them. And if he wants fine handsome girls and women to give his captains, I can send him great numbers."

Chapter 6

The Atlantic

Slave Trade:

Its Impact on

West Africa

(1600–1900)

Source 14 from letter of Samuel Crowther to William Jewett, 1837, in Journals of the Rev. James Frederick Schon and Mr. William Crowther *(London, 1842), pp. 381–384.*

14. Bishop Samuel Crowther, Rescue from a Portuguese Slave Vessel, 1822

[*Several months after being captured and enslaved in the interior, Crowther was taken to the coast near Lagos on the Bight of Benin, where he and other slaves waited to be shipped across the Atlantic.*]

. . . [W]e were embarked, at night, in canoes . . . to the beach; and on the following morning we were put on board the vessel, which immediately sailed away. . . . On the very same evening, we were surprised by two English men-of-war; and on the next morning found ourselves in the hands of new conquerors, whom we at first much dreaded, they being armed with long swords.

. . . Very soon after breakfast, we were divided into several of the vessels around us. This was now cause of new fears, not knowing where our misery would end. Being now, as it were, one family, we began to take leave of those who were first transshipped, not knowing what would become of them and ourselves. It was not long before we . . . were conveyed into the *Myrmidon,* in which we discovered not any trace of those who were transshipped before us. We soon came to a conclusion of what had become of them, when we saw parts of a hog hanging, the skin of which was white—a thing we never saw before; for a hog was always roasted on fire, to clear it of the hair, in my country; and a number of cannonshots were arranged along the deck. The former we supposed to be flesh, and the latter the heads of the individuals who had been killed for meat. But we were undeceived, by a close examination of the flesh with cloven foot, which resembled that of a hog; and, by a cautious approach to the shot, that they were iron. . . .

One of the brigs, which contained a part of the slaves, was wrecked on a sand-bank: happily, another vessel was near, and all the lives were saved. It was not long before another brig sunk, during a tempest, with all the slaves and sailors, with the exception of about five of the latter, who were found in a boat after four or five days, reduced to almost mere skeletons, and were so feeble, that they could not stand on their feet. One hundred and two of our number were lost on this occasion.

After nearly two months and a half cruising on the coast, we were landed at Sierra Leone, on the 17th of June 1822. The same day we were sent to Bathurst, formerly Leopold, under the care of Mr. [Thomas] Davey. Here we had the pleasure of meeting many of our country people, but none were known before. They assured us of our liberty and freedom; and we very soon believed them. But a few days after our arrival at Bathurst, we had the mortification of being sent for at Freetown, to testify against our Portuguese owner. It being hinted to us that we should be delivered up to him again, notwithstanding all the persuasion of Mr. Davey that we should return, we entirely refused to go ourselves, unless we were carried. . . .

QUESTIONS TO CONSIDER

In many ways, dealing with the evidence in this chapter will require you to draw a number of inferences from sometimes slender threads of evidence. This is not an uncommon task faced by historians, especially when the narrative record is incomplete, as it is in seeking African accounts of the slave trade. When they turn to statistical data, and the mathematical projections that may be derived from it, historians must also take care to consider only those kinds of questions that the evidence can help answer. Sometimes, the results of such inquiries must be, simply, that we do not know. Yet it would be an error to reach such a conclusion too quickly.

In approaching this evidence concerning the Atlantic slave trade, you will need to keep such considerations in mind. For example, based on the information you have here, it would be unproductive to consider how many Egba people (for example) were taken into slavery. Likewise, you should resist the temptation to make a quick judgment about general effects of the slave trade on Africa as compared to the rest of the world. But you should consider several other questions about numbers of slaves. What were the general time

patterns of the slave trade? Does it appear that these patterns coincide with other events in world history, such as major wars or revolutions?

You may also find it fruitful to break down the problem into smaller parts. When were the most slaves exported from each of the coastal regions? Does this correlate with any shifts in the population of those areas? Might some parts of western Africa have been affected more than others? Would this relate at all to the distance the slave trade penetrated into the interior?

Then, consider the narrative evidence. Was population change, specifically population loss, the most important cost of the slave trade? Did any African societies suffer other ill effects? How did those societies respond? Or was the slave trade more significant for individual Africans and their families? Did any Africans benefit from the slave trade? In what ways? Just as individuals? Or were there benefits to whole societies?

As you answer these questions, it may be helpful to group the evidence by region, accumulating both narrative and demographic data for each of the trading areas delineated in the sources. Do you have more, or even better, evidence from some areas than others? Apart from the limitations imposed by the selections made for this

Chapter 6

The Atlantic

Slave Trade:

Its Impact on

West Africa

(1600–1900)

chapter, can you suggest any reasons for such discrepancies? Is there any evidence to suggest that you might make broader generalizations from the information you have at hand?

Having worked through these questions, you may now be ready to examine some more subtle issues. Is there any evidence of social changes among these African societies? If so, what were they, and how extensive? Were they likely to have had long-term or short-term consequences? Think both about demographic shifts you identified as well as the depictions of African life contained in some of the narratives and illustrations. Then, use similar techniques to consider the political sphere. Can you see any evidence of political change wrought by the slave trade? Did the trade bring any political ad-vantages or shifts in power relationships? Keep in mind the descriptions of African societies you read early in this chapter as you answer this last group of questions.

Finally, consider the issue of winners and losers. In which category does West Africa better fit? Were there both gains and losses, winners and losers? On balance, do you think West Africans gained more than they lost? Or was the Atlantic slave trade more a destructive force on the continent and its peoples? When you have reached this point, you should be able to answer the central questions posed for this chapter: What were the costs of the slave trade to West Africa? Were there any benefits? And what was the overall effect of the Atlantic slave trade on the peoples and societies of West Africa?

EPILOGUE

The slave trade, like slavery itself, is a subject that sparks many emotions. Humanitarian—and moral—concerns have been a key element in the questions surrounding these topics for centuries. Yet historians must try to find ways to reduce the emotional elements in their study of the slave trade, while at the same time acknowledging the moral dimensions of the topic. That balance is essential to increasing our understanding.

By approaching the question of effects through examination of measurable change, and not merely descriptions of change, we can begin such a process. It is certainly true that numbers, and data derived from them, have no inherent moral authority. Neither do they have a distinct superiority as a kind of evidence. But statistical data and demographic information do give us an opportunity to step back from a question—such as the effects of the slave trade on West Africa—and think more clearly about what it means, free from the more volatile, emotional context of written and spoken words.

Doing this, we need not conclude that the Atlantic slave trade was a positive good; our moral conscience tells us it was not. Nor must we see it as an unmitigated evil. Looking at Africa itself and the place of the traffic in human beings on life within Africa, we are likely to find both. Suffering, without doubt, was both a personal and social result. Individual and societal potential most assuredly were left unfulfilled. And the slave trade undoubtedly limited the capacity for African cultural achievement and advancement.

But there were other consequences, as well. Without the slave trade, some African societies would not have achieved the fascinating cultural complexities admired by the world; the Ashanti, about whom you have read, are but one example. Without the slave trade, some individual Africans would never have achieved their potential as leaders of their people; Bishop William Crowther, part of whose autobiography you read, comes to mind. In one sense, then, the defenders of the slave trade were right: the institution did have a significant influence on Africans. But it was definitely not in providing them a new life away from the pernicious influences of their homeland. Rather, the Atlantic slave trade reshaped parts of Africa itself, some more than others, in ways ultimately determined by Africans themselves.

CHAPTER SEVEN

THE LIBERATOR-HERO AND

WESTERN REVOLUTIONS (1770s–1810s)

During the late eighteenth century, successful revolts, failed uprisings, and both real and imagined revolutionary plots swept across much of Europe and the Americas. While visiting her native city of Liège in 1791, Théroinge de Méricourt, a woman who sympathized with and participated in the early stages of the French Revolution, was arrested and imprisoned by the Austrians. Believing she was a spy, the Austrians interrogated her, without success, and then sent for the prison doctor, who diagnosed her as suffering from "revolutionary fever."[1] In the eyes of many, Méricourt was not the only person struck down with "revolutionary fe-

ver." Indeed, according to historian R. R. Palmer, English conservative Edmund Burke "was so afraid of invasion and revolution . . . that he gave orders for his remains to be secretly buried, lest triumphant democrats dig them up for desecration."[2]

Whatever their differences, the Western revolutionaries of the late eighteenth century were an extremely self-conscious lot. Convinced that they were altering history, for their own people as well as for all the world, these revolutionists wanted to justify their revolts as the fulfillment of a higher purpose (rather than a mere grab for power), as well as to pass on to future generations what they consid-

1. Théroinge de Méricourt, real name Anne-Joseph Méricourt (1762–1817), was one of the many fascinating participants in the French Revolution. See Simon Schama, *Citizens: A Chronicle of the French Revolution* (New York: Alfred A. Knopf, 1989), pp. 462–463, 530, 605, 611, 873–875.

2. R. R. Palmer, *The Age of the Democratic Revolution: A Political History of Europe and America, 1760–1800*, 2 vols. (Princeton: Princeton University Press, 1959), vol. I, p. 5. According to Palmer, revolutions, threats of revolutions, or plots took place in what was to become the United States as well as in France, Ireland, the Netherlands, Switzerland, Milan, Rome, Naples, Poland, Hungary, Greece, Ecuador, Brazil, what would become Haiti, and in some of the German states.

ered to be the true essence or meaning of their respective revolutions.

One way they were able to accomplish both objectives was through the creation of a *liberator-hero*, a person who could be a *symbol* of the revolution both to contemporaries and to future generations. Through the use of speeches, eulogies, memorials, pageants, paintings, and statuary, the major essences, goals, and events of the Western revolutions were personified, and myths about these revolutions were created and imbued in their liberator-heroes.

In this chapter you will examine the creation of three liberator-heroes: George Washington of the American Revolution, Jean-Paul Marat of the French Revolution, and Toussaint Louverture of the Haitian Revolution. Using eulogies and contemporary portraits, you will be asked to analyze how the participants in each revolution attempted to fashion a liberator-hero who symbolized the character, goals, and nature of the revolution as the participants themselves understood it *and* as they wanted others to see it. How was George Washington used by his contemporaries as a symbol of the American Revolution? Jean-Paul Marat of the French Revolution? Toussaint Louverture of the Haitian Revolution? Although these revolutions had much in common and in many ways were intertwined, the American, French, and Haitian revolutions were profoundly different.

BACKGROUND

In Britain's North American colonies, a struggle for home rule evolved into a war for separation. In the 1760s and early 1770s an increasing number of people in Britain's North American colonies began to oppose taxation by the mother country, as well as what they feared was an erosion of their political rights. In 1775 these protests erupted into open warfare, and in the next year the colonies declared their independence from Great Britain and their intention to form a new nation. Independence and nationhood, however, were not actually achieved until the British gave up the armed struggle in 1781 and grudgingly recognized the former colonies' independence in 1783. For their part, the colonial elites who had led the fight for independence (New England and Middle Colonies merchants and lawyers and southern planters) did not want the war to be accompanied by democratic reforms, and were able to prevent such an upsurge by forming a new government that favored rule by the elite, property qualifications for voting, and other conservative measures.

After the opening battles of what would become the American Revolution (at Lexington and Concord on April 19, 1775, later referred to by Ralph Waldo Emerson as "the shot heard 'round the world"), revolutionary leaders in Britain's North

Chapter 7

The Liberator-

Hero and

Western

Revolutions

(1770s–1810s)

American colonies[3] realized they needed a military leader who could organize the ragtag militia besieging the British forces in Boston into what would become the Continental Army. Reasoning that a man from the southern colonies would give the rebellion the unity it needed, Congress named forty-three-year-old George Washington of Virginia. Washington was born on February 11, 1732,[4] into Virginia's minor gentry. Trained as a surveyor, as a young man his goal was a commission in the regular British army. The intercession of a friend secured Washington an officership in the Virginia militia and the potentially dangerous assignment (at the age of only twenty-one) of delivering to the French, poised along the western frontier, an ultimatum to leave what Virginians believed was British territory. The following year (1754), Washington, now a colonel in the militia, returned to the frontier to challenge the French, but he was forced to surrender a fort he had constructed (Fort Necessity, in present-day western Pennsylvania) and to return to eastern Virginia.

In 1755 Washington became an aide to General Edward Braddock, who led a force of 1,400 British regulars and 450 colonial militiamen on an expedition to capture Fort Duquesne (present-day Pittsburgh) in western Pennsylvania. About eight miles below the fort, the army was attacked and defeated by a combined force of Frenchmen and Native Americans. Braddock was mortally wounded, and Washington led the remnant of the force to safety, an accomplishment that earned him an international reputation. But in 1758, frustrated by his inability to secure a commission in the British army as well as by insufficient support for the Virginia militia's campaign in the West, he resigned his militia post and retired to his home, Mount Vernon.

Although not in the forefront of colonial leaders who urged resistance to the mother country, Washington was so well-known that he was elected to most of the major colonial congresses that met to protest British policies and, as noted above, was a popular choice to command the American army formed after the outbreak of hostilities at Lexington and Concord.

George Washington's principal accomplishments were organizing what became the United States Army (called the Continental Line and never numbering more than 18,000 troops); preventing desertions from decimating that force (he once wrote, "We shall have to detach half of the army to look for the other half"); and keeping that force in the field for six years of skirmishes and battles, many of which were lost. The British, however, faced with the defeat of General Cornwallis at Yorktown in 1781 and mounting opposition to the war at

3. Canada was invited to join Britain's thirteen other North American colonies in the rebellion, but refused. See Justin H. Smith, *Our Struggle for the Fourteenth Colony: Canada and the American Revolution*, 2 vols. (New York: G. P. Putnam's Sons, 1907). See also George A. Rawlyk, *Revolution Rejected, 1775–1776* (Scarborough, Ont.: Prentice-Hall, 1968).

4. When the English changed from the Julian to the Gregorian calendar in 1752, eleven days were added to the calendar to realign it with the sun and stars. Therefore, Washington's birthday became February 22.

home, were forced to give up the struggle. After once again retiring to Mount Vernon, Washington was called back to service as the Constitutional government's first president (the article of the Constitution dealing with the executive branch was written with Washington in mind, hoping that he would accept the position). Having retired yet again in 1797, he died on December 14, 1799. By then, he was generally being referred to as the "father of his country," and was enshrined as the liberator-hero of the United States, the symbol of the successful American Revolution.

The French Revolution was the result of the convergence of several problems that overtook the French monarchy in the 1780s. The most critical of these problems was the government's fiscal bankruptcy. As a consequence of the costly wars of the eighteenth century and a system of taxation that virtually exempted the nobility and the clergy from fiscal obligations, the French monarchy was deeply in debt by 1787.[5] Several finance ministers struggled with the crown's debts (which by 1788 had reached 4 billion livres and took 51 percent of the government's total revenues just to make the interest payments), but eventually all of them arrived at the same conclusion: bankruptcy could be avoided only through fundamental reforms that

would tax the Church and nobility and not just the commoners.

In proposing such changes, however, the finance ministers encountered opposition from the noble judges of the great law courts (the *parlements*) who had to approve any new royal laws before they could be enforced. Such basic changes in taxation policy, they alleged, had to be approved by a nationwide representative body, and their objections forced the king to call for a meeting in 1789 of the Estates General, an elected assembly that had not met since 1614.

The election of 1789 was held in a country suffering from enormous economic problems. Since 1705 France's population had increased by 24.5 percent, with no corresponding increase in the food supply. Poor harvests in 1788 and 1789 and a commercial depression in 1789 only made matters worse. Inflation of prices had increased the cost of living for the working person by 62 percent over the eighteenth century, while wages for construction workers had risen only 24 percent and agricultural workers' wages a meager 16 percent. Nearly 40 percent of France's population in 1789 was destitute, living by squatting on land they did not own, begging, charity, or crime.

The result of France's economic and political problems was the election of an Estates General that was prepared to seek far more than tax reform. When Louis XVI refused to approve voting rules for the Estates General that would have assured the representatives of the commoners (known as the Third Estate) a chance

5. France's successful intervention in the American Revolution had cost the French government 2 billion livres, a figure that was four times the government's tax receipts in 1788.

Chapter 7

The Liberator-

Hero and

Western

Revolutions

(1770s–1810s)

at enacting tax reform and of realizing some degree of political equality with the clergy and the nobility (the First and Second Estates), the king encountered the first act of revolution. Declaring themselves a National Assembly and the rightful representatives of all the French people, the representatives of the Third Estate pledged to draft a written constitution that would clearly limit royal authority—in essence making Louis XVI a constitutional monarch. When the king countered by ordering troops to disperse the National Assembly, the people of Paris took up arms and seized the strategically important fort and prison the Bastille on July 14, 1789. In the countryside, peasants attacked the castles and manor houses of their noble lords and broke into grain storage facilities.

Faced with mounting opposition and rising violence, Louis XVI ostensibly agreed to live within a new constitutional order. Taking the king at his word, the National Assembly began work on a constitution that would have made France a constitutional monarchy. But Louis never really accepted the new constitutional order, and in 1791 he attempted to flee to eastern France to assume leadership of counterrevolutionary forces. Captured and forcibly returned to Paris where he was virtually made a prisoner in his own country, Louis's situation was hopeless. In September 1792, the republic was proclaimed, Louis XVI was tried for treason and condemned in December 1792, and the monarch went to the guillotine on January 16, 1793. His wife Marie An-

toinette (who probably never said, "Let them eat cake") followed soon thereafter and their son, next in line to the now nonexistent throne, died in prison in 1795.

Jean-Paul Marat was among the Jacobin radicals who were supported by the shopkeepers and craftsmen of Paris, known as *sans-culottes*,[6] in their regicide[7] and their search for other enemies of the revolution. Marat was born on May 24, 1743, the oldest of six children in a lower-middle-class family (the family's original name had been Mara, but Jean-Paul changed his name to appear more French). Later admitting that his dominant passion was a love of glory (*amour de la gloire*), Marat became a prosperous physician who treated the wealthy and published his research on the medical properties of electricity. His friends called him a brilliant doctor-scientist-philosopher, while his detractors dubbed him a desperate charlatan. Drifting toward radicalism (driven, perhaps, by his rejection for admission to the Academy of Sciences), in February 1789 Marat published an attack on the government, calling for a constitutional monarchy with full political rights to the peo-

6. *sans-culottes* (**without breeches**): the shopkeepers and craftsmen of Paris so named because they wore clothing characteristic of their social group. Their garb included pants that extended to their shoe tops and not the elegant knee breeches of aristocrats. This group was unified by more than just a common mode of dress, however. It espoused a political ideology of direct democracy and an economic policy of government regulation of wages and prices to protect its economic security.

7. **Regicide**: the killing of a king.

ple. In September 1789, he began to publish his newspaper *L'Ami du Peuple* (*The Friend of the People*).

From the first, *L'Ami du Peuple* echoed Marat's fears of plots against the Revolution by its enemies, and his responses to such plots became increasingly radical. As early as October 1789 he called for a revolutionary dictatorship that would preserve the Revolution's gains. One month earlier, Marat declared that "five or six hundred heads cut off would have assured you peace, liberty and happiness." But by May 27, 1791, he had raised that number: "today fifty thousand would be necessary" to protect the Revolution. Seen by his opponents as a dangerous radical and blamed by the police for instigating an October 1789 march on the royal palace at Versailles, Marat was forced into hiding and fled briefly to England, but he soon returned to France. Continuing to publish his newspaper, Marat gained more power when he was elected to the National Convention in 1792.

Marat supported *sans-culottes* ideals of direct democracy, aid to the economically disadvantaged funded by a progressive income tax, state-sponsored vocational schools, and shorter terms of military service. These positions won him the support of the Parisian *sans-culottes* and the enmity of the more moderate Girondin faction in the Convention. Indeed, the Girondins secured Marat's indictment on charges of inciting insurrection, but he was acquitted of these capital charges and gained his revenge by playing a major role in the Parisian insurrection that purged the Convention of its Girondin members on June 2, 1793.

After June 2, 1793, Marat was much less active politically. He was dying from skin and lung diseases, and was forced to spend long hours in medicinal baths in his Paris apartment. It was there that he was visited by a young woman named Charlotte Corday on July 13, 1793. Corday was a Girondist sympathizer who had become convinced that radicals like Marat were destroying the Revolution. Gaining admission to Marat's bathroom by claiming to have information on counterrevolutionary plots, she stabbed the revolutionary leader to death. Apprehended immediately, the twenty-five-year-old Corday was guillotined on July 17. A magnificent funeral and numerous eulogies turned Jean-Paul Marat into a revolutionary martyr and a liberator-hero. The ceremonies would have lasted longer but, in the hot Paris summer, Marat's body began to decompose. His embalmed heart was hung from the ceiling of the Cordeliers Club, but the remainder of Marat was quickly buried in the club's garden.

The search for enemies of the revolution led to the Reign of Terror of 1793–1794 in which perhaps as many as 40,000 citizens lost their lives. And their search for a secular state in which the Church would have no influence led the radicals to scrap the traditional calendar based on the Christian year in favor of a new revolutionary calendar that began counting years from 1791, when the new constitution came into force.

Chapter 7

The Liberator-

Hero and

Western

Revolutions

(1770s–1810s)

True stability, however, continued to elude France. Recurrent coups marked the rest of the decade until Napoleon Bonaparte's seizure of power in 1799 restored some measure of political stability.

Christopher Columbus had landed on the island he named Hispaniola (Little Spain) on December 6, 1492, and he claimed it for Spain.[8] French settlers began moving into the western part of the island in the late 1600s, and the Treaty of Ryswick (1697) officially divided the island between the two European nations, the French calling their portion Saint-Domingue and the Spanish calling theirs Santo Domingo. Gradually the French developed a plantation system with approximately 3,000 plantations that raised sugar, coffee, cotton, and indigo. The Native American population, not immune to European diseases, was virtually wiped out. The French planters, therefore, relied on slave labor from Africa, importing over 800,000 Africans between 1680 and 1776. By 1787, the population of Saint-Domingue was composed of around 24,000 whites, 408,000 black slaves (approximately two-thirds of whom were African born, largely from the Congo and Angola), and 20,000 *gens de couleur* (mulattos and free blacks).

The death toll among the slave population was enormous; thus planters had to import Africans con-tinuously to keep up the labor pool. Largely because a significant majority of the slave population had been born in freedom in Africa, slave resistance was a regular feature of life in the French colony. A large revolt took place in 1522 and four other armed conspiracies occurred between 1679 and 1704. Runaway slaves hid in the mountains, where, according to one European observer in 1705, "[t]hey gather together in the woods and live there exempt from service to their masters without any other leader but one elected among them." African culture among the slaves and run-aways remained both vital and durable, including the practice of voodoo, an African form of worship that the French tried in vain to eradicate but that formed an important bond among the blacks—even those who had nominally been converted to the Catholic faith. In 1757 another widespread rebellion, the Makandal conspiracy, broke out. Involving mostly African-born slaves, it sought to overthrow the white masters and win political independence. Crushed by the white planters, the conspirators were burned at the stake.

The French Revolution provided the opportunity for another revolt. Aware of revolutionary events in France, in 1791 mulattos sent a delegation to the National Assembly in Paris to secure the rights enumerated in France's Declaration of the Rights of Man and Citizen (1789). Being refused, mulattos rebelled against the white planters but were quickly overcome, as they had been in an earlier revolt in October 1790. Leaders of the

8. The origin of the name Haiti is somewhat unclear. Many scholars believe that the Native American Arawaks who were living on the island when Columbus arrived called the island Haiti. But other scholars of the region disagree.

uprising were executed and then decapitated, their heads placed on poles which were left standing for around three years as a warning to other would-be revolutionaries.

Once again, however, the French Revolution intruded on life in Saint-Domingue. Later in 1791, the National Assembly granted rights to all mulattos and all blacks born of free parents. When news of the National Assembly's actions reached the Caribbean colony (on June 30, 1791), whites were enraged. Civil war once again broke out between mulattos and whites.

In August 1791, the situation became even more complex—and bloody—by an uprising of the slaves. Many whites fled to U.S. seaports like Savannah, Charleston, and Baltimore, terrifying American plantation owners with reports of burning plantations, widespread killing, and atrocities. By 1793, slaves had built up an army of between 4,000 and 5,000 troops who were fierce, courageous, and tactically brilliant fighters. Led by Toussaint Louverture, this army beat back an attempted British invasion, a Spanish intrusion from Santo Domingo, and another uprising of mulattos in 1799.

François-Dominique Toussaint à Bréda was born on May 20, 1743, on the Bréda plantation in Saint-Domingue. The oldest of eight children, Toussaint's father had been born in Africa, captured in a war, and sold into slavery in the New World. Taught to read and write by a Roman Catholic priest, Toussaint was given more and more responsibility on the plantation until he was made coach-man and livestock steward; the plantation's overseer (the owner lived in Paris) gave him forty acres and thirteen slaves to manage. Permitted to marry (a rarity for slaves in Saint-Domingue), Toussaint wed Suzanne Simone Baptiste, and the union produced two sons. Therefore, although Toussaint was technically a slave and no manumission papers ever were drawn up, essentially he was looked upon and treated as a free man (*affranchi*).

When the slave rebellion first broke out in August 1791, Toussaint played only a minor role and was believed to be conservative in his thinking (he had helped his plantation's white factor, or agent, escape from a mob of ex-slaves). Gradually his powerful and articulate speeches to the troops (Toussaint spoke both the Creole patois and his father's African tribal language, in addition to French) and his charisma, tactical genius, and emphasis on training and discipline lifted him to the position of commander of the rebellion.

Seeing an opportunity to drive the French from Saint-Domingue, Toussaint briefly sided with the Spanish. It was at this time that he wrote a letter to blacks and signed it Toussaint Louverture, which means *the opening*. "I thought it was a good name for bravery," Toussaint reflected. But when he learned that the National Convention in Paris had abolished slavery (in February 1794), he switched sides and led his army against the Spanish and the British invaders, both of whom gave up the fight. In 1796 Toussaint was named lieutenant governor of Saint-Domingue, put down an uprising of the mulattos in

Chapter 7

The Liberator-

Hero and

Western

Revolutions

(1770s–1810s)

1800, and in 1801 issued a constitution for the republic.

And yet Toussaint believed that Haiti's economic future was tied to that of France. In 1802, Napoleon Bonaparte revived French ambitions for an empire in the Western Hemisphere. Intending to reap enormous profits from the sugar and coffee trade and determined to restore slavery in order to do it, Napoleon sent a French invading army to the island in 1802. When the French army invaded the island in 1802, Toussaint, foolishly, was prepared to welcome it. His two sons were being educated in France (they were received by the Empress Josephine) and he had tried to convince the ex-slaves to adopt French ways (he criticized the low necklines of Haitian women's dresses).

Tricked into surrendering, Toussaint was hustled off to a prison in France (Fort de Joux), where he died on April 7, 1803. His entreaties to meet with Napoleon had gone unheeded. Yet the Haitians ultimately won their independence from the French, and Toussaint Louverture became the symbol of the revolution, the liberator-hero.

The French army, decimated by yellow fever, was forced to withdraw from Haiti, ending Napoleon's dreams of an American empire. It was at that point that he offered to sell the Louisiana Territory to the United States. The Republic of Haiti (so named in 1804) had secured its independence, but the instability and terror of the revolution did not cease for decades.

Thus each revolution—the American, the French, and the Haitian—chose a person who could stand as the symbol and the essence of its respective revolution. Your task in this chapter is to analyze how each liberator-hero was portrayed by his contemporaries, through eulogies and portraits, and how each portrayal informs us about the nature of each of the momentous revolutions of the eighteenth century.

THE METHOD

In his provocative book *The Hero in History: A Study in Limitation and Possibility*, historian Sidney Hook observed that the "history of every nation is represented to its youth in terms of the exploits of great individuals— mythical or real. . . . The splendor, the power, the fame of the leader are shared imaginatively. New elements of meaning enter the lives of those who are emotionally impoverished."[9] When those nations are created by revolutions (as were the United States, France, and Haiti), the leader is portrayed as the liberator-hero.

Revolutions have several means at their disposal to create and shape the image of the liberator-hero that they want to pass on to their contempo-

9. Sidney Hook, *The Hero in History: A Study in Limitation and Possibility* (New York: Humanities Press, 1943), pp. 8, 22.

raries as well as to future generations. Special holidays, statuary, commemorative postage stamps, songs, and dramas are only a few of the ways that the image of the liberator-hero can be created and shaped. Two especially effective methods, however, are eulogies of the hero and paintings. How the liberator-hero is portrayed in eulogies and in comtemporary paintings can give us excellent clues as to how revolutionary leaders wanted others to see the essence or meaning of the revolution they had fomented.

Source 1, the eulogy to George Washington, is probably the most widely circulated of the more than four hundred that were delivered and published. It was commissioned by the Massachusetts legislature and delivered in Boston's Old South Meeting House by Fisher Ames on February 8, 1800.[10] Ames (1758–1808) was an attorney, a former congressman from Massachusetts, and a well-known conservative ally of Washington and Alexander Hamilton. How does Ames portray Washington? When he spoke of Washington conducting "a civil war with mildness, and a revolution with order," Ames was telling his listeners (and, later, his readers) how *he* wanted them to think about the nature of the American Revolution. How did he want people to view that revolution? To Ames, what was the true glory of the American Revolution? As you read

the eulogy carefully, think about how Ames was trying to portray Washington as the liberator-hero of the United States.

Jean-Paul Marat was murdered by Charlotte Corday when the French Revolution was in its most radical phase, the Terror of 1793–1794. Source 3 is the eulogy for Marat that was delivered to the National Convention by a Marat ally, F. E. Guiraut. Not much is known about Guiraut except that he was a member of the Paris Jacobin Club and a leader in the Social Contract Section of Paris. His eulogy of Marat seems to have been the most widely circulated tribute, appearing in pamphlet form and in the official bulletin of the Convention. How did Guiraut portray Marat as a liberator-hero? Using that portrayal, what did Guiraut (and, presumably, Marat) *want* the essence of the French Revolution to be? The name of the newspaper Marat published was *L'Ami du Peuple (The Friend of the People)*. How do Guiraut's word plays on that title give you some important clues?

No formal eulogy of Toussaint Louverture is known to exist and, since he died in a French prison, it is possible that none ever was delivered. Source 5, however, is quite close to a eulogy, part of an 1814 manifesto written by Henri Christophe (1767–1820). A follower of Toussaint, Christophe was born in the British West Indies (either Grenada or St. Kitts), taken to the French colony of Saint-Domingue, sold to a free black who owned a stable, was permitted to purchase his freedom, and became a waiter in a hotel. In 1811, eight years

---

10. The New York Public Library has collected 266 of the 440 Washington eulogies that still exist.

Chapter 7

The Liberator-

Hero and

Western

Revolutions

(1770s–1810s)

after Toussaint's death, Christophe proclaimed himself Henri I, King of Haiti. His 1814 manifesto was intended to rally Haitians to repulse a threatened French invasion of the island. What lessons did Christophe intend that his readers learn from the life of Toussaint? Toussaint attempted to create a Haiti in which whites, blacks, and mulattos could live in freedom and relative equality. What did Christophe think of Toussaint's goal? Finally, what does Christophe see as the true meaning of the Haitian Revolution?

With a bit of practice, portraits of liberator-heroes can be "read" by historians in order to understand how revolutionary leaders (through the artist) sought to create and shape the image of the liberator-hero and the image of the revolution as well. Examine each portrait carefully, noting how the subject is posed and dressed. Do other objects in the painting help to create and shape the image of the subject? Unlike photographs (especially those that appear in newspapers or magazines), nothing in a portrait is there by chance.

Source 2 is a painting of George Washington by Gilbert Stuart (1755–1828), one of the most noted portraitists of his time. Washington sat for the painting on April 12, 1796, and the work was finished the next year. Measuring almost eight feet by five feet, the painting is filled with clues. First of all, since Washington's role in the American Revolution was primarily a military one, why didn't Stuart choose to paint his subject in uniform and astride a horse (many portraitists of Washington did just that)? Also, examine closely Wash-

ington's facial expression. He had just purchased new dentures, which obviously did not fit well, but look beyond that. Look closely at his clothing, his pose, the books on the floor, the table leg, the chair in the background, the sheathed sword in Washington's hand. What clues do each of these provide? What is the overall image that Stuart sought to convey of Washington? Of the American Revolution?[11]

Source 4 is a painting of Marat by Jacques Louis David (1748–1825), undoubtedly France's best-known Neoclassical painter and an ardent supporter of the French Revolution. Given to oratorical outbursts almost as inflammatory as those of Marat himself, as an elected deputy to the National Convention he urged the statues of Louis XIV and Louis XV be destroyed and voted for the execution of Louis XVI. David arranged the pageant that accompanied Marat's funeral and presented his portrait of Marat to the National Convention on November 13, 1793. One knowledgeable critic has called it "one of the world's most skillfully executed propaganda pictures."[12]

11. Washington sat for Stuart to paint the portrait's head only. Various models later posed for Stuart to paint the body. This particular portrait (Stuart actually did three portraits of Washington, plus numerous copies), known as the Lansdowne portrait, was sold to William Bingham to be hung at his country house (Lansdowne) outside Philadelphia. A copy was painted for a British friend of America. In 1800 the U.S. government purchased the painting for $800.

12. David Lloyd Dowd, *Pageant-Master of the Republic: Jacques-Louis David and the French Revolution* (Lincoln: University of Nebraska, 1948), p. 107.

David could have painted Marat addressing the National Convention, or writing articles for his newspaper, or addressing a crowd of Paris *sansculottes*. And yet he chose to show his hero and political ally at the moment of his gruesome death, complete with bath water tinted with Marat's blood, the bloody wound, the knife on the floor, and the note Charlotte Corday had used to gain entrance to Marat's apartment in his hand. Why did he choose to do this? It is important to note that the macabre scene is historically inaccurate, since Marat's mistress and friends quickly carried him to his bed, where he expired. Why did David ignore the truth in his painting? What image of Marat did David seek to communicate? What image of the French Revolution did the thousands who viewed the painting receive? Thousands of cheap reproductions of this painting were distributed throughout France. Why was this done?

Unfortunately, no contemporary portrait of Toussaint Louverture by a Haitian artist is known to exist, and it is possible that one was never done. Source 6 is from the book *An Historical Account of the Black Empire of Hayti*, written in 1802 by Marcus Rainsford, a British officer, and published in London in 1805.[13] Rainsford had met and interviewed Toussaint and obviously admired him. The artist is identified only as J. Barlow, and about him we know nothing. There is no evidence that Barlow ever met Toussaint, and he may have been commissioned in London to illustrate Rainsford's book. But Rainsford almost certainly conferred with Barlow about how Toussaint should have been portrayed.

This presents the historian with a very difficult problem, for we cannot be sure that Barlow's portrait of Toussaint would have been similar to portraits by contemporary Haitian artists. How, then, can we use Barlow's portrait to analyze what Haitians thought of Toussaint as a liberator-hero? And yet, since Rainsford knew Toussaint and admired him, we can suppose that Rainsford instructed Barlow to paint Toussaint Louverture *as Toussaint himself wanted to be portrayed*—as a liberator-hero.

Keeping that problem in mind, examine Barlow's illustration carefully, noting Toussaint's clothing, the fact that his right hand rests on his sword while his left hand holds a copy of Haiti's constitution, and the background matter. What image of Toussaint Louverture did Barlow seek to communicate? What image of the Haitian Revolution?

13. Marcus Rainsford, *An Historical Account of the Black Empire of Hayti* (London: James Cunde, 1805). The portrait is opposite page 241.

Chapter 7
The Liberator-
Hero and
Western
Revolutions
(1770s–1810s)

Source 1 from Fisher Ames, Works of Fisher Ames (Boston: T. B. Wait and Co., 1809), pp. 115–133.

1. Fisher Ames's Eulogy on Washington, Boston, February 8, 1800

Rome did not owe more to Fabius,[14] than America to Washington. Our nation shares with him the singular glory of having conducted a civil war with mildness, and a revolution with order.

The event of that war seemed to crown the felicity and glory both of America and its chief. Until that contest, a great part of the civilized world had been surprisingly ignorant of the force and character, and almost of the existence, of the British colonies. They had not retained what they knew, nor felt curiosity to know the state of thirteen wretched settlements, which vast woods enclosed, and still vaster woods divided from each other. They did not view the colonists so much a people, as a race of fugitives, whom want, and solitude, and intermixture with the savages, had made barbarians.

At this time, while Great Britain wielded a force truly formidable to the most powerful states, suddenly, astonished Europe beheld a feeble people, till then unknown, stand forth, and defy this giant to the combat. It was no unequal, all expected it would be short. Our final success exalted their admiration to its highest point: they allowed to Washington all that is due to transcendent virtue, and to the Americans more than is due to human nature. They considered us a race of Washingtons, and admitted that nature in America was fruitful only in prodigies. . . .

Washington retired to Mount Vernon, and the eyes of the world followed him. He left his countrymen to their simplicity and their passions, and their glory soon departed. Europe began to be undeceived, and it seemed, for a time, as if, by the acquisition of independence, our citizens were disappointed. The confederation was then the only compact made "to form a perfect union of the states, to establish justice, to ensure the tranquillity, and provide for the security, of a nation;" and, accordingly, union was a name that still commanded reverence, though not obedience. The system called justice was, in some of the states, inequity reduced to elementary principles; and the publick tranquillity was such a portentous calm, as rings in deep caverns before the explosion of an earthquake. Most of the states then were in fact, though not in form, unbalanced democracies. Reason, it is true, spoke audibly

14. Fabius Maximus, hero of the Second Punic War, who adopted the military strategy whereby Rome was able to retain control of Italy in spite of the major successes of Hannibal.

in their constitutions; passion and prejudice louder in their laws. . . . It was scarcely possible that such governments should not be agitated by parties, and that prevailing parties should not be vindictive and unjust. Accordingly, in some of the states, creditors were treated as outlaws; bankrupts were armed with legal authority to be persecutors; and, by the shock of all confidence and faith, society was shaken to its foundations. Liberty we had, but we dreaded its abuse almost as much as its loss; and the wise, who deplored the one, clearly foresaw the other.

The peace of America hung by a thread, and factions were already sharpening their weapons to cut it. The project of three separate empires in America was beginning to be broached, and the progress of licentiousness[15] would have soon rendered her citizens unfit for liberty in either of them. An age of blood and misery would have punished our disunion: but these were not the considerations to deter ambition from its purpose, while there were so many circumstances in our political situation to favour it.

At this awful crisis, which all the wise so much dreaded at the time, yet which appears, on a retrospect, so much more dreadful than their fears; some man was wanting who possessed a commanding power over the popular passions, but over whom those passions had no power. That man was Washington.

His name, at the head of such a list of worthies as would reflect honour on any country, had its proper weight with all the enlightened, and with almost all the well disposed among the less informed citizens, and blessed be God! the constitution was adopted. Yes, to the eternal honour of America among the nations of the earth, it was adopted, in spite of the obstacles, which, in any other country, and, perhaps, in any other age of *this*, would have been insurmountable; in spite of the doubts and fears, which well-meaning prejudice creates for itself, and which party so artfully inflames into stubbornness; in spite of the vice, which it has subjected to restraint, and which is therefore its immortal and implacable foe; in spite of the oligarchies in some of the states, from whom it snatched dominion; it was adopted, and our country enjoys one more invaluable chance for its union and happiness: invaluable!

No sooner did the new government begin its auspicious course, than order seemed to arise out of confusion. Commerce and industry awoke, and were cheerful at their labours; for credit and confidence awoke with them. Every where was the appearance of prosperity; and the only fear was, that its progress was too rapid to consist with the purity and simplicity of ancient manners. The cares and labours of the president were incessant: his exhortations, example, and authority, were employed to excite zeal and activity for the publick service: able officers were selected, only for their merits; and some of them remarkably distinguished themselves by their successful management of the publick business. Government was administered with such

15. The lack of moral discipline or restraint.

Chapter 7

The Liberator-

Hero and

Western

Revolutions

(1770s–1810s)

integrity, without mystery, and in so prosperous a course, that it seemed to be wholly employed in acts of beneficence. Though it has made many thousand malcontents, it has never, by its rigour or injustice, made one man wretched.

Such was the state of publick affairs: and did it not seem perfectly to ensure uninterrupted harmony to the citizens? Did they not, in respect to their government and its administration, possess their whole heart's desire? They had seen and suffered long the want of an efficient constitution; they had freely ratified it; they saw Washington, their tired friend, the father of his country, invested with its powers: they knew that he could not exceed or betray them, without forfeiting his own reputation. Consider, for a moment, what a reputation it was: such as no man ever before possessed by so clear a title, and in so high a degree. His fame seemed in its purity to exceed even its brightness: office took honour from his acceptance, but conferred none. Ambition stood awed and darkened by his shadow. For where, through the wide earth, was the man so vain as to dispute precedence with him; or what were the honours that could make the possessor Washington's superior? Refined and complex as the ideas of virtue are, even the gross could discern in his life the infinite superiority of her rewards. Mankind perceived some change in their ideas of greatness: the splendor of power, and even of the name of conqueror, had grown dim in their eyes. They did not know that Washington could augment his fame; but they knew and felt, that the world's wealth, and its empire too, would be a bribe far beneath his acceptance.

While the president was thus administering the government in so wise and just a manner, as to engage the great majority of the enlightened and virtuous citizens to co-operate with him for its support, and while he indulged the hope that time and habit were confirming their attachment, the French revolution had reached that point in its progress, when its terrible principles began to agitate all civilized nations. I will not, on this occasion, detain you to express, though my thoughts teem with it, my deep abhorrence of that revolution; its despotism, by the mob or the military, from the first, and its hypocrisy of morals to the last. Scenes have passed there which exceed description, and which, for other reasons, I will not attempt to describe; for it would not be possible, even at this distance of time, and with the sea between us and France, to go through with the recital of them, without perceiving horrour gather, like a frost, about the heart, and almost stop its pulse. That revolution has been constant in nothing but its vicissitudes, and its promises; always delusive, but always renewed, to establish philosophy by crimes, and liberty by the sword. . . .

Who then, on careful reflection, will be surprised, that the French and their partisans instantly conceived the desire, and made the most powerful attempts, to revolutionize the American government? But it will hereafter seem strange that their excesses should be excused, as the effects of a struggle for liberty; and that so many of our citizens should be flattered, while they were insulted with the idea, that our example was copied, and our principles pursued. Nothing was ever more false, or more fascinating. Our liberty depends on our education, our laws, and habits, to which even prejudices yield; on the dispersion of our people on farms, and on the almost equal diffusion of property; it is founded on morals and religion, whose authority reigns in the heart; and on the influence all these produce on publick opinion, before *that* opinion governs rulers. *Here* liberty is restraint; *there* it is violence: *here* it is mild and cheering, like the morning sun of our summer, brightening the hills, and making the vallies green; *there* it is like the sun, when his rays dart pestilence on the sands of Africa. American liberty calms and restrains the licentious passions, like an angel that says to the winds and troubled seas, be still. . . .

It is not impossible, that some will affect to consider the honours paid to this great patriot by the nation, as excessive, idolatrous, and degrading to freemen, who are all equal. I answer, that refusing to virtue its legitimate honours would not prevent their being lavished, in future, on any worthless and ambitious favourite. If this day's example should have its natural effect, it will be salutary. Let such honours be so conferred only when, in future, they shall be so merited: then the publick sentiment will not be misled, nor the principles of a just equality corrupted. . . .

But such a chief magistrate as Washington appears like the pole star in a clear sky, to direct the skilful statesman. His presidency will form an epoch, and be distinguished as the age of Washington. Already it assumes its high place in the political region. Like the milky way, it whitens along its allotted portion of the hemisphere. The latest generations of men will survey, through the telescope of history, the space where so many virtues blend their rays, and delight to separate them into groups and distinct virtues. As the best illustration of them, the living monument, to which the first of patriots would have chosen to consign his fame, it is my earnest prayer to heaven, that our country may subsist, even to that late day, in the plenitude of its liberty and happiness, and mingle its mild glory with Washington's.

Chapter 7
The Liberator-
Hero and
Western
Revolutions
(1770s–1810s)

Source 2 from the White House Historical Association.

2. Gilbert Stuart, *George Washington* (The Lansdowne Portrait), 1797

Source 3 from J. Mavidal and E. Laurent, eds., Archives parlementaires de 1787 à 1860. Recueil complet des débats législatifs et politiques des chambres francaises, *1st series, volume 73 (Paris: Librairie administrative Paul Dupont, 1908), pp. 302–305. Translated by Julius R. Ruff.*

3. F. E. Guiraut, Funeral Oration for Marat, Paris, July 1793

Citizens:

A hideous night has just stretched its funeral crepe over us; the intrepid defender of liberty has become its martyr. Marat, Marat is no more.

People! It is true that you have lost your friend.[16] A monster vomitted up by tyranny has come to pierce his breast. You have seen his mortal wounds with your own eyes;[17] his body was cold and bloodied, sad remains which for you are the last witnesses of his fidelity.

His funeral, it is true, was one filled with our gratitude! You have carefully placed him in a tomb, you have covered him with garlands and flowers; and you have done more: you bathed him in your tears. Oh Marat, how glorious it is to die in the middle of your brothers! . . .

Marat was born, the son of a doctor, on May 24, 1743, in Boudry near Neuchâtel in a republican land, at the base of mountains that pierce the clouds and hold down Hell, near that city[18] where liberty has resided since its departure from Greece and Rome. . . .

He had a sickly childhood and a meticulous education. His mother enjoyed allowing him to taste the sweetness of philanthropy. From the age of eight, he could not bear any aspect of injustice or cruelty. Obedient, hardworking, he never knew the play of childhood, but made rapid progress in his studies. Reflective at fifteen, observant at eighteen, thinker at twenty-one, work was a basic need for him.

He spent twenty-five years in an intellectual retreat, engaged in the reading of the best books; he exhaustively studied morality, philosophy and politics. Like Plato he sometimes listened to his soul speak and at these moments, when filled with respect for the Creator and with admiration for all living beings, he weighed the vanity of human glory, searched the somber future, and looked for the man beyond the monument, . . . and like the famous Locke he, too, had a medical degree. He used his medical knowledge to enlighten, but practiced his profession little.

---

16. Note Guiraut's play on words here.

17. Marat's body was on view in the Church of the Cordeliers on July 16, along with the bathtub in which he was murdered and his bloody shirt.

18. The city here probably is Rousseau's hometown of Geneva.

Chapter 7

The Liberator-

Hero and

Western

Revolutions

(1770s–1810s)

Citizens! Follow Marat! Born for liberty, he early experienced acts of despotism caused by ignorance. He could not stand ignorance and, having identified it, would have abolished it in the twinkling of an eye if he could have. Instead, his imagination was kindled, and, impelled by his love of fame, he took his pen in a firm hand and set forth his metaphysical, anatomical and physiological works on man in eight volumes. . . .

Under the blissful influence of freedom, he extended his knowledge of human affairs to social relations. For Marat governments were a monstrosity, nothing but a mixture of extortions, crimes, and impudence. He knew governments' politics and he tried to overthrow their monstrous abuses. His stay in England furnished a good opportunity for such an attempt at the time of the Parliamentary election of 1774. Indeed Marat enjoyed this. Citizen of the world, he wrote of the state's attacks against liberty and the people, the ruses it employed, and the bloody scenes which accompany despotism. Finished and printed under the title *The Chains of Slavery*, his work could not be published. The English ministry had corrupted all, bought printers, publishers, and journalists, its gold infiltrating everywhere. The genius of Marat had shaken the operation of the throne. . . .

Then in 1789 the earthshaking reveille of liberty sounded. The people rose up, stamped its foot on the ground and the throne started to shake. Marat saw it already toppled. "Be watchful," he wrote to his fellow citizens, "the laurels are for you." Intrepid, courageous, he took responsibility for assuring the victory of the Revolution. He advised the people's representatives meeting at Versailles; in Paris he kept the people stirred up, and he was everywhere in the streets and roads fearing that liberty would escape his grasp. Marat was indignant at the deceptive scheme for double representation,[19] and he planned a constitution. He observed events. The people, he concluded, had been deceived, betrayed by its representatives, and he mounted a war to the death against the traitors.

Ignoring all other sentiments than the wish to see his homeland happy, Marat saw all the perils. He feared nothing. He resolved to fight all vices with a daily newspaper whose austere language would remind legislators of their principles, unmask scoundrels and corrupt officials, reveal their plots and sound the alarm bell in moments of danger.

Scarcely had he cast his glance on the Constituent Assembly, than innumerable plots were directed against him. He spoke the truth, his enemies wished

---

19. **double representation:** In late 1788 Louis XVI conceded a doubling of the number of Third Estate representatives in the Estates General to be elected in February–April 1789. This would have given the commoners a number of representatives roughly equal to those of the clergy and the nobility. What was not conceded was vote by head in place of vote by house. Because the Estates General was, in essence, a three-house legislature that required positive votes by all three estates or houses (the First Estate representing the clergy, the Second Estate the nobility, and the Third Estate the commoners), the maintenance of vote by house meant that the privileged groups could block reform legislation proposed by the commoners of the Third Estate.

to buy his silence. Necker[20] offered him a million in gold, but he refused it. They seized his presses, ordered his arrest, put a price on his head in vain efforts to silence him. His courage sustained him, his paper continued, his energy grew.

Lafayette beseiged his home with 12,000 men but Marat escaped, though his home was pillaged and he was reduced to misery.

In this dreadful situation, he was without domicile and soon without friends. Wandering from one neighborhood on the outskirts of Paris to another, pursued relentlessly, heaped with venom and pain, he was only the more formidable. Everywhere spied on, everywhere he escaped the fury of his enemies' knives. They could not silence him.

Lafayette spared no sacrifice in his search for Marat, stirring everyone out of their indifference. Marat found no refuge. He looked for an underground tunnel and took refuge in quarries of Montmartre. There, some good citizens were pleased to keep him; they brought him food which he received with gratitude. He clasped his bread, bathed it in his tears and gave to the state the life that had been sustained by hands of brotherhood.

When the constitution was proclaimed, Marat sensed that the new order of things could not last a long time. His eye discovered secret plots, and he told the people that the plotters wished to subjugate them and to restore Louis XVI to his former authority. He pursued the deputies of the Legislative Assembly, denouncing their treachery and venality, and found himself charged with a crime and the crowd at his heels. Passion dictated his actions. Didn't he write that "The defense of the people's rights is my supreme law"? Stronger than all the plotters together he defied them, scorned them, revealed conspiracies, and showed the need to exclude priests, nobles, financiers, creatures of the court, and tricksters from all public office.

The Revolution took some reactionary steps and public spirit seemed to weaken. Marat shook with indignation at the inactivity of patriots. He worried, he wished to electrify all souls and to achieve liberty. You should have seen him thus reduced, citizens, more unhappy than Diogenes[21] in his tub deprived of his light. Often in wet places, he had nothing to sleep on. Wasted by the most dreadful misery, he covered his body with a simple blue frock coat and his head with a handkerchief. With a handkerchief, alas, almost always soaked in vinegar in order to cool the ardor of his mind which could not allow the friends of liberty to sleep. He wrote with a writing case in his hand and his knees, supporting some sheets of paper, served

20. Jacques Necker was a Swiss banker who was made director of finances by Louis XVI in 1777, but who was dismissed when he attempted to reform France's tax structure. During the revolution he played a major role in trying to restructure the nation's finances.

21. Diogenes (412–323 B.C.E.) was a Greek philosopher who believed the only virtuous life was a simple one. He demonstrated this by discarding all his worldly possessions and living in a tub. Diogenes showed his contempt for his fellow Greeks by conducting daylight searches, complete with a lantern, for an honest man.

Chapter 7

The Liberator-

Hero and

Western

Revolutions

(1770s–1810s)

as his desk. His work was sold, people gave to him, and he lived on an *écu*. . . .[22]

Disgusted by bitterness, with France inundated by ministerial placards describing him as a ferocious beast, his latest efforts without effect, Marat recalled his reception in England. He left for that country, but was recognized at Amiens and an armed force was immediately assembled. He was surrounded but burst through the ranks of men and escaped. Heaven protected his life, the countryside aided his flight, and he arrived in Paris without shoes, his feet stained with his blood. Having barely survived, he sacrificed himself entirely for his cause and swore to conquer.

On August 10[23] the voice of the people made itself heard and toppled not enormous stones wet with the tears of the oppressed[24] but crowns, *fleurs de lis*[25] and gilded corridors. . . .

Marat was a lone mountain[26] and it was necessary to destroy him at any price. . . .

Respond, assassins of Marat! You who thrust the knife into his chest, have you, like him, any virtues to offer? Did you ever know this extraordinary mortal? He spent all his life in seclusion and thought but was persecuted by the envious and jealous, pursued by the forces of despotism, abandoned by the timid and weak, hated by those who are evil and corrupt, feared by the ambitious and conspirators, esteemed by the people, and slain by agents of fanaticism. Answer, assassins! Did you know him? . . .

Listen to the last words of this philosopher, citizens:

People! I was your representative. I defended your rights. I lived in misery, and I died in misery. People! Your confidence was too great and was always your misfortune. Cease to acclaim false idols. Your welfare depends on you. Know your dignity and your strength. Calculate your needs coldly. Faithful observer, no longer allow yourself to be enslaved. Crush intrigue, suppress ambition, scorn evil, esteem talent, honor virtue. . . .

People, do not let yourselves be led astray. Be on guard against those who would deceive you. Never again become the instrument of passion. Do not arm yourselves against your brothers but employ toward them all those means of reconciliation worthy of you. Everywhere arrest the most culpable enemies; they alone deserve to be punished.

People, cherish your liberty! All the social virtues should reign with it. Among you it is in an embryonic state. Be happy and enjoy the charms of philanthropy. Think sometimes of your friend; I make you the trustee of my heart.

22. **écu**: A coin of the Old Regime.

23. On August 10, 1792, Parisian crowds stormed the Tuileries Palace and effectively ended the monarchy founded by the Constitution of 1791.

24. Guiraut refers here to the crowd's capture of the Bastille prison in Paris on July 14, 1789.

25. **fleurs de lis**: A three-leaf lily that symbolized the Old Regime monarchy.

26. A clever reference on Marat's political faction, the Montagnard (mountain).

Oh Marat, the ever watchful and vigilant sentinel before our gate, we will never again hear: "Here is Marat, the friend of the people!"

Always present in our thought, we will never forget what you have done for us. . . .

Source 4 from Château de Versailles/Cliché des Musées Nationaux-Paris.

4. Jacques Louis David, *Portrait of Marat*, 1793

Chapter 7

The Liberator-

Hero and

Western

Revolutions

(1770s–1810s)

Source 5 from Toussaint L'Ouverture: Biography and Autobiography (Boston: James Red-path, 1863), pp. 331–336.

5. Henri Christophe, Manifesto, 1814

We have deserved the favors of liberty, by our indissoluble attachment to the mother country. We have proved to her our gratitude.

At the time when, reduced to our own private resources, cut off from all communication with France, we resisted every allurement; when, inflexible to menaces, deaf to proposals, inaccessible to artifice, we braved misery, famine, and privation of every kind, and finally triumphed over our enemies both within and without.

We were then far from perceiving that twelve years after, as the price of so much perseverance, sacrifice, and blood, France would deprive us in a most barbarous manner of the most precious of our possessions,—liberty.

Under the administration of Governor-General Toussaint L'Ouverture, Hayti arose from her ruins, and everything seemed to promise a happy future. The arrival of General Hédouville[27] completely changed the aspect of affairs, and struck a deadly blow to public tranquillity. We will not enter into the detail of his intrigues with the Haytian General, Rigaud,[28] whom he persuaded to revolt against the legitimate chief. We will only say, that before leaving the island, Hédouville had put everything into confusion, by casting among us the firebrands of discord, and lighting the torch of civil war.

Ever zealous for the reëstablishment of order and of peace, Toussaint L'Ouverture, by a paternal government, restored their original energy to law, morality, religion, education, and industry. Agriculture and commerce were flourishing; he was favorable to white colonists, especially to those who occupied new possessions; and the care and partiality which he felt for them went so far that he was severely censured as being more attached to them than to people of his own color. This negro wail was not without reason; for some months previous to the arrival of the French, he put to death his own nephew, General Moise, for having disregarded his orders relative to the protection of the colonists. This act of the Governor, and the great confidence which he had in the French Government, were the chief causes of the weak resistance which the French met with in Hayti. In reality, his confidence in that Government was

27. Hedouville was the commander of the French forces that Toussaint ultimately defeated in 1797–1798, forcing the French to abandon Haiti until the French invasion of 1802.

28. Rigaud had been second in command to Toussaint but broke with him and led the mulattos in a civil war against Toussaint in 1799–1800. Rigaud's revolt was brutally repressed and approximately 2,000 people were put to death.

so great, that the General had disbanded the greater part of the regular troops, and employed them in the cultivation of the ground.

Such was the state of affairs whilst the peace of Amiens[29] was being negotiated; it was scarcely concluded, when a powerful armament landed on our coasts a large army, which, attacking us by surprise, when we thought ourselves perfectly secure, plunged us suddenly into an abyss of evils.[30]

Posterity will find a difficulty in believing that, in so enlightened and philosophic an age, such an abominable enterprise could possibly have been conceived. In the midst of a civilized people, a horde of barbarians suddenly set out with the design of exterminating an innocent and peaceable nation, or at least of loading them anew with the chains of national slavery.

It was not enough that they employed violence; they also thought it necessary to use perfidy and villainy,—they were compelled to sow dissension among us. Every means was put in requisition to carry out this abominable scheme. The leaders of all political parties in France, even the sons of the Governor Toussaint, were invited to take part in the expedition. They, as well as ourselves, were deceived by that *chef-d'oeuvre*[31] of perfidy, the proclamation of the First Consul,[32] in which he said to us, 'You are all equal and free before God and the Republic;' such was his declaration, at the same time that his private instructions to General Leclerc[33] were to reëstablish slavery.

The greater part of the population, deceived by these fallacious promises, and for a long time accustomed to consider itself as French, submitted without resistance. The Governor so little expected the appearance of an enemy that he had not even ordered his generals to resist in case of an attack being made; and, when the armament arrived, he himself was on a journey toward the eastern coast. If some few generals did resist, it was owing only to the hostile and menacing manner in which they were summoned to surrender, which compelled them to respect their duty, their honor, and the present circumstances.

After a resistance of some months, the Governor-General yielded to the pressing entreaties and the solemn protestations of Leclerc, 'that he intended to protect the liberties of every one, and that France would never destroy so noble a work.' On this footing, peace was negotiated with France; and the Governor Toussaint, laying aside his power, peaceably retired to the retreat he had prepared for himself.

---

29. The Peace of Amiens (1802) brought a temporary end to the war between France and Great Britain, thus allowing Napoleon to plan an invasion of Haiti.

30. The French invasion of 1802.

31. *chef-d'oeuvre:* masterpiece.

32. Napoleon Bonaparte.

33. Leclerc was the commander of the 1802 French invasion force.

Chapter 7

The Liberator-

Hero and

Western

Revolutions

(1770s–1810s)

Scarcely had the French extended their dominion over the whole island and that more by roguery and deceit than by force of arms, than they began to put in execution their horrible system of slavery and destruction.

To hasten the accomplishment of their projects, mercenary and Machiavellian writers fabricated fictitious narratives, and attributed to Toussaint designs that he had never entertained. While he was remaining peaceably at home, on the faith of solemn treaties, he was seized, loaded with irons, dragged away with the whole of his family, and transported to France. The whole of Europe knows how he ended his unfortunate career in torture and in prayer, in the dungeon of the Château de Joux.

Such was the recompense reserved for his attachment to France, and for the eminent services he had rendered to the colony.

At the same time, notice was given to arrest all suspected persons throughout the island. All those who had shown brave and enlightened souls, when we claimed for ourselves the rights of men, were the first to be seized. Even the traitors who had most contributed to the success of the French army, by serving as guides to their advanced guard, and by exciting their compatriots to take vengeance, were not spared. At first they desired to sell them into strange colonies; but, as this plan did not succeed, they resolved to transport them to France, where overpowering labor, the galleys, chains, and prisons, were awaiting them.

Then the white colonists, whose numbers have continually increased, seeing their power sufficiently established, discarded the mask of dissimulation, openly declared the reëstablishment of slavery, and acted in accordance with their declaration. They had the impudence to claim as their slaves men who had made themselves eminent by the most brilliant services to their country, in both the civil and military departments. Virtuous and honorable magistrates, warriors covered with wounds, whose blood had been poured out for France and for liberty, were compelled to fall back into the bonds of slavery. These colonists, scarcely established in the possession of their land, whose power was liable to be overthrown by the slightest cause, already marked out and chose in the distance those whom they determined should be the first victims of their vengeance.

The proud and liberty-hating faction of the colonists, of those traffickers in human flesh, who, since the commencement of the revolution, had not ceased to impregnate the successive Governments in France with their plans, their projects, their atrocious and extravagant memorials, and everything tending to our ruin,—these factious men, tormented by the recollection of the despotism which they had formerly exercised at Hayti, a prey to their low and cruel passions, exerted all their efforts to repossess themselves of the prey which had escaped from their clutches. In favor of independence under the constitutional assembly, terrorists under the Jacobins, and finally, zealous Bonapartists, they knew how to assume the mask of any party, in order to obtain place and favor. It was thus, by their insidious counsels, they urged Bonaparte to undertake this iniquitous expedition to Hayti. It was this faction who, after having advised the expedition, furnished the pecuniary resources which were necessary, by means of subscriptions which were at this time commenced. In a word, it was this faction which caused the blood of our compatriots to flow in torrents,—which invented the exhausting tortures to which we were subjected; it is to these colonists that France owes the loss of a powerful army, which perished in the plains and marshes of Hayti; it is to them she owes the shame of an enterprise which has fixed an indelible stain on the French name. . . .

Chapter 7
The Liberator-
Hero and
Western
Revolutions
(1770s–1810s)

Source 6 from Marcus Rainsford, An Historical Account of the Black Empire of Hayti *(London: James Cundee, 1805), facing p. 241. Photo from Stock Montage, Inc.*

6. J. Barlow, *Portrait of Toussaint Louverture*, c. 1805

QUESTIONS TO CONSIDER

In this chapter, your task is *not* to find out what each revolutionary leader (Washington, Marat, and Toussaint) was *really* like. Instead, your task is to analyze how each leader's fellow revolutionists or contemporaries created and shaped an *image* of a liberator-hero, and through that image communicated to their contemporaries and to future generations the nature or essence of the revolution.

Fisher Ames's eulogy to George Washington is an excellent case in point. In spite of the fact that Washington's initial prominence came from his military leadership of the Continental Line, Ames spends almost no time on that aspect of Washington's life. Why do you think this is so? Instead, Ames concentrates on the years *after* the War for Independence, saying only that Washington and his fellow revolutionists (including Ames himself) "conducted a civil war with mildness, and a revolution with order." What did Ames mean by that statement?

Ames pictured a postwar decade of "awful crisis" and filled with "popular passions." To what was he referring? How did the Constitution solve those problems? Was the acceptance of the presidency by Washington a key factor in overcoming the crisis? How?

Washington was president when the French Revolution broke out in 1789. What opinions does Ames have of that revolution? What dangers does he see in it? On a related note, what does Ames consider the principal threat to the American Revolu-

tion? And, from that, what does Fisher Ames see as the true nature of the American Revolution? How can Washington be used to personify or symbolize that true nature?

Of Gilbert Stuart's 1797 portrait of Washington, William Kloss has remarked that no "other portrait conveys the unyielding resolve and severe dignity that made him the embodiment of the young Republic."[34] As you examine the painting, look first at the central figure. What is the expression on Washington's face? What is the significance of the body's pose? Why was he dressed in civilian clothes (the majority of paintings of Washington show him in military garb)? What is the significance of the sheathed sword in his left hand?

The table leg is formed to resemble a *fasces*, a band of rods that symbolized authority and justice in the Roman Republic. Does the chair behind Washington contain symbols equal to those of the table leg? What are the titles of the books in the painting and what is their importance? Is there anything else in the background that Stuart intended to be used as a symbol? Finally, by looking at Stuart's portrait what did he hope that viewers would see about George Washington? About the American Revolution?

The funeral oration for Jean-Paul Marat is a dramatically different eulogy from Fisher Ames's address. Guiraut begins by referring to Marat as a "martyr." A martyr to what? If Marat was a martyr to the French

34. William Kloss et al., *Art in the White House: A Nation's Pride* (Washington, D.C.: White House Historical Association, 1992), p. 66.

Chapter 7

The Liberator-

Hero and

Western

Revolutions

(1770s–1810s)

Revolution, what *particular aspect* of the revolution did he symbolize?

Guiraut intersperses his biographical sketch of his subject with numerous observations and judgments, as if Marat's early life was preparing him for the revolution. How does Guiraut accomplish this? What phases are particularly significant?

As the revolution began, what does Guiraut assert was Marat's warning? What did Marat fear? What message is Guiraut intending to communicate? Why were plots hatched against Marat? What lessons does Guiraut see in those conspiracies? What kind of French Revolution did Marat seek?

The "last words" attributed to Marat were actually those of Guiraut.[35] Through Marat, what does Guiraut see as true goals of the French Revolution? What are the dangers? Finally, how does Guiraut use the image of Marat to make him into a liberator-hero? What, in Guiraut's view, is the nature of the French Revolution?

As noted above, David's painting of Marat is a magnificent piece of political propaganda. In what ways is it so? Why did David choose to portray Marat in this way, in his grisly death? Why does David have Marat holding the note from Charlotte Corday? What does that say about David's view of the revolution?

At the bottom of the wooden box, David has painted the words *L'An Deux* (the Year Two). Since it was 1793, what is the significance of David's date? Finally, what reaction did David

35. Marat's actual last words were "Help, my dear, help!" Edward S. LeCompte, comp., *Dictionary of Last Words* (New York: Philosophical Library, 1955), p. 144.

hope viewers of the painting would have? How could Marat be used as a liberator-hero of the French Revolution?

Henri Christophe, like the preceding two eulogists, is using the career, the accomplishments, and the ideas of Toussaint Louverture to make a point. What is that point? In Christophe's view, what was Toussaint's fatal blunder? (It was *not* his being duped into surrendering.)

Toussaint Louverture tried to build a nation in which whites, blacks, and mulattos would live in peace and mutual trust. What does Henri Christophe think of that goal? How does Christophe use Toussaint as a *negative example* of the liberator-hero? What does that say about Christophe's notion of the true nature of the Haitian Revolution—or what that true nature *should* be?

Unlike Stuart and David, the artist who portrayed Toussaint Louverture probably never met his subject. Yet Marcus Rainsford may well have given Barlow enough details to make this a reasonably accurate portrait—at least according to Rainsford. Examine the artist's representation of Toussaint: his face, his physique, his clothing. What impressions was the artist seeking to convey? What is the significance of the sword and the document (Haiti's constitution, issued by Toussaint in 1801) in his hand? Of the Haitian Revolution?

Revolutionists face a dual challenge. The first challenge is to win their revolution. The second challenge is to preserve it and to pass it down to future generations. How do the three eulogists and the three artists attempt to do this?

EPILOGUE

As the "revolutionary fever" that "afflicted" Théroigne de Méricourt swept across the Western world in the late eighteenth century, revolutionists sought to justify, legitimate, and explain the true natures of their respective uprisings to their wary contemporaries as well as to generations yet unborn. To do this, they created the images of liberator-heroes, men and (occasionally) women who could be used as symbols of the revolution and through whose lives the true nature or essence of the revolution could be seen. Some, like Washington, became symbols of revolts that succeeded. Others, like Marat and Toussaint Louverture, became martyrs to a revolution not yet fulfilled. Nevertheless, each one became a liberator-hero, a construction through which the message of the revolution could be communicated.

George Washington became a symbol of a revolution that stopped (according to Fisher Ames) at precisely the right moment—not falling back into monarchy nor veering wildly into democracy. It was a revolution out of which reform and democratization would come gradually, wrenched by only one (albeit bloody) civil war. After his death in 1799, biographers made Washington into a symbol of that revolution. From the wildly creative biography by Mason Locke "Parson" Weems to the magisterial seven-volume work by Douglas Southall Freeman, George Washington continues to reign as the "Father of His Country."

Gilbert Stuart moved to Washington, D.C., soon after the nation's capital was relocated there. He continued to receive enormous fees for painting portraits of the new nation's political and commercial leaders, but died in debt in 1823. When British troops invaded Washington in 1814 (during the War of 1812 between the United States and Great Britain), Dolley Madison, wife of President James Madison, broke the Lansdowne portrait's frame and carried the canvas on its stretcher out of the city to save it from British mutilation. It was returned to the White House in 1817 and hangs there today, in the city that bears its subject's name.

Charlotte Corday went silently to the guillotine, refusing to disclose information on any plot against Jean-Paul Marat. The liberator-hero of the radicals at first was placed in a cave-like tomb on the grounds of the radical Cordeliers Club in Paris. Later Marat's body was moved to the Pantheon, the burial place of France's great figures. But in the conservative Thermidorian Reaction, it was once again moved to the Sainte-Genevieve Cemetery.

Jacques Louis David survived the French Revolution and became Napoleon Bonaparte's favorite painter (David did several famous paintings of Napoleon), in 1803 was made a knight of the French Legion of Honor, and in 1804 was named First Painter to the Emperor.[36] When Napoleon fell at Waterloo, David went into exile, continued to paint, and died in exile in Belgium in 1825.

36. David's 1808 portrait of Napoleon in his study has the well-known pose of the subject with his right hand inserted in his vest.

Chapter 7
The Liberator-
Hero and
Western
Revolutions
(1770s–1810s)

The popular revolution Marat, Guiraut, and David hoped for did not come. The French Revolution began to move into more conservative channels in 1795, capped by the coup d'etat of Napoleon Bonaparte in 1799. Napoleon's fall in 1815 restored the Bourbon monarchy to France, and the nation struggled gradually but perceptibly toward stability throughout the rest of the nineteenth and part of the twentieth centuries. Only after decades would Marat's goal of a democratic republic finally be achieved.

The French invasion of Haiti in 1802 was broken by a yellow fever epidemic which ravaged the French army. In 1804, Jean Jacques Dessalines, a black general, assumed the title of Emperor of Haiti, but was soon assassinated, to be followed by Henri Christophe. Henri I maintained power until 1820, when a paralytic stroke and yet another uprising led to his suicide (October 8, 1820). Since that time, the history of Haiti has been one of grinding poverty, political tyranny, and instability. In 1980 Haiti's illiteracy rate was 85 percent, its infant mortality rate 20 percent, and its per capita income a meager $219 per year. More recently, the United States has intervened in Haiti to install and prop up the government of President Jean Bertrand Aristide. A statue of Toussaint Louverture still stands in Port-au-Prince, a symbol to those who seek to continue the revolutionary struggle. In France, his grave was destroyed between 1876 and 1880 when alterations were made to the prison chapel.

CHAPTER EIGHT

ISLAMIC FUNDAMENTALISM AND

RENEWAL IN WEST AFRICA (CA. 1775–1820)

Among people in the Western world, and especially the United States and much of Europe, many images of Islam equate that faith with fanaticism. These notions have deep roots, extending to the time of the medieval Crusades when accounts of Muslim warriors were frequently exaggerated in an effort to recruit soldiers and others to the ranks of the Christian crusaders. In our own time, similar ideas have found their way into our popular image of Islam. Certainly Palestinian resistance to the creation of the state of Israel, the Iranian revolution of the 1970s, and Iraqi attempts at regional conquest in the 1990s have reinforced these images.

Perhaps even more, the terrorist activities of small, militant Islamic groups have further contributed to fanatical images of Islam. The slaying of Israeli athletes at the 1972 Munich Olympic games, threats against and attacks on commercial civilian aviation and shipping, and such events as the 1993 bombing of the New York World Trade Center, have made us more suspicious of what is often described as Islamic fundamentalism. Despite protestations of many Islamic religious and political leaders that these actions are the work of only a few disaffected members of their faith, we often wonder why those terrorists justify their actions in the name of a reformed and revitalized Islam.

Confronting these images of Islam, the president of the United States has explicitly said that "those who insist that between America and the Middle East there are impassable religious barriers to harmony, that our beliefs and cultures must somehow inevitably clash . . . are wrong." Mr. Clinton went on to describe "the forces of terror and extremism" within the Islamic world as a decided minority "who cloak themselves in the rhetoric of religion and national-

Chapter 8

Islamic

Fundamentalism

and Renewal in

West Africa

(ca. 1775–1820)

ism, but behave in ways that contradict the very teachings of their faith."[1]

Still further complicating the visions of Islamic extremism which the president addressed is the concept of *jihad*, often translated as "holy war." More accurately, the term means "struggle for the faith," although this perception of the concept is often not understood in the West. Thus when we read or hear that one Islamic leader or another has proclaimed a jihad against certain individuals or countries, it may seem to be yet another act of fundamentalist extremism. But how do we understand what a jihad means if it can be waged against other Islamic countries or fellow Muslims?

Indeed, such movements to change the Islamic practice of fellow Muslims has long been a part of the history of Islam. Generally, such efforts have had as their purpose convincing co-religionists to return to the "true faith," to abide by the supposed original intentions of Allah as revealed to the Prophet Muhammad and recorded in

1. "Remarks by the President to the Jordanian Parliament," October 26, 1994, The White House, Office of the Press Secretary.

the Qur'an. In that sense (but not in all ways), such Islamic reform movements have parallels in the Reformation and Counter Reformation movements within European Christianity. Similar Islamic efforts at reform have occurred at many times and places within the *umma* (Islamic community), yet perhaps none have had such striking effects as those undertaken in West Africa in the early nineteenth century. Largely inspired by a great Islamic teacher, 'Uthman dan Fodio, they changed the political and religious face of interior West Africa even more than the arrival of European colonialists shortly thereafter.

In this chapter you will read selections from participants in these jihads, as well as the writings of Islamic teachers who both inspired and participated in these movements. Through their writings and other evidence, you will approach the central questions of this chapter: Were 'Uthman dan Fodio and his followers Islamic extremists? What effects did their movement have on early nineteenth-century West Africa? And finally, what does their experience tell you about the basis of Islamic fundamentalism?

BACKGROUND

Islam itself grew from revelations, said to have been delivered by the angel Gabriel, to an illiterate Arab merchant who thus became the Prophet Muhammad. These revelations were recorded by friends and

followers of Muhammad who collected them into a single written work. This was the Qur'an, the holy book of those who would submit to the will of God expressed therein. Thus, this was a faith of submission, called Islam and its followers Muslims, both terms being derived from the Arabic word for submission.

Muhammad himself began to tell others, mostly in the city of Mecca, about the revelations. In his preaching he called upon his listeners to accept the monotheism of Allah and to reject the natural spirits, called *jinn*, that had long been the basis of most Arab beliefs. Strong objections to his teaching from the political leaders in Mecca led to persecutions and finally the Prophet's flight from Mecca north to Medina. This event, known to Islam as the *hegira*, or journey, was a crucial turning point in the history of the faith. In Medina, Muhammad began to attract many more followers whom he organized into a community (*umma*) and led in the conquest of Mecca and much of Arabia.

Only a few years after the death of Prophet Muhammad in 632 C.E., disagreements began to surface among members of the Islamic *umma*. Of course, competing understandings of a new faith were not uncommon in many religious communities. Certainly it was true of those who followed Jesus a few centuries earlier; among the followers of both faiths a variety of interpretations of the founders' teachings circulated and gained adherents. Within the Muslim community, many of these divergent interpretations were somewhat legalistic disagreements about the meaning of the Qur'an, whereas others of the new ideas about the faith revolved around visions and dreams of extremely pious followers of Allah and his Prophet.

Within Islam the visionary challengers were known as *sufis;* their special claim to understanding the faith proclaimed by the Prophet lay in the mystical revelations through which they professed also to receive divine inspiration. In this they saw themselves as having experiences similar to those of the Prophet himself, although none claimed exactly the same level of divine intervention as Muhammad. Indeed, many *sufis* revered the Prophet as second only to God as a source of their religious inspiration.

Despite these internal disagreements, the outstanding fact of Islam in the century after Muhammad's death was the expansion of the faith beyond Arabia to Africa, India, and Europe. As its followers spread their new faith and their political dominance across North Africa, merchants and teachers also ventured south, across the Sahara. By the tenth century, the new religion had made an impact on the rulers of the commercial empires in the grasslands just south of the Sahara desert. Some evidence suggests Islamic ideas may have reached the interior West African kingdom of Ghana as early as the eighth century C.E. Without doubt the new faith steadily found adherents, but it did not fully replace the traditional beliefs of the peoples living in the sudanic belt south of the desert but north of the forest zone along the West African coast.

By the fourteenth century, Islam had made serious inroads into the leadership classes of the sudanic kingdoms. Mansa (that is, emperor or supreme ruler) Musa, the leader of Mali (which succeeded Ghana as the dominant state in the region) became famous in Africa and Europe, as well as Arabia, for his *hajj* (pilgrimage to

Chapter 8

Islamic

Fundamentalism

and Renewal in

West Africa

(ca. 1775–1820)

Mecca) in 1324 C.E. Yet he made that religious journey at some risk, since many of his followers were much more impressed by his status in African customary law than they were by his devotion to one of the "five pillars" of the new faith.[2]

It was only by the sixteenth century C.E., after the kingdom of Songhai supplanted Mali as the preeminent state in the western sudan, that the rulers became more committed to Islam: the former African "magician-kings" were gradually replaced by "pilgrim-kings" whose greatest allegiance was to their new faith.[3] The position of Songhai's rulers was not significantly improved by these developments. In fact, by the sixteenth century C.E., Songhai passed the pinnacle of its strength and, following an invasion by Moroccans in 1591, there was no other state powerful enough to exercise the political hegemony that had been exercised successively by Ghana, Mali, and then Songhai.

The political vacuum created throughout the West African Sudan made it easy for new groups of people to move into the region and expand their influence. From the west Fulfulde-speaking people, better known as Fulani, continued a gradual migration from the middle

Senegal River Valley that had probably begun in the tenth century C.E. Many of these Fulani were pastoralists who grazed their cattle on the abundant grasslands. A smaller number of Fulani, however, had adopted Islam; their conversions certainly had begun by the fourteenth century (and perhaps earlier). Within this Fulani Muslim community were a sizable number of teachers and clerics who served to both sustain and extend Islam among their fellow Fulani and their neighbors.

Known as the *ulama*, this educated and literate class was instrumental to the expansion of Islam in the region. Their efforts depended on a two-tiered educational system that was common in much of the Islamic world. At its core were the *kitatib*, or Qur'anic schools, in which young male pupils were taught the Arabic alphabet and recitations from the Qur'an. Many boys spent some time in the *kitatib*, with a much smaller number continuing their education in the *madaris*, advanced schools where instruction depended upon learned and respected *shaykhs* (teachers). A few of these *madaris* were fairly large institutions, mostly in the urban centers, but many were little more than annexes to the homes of the *shaykhs* themselves.

Students would stay with a particular *shaykh*, often living in his home or following him in his travels along the trade routes, until they had learned the knowledge he had to teach: a particular text, an interpretation of the *hadith* (written records of the Prophet Muhammad's deeds and

2. In addition to the *hajj,* those five basic principles of Islamic belief include a simple profession of faith ("There is no god but Allah and Muhammad is his Prophet."), prayer five times a day, giving alms to the poor, and fasting from sunup to sundown during the month of Ramadan.

3. These terms are more fully explained by Nehemia Levtzion in the *Cambridge History of Africa* (1977), vol. 3, p. 428.

sayings), or some aspect of the law (*sharia*). Having mastered the knowledge of a particular *shaykh,* the students would move on to another teacher, hoping to gain additional insights. The competence of any who would become teachers themselves was measured in large part by the reputations of the *shaykhs* with whom they had studied. In this way, literacy and the networks of schools and *shaykhs* that supported it, became crucial to Islam amongst the Fulani, as well as other Muslim peoples in the western sudan.

The Fulani *ulama* frequently came into conflict with Hausa-speaking rulers in the central Sudan. The Hausa, an ethnically mixed group of largely agricultural peoples, began moving into the region at about the same time as the Fulani. They congregated in settlements, some of which became towns that dominated small states in the region. Many of the Hausa cities, such as Kano and Zaria, also became the focus of long-distance trade, which had previously been concentrated in the capitals of Ghana, Mali, and Songhai. Like the rulers of those previous states, many Hausa political and economic leaders found Islam useful in their commercial dealings, but few were committed converts to the faith.

Differences in their approach to the faith served to increase tensions between the Fulani—both the *ulama* and their pastoralist brethren—and the rulers of the various Hausa states, whose influence in the region waxed and waned. During the latter half of the eighteenth century the state of Gobir, in the northern reaches of Hausaland, expanded significantly and exerted considerable influence over its neighboring Hausa states. Although Gobir's expansion was perhaps the most significant political development in eighteenth-century Hausaland, it did little to ease the tensions between the Fulani Muslims and the Hausa state within which many of them lived.

This was the environment into which 'Uthman dan Fodio was born in 1754, son of a Qur'anic school teacher who was usually known simply as "Fodio," or the teacher. Thus the young 'Uthman was known as "the son of the teacher." It was a fitting name, as he later gained wide renown as a teacher in his own right, becoming himself a *shaykh* (or *shehu,* in the vernacular). As this was also a time when the wider Islamic world witnessed a revival of *sufism,* it is not surprising 'Uthman was exposed to many of its teachings. He was certainly aware of the expectations of a coming *Mahdi* who would deliver Islam from the many challenges it faced, ushering in the end of time. He also entered his thirtieth year just before the coming of a new Islamic century [1200 A.H. (after hegira)], a time when many around him expected a prophet (*mujaddid,* or "renewer") who would pave the way for the coming *Mahdi.*

Certainly, 'Uthman dan Fodio became enmeshed in the religious and political controversies of his time, both within the wider Islamic world and his own particular part of Africa. Although his motives were undoubt-

Chapter 8

Islamic

Fundamentalism

and Renewal in

West Africa

(ca. 1775–1820)

edly complex, there were important reasons that he choose to preach a jihad to the people of the central Sudan. These are important aspects of the first two questions you will address in this chapter: Were 'Uthman dan Fodio and his followers Islamic extremists? And what effects did their movement have on early-nineteenth-century West Africa?

THE METHOD

Most of the sources included in this chapter are translated from documents written or dictated in either the Arabic or Hausa languages. As is true in Western Europe, some of these documents are the product of many scribes and have been rewritten many times. But most of them also have an accepted validity in the oral traditions still found in Hausaland. Although most are the work of 'Uthman dan Fodio, his relatives, and supporters, a few represent the voices of his critics. To better understand the fundamental basis of the call for a jihad, you will begin in Source 1 with the Qur'an. Keep in mind the injunctions of this foundational Islamic document as you approach some of the later sources.

The next group of selections (Sources 2 through 5) concern the life and beliefs of 'Uthman dan Fodio himself. In Source 2 his older brother, 'Aba Allah bin Muhammad, describes the education of *shaykh* 'Uthman, including his early failure to make the *hajj*. Then in Source 3 you will read about 'Uthman's own thoughts on the pilgrimage and the place of the Prophet Muhammad in his life. Do you see any connection between his experience and his belief about the *hajj*? This is followed by a section from a sort of spiritual autobiography (Source 4) written late in his life, in which 'Uthman dan Fodio describes some of the formative influences on his thinking. What can you conclude about the most important of these influences? Source 5 is part of a verse in which 'Uthman discusses his place and role within the *umma*. How would you characterize his understanding of his relationship to the community of faith? Do you think 'Uthman dan Fodio was an extremist? Why?

Next you will find two sources that describe the state of affairs in Hausaland while 'Uthman was engaged in his teaching. Source 6 was written in 1940 by descendants of the rulers of Abuja, a state formed by Hausa kings in the aftermath of 'Uthman dan Fodio's jihad. Although based on tradition, most historians of West Africa accept this as a fairly accurate description of how the Hausa states functioned from at least the late eighteenth century. This is followed by 'Uthman dan Fodio's own description in Source 7 of the governments of the Hausa states. To what extent do the descriptions in Sources 6 and 7 agree? How might you explain any differences?

As *Shehu* 'Uthman took his teaching into the city of Gobir itself, he began to arouse opposition. Muhammad Bello, 'Uthman's second son and successor, describes some of the reactions

[228]

to his father's teaching (Source 8), including some of the rulings made by the ruler (*sarkir*) of Gobir, Nafata. Then in Source 9 you will find an Islamic criticism of *shaykh* 'Uthman voiced by some of the Islamic followers of the *sarkir* of Gobir, as recorded by 'Abdullah, younger brother of the *shaykh*. This opposition was undoubtedly significant, for it caused 'Uthman and his followers to move north of Gobir into territory where they could operate more independently.

Having found that his *jihad al-gawl* (jihad of preaching) was not having the effects he desired, *Shehu* 'Uthman then called for *jihad al-sayf* (jihad of the sword) against Gobir and other Hausa states. His formal proclamation is excerpted in Source 10. Taking up the sword, his followers campaigned with marked success against the Hausa and others. Source 11 is a poetic description of one of their battles, composed by 'Uthman's younger brother. The immediate effects of their victories were widely significant and resulted in many changes in the central Sudan. Excerpts from the Kano Chronicle (a lengthy history of that city) concerning this period (Source 12) give some indication of the effects of the jihad on the Hausa states.

Yet in extending the jihad further, 'Uthman and his followers met serious opposition, not only military resistance but also objections to the intellectual basis of the jihad itself. Source 13 is part of a letter from Muhammad al-Amin Muhammad al-Kanemi, one of the leaders of Bornu, to the east of Hausaland. Al-Kanemi writes to Muhammad Bello, son of 'Uthman, whom the *shehu* had appointed one of the military commanders of the jihad forces. Do you find anything of particular interest in al-Kanemi's objections to the Fulani attack on his state?

There were even reservations among the Fulani about what their jihad had wrought. In Source 14 you will find some hints of this uncertainty from one of those closest to 'Uthman dan Fodio, his younger brother 'Abdullah ibn Muhammad. What seem to be his greatest concerns about the Fulani community after their success? In thinking about this question, you will be aided by Source 15, reflections of an English visitor to Hausaland. Having come to Sokoto—the capital (and namesake) of the state created by the jihad of 'Uthman dan Fodio—two years before, Hugh Clapperton seems to have been less than impressed on his return in 1826. Does he seem to feel that the jihad reached its objectives?

After reading these sources, you will be in a better position to answer the central questions posed in this chapter. First, think about the West Africans involved in this jihad. Were 'Uthman dan Fodio and his followers Islamic extremists? And what effects did their movement have on early nineteenth-century West Africa?

Then consider again the teachings of the Qur'an and the writings of the principal West African Muslims you have read. Think of them as in many ways typical of Islamic reform and revival movements, even in our own time. Now consider the last of the central questions: What is the basis of Islamic fundamentalism?

Chapter 8

Islamic

Fundamentalism

and Renewal in

West Africa

(ca. 1775–1820)

THE EVIDENCE

Source 1 from The Qur'an: Selections from the Noble Reading, *2nd rev. ed., trans. T. B. Irving (Cedar Rapids, Iowa: Lawrence Press, 1980).*

1. From the Qur'an

Fight in the cause of God against those who fight against you, but do not begin hostilities. Surely, God loves not the aggressors. Once they start the fighting, kill them wherever you meet them, and drive them out from where they have driven you out; for aggression is more heinous than killing. But fight them not in the proximity of the Sacred Mosque unless they fight you therein; should they fight you even there, then fight them: such is the requital of these disbelievers. Then if they desist, surely God is Most Forgiving, Ever Merciful. Fight them until all aggression ceases and religion is professed for the pleasure of God alone. If they desist, then be mindful that no retaliation is permissible except against the aggressors. (2:190–193)

Do not acount those who are slain in the cause of God, as dead. Indeed, they are living in the presence of their Lord and are provided for. They are jubilant over that which god has bestowed upon them of His bounty, and rejoice for those who have not yet joined them out of such as they left behind, because on them shall come no fear, nor shall they grieve. They rejoice at the favour of God and His bounty, and at the realisation that God suffers not the reward of the faithful to be lost. (3:169–171)

Source 2 slightly modified from Mervyn Hiskett, "Material Relating to the State of Learning among the Fulani," Bulletin of the School of Oriental and African Studies *19 (1957): 563–565.*

2. 'Abd Allah bin Muhammad on the Education of his Brother, 'Uthman dan Fodio, early 19th century

The *shaykh* ['Uthman dan Fodio] read the Koran with his father, and learnt *al-'Ishrīniyāt* and similar works from his *shaykh,* known as Biddu al-Kabawī. . . . He read *al-Mukhtaṣar* with our paternal and maternal uncle 'Uthmān, known as Biddūrī b. al-Amīn b. 'Uthmān b. Hamm b. 'Alī, etc. This *shaykh* of his was learned and pious. . . . He it was whom our *shaykh* 'Uthmān imitated in states [probably Sufi practices] and deeds. He accompanied him for nearly two years, moulding himself according to his pattern in piety. . . . [Our maternal uncle, Muḥammad Thanbu] . . . was learned, having success-fully memorised most of what he had read, and it was he who read to them the commentary of al-Karāshī. If [Shehu 'Uthman] made a mistake, or let any-thing slip, this maternal uncle of ours would correct it for him without look-ing in a book, for he knew the commentary of al-Karāshī by heart. Then he went to the country of the two Holy Places, performed the Pilgrimage, and re-mained there for over ten years. He then returned and reached the town of Agades, and there he died. . . . Then the *shaykh* 'Uthmān [dan Fodio] went to seek knowledge to our *shaykh* Jibrīl [Jibrīl b. 'Umar] and he accompanied him for almost a year, learning from him until he came with him to the town of Agades. Then the *shaykh* Jibrīl returned him to his father and went on Pilgrim-age for ['Uthman's] father had not given him permission to go on pilgrim-age. . . . In short, the *shaykhs* of the *shaykh* ['Uthman] were many. I knew some of them, and some I did not know.

Sources 3 and 4 from Mervyn Hiskett, The Sword of Truth: The Life and Times of Shehu Usuman dan Fodio *(New York: Oxford University Press, 1973), p. 33; pp. 64–66. Translated by Mervyn Hiskett.*

3. 'Uthman dan Fodio, *Qasidat al-daliyya,* 1774

Is there a way for me to Tayba [Medina], swiftly,
　　To visit the tomb of the Hashimite, Muhammad [the Prophet],
When his sweet perfume diffuses in its sheltered places,
　　And the star of Muhammad urges on the pilgrims?
I wept, and tears poured down like heavy rain
　　In longing for this Prophet, Muhammad.
I swear by the Merciful God, nothing graces me
　　Save my desire to love the Prophet Muhammad.
I am as one afflicted with longing for him, for whom it befell
　　There is no joy in life without Muhammad.
Through longing I almost flew to his tomb—
　　There is no joy for me without a visit to my master—
The sun of the forenoon, crown of right guidance, sea of generosity,
　　There is no other good than following Muhammad,
He is the most generous, his favours cover all mankind, nay,
　　All God's creation is beneath Muhammad.
Were I to visit Tayba, I would achieve the height of my ambition,
　　Sprinkling myself with the dust of Muhammad's sandal.

Chapter 8
Islamic
Fundamentalism
and Renewal in
West Africa
(ca. 1775–1820)

4. 'Uthman dan Fodio, *Wird*, ca. 1815

When I reached thirty-six years of age, God removed the veil from my sight, and the dullness from my hearing and my smell, and the thickness from my taste, and the cramp from my two hands, and the restraint from my two feet, and the heaviness from my body. And I was able to see the near like the far, and hear the far like the near, and smell the scent of him who worshipped God, sweeter than any sweetness; and the stink of the sinner, more foul than any stench. And I could recognize what was lawful to eat by the taste, before I swallowed it; and likewise what was unlawful to eat. I could pick up what was far away with my two hands while I was sitting in my place; and I could travel on my two feet [a distance] that a fleet horse could not cover in the space of years. That was a favour from God that He gives to whom He will. And I knew by my body, limb by limb, bone by bone, sinew by sinew, muscle by muscle, hair by hair, each one by its rank, and what was entrusted to it. Then I found written upon my fifth rib, on the right side, by the Pen of Power, "Praise be to God, Lord of the Created Worlds" ten times; and "O God, bless our Lord Muhammad, and the Family of Muhammad, and give them peace" ten times; and "I beg forgiveness from the Glorious God" ten times; and I marvelled greatly at that. . . .

When I reached forty years, five months and some days, God drew me to him, and I found the Lord of djinns [spirits] and men, our Lord Muhammad—may God bless him and given him peace. With him were the Companions, and the prophets, and the saints. Then they welcomed me, and sat me down in their midst. Then the Saviour of djinns and men, our Lord 'Abd al-Qadir al-Jilani,[4] brought a green robe embroidered with the words "There is no god but God; Muhammad is the Messenger of God"—May God bless him and give him peace—and a turban embroidered with the words, "He is God, the One."

He sat me down, and clothed me and enturbaned me. Then he addressed me as "Imam of the saints" and commanded me to do what is approved of and forbade me to do what is disapproved of; and he girded me with the Sword of Truth, to unsheath it against the enemies of God. Then they commanded me with what they commanded me; and at the same time gave me leave to make this litany that is written upon my ribs widely known, and promised me that whoever adhered to it, God would intercede for every one of his disciples.

4. **Abd al-Qadir al-Jilani:** twelfth-century *sufi* founder of the Qadiriyya *tariga* [religious order or brotherhood]; his ideas and his following spread from Baghdad to North Africa by the fourteenth century and south into the central Sudan not long after, certainly by the sixteenth century.

Source 5 from R. A. Adeleye and I. Mukoshy, trans. and eds., Center of Arabic Documentation (Ibadan), Research Bulletin 2, no. 1 (January 1966): 26–27.

5. 'Uthman dan Fodio, *Sifofin*
Shehu, ca. 1810

I say, "Peace be upon our prophet,"
    Know that I have obtained many of his characteristics.
These will I mention in gratitude to Allah
    That Muslims may know them, East and West. . . .
After summoning people to the religion he made the *hijra* [*hegira*];
    When I made mine it cost me great effort.
At that place where the enemies came out
    As they failed against him, so also against me, did they fail.
By making the *hijra* he was indeed saved from them,
    I did the same and the same has been repeated.
He made it at the beginning of the sixth decade of his life;
    Of a truth, mine was indeed made at the same time.
No sooner had he made the *hijra* than he waged the *jihād;*
    Likewise did I, keeping the pattern. . . .
Because our time has become that of the Mahdī,
    Thus, in it, have I come, in the cause of peace.
He is endowed with the abundant goodness belonging to the Mahdī;
    Hear ye, the same is true of me, there is no controversy.
He is appointed customarily to office at a time of upheaval;
    Truly, during it [a time of upheaval] did I obtain leadership.
When injustice has become excessive, he is made to appear;
    Indeed, I have also appeared at a time of tyranny.
He is made to appear during a time of religious degeneration;
    At such a time have I appeared; you have heard the word of wisdom. . . .
Note that I am not the Mahdī, duly appointed;
    I have been clothed with his mantle in keeping with the pattern.
Verily I do not disbelieve in Mahdism;
    At these times have I obtained my spiritual powers.
Because every epoch has a Mahdī;
    It is already a thousand years and over; for this reason I am informing you.
Like the wind heralding the raincloud;
    Almost exactly so am I in relation to the Mahdī.

Chapter 8

Islamic

Fundamentalism

and Renewal in

West Africa

(ca. 1775–1820)

Source 6 from Alhaji Hassan and Mallam Shuaibu Ha'ibi, A Chronicle of Abuja, *trans. F. Heath (Ibadan: Ibadan University Press, 1952), pp. 78–79.*

6. From *The Chronicle of Abuja*

The Chiefs of all these towns and the Headmen of all the smaller places used to pay tribute to the Emir [local ruler] in money and in slaves. Each of them sent one slave or more to him, together with one hundred thousand cowries, or more; this they would pay once a year, or sometimes more often. . . . The people would give a part of the produce of their home industries. . . .

All traders who came in with cattle, horses, sheep, goats, potash, salt, onions or whatever it was they brought, would take some of each kind to the Emir; and those who stopped in the Madawaki's or the Galadima's Ward gave them also a share. Besides this, the Emir received money from the Councillors and title-holders on their installation: from the Madawaki and the Galadima he had one million cowries each; from the Wambai and the Dallatu, five hundred thousand; from each of the rest of the Councillors about two hundred thousand; and from the other title-holders according to their position and means. A share of the spoil of any raid came always to their Emir and to the Madawaki; and when the Fulani were allowed to come, they paid a tax of ten thousand cowries on each head of cattle.

In return, the Emir had many obligations to his chiefs and people. . . .

Whenever the Chief of any town or district sent word that they were threatened by enemies, he would send warriors to help them fight; and he provided horses for his warriors and rewarded them for their bravery. If it was reported to him that any one was robbing or oppressing his people, he would send to seize the man and pass judgement on him. . . .

He provided gifts at the completion of the readings of the Koran; and when a young man had finished his first learning of the Koran, he was brought before the Emir who gave him a fez [characteristic Islamic hat] and a robe—but first he would see if the youth could read what was written on his writing board.

Source 7 from Mervyn Hiskett, trans., "Kitab al-farq: A Work on the Habe [Hausa] Kingdoms," Bulletin of the School of Oriental and African Studies 23 (1960): 567–570.

7. 'Uthman dan Fodio, *Kitab al-farq*, ca. 1808

I say—and help is with God—indeed the intention of the unbelievers in their governments is only the fulfilling of their lusts, for they are like the beasts. . . . One of the ways of their [Hausa] government is succession to the

emirate by hereditary right and by force to the exclusion of consultation. . . . One of the ways of their governments is their intentionally eating
whatever food they wish, whether it is religiously permitted or forbidden,
and wearing whatever clothes they wish, whether religiously permitted or
forbidden, and drinking what beverages they wish, whether religiously permitted or forbidden, and riding whatever riding beasts they wish, whether religiously permitted or forbidden, and taking what women they wish without
marriage contract, and living in decorated palaces, whether religiously permitted or forbidden, and spreading soft carpets as they wish, whether religiously permitted or forbidden. . . . One of the ways of their governments is to
place many women in their houses, until the number of women of some of
them amounts to one thousand or more. One of the ways of their governments is that (a man) puts the affairs of his women into the hands of the oldest
one, and every one (of the others) is like a slave-woman under her. One of the
ways of their government is to delay in the paying of a debt, and this is injustice. . . . One of the ways of their government is to change the laws of God,
and an example of that is that the *Sharī'a* decrees that the adulterer shall be
flogged if he is not married, and stoned if he is married, and that the thief
shall have his hand cut off, and that he who kills a person deliberately shall be
killed, or if the killing was unintentional, shall be ordered to pay the blood
money, which shall be divided among the heirs of the slain man. The *Sharī'a*
also decrees that one who destroys one of the limbs of the body, a similar limb
of his shall be destroyed. And for wounding it lays down retaliation in so far
as retaliation is possible, and compensation where retaliation is not possible.
They have changed all that has been mentioned, and turned it to devouring
the property of the people. . . . One of the ways of their governments is their
forbidding to the worshippers of God part of that which is legal for them,
such as the veiling of women, which is incumbent upon them, and turbans for
men. . . . One of the ways of their government which is also well known is
that they will not abandon the custom which they found their forebears prac-
tising, even though it is evil. . . . One of the ways of their governments is lying
and treachery and pride, and you cannot see one of them who does not give
himself airs, and anyone who shows the least lack of respect (for them), they
punish him for that: and these characteristics which have been mentioned, all
of them are according to the way of the unbelievers in their governments, and
everyone who follows their way in his emirship then he has in truth followed
the way of Hell fire. . . .

I say—and help is with God—the purpose of the Muslims in their governments is to strip evil things from religious and temporal affairs, and introduce
reforms into religious and temporal affairs, and an example of stripping evil
things from religious and temporal affairs is that every governor of a province
should strive to fortify strongholds and wage holy war against the unbelievers, and the war-makers and the oppressors, and set up a military station on
every frontier, and combat every cause of corruption which occurs in his

Chapter 8

Islamic

Fundamentalism

and Renewal in

West Africa

(ca. 1775–1820)

country, and forbid every disapproved thing. An example of introducing reforms into religious and temporal affairs is that the governor of every country shall strive to repair the mosques, and establish the five prayers in them, and order the people to strive to read the Qur'ān, and make (others) read it, and learn knowledge, and teach it; and that he should strive to reform the markets and set to rights the affairs of the poor and the needy, and order the doing of every approved thing. These . . . are the qualities of the way of the Muslims in their governments, and he who follows them in his emirship, has followed the way of Paradise, which is the straight way.

Source 8 from E. J. Arnett, The Rise of the Sokoto Fulani *(Kano, 1922), pp. 47–48; translated and paraphrased by E. J. Arnett.*

8. Muhammad Bello, *Infaq al-Maisur*, ca. 1813

Again when they saw that Shehu did not cease from what he was upon and that his affairs only grew in strength and the multitude of his people was not diminished, but entered the faith in multitudes then they began to fear him on account of their actions. For their actions were not in accord with what he practised. In truth their authority was not in accordance with the Law. For so far as the Law is concerned they held to it in the measure of their washings and the fashion of their clothes; they said prayers and fasted and paid zakka and made the profession of faith. But in all this they knew not the Law thoroughly. And as for their judgments they followed the practice of their fathers who knew [not] Mohamedanism. Most of their judgments were contrary to the book so far as we are acquainted with them. And much of their speech and their actions were those of heathens only. In truth the revelation of religion and the maintenance of the Law could not be reconciled with their deeds. For this reason they began to make plans for war with Mallam Shehu and his people. They did not doubt that the victory would be with them because they saw that the followers of Shehu were poor and not fit for fighting. They gathered together and took counsel and said that the man must be prevented from calling to religion and from preaching in public and that every man must be commanded to return to what he had inherited from his father and grandfather.

There was nothing that caused us so much fear as the proclamation made by Sarkin Gobir Nafata. He proclaimed three things: First, that he would not permit any man to preach to the people except Shehu alone. Second, that he would not permit any man to be a Mohamedan except he who had inherited it from his father, and he who had not inherited Mohamedanism must return to what he had inherited from his father and grandfather. Thirdly, that no man henceforward must be seen wearing a turban and no woman veil her body.

Source 9 from Mervyn Hiskett, ed. and trans., Tazyin al-Waraqat of 'Abdullah ibn Muhammad *(Ibadan: Ibadan University Press, 1963), p. 87.*

9. An Objection to the Preaching of 'Uthman dan Fodio, late 18th century

O you who have come to guide us aright,
We have heard what you have said. Listen to what we say.
You gave advice to the best of your ability,
But would that you had freed us from blame!
And you spoke—Glory be to God, it was evil-speaking—
Indeed, devils, if they come to our gathering,
Spread evil talk, exceeding all bounds!
We have not mixed freely with women
[by allowing them to listen to our preaching],
how should that be!

Source 10 from A. D. H. Bivar, trans., "The Wathiqat Ahl al-Sudan: A Manifesto of the Fulani *jihad," Journal of African History 2 (1961): 239–241.*

10. 'Uthman dan Fodio, "Dispatch to the People of the Sudan," ca. 1804

In the name of God, the Merciful, the Compassionate. May God bless our master Muhammad, with his family and his companions, and welcome [them] with greetings.

Praise be to God who has bestowed upon us his dispensation of Islam, and guided us by our lord and master Muhammad, on whom from God the Exalted be most gracious blessings and noble salutation.

After which, this is a dispatch from Ibn Fūdī, the Commander of the Faithful, 'Uthmān, to all the folk of the Sudan, and to whomso God wills of the brethren in the (Hausa) States; it is a dispatch advantageous in the present times. Thus speak I, and success comes of God.

Know then, my Brethren:

(i) That the commanding of righteousness is obligatory by assent [*ijmā'*][5];

5. **obligatory by assent:** the Muslim legal concept of *ijmā'* may be defined as the unanimous agreement of those qualified in the law; it forms one of the sources of Muslim legislation.

Chapter 8

Islamic

Fundamentalism

and Renewal in

West Africa

(ca. 1775–1820)

(ii) And that the prohibition of evil is obligatory by assent;

(iii) And that Flight [*al-hijra*] from the land of the heathen is obligatory by assent;

(iv) And that the befriending of the Faithful is obligatory by assent;

(v) And that the appointment of the Commander of the Faithful is obligatory by assent;

(vi) And that obedience to him and to all his deputies is obligatory by assent;

(vii) And that the waging of Holy War [*al-jihād*] is obligatory by assent;

(viii) And that the appointment of Emirs in the States is obligatory by assent;

(ix) And that the appointment of judges is obligatory by assent;

(x) And that their enforcement of the divine laws is obligatory by assent;

(xi) And that by assent the status of a town is the status of its ruler: if he be Muslim, the town belongs to Islam; but if he be heathen the town is a town of heathendom from which Flight is obligatory;

(xii) And that to make war upon the heathen king who will not say "There is no God but Allah" is obligatory by assent, and that to take the government from him is obligatory by assent;

(xiii) And that to make war upon the heathen king who does not say "There is no God but Allah" on account of the custom of his town, and who makes no profession of Islam, is [also] obligatory by assent; and that to take the government from him is obligatory by assent;

(xiv) And that to make war upon the king who is an apostate, and who has abandoned the religion of Islam for the religion of heathendom, is obligatory by assent, and that to take the government from him is obligatory by assent;

(xv) And that to make war against the king who is an apostate—who has not abandoned the religion of Islam as far as the profession of it is concerned, but who mingles the observances of Islam with the observances of heathendom, like the kings of Hausaland for the most part—is [also] obligatory by assent, and that to take the government from him is obligatory by assent;

(xvi) And that to make war upon backsliding Muslims who do not own allegiance to any of the Emirs of the Faithful is obligatory by assent, if they be summoned to give allegiance and they refuse, until they enter into allegiance; . . .

(xxii) And that to enslave the freeborn amongst the Muslims is unlawful by assent, whether they reside in the territory of Islam, or in enemy territory; . . .

(xxiv) And that to make war upon the congregation of the apostates is obligatory by assent, and that their property is booty, and that in the matter of their enslavement there are two opinions, the widespread one being its prohibition.

Source 11 from Mervyn Hiskett, ed. and trans., Tazyin al-Waraqat of 'Abdullah ibn Muhammad *(Ibadan: Ibadan University Press, 1963), pp. 112–113.*

11. 'Abdullah ibn Muhammad, *Tazyin al-Waraqat*, Describing Events of 1804

And we came upon them on Thursday,
At Qurdam[6] before midday, in the high places;
And they had spitted meats around the fire,
And gathered ready in tents
Fine vestments in a chest,
And all kinds of carpets, with cushions.

. . .

They rose up, and made everything ready for war.
Then they formed up in ranks, according to size.
Our banner began to draw near to them,
And it seemed to them like an ogre in striped clothing.
We fired at them, and they fired naphtha.[7]
Their fire became like ashes and it was
As if their arrows had no heads to them;
And as if their swords were in the hands of inanimate things,
As if their lances were in the hands of the blind.
They turned in flight, without provision,
And their army was scattered, and they were thirsty,
Confused, like young locusts.
We slew them, and collected all their wealth
Which they had left strewn in the valley.

6. **Qurdam:** site of a June 1804 battle between the jihadists and the forces of Gobir.

7. **naphtha:** refers to "Greek fire"—burning petroleum cast onto enemies—which had been used in battle throughout the Mediterranean world for centuries; in this context, probably means muskets or other firearms.

Chapter 8

Islamic

Fundamentalism

and Renewal in

West Africa

(ca. 1775–1820)

Source 12 from H. R. Palmer, ed. and trans., Sudanese Memoirs *(Lagos, 1928), vol. 3, pp. 127–129.*

12. From "The Kano Chronicle," ca. 1880s

XLIII. MOHAMMA ALWALI, SON OF YAJI (A.H. 1195–1222; A.D. 1781–1807)

The forty-third Sarki [ruler of Kano] was Mohamma Alwali, son of Yaji. His mother's name was Baiwa. As soon as he became Sarki he collected stores of "Gero" [millet] and "Dawa" [guinea corn] in case of war and famine. Nevertheless famine overtook him. . . .

In Alwali's time the Fulani conquered the seven Hausa States on the plea of reviving the Muhammadan religion. The Fulani attacked Alwali and drove him from Kano, whence he fled to Zaria. The men of Zaria said, "Why have you left Kano?" He said, "The same cause which drove me out of Kano will probably drive you out of Zaria." He said, "I saw the truth with my eyes, I left because I was afraid of my life, not to save my wives and property." The men of Zaria drove him out with curses. So he fled to Rano, but the Fulani followed him to Burum-Burum and killed him there. He ruled Kano twenty-seven years, three of which were spent in fighting the Fulani.

XLIV. SULIMANU, SON OF ABAHAMA (A.H. 1222–1235; A.D. 1807–1819)

The forty-fourth Sarki was Sulimanu, son of Abahama, a Fulani. His mother's name was Adama Modi. When he became Sarkin Kano, the Fulani prevented him from entering the palace. . . . One of the remaining Kanawa said to Sulimanu, "If you do not enter the Giddan Rimfa [royal palace], you will not really be the Sarki of city and country." When Sulimanu heard this he called the chief Fulani, but they refused to answer his summons. . . . Sulimanu said nothing but set off to Shehu-Osuman Dan Hodio ['Uthman dan Fodio] asking to be allowed to enter the Gidden Rimfa. Shehu Dan Hodio gave him a sword and a knife and gave him leave to enter the Giddan Rimfa, telling him to kill all who opposed him. He entered the house, and lived there. All the Kano towns submitted to him, except Faggam, which he attacked. He took many spoils there.

Source 13 from Thomas Hodgkin, Nigerian Perspectives, *2nd ed. (London: Oxford University Press, 1975), pp. 261–264; translated by H. F. C. Smith.*

13. Al-Kanemi, Letter to Muhammad Bello, ca. 1808

From him who is filthy with the dust of sin, wrapped in the cloak of shame, base and contemptible, Muḥammad al-Amīn ibn Muhammad al-Kanemi to the Fulani *'ulamā'* and of their chiefs. Peace be on him who follows His guidance.

The reason for writing this letter is that when fate brought me to this country, I found the fire which was blazing between you and the people of the land. I asked the reason, and it was given as injustice by some and as religion by others. We were perplexed, so I wrote to those of your brothers who live near to us asking them the reason and instigation of their transgression, and they returned me a weak answer, not such as comes from an intelligent man, much less from a learned person, let alone a reformer. . . . Then, while we were still perplexed, some of them attacked our capital, and the neighbouring Fulani came and camped near us. So we wrote to them a second time beseeching them in the name of God and Islam to desist from their evil doing. But they refused and attacked us. So, when our land was thus confined and we found no place even to dwell in, we rose in defence of ourselves, praying God to deliver us from the evil of their deeds; and we did what we did. Then when we found some respite at the present time—the future is in the hands of God—we decided to write to you, because we believe that writing is better than silence, even if it makes no impression on you.

Tell us therefore why you are fighting us and enslaving our free people. If you say that you have done this to us because of our paganism, then I say that we are innocent of paganism, and it is far from our compound. If praying and the giving of alms, knowledge of God, fasting in Ramaḍān and the building of mosques is paganism, what is Islam? These buildings in which you have performed the Friday prayer, are they churches or synagogues or fire temples? If they were other than Muslim places of worship, then why did you pray in them when you captured them? Is this not a contradiction?

Among the biggest of your arguments for the paganism of the believers generally is the practice of the amirs of riding to certain places for the purpose of making alms-giving sacrifices there; the uncovering of the heads of free women; the taking of bribes; embezzlement of the property of orphans; injustice in the courts. But these five charges do not require you to do the things you are doing. . . .

Acts of immorality and disobedience without number have long been committed in all countries. Egypt is like Bornu, or even worse. So also is Syria and all the cities of Islam. There has been corruption, embezzlement of the property of orphans, oppression and heresy in these places from the time of the

Chapter 8

Islamic

Fundamentalism

and Renewal in

West Africa

(ca. 1775–1820)

Bani Umayya [the Umayyad dynasty, 661–750 C.E.] right down to our own day. No age and no country is free from its share of heresy and sin. If, thereby, they all become pagan, then surely their books are useless. So how can you construct arguments based on what they say who are infidel according to you?

Source 14 from Mervyn Hiskett, ed. and trans., Tazyin al-Waraqat of 'Abdullah ibn Muhammad *(Ibadan: Ibadan University Press, 1963), p. 120.*

14. 'Abdullah ibn Muhammad, *Tazyin al-Waraqat*, Describing Events of about 1808

And when God had driven the enemy from us, we began to raid and to attack those who had rebelled against us. . . . Then there came to me from God the sudden thought to shun the homelands, and my brothers, and turn towards the best of God's creation, in order to seek approval, because of what I had seen of the changing times, and (my) brothers, and their inclination towards the world, and their squabbling over its possession, and its wealth, and its regard, together with their abandoning the upkeep of the mosques and the schools, and other things besides that. I knew that I was the worst of them, and that what I had seen from others would not deter me. I considered flight incumbent upon me, and I left the army and occupied myself with my own (affairs) and faced towards the East, towards the Chosen One—may God bless him and give him peace—if God would make that easy.

Source 15 from Hugh Clapperton, Journal of a Second Expedition into the Interior of Africa *(London: John Murray, 1829), pp. 223–224.*

15. From Hugh Clapperton, *Journal of a Second Expedition into the Interior of Africa,* 1826

These Africans keep up the appearance of religion. They pray five times a day. They seldom take the trouble to wash before prayers, except in the morning; but they go through the motions of washing, clapping their hands on the ground as if in water, and muttering a prayer. This done, as if they had washed, they untie their breeches and let them fall off; then, facing the east, let the sleeves of their larger shirt, or tobe, fall over their hands, and assuming at the same time a grave countenance, begin by calling out, in an audible voice,

"Allahu Akber!" &c. kneeling down and touching the ground with the fore-head. When they have finished repeating this prayer, they sit down, leaning over on the left thigh and leg, and count or pass the beads through their fingers. All their prayers and religious expressions are in Arabic; and I may say without exaggeration, taking Negroes and Fellatas [Fulani] together, that not one in a thousand know what they are saying. All they know of their religion is to repeat their prayers by rote in Arabic, first from sunrise to sunset in the Rhamadan, and a firm belief that the goods and chattels, wives and children of all people differing with them in faith, belong to them; and that it is quite lawful in any way to abuse, rob, or kill an unbeliever. Of the Fellatas, I should suppose about one in ten are able to read and write. They believe, they say, in predestination; but it is all a farce; they show not the least of such belief in any of their actions.

QUESTIONS TO CONSIDER

After reading the sources, try to remember that they represent the thinking and actions not only of Africans, but also of Muslims. In what ways were 'Uthman dan Fodio and his followers African, and in what ways were they Muslim? What does that say about the nature of Islam as a way of life as well as a religion, and about the nature of the *umma,* the community of faith? Answering these questions will be important to your approach to the central questions of the chapter.

Think about the situation in which the Fulani found themselves, most of them pastoralists within states formed largely by Hausa-speaking agriculturalists. For whom was Islam more compatible? Why? Whom do you think 'Uthman dan Fodio had in mind when he made his call for the jihad? What were his motives? In answering that question, compare the teaching of the Qur'an (Source 1) with the writings of the *shehu* himself, especially Sources 5, 7, and 10. What do you think he means by "succession to the emirate by hereditary right and by force to the exclusions of consultation" (Source 7)? Compare this to the experience of Solomon, *Sari* of Kano (Source 12). Also consider the post-jihad observations of 'Uthman's younger brother 'Abdullah (Source 14), and those of the English visitor Clapperton (Source 15). Can the results actually achieved by a movement of this sort provide any clues to its motives? Do they in this case?

You now may be in a position to answer the first of the central questions posed in this chapter. Were 'Uthman dan Fodio and his followers reformers? Were they extremists? And what impact did they have on the central African Sudan in the early nineteenth century? In answering the last of these, think again about the questions raised by al-Kanemi of

Chapter 8
Islamic
Fundamentalism
and Renewal in
West Africa
(ca. 1775–1820)

Bornu (Source 13). What concerns for the future does he express?

Now, turn your attention to the other set of central questions in this chapter. What were the primary sources of 'Uthman dan Fodio's beliefs? From what types of Islamic learning and thinking did they derive? Consider especially Sources 2 through 5. What seem to be the most important sources of authority that informed *shaykh* 'Uthman's opinions?

Do they fall within any particular Islamic traditions? Do they suggest anything about the roots of Islamic fundamentalism? Do you see any parallels with the experiences of Europe and the United States? Perhaps after answering these questions, you will come to concur with President Clinton's declaration that the "beliefs and cultures" of the West and Islam are not inevitably bound for conflict.

EPILOGUE

There can be little doubt that the jihad of *shaykh* 'Uthman dan Fodio brought many significant changes to West Africa, and especially to the central Sudan. Certainly Islam became much more significant in the lives of many more people; in many places it became something of an "official state ideology," no longer just tolerated, but the basis upon which rulers wanted their people to live.[8] This development was paralleled by the expansion of the *sufi tariqas* as well, especially the Qadiriyya of 'Uthman dan Fodio and the newer Tijaniyya. In fact, during the nineteenth century in the central Sudan, to be a Muslim was in most cases to be a member of one of the *tariqas*.

The use of Islam as a state ideology meant that greater influence, and even the opportunity to rule, was extended to the *ulama*, that class of Islamic clerics and teachers who had

8. Mervyn Hiskett, *The Development of Islam in West Africa* (London: Longman, 1984), p. 166.

been little respected by the former Hausa rulers. At first unified in the Sokoto caliphate, their efforts—despite later disagreements—led to the expansion of the theocratic rule, a major extension in the *Dar al-Islam* [territory of Islam] in West Africa. This show of strength also encouraged others to respond with new calls for jihads, which became a major fact of life in nineteenth-century West Africa, more important in some areas than the arrival of growing numbers of Europeans and the imposition of colonial rule. The new cities and states within the *Dar al-Islam* also became the focus of increasing economic activity as traders gravitated to the sources of power, wealth, and the valuable markets they also found there.

These patterns of change among the peoples of West Africa in the nineteenth century reflected common occurrences within the Islamic world of that time; they also parallel much of the religious discourse and political tone within Islam during the twentieth century. The degeneration of the Ottoman Empire, and its collapse during World War I, created another vacuum in the Islamic world; throughout the century other factors—particularly the globalization of Western culture—continued to challenge Islamic values. Muslim religious leaders emerged with messages startlingly similar to those of 'Uthman dan Fodio and the West African *ulama,* condemning breaches in Islamic practice and calling for a renewal of the faith.

Just as *shaykh* 'Uthman responded to the expectations of the appearance of a *mujaddid,* or new prophet, to prepare the way for a *Mahdi* who would deliver Islam from its troubles, so in the twentieth century have similar figures emerged to offer new leadership for the *umma.* The dilemma faced by these new leaders has, in many ways, been the same as that faced by 'Uthman dan Fodio. Historian John Hunwick has framed the question simply: "How to build truly modern societies using not just the moral and ethical principles of an ancient religion, but retaining a frame of reference for social action which evolved in a bygone era," the time of the Prophet Muhammad himself.[9]

In the last decades of the twentieth century—as Hollywood movies, Coca-Cola, Levi jeans, and satellite television blaring MTV and CNN have enraptured so much of the world—many Muslim clerics have increased the intensity of their pronouncements against deviations from the core teachings of Islam. Like 'Uthman dan Fodio, they find much to criticize in the contemporary world, and they seek a return to simpler ways they associate with the original faith. Thus, it is not surprising that the clerics' calls for renewal—even for jihad—seem at the same time both reasonable to themselves and yet outrageous and extreme to many in the West.

9. John Hunwick, "Africa and Islamic Revival: Historical and Contemporary Perspectives," lecture delivered at James Madison University, March 25, 1996. <URL: http://www.mynet.net/~msanews/MSANEWS/199606/19960616.0.html>. (read: 20 August 1996).

CHAPTER NINE

INDUSTRIALIZING THE NATION:

GERMANY AND JAPAN (1860–1900)

The nation-state by and large has been seen as the main actor or agent of modern history. Beginning in Western Europe, where it originated in early modern times, this unique form of state won nearly worldwide acceptance during the course of Europe's rise to global dominance. In ideal form, such a state represents a distinct "nation" or people whose interests it promotes over those of others. It presupposes a homogeneous population bound together by a common language, culture, and historical tradition and possessed of a collective will. "To achieve this state is the highest moral duty for nation and individual alike," proclaimed one of the nineteenth century's greatest promoters of the ideal, the German historian Heinrich von Treischke, who added that "all private quarrels must be forgotten" in the face of it.[1] Such unanimity was rare, however, and modern leaders more often found

that far from finding a ready-made sense of national identity among their people, they had to cultivate it. The onset of the Industrial Revolution immensely complicated this task, for it created powerful tensions within modernizing societies that strained national unity even as it offered opportunities for mobilizing people behind new national goals.

Leaders in Britain, France, and the United States—the first major countries to industrialize—were able to take the relationship between national unity and economic development for granted because of their early start and their unique political traditions. Already beginning to industrialize by the start of the nineteenth century, these countries underwent the process at a relatively slow pace that took generations to complete. Moreover, they benefited

1. From Heinrich von Treischke, *German History in the Nineteenth Century,* in *Documents of German History,* ed. Louis Snyder (New Brunswick, N.J.: Rutgers University Press, 1958).

from earlier revolutions and reform movements that modernized their societies and provided them with representative governments founded on the liberal ideals of the European Enlightenment, such as the doctrines of popular sovereignty and individual rights. These changes helped to allay many of the tensions created by industrialization and inspired great optimism about national progress among their leaders. Convinced that an "invisible hand" of providence promoted their improvement, they confidently relinquished the direction of industrialization and subsequent national adjustment mainly to private initiatives.

By the mid-nineteenth century, impressive gains in these states won them the attention and envy of people elsewhere. But because leaders of other countries regarded them as atypical, few sought to adopt their approach. By then the human and material costs of industrializing had grown greater; and the need to speed up economic change while simultaneously introducing social and political modernization posed more of a threat to stability. This chapter thus looks at the way in which Germany and Japan attempted to meet this challenge by finding their own paths to industrial development. As the two dominant states in Europe and East Asia respectively throughout most of the twentieth century they, of course, merit special attention. But more important, Germany and Japan stand out as two of the earliest examples of states whose governments actively sought to manage industrial-

ization, an approach that increasingly became the norm among developing countries in the twentieth century. As such, they may provide more typical cases of industrialization than Britain or the United States. They may also afford more insight into the ways in which industrialization complicated nation building, for both German and Japanese government efforts to guide economic growth forced frequent and deliberate public debate on the broader impact of industrialization.

Your task here is to assess how industrialization affected efforts to build a sense of national unity in modern Germany and Japan. Industrialization brought profound social changes, creating new groups in the population with new social and political aspirations as well as new economic interests. On the one hand, their competing demands and conflicts could destroy the unity so essential to the nation-state and undermine its stability. On the other, of course, industrialization also posed opportunities for uniting the nation. As a way to increase living standards, strengthen national defense, or enhance a nation's international stature, industrialization promised benefits to all and could be used to mobilize the population behind common goals. Economic achievement, serving as a measure of national success, could give citizens a sense of common pride and accomplishment. In the material that follows, try then to answer this central question: What impact did industrialization have on national unity in modern Germany and Japan?

Chapter 9

Industrializing

the Nation:

Germany

and Japan

(1860–1900)

BACKGROUND

Both Germany and Japan represent a second wave of modernizing nations. Their late start in the second half of the nineteenth century, which came nearly a century after the French Revolution and the beginning of British industrialization, had both advantages and disadvantages. Obviously, they could learn from those who had begun to modernize earlier, both in anticipating their difficulties and in following their models. They could also import technology, experts, and even capital to help them through the initial stages. But they often faced new and unknown problems, for the costs of modernization had become much greater by the century's end.

A major technological shift occurred during the 1860s and 1870s, boosting the cost of development enormously. In the early stage of industrialization, local entrepreneurs and artisans with only modest capital and skill were sufficient to mechanize a small number of pioneer industries with steam power. But the rise of new steel, petrochemical, and electrical industries and the increasing scope of manufacturing in the late nineteenth century demanded large outlays of capital and sophisticated expertise. Huge plants, extensive networks of transport, and armies of skilled workers were now needed as well as a whole range of new institutions from central banks to public systems of education. Besides such infrastructure, countries that modernized at this time also had to sustain high military expenditures.

For it was an age of extreme nationalism in which the Darwinian concept of a "struggle for survival" became a metaphor for international relations. Besides high material costs, the industrialization of this era entailed a great deal of social change, as rural people poured into industrial cities to form new classes of business people and factory workers, creating all kinds of tensions. Fear of riot and rebellion, if not the welfare of its citizenry, forced governments to spend resources on social issues.

Despite such costs, Germany and Japan succeeded in building powerful new nation-states in less than fifty years, half the time it took Britain, France, or the United States. One reason for their quicker development was the active role played by their governments in encouraging and directing change. Fast change, however, imposes severe strains on a population, and the disorienting effect of over-rapid growth under the direction of a powerful state may help to explain the behavior of both countries in the twentieth century. In many ways the pace of change may have outrun the ability of people to adjust, leaving them vulnerable to new forms of mass mobilization and manipulation. Few of the founders of modern Germany and Japan, however, could have foreseen this danger, for disunity and weakness were the dominant problems of their day.

Germany, for example, did not exist as a political entity in the first half of the nineteenth century. Instead of one nation, Germans lived in nearly thirty separate states, each with its own rulers and laws. Although an emerging middle class, inspired by the example of French unity and power, began to call for a "Greater Germany," the liberal beliefs that they adopted from French and British counterparts made them suspect in the eyes of more traditionally minded Germans. The rulers of the two largest German states, Austria and Prussia, thus took over the cause of nationalism, hoping to win popular support against middle-class challenges to their power. But each envisioned only a "Little Germany" united around a core of its own lands, rather than the Greater Germany of all German-speaking lands favored by liberals. The Austrians had an early advantage in this rivalry. After Napoleon's defeat (1814) they headed a loose German Confederation that offered a potential framework for national unity. But in the end, they were foiled by the Prussians.

The groundwork for Prussian success was laid by Frederick Wilhelm IV, who pushed for military and economic modernization soon after becoming king in 1840. During his reign, the monarchy allowed a limited amount of political reform, tolerating the creation of both a Prussian constitution and a Diet or parliament whose elected lower house came to be dominated by liberals. But decisive moves came later, following the ascension of King Wilhelm II in 1861. As prince regent from 1859 to 1861, he championed German unification by organizing a *Zollverein*, or Customs Union, to create a German free trade area. Then on his ascension in 1862, Wilhelm appointed a gifted diplomat, Otto von Bismarck, as Prussian chancellor to help him unite Germany politically.

Otto von Bismarck reflected the conservative values of the distinctive Prussian elite, a class of landowning aristocrats known as *Junkers*, of whom he was a member. Originally a feudal nobility with hereditary control of land and serfs, this privileged class supplied the bulk of the civil service and officer corps when the Prussian state began to modernize in the eighteenth century. It thus retained political dominance well into the modern era, eventually gaining control of the upper house of the Diet as well as the state's administrative apparatus. As a class of big land owners, who looked abroad for markets in which to sell the produce of their estates, the *Junkers* favored the liberal ideal of free trade. In most other respects, however, *Junkers* held conservative social and political ideas and firmly rejected middle-class attempts to broaden participation in politics. Wilhelm's choice of Bismarck signaled his rejection of liberal, middle-class aspirations and an intention to bolster the traditional alliance of crown and *Junker* conservatism.

For the next thirty years, during which he directed first Prussian and then ultimately German policy, Bismarck posed as the defender of the existing power structure whose chief task was to keep liberals from weakening the monarchy and its traditional supports, the *Junker*-dominated bureaucracy and army. He was helped by the fact that the Prussian constitution severely restricted the

Chapter 9

Industrializing

the Nation:

Germany

and Japan

(1860–1900)

authority of the Diet. By its writ, a prime minister was responsible only to the crown, not the Diet or the populace, and needed no parliamentary majority for support. This provision reduced the Prussian Diet to little more than a forum for middle-class and elite opinion, allowing Bismarck to formulate programs in an autocratic manner.

Despite his opposition to liberals, Bismarck did share their interest in German unification, if only to strengthen Prussia. He thus started wars in which Prussia could pose as the protector of German-speaking people and win acceptance of a Little Germany united around and dominated by Prussia. In 1864 he went to war with Denmark to wrest two German duchies from its control. Then in 1866 he risked a more dangerous conflict with Austria to force it to abandon the old German Confederation so that he could replace it with a new North German Confederation under Prussian hegemony. Finally in 1870, he goaded France, then considered the Germans' greatest enemy, into the Franco-Prussian War to arouse German interest in unification. Prussia's overwhelming defeat of France won Bismarck the acclaim of most nationalistic-minded Germans, including liberals. On the occasion of the French surrender in 1871, Bismarck thus proclaimed the Prussian king, Wilhelm II, *Kaiser,* or emperor, of a new empire embracing all German states save Austria.

The German "empire" heralded in 1871 was far from a cohesive nationstate. As spelled out in a new constitution, it was only a loose union of states still retaining their individual identities and most of their former powers over local administrations, schools, and state enterprises such as railroads and utilities. Sovereignty was vested in a Federal Council, or *Bundesrat,* made up of delegates appointed by the member states. But the imperial monarchy (hereditarily held by the Prussian royal house) quickly emerged as a more significant institution because Bismarck, assuming the role of imperial chancellor, staffed the new government with Prussians loyal to Wilhelm. The constitution also called for an elected parliament, known as the Reichstag, but subjected to the same limitations as the old Prussian Diet, it had little real power. Given the weakness of the legislature—and the emperor's deference to Bismarck—the imperial chancellor dominated the new government, using the threat of lower-class unrest, the "red specter" of revolution, to win liberal and middle-class acceptance of his authoritarian ways.

Bismarck's autocratic rule led him to chart a course for the new Germany that included incongruent elements. On one hand, as a believer in aristocratic rather than democratic rule, he tried to strengthen traditional elites like the *Junkers* and bar emerging social groups from political power. Yet he was wise enough to see that oppression alone could not stave off revolution from below and sought to relieve popular discontent. He thus allowed elections to placate liberals and initiated reforms to improve middle- and lower-class life. Deeply concerned with domestic affairs, he tried to forestall further foreign conflicts by supporting, rather than challenging, the international status quo. Nevertheless, he worked closely with the heads of the armed forces to build a modern army and navy designed to make Germany the most powerful military nation of the day.

Such power required advanced industry. Industrialization, of course, had begun decades earlier in some German states, notably in the Rhine Valley. But the creation of a unified empire with an integrated market greatly accelerated the process, and in a single generation from 1873 to 1895, Germany changed from an agrarian to an industrial nation. German industrialization began under the same system of private capitalism that emerged in England, but the imperial government did more than its British or American counterparts to foster industry. Like them, it created a common commercial code, a common currency system—based on the mark—and a new Imperial Bank to regulate the money supply and raise funds through the sale of bonds. But it also built the bulk of modern communication and transportation links at state expense; and it pioneered in setting up a system of secular, state schools from kindergartens to research universities (both German innovations) to allow true mass education.

Germany also departed from Anglo-American practices by abandoning free trade policies in favor of state-guided economic development. Hurt by the prolonged depression of 1873 to 1879, businessmen in key industries called on the government to create protective customs behind which they could complete German indus-

trialization without foreign competition. The government complied by adopting a new tariff policy in 1879. It also assumed an increasingly paternalistic relationship with businesses, offering them frequent aid at the cost of growing state regulation and management of industry. Far from opposing concentrations in industry, therefore, the imperial government promoted it, encouraging the formation of giant interlocking combines called *Kartels*, through which government leaders could informally influence and guide economic development. Germany thus completed its industrialization under a system of managed capitalism characterized by limited competition and active government involvement in business.

The German government also sought to play an active role in managing the whole of industrial society. Here, too, the depression of 1873–1879 proved decisive, for the labor unrest stirred by sinking wages led to the growth of unions and a socialist movement. Pleading the danger of lower-class revolt in 1878, Bismarck persuaded the Reichstag to outlaw socialist parties and their activities, bringing years of police suppression and censorship. In doing so, he skillfully turned liberals and the middle class against the left. But to placate workers and forestall further turmoil, he followed this move with a bold, positive step: the creation of the first comprehensive system of state welfare. He began by introducing compulsory health insurance in 1883, following it the next year with a program for workmen's accident insurance and compensation, and then in

Chapter 9
Industrializing
the Nation:
Germany
and Japan
(1860–1900)

1889, provisions for old-age coverage and a pension plan. Later, in 1891, the government began to regulate the hours of employment as well as working conditions. Although industrial booms in the late 1880s and 1890s probably did more to raise the wages and living standards of German workers, Bismarck's welfare programs helped Germany reduce the human cost of industrialization better than many other modernizing states.

Unlike Germany, Japan began its modernization as a unified state. The unity of mid-nineteenth-century Japan, however, was loose, for the feudal military regime that ruled the country left most power at the local level. Its head, a military leader called the *Shogun,* nominally ruled in the name of an emperor residing in the ancient city of Kyoto. But the position, hereditarily held in the Tokugawa family, really derived its power from the Shogun's personal lordship over the territorial magnates who controlled local land and people. These vassals, known as *daimyo,* ruled their domains autonomously with the aid of hereditary retainers drawn from the *bushi,* or warrior, class. The shogunate, based in the city of Edo, thus did not have much governing to do other than to keep peace among the *daimyo,* deal with foreign powers, and respond to problems that threatened the overall security or stability of the system. National unity thus rested upon a delicate balance of regional and central power.

Anxious about this balance from its inception in 1600, the Tokugawa shogunate looked askance at most

change, using what powers it had to preserve the status quo—a task made difficult by increasing pressures for economic and social change. A commercial revolution was slowly engulfing the country in a market economy and promoting urbanization, trends that undermined the feudal, agrarian base of the shogunal system. As cities grew in size and prosperity, a new urban class of merchants and manufacturers emerged who ill fit within the hierarchy of feudal, military arrangements but who garnered much of the country's wealth. Rather than adjust to these changes, the shogunate tried to stifle them, relying on rigid class rules, property restrictions, and sumptuary laws to bolster traditional arrangements and secure the rule of the military class. The regime similarly refused to adapt to change in the outside world.

Unsympathetic to foreign trade from the start, the Tokugawa regime became even more wary of international contacts following a rebellion of some of its vassals in the early seventeenth century. Because a few of these insurgents had not only traded with Europeans but embraced Christianity, the shogunate came to view European influence as a source of dangerous ferment. Gradually it broke off relations with outside powers, by 1641 banning all foreign contact except for a limited trade with the Chinese and Dutch on a single island. This policy of *sakoku,* or seclusion, became the bedrock of Tokugawa foreign policy. Though initially accepted by other countries, who largely ignored Japan over the next two centuries, this policy led to a crisis in the mid-nineteenth century when out-siders attempted to "open" the country. Foreign affairs thus became the dominant issue of nineteenth-century Japan, setting the stage for modernization.

The problem arose because of new Western interest in the Pacific and a disparity of power created by the rapid industrial and technological development of the West. While the British and French turned to Qing China following England's victory there in the Opium War of 1839–1842, the United States, then pursuing a "manifest destiny" in the Pacific after the annexation of California in the 1840s, focused its attention on Japan. In 1853, President Fillmore sent an American naval squadron under Commodore Matthew C. Perry to demand Western-style diplomatic and trade relations. Though aware that the British had started a war with China when refused a similar request, the shogunate temporized. Perry thus had to return for a reply the next year with nearly a quarter of the U.S. Navy to force compliance. Fearful of the military might revealed by Anglo-French victories over Qing China in the Arrow War, the Tokugawa shogunate signed an additional round of treaties with Britain, France, Holland, and Russia, as well as the United States, in 1858. Termed the five-nation "unequal treaties" because they infringed on Japan's sovereignty, these agreements ended Tokugawa isolationism.

Fear of Western power provided an impetus for change. The shogunate, deeply humiliated at succumbing to foreign pressure, tried to strengthen itself by turning first to the Americans and then ultimately to the French for assistance. Many of the elite, however, objected to this receptivity to foreign ways. Some spoke seditiously of turning to the emperor at Kyoto for alternate leadership, touting the slogan *sonno joi,* or "Revere the emperor and expel the barbarian." Anti-shogunal groups found strong support in western Japan where they built new local governments with westernized forces of their own and began to challenge the Tokugawa regime in the 1860s. But neither side achieved a decisive victory until 1868. That January forces from half a dozen rebellious domains seized control of Kyoto and prevailed upon the recently enthroned Emperor Mutsuhito, still a boy of fifteen, to reassert imperial authority and outlaw the Tokugawa regime. With his sanction, rebel forces marched on Edo where the demoralized Shogun, himself only recently installed, prudently abdicated. Promising a new era of Meiji, or "enlightened rule," under the emperor, the rebels set out to revitalize the nation and regain its lost honor.

This Meiji Restoration of 1868, though nominally a return to tradition, actually proved a revolution that transformed Japan and began its modern age. It brought a new group of leaders, mainly young samurai, to the forefront of national politics. Together with the young emperor Mutsuhito, they formed a cohesive oligarchy at the center of the new regime. For all their original opposition to foreign ways, these pragmatists quickly saw that they could

Chapter 9

Industrializing

the Nation:

Germany

and Japan

(1860–1900)

never reverse the humiliating un-equal treaties and compete success-fully in the new world order without modern military power. And this power, they realized, depended on the latest technology and an indus-trial base, which in turn required the modernization of society and culture. Guided by an old Chinese adage, *fukoku kyohei,* meaning "enrich the country to strengthen the military," they set out to refashion the basis of national power, even if it meant fol-lowing foreign models.

First on their agenda was the cre-ation of a stable government in Edo, now renamed Tokyo. By June 1868, Meiji leaders unveiled a brief consti-tution, inspired by the American ex-ample, establishing a Council of State with a Western-style cabinet of minis-ters. Construction of a centralized system of local administration based on French models followed. In 1871 they induced all *daimyo* to return their lands and authority to the em-peror in return for appointment as prefectural governors with annual stipends. They then introduced a standard land tax to generate steady revenue. Interest in financial security also led them to create a new, decimal monetary system based on the yen and a modern national bank to regu-late the supply and circulation of money. Meanwhile, to build an effec-tive new military system, they na-tionalized all domainal forces in 1872, reorganizing them into a West-ern-style army and navy. The Meiji also developed a modern system of state education based on the latest European examples and a revamped legal system modeled after the Na-poleonic Code of France.

Because of the critical importance of new technology and manufactur-ing to defense, Meiji leaders soon grew interested in industrialization. To foster the process, they set up a postal service and introduced other forms of communication and trans-portation like telegraph lines and railroads. But initial hopes that tradi-tional merchant firms would com-plete industrial development proved vain. The high start-up costs, to-gether with lack of familiarity, dis-suaded traditional merchants from taking up the challenge. As a result, the state decided to build pilot indus-tries to demonstrate their feasibility. Although it concentrated heavily on strategic industries like steel foun-dries that supplied materials needed in state shipyards and arsenals, it also set up some nonstrategic enter-prises like silk mills to offset the chronic trade imbalances caused by Western imports. Nearly bankrupted by this attempt, the regime sold most off at great discount to a handful of private *zaibatsu,* or "financial groups," largely run by members of the old military elite. Small in num-ber, they gave Japan's industrial sec-tor an oligopolistic character parallel to the Meiji political oligarchy.

Along with efforts to build up na-tional power and wealth, the regime also undertook a program of radical social reform to eradicate surviving vestiges of feudalism. As early as 1869, it outlawed old occupational re-strictions and, in 1871, began a wave of legislation that abolished feudal tenure and the old class structure, ef-fectively ending the legal status of the former military elite. By 1876 the regime felt confident enough to commute annual payments to former *daimyo* and their retainers into lump sum settlements, undercutting their economic privileges. Even more telling was the government's decision in 1873 to introduce a European system of universal male conscription for military recruitment, a measure that ended the elite's monopoly of military power. In 1877 some more traditional samurai, resentful of such reforms, took up arms against the regime. Suppression of this uprising, known as the Satsuma Rebellion, ended serious opposition allowing Meiji leaders to contemplate further changes in national life.

One of the issues that disturbed the rebels, who remained true to the original principles of the restoration, was the growing Meiji adoption of Western ways. Their resentment reflected a dilemma that troubled others, too: in Japan institutional modernization unleashed a parallel trend of cultural Westernization. People who accepted the former in order to strengthen Japan against Western encroachment often feared the latter would undermine their efforts. Government adoption of European uniforms, Victorian architecture, and the metric system, for example, troubled the more conservative as did popular fads, promoted by a Western-style press that provided information on all aspects of foreign life. Even the Meiji leaders themselves had trouble accepting certain Western ways, especially those related to democratic politics.

Nonetheless, the introduction of French and British ideas in the 1870s led a group called the Society of Patriots to launch a "People's Rights" campaign to establish elected assemblies. On the recommendation of prefectural governors, the regime agreed in 1878 to allow local assemblies as advisory bodies. But it continued to reject calls for a national assembly until 1881, when a prominent member broke ranks and petitioned the emperor for a parliament. The next year top officials went to Europe to study Western examples. Impressed by Germany, they set up a Bismarckian-style imperial cabinet under Ito Hirobumi as prime minister in 1885 and went on to promulgate a constitution modeled on German lines in 1889. Declaring the emperor the "sacred and inviolable" source of authority, it empowered him personally to select all top officials and to set policy in consultation with a civil cabinet under a prime minister, and a general staff under a chief of staff. The bicameral Diet, made up of an appointed House of Peers and an elected House of Representatives, had only an advisory role like its Prussian namesake. Restrictions limited those who could vote for candidates to the one elected branch, the House of Representatives, to only 450,000 males. But this recast balance of political forces brought a decade and a half of stable government in which parties gained a measure of influence.

Foreign affairs helped to promote domestic unity. Unlike modern Germany, which from the time of its birth enjoyed a reputation of military superiority thanks to Prussia's victories, Meiji Japan began as a weak power vulnerable before even the lesser Western states. Far from content to maintain the status quo in East Asia, therefore, its leaders resolved early on to take aggressive measures

Chapter 9

Industrializing

the Nation:

Germany

and Japan

(1860–1900)

to enhance national power and prestige. In pursuit of a dominant role in Korea, they deliberately started two wars, one with Qing China in 1894 and another with the Russian Empire in 1904. Spectacular victories in both instances led to a dramatic reversal in Japan's international position. Suddenly Japan not only exerted colonial control over Korea and an island empire stretching from Taiwan to Sakhalin off the Siberian coast, but earned Western recognition as a major regional power. By the time the Meiji emperor died in 1912 a powerful new industrial Japan was emerging, belying the idea that modernization was a purely Western phenomenon.

THE METHOD

The question at issue here—how industrialization affected efforts to build a sense of national unity in modern Germany and Japan—certainly involves economic factors, but the problem is not primarily one of economic history. It focuses more on the social and political consequences of industrialization than on its economic ramifications. For this reason, the sources that follow in the Evidence section do not comprise statistical tables and graphs, the usual stock in trade of economic historians. They instead consist of public statements of one sort or another giving different perspectives on the impact of industrialization within Germany and Japan from the final decades of the nineteenth century through the start of the twentieth century. And as you might expect, they occur in two sets, one for Germany and one for Japan.

During this period, rapid industrial growth contributed to the rise of mass society and aroused interest in public opinion in both societies. Political parties in the recently formed parliaments were beginning to challenge the authoritarian ways of the past, and both they and government leaders, who often remained aloof from them, sought ever-increasing popular support for their views. As the Japanese statesman Ito Hirobumi observed in one of the items included here, not only did the populace gain the right "to voice their opinions on the advisability and the faults of their country's administration," but governments found they had "to inform them well so that they will serve well." All of the sources presented here reveal the broadening scope of public debate within mass industrial society—even in such relatively authoritarian states as imperial Germany and Japan—and the growing diversity of opinion within such a society. Those that are graphic in nature especially attest to this trend, for they deliver their message in simple, direct terms accessible to all.

Sources 1 and 2, pictures commissioned by German factory owners to impress the public with their success, vividly depict the changing nature of industrial development during the late nineteenth century. The social and political consequences of these material changes can be gleaned from Source 3, an excerpt from a lecture by the noted German sociologist Max

Weber. As Weber's remarks imply, these consequences unleashed a national debate over how to adjust to new social and political realities. In this debate, the new media often sought to shape opinions through simple, visual statements like Source 4, a German political cartoon from the satirical magazine *Simplicissimus*, or Source 5, one of a series of emotionally intense photographs exposing the nature of working-class life in Berlin. Political leaders, too, often gave in to simplification and overstatement, as you can see in Source 6, the famous Erfurt Programme—or manifesto—of the German Social Democrats, and Source 7, one of Bismarck's parliamentary speeches.

Similar conditions prevailed in Japan. For all the cherry blossoms displayed in Source 8, a traditional Japanese woodblock print, this scene of the 1870s already focuses on the railway, one of the key symbols of modern industrialization. In his celebrated memo to the emperor proposing industrialization (Source 9), one of the key Meiji leaders, Okubo Toshimichi, claimed it was imperative that all Japanese embrace this new direction as a national "duty." For a while most did. As Source 10, a print showing the emperor's open visit to the Tokyo Industrial Fair of 1877, indicates, even the Meiji emperor complied. Over twenty years later, despite the evolution of a Western-style parliamentary system and contending political parties, Japan's first prime minister, Ito Hirobumi, still echoed that demand in his public speeches (Source 11). But by then parliamentary discussions and a mass media gave voice to other views. Cartoons and prints like Sources 12 and 13 publicized some of the human costs of change. And the exposure of conditions like those revealed in Source 14 through the recollections of some of the victims of industrialization made it clear that certain citizens bore a disproportionately higher share of the cost of change.

In both Germany and Japan, therefore, public debate revealed that industrialization complicated the process of building a modern nation. In theory the populace of a modern nation-state was supposed to be (or to become) a single, homogeneous body. The challenge of building up national industry could, of course, enhance that unity by providing a common purpose. But, as you can see from sources like the one giving voice to the women who crossed Nogumi Pass, many groups of people found themselves set apart from the rest of the population as a result of industrial development and the changes it set in motion. As you read over these sources, therefore, make two lists, indicating ways in which industrialization served to (1) unify or (2) divide the nation. Note any significant groups or categories of people whom the sources mention as either benefactors or victims of industrialization. Pay particular heed to those who became alienated from the rest of the nation, and observe how this affected social and political life. With your list as a guide, you should be able to decide for yourself the impact industrialization had on the development of national unity in modern Germany and Japan.

Chapter 9
Industrializing
the Nation:
Germany
and Japan
(1860–1900)

THE EVIDENCE

Sources 1 and 2 from Questions on German History (catalog of the Historical Exhibition in the Berlin Reichstag) (Bonn: German Bundestag Press, 1984), illustration 102, p. 167; color plate XVI. Photographs: Source 1 from Bildarchiv Preussischer Kulturbesitz; Source 2 from Historische Archiv, Fried. Krupp H GmbH, Essen.

1. Hagen Rolling Mill, 1860s

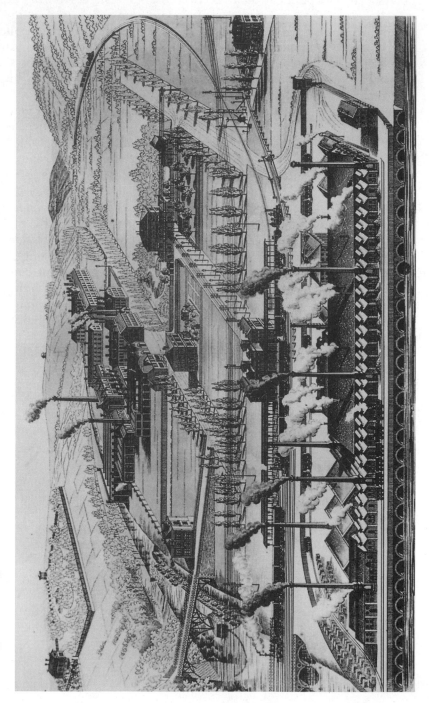

2. **Krupp Steel Works, 1912**

Chapter 9

Industrializing

the Nation:

Germany

and Japan

(1860–1900)

Source 3 from Nineteenth Century Europe: Liberalism and Its Critics, *trans. Paul Silverman (Chicago and London: University of Chicago Press, 1979), pp. 438–460 ff.*

3. From Max Weber, Inaugural Lecture at Freiberg University, 1895

During the first half of the century, the Polish element in the east appears to have been slowly and continuously pushed back. Since the 1860s, however, as is well known, it has been just as slowly and continuously on the advance. Despite their faulty foundations, linguistic inquiries establish this latter fact for West Prussia in the clearest possible manner. Now a shift of the boundary between two nationalities can come about in two fundamentally distinct ways. One way is for national minorities in a nationally mixed region to have the language and customs of the majority gradually imposed upon them, for them to be "absorbed." This phenomenon can be found in the east. It is statistically demonstrable in the case of German Catholics. The bond of the church is stronger here than that of the nation, memories of the *Kulturkampf* also play a part, and the lack of a German-educated clergy permits them to be lost to the cultural community of the nation. More important, however, and more interesting for us, is the second form in which shifts of nationalities take place— *economic displacement.* This is what we are dealing with here.

One is dealing here with a process of a mass-psychological kind: German agricultural workers can no longer adapt to the *social* living conditions of their home. Reports out of West Prussia from the lords of the estates complain of the "self-assurance" of the workers. The old patriarchical relationship between lord and smallholder, which attached the day laborer directly to the interests of agricultural production as a small cultivator entitled to a portion of the crop, is disappearing. Seasonal work in the beet-growing districts requires seasonal workers and money wages. These workers face a purely proletarian existence, but without the possibility of the sort of vigorous ascent to economic independence that fills the industrial proletariat, crowded together in the cities, with self-confidence. It is those who take the place of the Germans who are better able to accommodate themselves to these living conditions— the Polish migrant workers, bands of nomads recruited by agents in Russia, who cross the border in tens of thousands in the spring and then depart in the autumn.

But, as I have already said, I do not wish to discuss today this practical question of Prussian agrarian policy. I would much prefer to take up the fact that this question has arisen for us at all, that we consider the German element in the east to be something that *ought* to be protected and in defense of which the economic policy of the state *ought* to enter into the lists. It is the fact that our state is constituted as a *national state* that allows us to feel we have the right to make this demand.

In the final analysis, processes of economic development are also *power* struggles; they are *power* interests of the nation, and, where they are placed in question, they are the ultimate and decisive interests in whose service the nation's economic policy has to place itself. The science of economic policy is a *political* science. It is a servant of politics, not of the day-to-day politics of whichever rulers and classes may be in power at the moment, but of the long-term power political interests of the nation. And the *national state* is not a vague something for us that some believe is made all the more majestic the more one shrouds its nature in mystical darkness. It is rather the temporal institution that organizes the nation's power, and in such an institution the ultimate standard of value for us in inquiries regarding economic policy is, as in everything else, "*reason of state.*" This does not mean for us, as an odd misunderstanding has led some to believe, "state assistance" instead of "self-help," state regulation of economic life instead of the free play of economic forces. Rather, by means of this term we want to raise the demand that in questions of German economic policy—including, among others, whether and to what degree the state ought to intervene in economic life, and whether and when, on the contrary, the state ought to tear down the barriers standing in the way of the economic powers of the nation and let them loose to develop freely on their own—in individual cases the last and decisive vote ought to belong to the economic and political power interests of our nation and the entity responsible for them, the German national state.

The *attainment of economic power* has, in all times, engendered in a class the notion that it *can expect to assume political leadership.* It is dangerous and, in the long run, incompatible with the interests of the nation when a class that is economically on the decline holds the nation's political power in its hands. But it is still more dangerous when classes that are beginning to *attract* economic power and thus the expectation of gaining political command are not yet politically mature enough to assume the leadership of the state. Both of these things are threatening Germany at the present time and in fact are the key to the present dangers in our situation. Moreover, the upheavals in the social structure of the east connected with the phenomena discussed at the outset also belong within this larger context.

In the Prussian state right up into the present, the dynasty has depended politically on the caste of the Prussian *Junkers.* Admittedly, the dynasty moved against them when creating the Prussian state, but, all the same, it was only with their assistance that its creation was possible. I am well aware that the Junkers' name has an unpleasant sound to South German ears. It may be felt that I am speaking a "Prussian" language if I say a word in their favor. I would not know. In Prussia even today the Junkers have open to them many paths to influence and power as well as many paths to the monarch's ear,

Chapter 9
Industrializing
the Nation:
Germany
and Japan
(1860–1900)

which are not accessible to every citizen. They have not always used this power in such a way as to allow them to answer for themselves before history, and I see no reason why a bourgeois scholar ought to have any particular fondness for them. Nonetheless, the strength of their political instincts was one of the most powerful resources that could be applied in the service of the power interests of the state. Now their work is done, and today they lie in the throes of an economic death from which no economic policy of the state could ever retrieve them and lead them back to their old social status. Moreover, the tasks of the present are different from those that could be solved by them. For a quarter of a century the last and greatest of the Junkers [Bismarck] stood at the head of Germany, and, although today some are still unable to see it, the tragic element that, alongside the incomparable greatness, was inherent in his career as a statesman will be discovered by the future in the fact that the work of his hands, the nation to which he gave unity, slowly and irresistibly changed its economic structure under him and became something other than what it was, a people who must demand social forms different from those he was able to provide it and to which his caesarist nature was able to adapt. In the final analysis, this is what brought about the partial failure of his life's work, for this life's work surely ought to have led not only to the outer but also to the inner unification of the nation, and every one of us knows that that has not been achieved. With the means he used it could not be achieved.

I am a member of the bourgeoisie, feel myself to be such, and have been brought up to share in its attitudes and ideals. But it is the calling of precisely our science to say what one would rather not hear—on high, down below, and in our own class too—and when I ask myself whether the German bourgeoisie is at present mature enough to become the nation's political governing class, I cannot *today* answer this question in the affirmative.

The political immaturity of broad sections of the German bourgeoisie is not due to economic causes, nor is it due to "interest politics," something that is often mentioned but that other nations are no less familiar with than we are. The cause lies in this class's unpolitical past, in the fact that a century's worth of political education cannot be made up for in a decade, and in the fact that rule by a great man is not always the best means of political education. The important question for the political future of the German bourgeoisie is whether or not it is now too *late* to make up for this missed political education. No *economic* factor can serve as a substitute for it.

Will other classes become the champions of a politically greater future? The modern proletariat is self-confidently stepping forward as the heir to bourgeois ideals. What can be said of its prospective claim to the political leadership of the nation?

The danger does *not* lie with the *masses*, as those who stare hypnotically into the depths of society believe. The ultimate content of the problem of *social* policy is not a question of the *economic* condition of the *ruled*, but on the contrary a question of the *political* qualifications of the *ruling* classes and those *on the rise*. The goal of our work in the field of social policy is not the spreading of happiness throughout the world but, rather, the *social unification* of the nation—a condition that modern economic development split apart—so that it will be possible to face the arduous struggles of the future. If a "labor aristocracy" were in fact created that would be the bearer of the political understanding we cannot now see in the workers' movement, then the spear that the arm of the bourgeoisie seems still not strong enough to carry might be transferred to those broader shoulders. But there appears to be a long way to go before that happens.

Chapter 9

Industrializing

the Nation:

Germany

and Japan

(1860–1900)

Source 4 from Simplicissimus, *vol. 4 (1899/1900), number 29. Courtesy of the Boston Public Library.*

4. Cartoon, "Through Darkest Germany, a View Inland," 1899

Source 5 from Barbara Franzoi, At the Very Least She Pays the Rent: Women and German Industrialization, 1871–1914 (Westport, Conn.: Greenwood Press, 1994), figure 10. Photograph: AKG Photo London.

5. A German Worker's Apartment, 1910

Chapter 9

Industrializing

the Nation:

Germany

and Japan

(1860–1900)

Source 6 from Susanne Miller and Heinrich Potthoff, A History of German Social Democracy From 1848 to the Present, *trans. J. A. Underwood (Hamburg and New York: Berg), Appendix 3.*

6. The Erfurt Social Democratic Party Program, 1890

The economic development of bourgeois society inevitably leads to the destruction of the small enterprise, the basis of which is private ownership by the worker of his means of production. It separates the worker from his means of production and turns him into an unpropertied proletarian, while the means of production become the monopoly of a relatively small number of capitalists and large landowners.

Hand in hand with this monopolisation of the means of production go the displacement of the fragmented small-business sector by gigantic big businesses, the evolution of the tool into the machine, and an enormous growth in the productivity of human labour. All the advantages of this change, however, are monopolised by the capitalists and large landowners. For the proletariat and the sinking middle orders—petty bourgeoisie, peasant farmers—it means a growing increase in the uncertainty of their livelihood and in poverty, pressure, enslavement, degradation, and exploitation.

The number of proletarians becomes ever greater, the army of surplus workers becomes ever more massive, the contrast between exploiters and exploited becomes ever sharper, and the class struggle between bourgeoisie and proletariat, which divides modern society into two hostile camps and is the common feature of all industrialised countries, becomes ever more vehement.

The gap between propertied and unpropertied is further widened by the crises inherent in the nature of the capitalist mode of production, which become more and more expensive and devastating, make the normal condition of society one of generalised insecurity, and prove that the forces of production have got beyond the control of present-day society and that private ownership of the means of production has become incompatible with their being utilised appropriately and developed to the full.

Private ownership of the means of production, once the means of protecting the producer's ownership of his products, has today become a means of expropriating peasant farmers, craft-tradesmen, and retailers and placing the non-workers—capitalists, large landowners—in possession of the product of the workers. Only the transformation of the capitalist private ownership of the means of production—land, mines, raw materials, tools, machinery, transport—into social ownership and the conversion of commodity production into socialist production, pursued by society for society's benefit, is capable of bringing it about that big business and the constantly increasing yield capac-

ity of social labour cease to be a source of poverty and oppression for the hitherto exploited classes and become a source of supreme welfare and all-round,
harmonious improvement. This social transformation means the emancipa-
tion not only of the proletariat but of the whole human race as suffering under
present circumstances. It can only be achieved by the working class, however,
because all other classes, despite conflicts of interest between them, take their
stand on the private ownership of the means of production and have as their
common goal the preservation of the foundations of present-day society.

The struggle of the working class against capitalist exploitation is of necessity a political struggle. The working class cannot wage its economic struggles
and develop its economic organisation without political rights. It cannot effect the switch of the means of production to common ownership without first
acquiring political power.

The task of the Social Democratic Party is to mould that struggle of the
working class into a conscious, uniform process and direct it towards its im-
mutable goal.

The interests of the working class in all countries with a capitalist mode of
production are the same. With the growth of world trade and production for
the world market the position of workers in one country is becoming increasingly dependent on the position of workers in all other countries. The emanci-
pation of the working class is thus a task in which the workers of all civilised
countries are equally involved. Recognising this, the Social Democratic Party
of Germany feels and declares itself to be one with the class-conscious workers of all other countries.

The Social Democratic Party of Germany is thus fighting not for new class
privileges and prerogatives but for the abolition of class rule and of classes
themselves and for equal rights and equal obligations for all without distinction of sex and birth. Armed with these opinions it campaigns in present-day
society not only against the exploitation and oppression of wage workers but
against every kind of exploitation and oppression, be it directed against a
class, a party, a sex, or a race.

On the basis of these principles the Social Democratic Party of Germany demands firstly:

1. Universal, equal, direct suffrage with secret balloting for all German citizens of twenty and over without distinction of sex for all elections and votes.
A proportional-representation system, and until that is introduced the statutory re-drawing of constituency boundaries after every census. Two-year legislative periods. Elections and votes to be held on a statutory public holiday.
Remuneration of elected representatives. The abolition of any restriction of
political rights except in the event of legal incapacitation.

2. Direct legislation by the people through the medium of rights of proposal and rejection. Self-determination and self-government of the people at

Chapter 9

Industrializing

the Nation:

Germany

and Japan

(1860–1900)

national, state, provincial, and municipal level. The election of public authorities by the people, those authorities to be accountable and liable. An annual grant of supply.

3. Training for universal fitness to fight. A citizen army in place of the regular army. Decisions regarding war and peace to be made by parliament. All international disputes to be settled by arbitration.

4. The repeal of all laws restricting or suppressing the free expression of opinion and the right of association and combination.

5. The repeal of all laws placing women at a disadvantage in terms of public and private law as compared with men.

6. Religion to be declared a private matter. The abolition of all expenditure out of public funds for ecclesiastical and religious purposes. Ecclesiastical and religious communities to be regarded as private associations that order their affairs in complete independence.

7. Secular schooling. Compulsory attendance at public elementary schools. Free education, teaching aids, and food in public elementary schools as well as in more advanced educational institutions for those pupils whose abilities are such that they are considered suitable for higher education.

8. Free justice and legal advice. Jurisdiction by judges elected by the people. Appeal in criminal cases. Compensation for those indicted, arrested, and convicted and subsequently proved innocent. The abolition of the death penalty.

9. Free medical attention including midwifery and medication. Free burial.

10. A graduated income and property tax to defray all public expenditure where this is to be covered by taxation. Compulsory self-assessment. Death duties, graduated according to size of inheritance and degree of kinship. The abolition of all indirect taxes, duties, and other politico-economic measures that sacrifice the interests of the people as a whole to the interests of a privileged minority.

To safeguard the working class the Social Democratic Party of Germany demands firstly:

1. Effective national and international legislation for the protection of labour on the following bases: a) the standard working day to be fixed at a maximum of eight hours; b) paid labour to be prohibited for children under fourteen; c) night work to be prohibited except in those branches of industry that require it by their very nature, whether for technical reasons or for rea-

sons of public welfare; d) a continuous break of at least thirty-six hours in each week for every worker; e) the truck system to be prohibited.

2. The supervision of all industrial and commercial establishments and the study and regulation of labour relations in town and country by national and regional departments of labour and chambers of labour. Effective industrial hygiene.

3. The same legal status for agricultural workers and domestic staff as for industrial workers; the abolition of the special regulations for servants.

4. Guaranteed right of combination.

5. The assumption of all labour insurances by the state with workers playing a decisive part in the administration of it.

Source 7 from Louis L. Snyder, The Blood and Iron Chancellor: A Documentary-Biography of Otto von Bismarck *(Princeton, N.J.: D. Van Nostrand Company, 1967), pp. 280–283.*

7. From Otto von Bismarck, Address to the Reichstag Proposing State Social Insurance, 1881

The field of legislation—justly pronounced by Deputy Richter to be one commanding a vast perspective—opened up by this measure has to do with a question which, in all probability, will not vanish from the order of the day very speedily. For the last fifty years we have been talking about the social question. Since the Socialist Law was passed, I have been repeatedly reminded, in high quarters as well as low, of the promise I then gave that something positive should be done to remove the causes of socialism. Hints of this sort have been imparted to me *toto die;* but I do not believe that our sons, or even our grandsons, will be able finally to solve the question. Indeed, no political questions can ever be mathematically settled, as books are balanced in business; they crop up, have their time, and give way to other questions propounded by history. Organic development wills that it shall be so. I consider it my duty to take up these questions without party feeling or excitement, because I know not who is to do so, if not the imperial government.

Deputy Richter has pointed out the responsibility of the state for what it is now doing. Well, gentlemen, I feel that the state should also be responsible for what it leaves undone. I am not of opinion that *laissez faire, laissez aller,* "pure Manchester policy," "everybody takes care of himself," "the weakest must go

Chapter 9

Industrializing

the Nation:

Germany

and Japan

(1860–1900)

to the wall," "to him who hath shall be given, from him who hath not shall be taken even that which he hath," can be practiced in a monarchically, patriarchically governed state. . . .

For my part, I should not have the courage to proceed with this measure if the outlay it involves were to be exclusively borne by industrialists. Were state assistance, in every form now obtaining, to be cut off, I should not venture to assume the responsibility of imposing the bill upon German industry. We may limit the state subvention to a period of three years, or otherwise, as you please; but, without having made any experiment by which we can appraise what is before us, I do not feel justified in saddling our industrialists with the whole cost of these state institutions, or in burdening them more heavily than heretofore with the outlay for injured operatives that has hitherto been defrayed by local poor relief, and will at some future time be disbursed to a greater, completer, and more dignified extent by the insured themselves in partnership with the state. . . .

The invalid workman is saved from starvation by the measure we now advocate. That, however, is not sufficient to make him look forward contentedly to old age. And the bill is animated by a desire to keep alive the sense of human dignity, which I hope the poorest German will preserve, and which prescribes that he should not be forced to accept eleemosynary assistance [charity] (to which he has no right) but should be entitled to something of which nobody can dispose but himself, and of which nobody can deprive him; that doors, hitherto closed to him, should open readily when he knocks, and that better treatment should be accorded to him in his place of refuge by reason of the additional means he brings into it with him.

Whosoever has looked closely into the state of the poor in large towns, or into the arrangements made for paupers in country communes, and has seen for himself how—even in the best-managed villages—a poor wretch is sometimes treated when weakly and crippled, must admit that any healthy operative, contemplating that spectacle, is fully justified in exclaiming: "It is simply horrible that a human being should be treated worse than a dog in his own house!" I say, therefore, our first object in bringing forward this bill is to ensure kindlier treatment to this class of the poor; and next year I will do my best to give Deputy Richter full satisfaction as to the extent of the provision proposed to be made by the state for the better usage of the unemployed. For the present this measure must be regarded as an experiment—an attempt to find out the depth of the financial water into which we ask the country to plunge. . . .

An appropriate title for our enterprise would be "Practical Christianity," but we do not want to feed poor people with figures of speech, but with something solid. Death costs nothing; but unless you will put your hands in your pockets and into the state exchequer, you will not do much good. To saddle our industry with the whole affair—well, I don't know that it could bear the burden. All manufacturers are having hard times. . . .

Source 8 from the Tsuneo Tamba Collection, Yokohama/Laurie Platt Winfrey, Inc.

8. Ando Hiroshíge, Woodblock Print of Tokyo's First Railway Station, 1870s

Chapter 9

Industrializing

the Nation:

Germany

and Japan

(1860–1900)

Source 9 from David John Lu, Sources of Japanese History *(New York: McGraw Hill Book Company, 1974), vol. 2, pp. 48–49.*

9. From Okubo Toshimichi, Recommendation on Industrialization, 1874

Generally speaking, the strength or weakness of a country is dependent on the wealth or poverty of its people, and the people's wealth or poverty derives from the amount of available products. The diligence of the people is a major factor in determining the amount of products available, but in the final analysis, it can all be traced to the guidance and encouragement given by the government and its officials. . . .

We have come to a point where all the internal conflicts have ceased, and the people can now enjoy peace and can securely engage in their respective callings. This is the most opportune time for the government and its officials to adopt a protective policy which has as its goal the enhancement of people's livelihood. . . .

Anyone who is responsible for a nation or its people must give careful consideration to the matters which can enhance the livelihood of the people, including the benefits to be gained from industrial production and the convenience derived from maritime and land transportation. He must set up a system suitable to the country's natural features and convention, taking into account the characteristics and intelligence of its people. Once that system is established it must be made the pivot of the country's administrative policies. Those industries which are already developed must be preserved, and those which are not in existence must be brought into being.

An example can be found in England which is a very small country. However, she is an island nation and has excellent harbors. She is also richly endowed with mineral resources. Her government and its officials have considered it the greatest fulfillment of their duties when they have made full use of their natural advantages, and have brought about maximum [industrial] development. In this endeavor the Queen [Victoria] and her subjects have put together their ingenuity and created an unprecedented maritime law in order to monopolize the maritime transportation of the world and to enhance her national industries. . . .

In this way her industries have prospered, and there has always been a surplus after providing the necessary commodities to her people. . . .

It is true that time, location, natural features and convention are not the same for each country, and one must not always be dazzled by the accomplishments of England and seek to imitate her blindly. . . .

However, our topography and natural conditions show similarities to those of England. What differs most is the feebleness in the temperament of our people. It is the responsibility of those who are in the administrative positions in the government to guide and importune those who are weak in spirit to work diligently in the industries and to endure them. Your subject respectfully recommends that a clear-cut plan be established to find the natural advantages we enjoy, to measure the amount by which production can be increased, and to determine the priorities under which industries may be encouraged [e.g., subsidized]. It is further recommended that the characteristics of our people and the degree of their intelligence may be taken into account in establishing legislation aimed at encouraging development of industries. Let there not be a person who is derelict in performing his work. Let there not be a fear of anyone unable to have his occupation. If these goals can be attained the people can reach a position of adequate wealth. If the people are adequately wealthy, it follows naturally that the country will become strong and wealthy. . . . If so, it will not be difficult for us to compete effectively against major powers. This has always been your subject's sincere desire. He is even more convinced of the necessity of its implementation today, and is therefore submitting humbly his recommendations for Your Majesty's august decision.

Source 10 from the Local History Archives, Ministry of Education, Tokyo/Laurie Platt Winfrey, Inc.

10. Kawanabe Gyosai, Woodblock Print of Trade Fair of 1877

Source 11 from Sources of Japanese Tradition, *compiled by Ryusaku Tsunoda, Wm. Theodore de Bary, and Donald Keene (New York: Columbia University Press, 1960), pp. 676–679.*

11. From Ito Hirobumi, Speech at a Homecoming Celebration, 1895

Oriental countries—China and Japan included—have the habit of holding foreign countries in contempt and of holding their own country in esteem. But in carrying on relations according to civilized standards of common justice, it is done according to a procedure of mutual equality without contempt for the other and esteem for oneself, or vice versa. . . .

From the standpoint of the sovereign power, that is, the emperor's prerogative to rule the country, the people are one and equal under the constitutional government. They are all direct subjects of the emperor. The so-called "indirect subjects" no longer exist. This means that the Japanese people have been able to raise their status and to achieve for themselves a great honor. They now have the right to share in legislative rights, which come from the emperor's sovereign powers, and to elect and send representatives. Having the right to send representatives they can, indirectly, voice their opinions on the advisability and the faults of their country's administration. Thus, every member of the nation—be he a farmer, craftsman, or merchant—must become familiar beforehand with the merits and demerits of questions of government. Not only on questions of government, but also on matters concerning his own occupation, the citizen must give due thought and become prosperous. When every man becomes wealthy, the village, the county, and the prefecture in turn become wealthy, and the accumulated total of that wealth becomes the wealth of Japan. The expansion of military strength and the promotion of national prestige depend upon the power of the individual members of the country. Therefore, in order to promote the development of military strength and national prestige, it is only proper and necessary to diffuse education so that the people can understand the changes and improvements with respect to their government and their society. In a constitutional government the occasions for secrecy are few—except for laws not yet proclaimed—in contradistinction to a despotic government. The principle of keeping the people uninformed in order to make them obedient has no place here. To inform them well so that they will serve well is the way of constitutional government. . . .

Since government is concerned with the administration of the country as a whole it does not follow that its acts are always favorable to all individuals. The nation's affairs, of their own nature, are not personal and concerned with the individual. They must be carried out according to the nation's aims, the nation's prestige, and the nation's honor. It is for this reason that the people have an obligation to understand the nation's aims. They must regard the nation as their own, meet the military obligation to defend it and to pay for the cost of defending it.

Chapter 9
Industrializing
the Nation:
Germany
and Japan
(1860–1900)

When our enlightened emperor decided to accept the open-door principle as an imperial policy . . . it became a matter of urgent necessity to develop the intellectual faculties of our people and to increase their business activities. This led to the abolition of the feudal system and made it possible for the Japanese people to live in a new political environment and to have diverse freedoms. . . . The first of these freedoms was the freedom of movement, followed by the freedom to pursue an occupation of one's own choosing. Moreover, the freedom to study at any place of one's choosing was given to all. There was also granted freedom of speech in political affairs. Thus, the Japanese today enjoy freedom, each according to his own desires, within the limits of the law. These rights belong to people who live in a civilized government. If these rights are withheld and their enjoyment refused, a people cannot develop. And if the people cannot develop, the nation's wealth and the nation's strength cannot develop. . . . But the fact is that because of the imperial policy of the open-door, we have established a government which is civilized. And as we have advanced to such a position, it has become necessary to establish a fixed definition of the fundamental laws. This, in short, is the reason for the establishment of constitutional government.

A constitutional government makes a clear distinction between the realms of the ruler and the ruled, and thereby defines what the people and the sovereign should do; that is, the rights which the sovereign should exercise and the rights which the people should enjoy, followed by the procedure for the management of the government. According to the Constitution the people have the right to participate in government, but this right is at once an important obligation as well as a right. Government is a prerogative of the emperor. As you will be participating in government—which is the emperor's prerogative—you must regard this right as the responsibility of the people, the honor of the people, and the glory of the people. It is therefore a matter of the greatest importance.

In this connection what all Japanese must bear in mind is Japan's national polity. It is history which defines the national polity; thus the Japanese people have a duty to know their history. . . . The national polity of the various countries differs one from another, but it is the testimony of the history of Japan to this day that the unification of the country was achieved around the Imperial House. So I say that the understanding of the national polity of Japan is the first important duty of our people.

In the next place we must know the aims and the policies of our country. Political parties may have their arguments, and others may have their views about the government, but they must be kept within the bounds of the aims and policies of the government. What then is the aim of the nation? It is the imperial aim decided upon at the time of the [Meiji] Restoration of imperial rule. . . . The aim of our country has been from the very beginning, to attain among the nations of the world the status of a civilized nation and to become a member of the comity of European and American nations which occupy the position of civilized countries.

Source 12 from the Omiya Municipal Cartoon Art Museum, Japan.

12. Cartoon from *Tokyo Puck*, "Taxes Rise After the Russo-Japanese War," 1905

13. Ichiyosai Kuniteru, Woodblock Print of an Early Japanese Silk Mill, 19th century

Source 14 from Mikiso Hane, Peasants, Rebels, and Outcastes: The Underside of Modern
Japan (New York: Pantheon, 1982), pp. 178–193 ff.

14. Oral Records of "Crossing
Nomugi Pass" to Work in the
Suma Mills, ca. 1900

Where do the cheap workers come from? They all come from the farming
communities. . . . People from families that are working their own land, or are
engaged in tenant farming but have surplus workers, come to the cities and
the industrial centers to become factory workers. . . . Income from the farms
provides for the family needs and subsistence of the parents and siblings. The
person who takes employment in the factory is an unattached component of
the family. All he or she has to do is earn enough to maintain his or her own
living. This is why the workers' wages are low. This shows how important
a force agriculture is for the development of our nation's commerce and
industry.

The money that the factory girls brought back by climbing over Nomugi Pass
was often more than a "water-drinking" farmer's income for the entire year.
For these families, the girls were an invaluable source of income. The poor
peasants of those days had to turn 60 percent of their yield over to the landlord. Thus, the peasants had only broken bits of rice mixed with weeds for
food. . . . The poor peasants of this region had a saying: "Shall I hang myself
or cross Nomugi Pass?" These were the only alternatives they had. Their only
salvation was the girls who went to work in the factories.

Nomugi Pass is where many factory girls fell down into the ravine. When
someone slipped and fell down, we would untie our sashes, tie them together
to make a rope, and lower it down to the person in the ravine. . . . I can't tell
you how many girls died in that ravine. . . . We used to tie ourselves to the
girls ahead of us so as not to get left behind. Each step of the way we prayed
for our lives.

The wish to make my parents happy with the money I earned with my tears
during the year . . . made me cross Nomugi Pass at the end of the year full of
joyous expectations. I used to walk 85 miles over the pass in my straw sandals
to come home. We didn't have mittens in those days, so we tucked our hands
in our sleeves, linked ourselves together with cords, and crossed the pass.

Soon after I went to work in the Yamaichi silk factory in Shinshū [Nagano pre-
fecture], my younger sister Aki came to work there, too. I think she worked
for about two years. Then she took to bed because of peritonitis. At that time
there were about thirty sick people. Those who clearly had lung trouble were

Chapter 9

Industrializing

the Nation:

Germany

and Japan

(1860–1900)

sent home right away. . . . Everybody feared tuberculosis and no one would come near such patients. My sister Aki was also sent home before long, and she died soon after. She was in her thirteenth year. She had come to the factory determined to become a 100 yen worker and make our mother happy. I can never forget her sad eyes as she left the factory wan and pale. . . . It would be impossible, I felt, for a person as sick as she was to travel over 30 *ri* or more and cross Nomugi Pass. But they would not let her stay in the factory. There was no money to send her to the hospital. There was nothing for her to do but go home.

From morning, while it was still dark, we worked in the lamplit factory till ten at night. After work, we hardly had the strength to stand on our feet. When we worked late into the night, they occasionally gave us a yam. We then had to do our washing, fix our hair, and so on. By then it would be eleven o'clock. There was no heat even in the winter, and so we had to sleep huddled together. Several of the girls ran back to Hida. I was told that girls who went to work before my time had a harder time. We were not paid the first year. In the second year I got 35 yen, and the following year, 50 yen. I felt that it was not a place for a weak-willed person like me. If we didn't do the job right we were scolded, and, if we did better than others, the others resented it. The life of a woman is really awful.

QUESTIONS TO CONSIDER

An important issue to consider as you assess the impact industrialization had on national unity in Germany and Japan is how the process intensified over time with broadening effects. The first two sources demonstrate the changing nature of industry as a result of the technological and organizational innovations of the late nineteenth century. The Hagen rolling mill shown in Source 1 shows a German iron foundry of the 1860s. It clearly belongs to an older phase of small-scale operations. Notice not only its size and rural setting but its location on a river, probably its original form of energy. Who do you think lived in the fenced-in villa on the hill? Small mills of this sort were often family-owned and -run. How would this affect relations with the workers?

Compare this facility to the early twentieth-century Krupp steel mill (Source 2). Obviously bigger, it indicates the greater complexity and urban nature of the massive industrial plants built around the turn of the century. What do these differences suggest about the changing nature of industrial production and its social impact? How would enough workers be found to operate such a mill? Where would they live and what might their lives be like in this setting? Is the lack of an adjoining villa here surprising? How might labor relations be affected by the shift to cities?

Source 3 suggests how urban mills obtained workers. These remarks by one of Germany's most renowned social scientists and liberals, Max Weber, are part of a lecture he gave in 1895. At the time, nationalistic Germans worried about Polish migrants recruited into the eastern portions of the empire by *Junker* landlords to replace German farm workers who were drifting into the cities for factory jobs. Weber uses this issue to show how the "economic dislocation" entailed by development created diversity and divisions in German society, resulting in *"power struggles."* What groups does Weber say economic development has made into rivals? How has the growth of urban industry specifically affected them? An earlier German, Karl Marx, argued that industrialization would precipitate a class war between the bourgeoisie—the middle-class professional and business people who owned and ran the factories—and the proletariat or mill hands who worked in them. Marx believed the latter would win and so dominate modern society. How does Weber think the struggle will end? Why? Who does he say should govern Germany in "the power interests of the nation"? Concern for national unity leads this acknowledged liberal to advocate a powerful state capable of decisive intervention in national life. Why?

State supervision of economic life continued to be debated in German politics during the 1890s. Source 4, a satiric cartoon of 1899, compares such oversight to contemporary efforts of the imperial government to manage recently acquired African colonies. The figures flying over the smoky industries of the Ruhr Valley represent the two chief divisions of the imperial government, the bureaucracy and the army. Their troubled expressions are explained by the caption "Through Darkest Germany, A View Inland," an allusion to the European conceit that the interior of Africa was a dark land. What makes industrial Germany "dark," too?

Germany's industrial leaders on the whole shared the belief that development required strict control from the top down. Many thus adopted an authoritarian stance in dealing with their own subordinates and workers, equating the management of a firm with the emperor's rule over the nation and workers' obedience with patriotism. In return, some accepted responsibility for the welfare of their employees. German industrial workers of the time thus generally fared better than many others elsewhere, but salaries were often insufficient to support families. You can gain some sense of the material standard of living of German workers from Source 5, a photograph of a typical workman's home in Berlin around the turn of the century. How do their living conditions in tenement rooms like this compare to those of workers today? Notice what the women are doing. Working-class women often had to take in sewing or other handwork to supplement a meager family income. How might that have affected their role in the household—and society?

Low wages, insecurity, and the intrusive authority distressed most German industrial workers. Along with

Chapter 9

Industrializing

the Nation:

Germany

and Japan

(1860–1900)

the growing number of unemployed artisans whose labor machine-made goods made obsolete, they agitated for improvement, raising the "social question" of inequity between classes. Although hampered by the antisocialist law, working-class efforts to unionize and form parties persisted, and by 1890 the largest of the workers' parties, the Social Democrats, took control of the lower house of the Reichstag. Party leaders met the following year to draw up an idealistic program of national reforms.

Source 6 presents excerpts from this Erfurt Program. Notice how it echoes Karl Marx, rejecting not only bourgeois control of industrial wealth but even the nation's claim on its citizens' loyalty. What other group does the manifesto celebrate in place of the nation? Compare this view to Weber's argument that national interests must outweigh class interests. Look at the specific demands for improvement. What problems in the workplace does it single out for reform? What can you infer about working conditions in German industry from the grievances? The program also addresses more universal problems, declaring itself opposed to "every kind of exploitation and oppression." What does it say about sexual discrimination? How did industrialization give this issue new meaning?

The growth of the German socialist movement deeply troubled the imperial government. Bismarck tried to check the threat by a combination of tactics, restricting the party's political activity while reducing the working-class discontent that nourished it. Beginning in the 1880s, he introduced

a series of state-run insurance services that by 1911 gave Germany the world's first comprehensive welfare program, a program Bismarck characterized as "state socialism." Source 7, a speech he made to the Reichstag in 1881 when first launching "social insurance," offers his rationale for it. Observe how the chancellor openly rejects socialist demands for reforms that benefit a single class as well as the liberal call for *laissez faire* policies. How does he justify government economic regulation and welfare? Bismarck assumes that the state must transcend narrow interests and protect the weak and poor. Why? What does this tell about actual national unity of the time?

Although industrialization occurred more slowly in Japan than in Germany, changes often proved more disturbing because they provoked radical cultural as well as social adjustment. What in Germany seemed merely "modern," had an alien quality in Japan where it was also seen as "Western." Woodblock prints made in the late nineteenth century like the one reproduced as Source 8 display this discordance. The scene is a terminal on Japan's first railroad, a line built from Yokahama to Tokyo in the 1870s. Western-style structures contrast sharply with the older Japanese buildings in the background. The mix of traditional and European costumes provides another sign of acculturation. Look carefully at who wears Western clothing. People working in new industries and institutions adopted Western dress first—like the railway workers here, many of whose early customers were Europeans. Notice, too, the telegraph wires. They and the train reflect the revolution in transportation and communication that industrialization unleashed here as well as in Germany.

Unlike Germany's industrialization, which began through piecemeal private ventures launched before the birth of the modern imperial state, Japan's came through the initiative of the new Meiji regime. In Source 9, a government memorial of 1874, the oligarch Okubo Toshimichi gives its reasons. His insistence on government responsibility for national prosperity reflects traditional Confucian belief that the state must benefit the people. But his desire to seek prosperity through modern industry and transportation reveals Western ideas. Why does he single out England as a model for Japan? England's industrial wealth gave it imperial might. How would such might satisfy Okubo's desire "to compete effectively against major powers"—and reverse the humiliating unequal treaties? Given the "feebleness in the temperament" of the Japanese people Okubo notes, how does he think industrialization much be launched?

After modest state pilot projects proved the feasibility of transplanting factories to Japan, Meiji leaders decided to call attention to their efforts by hosting an industrial fair in Tokyo. Such fairs, which began in Europe earlier in the century, had become an acknowledged way of showcasing national development to the world. But Meiji oligarchs were taking a bold step in 1877 when they staged the first industrial fair held outside the West. As Source 10, a print of the fair, shows, traditional architecture and exhibits predomi-nated, for the Japanese still had only modest industrial products to display. But they had already learned how to use the event to celebrate and strengthen national identity in Western terms. Look at the emperor, shown here riding in a foreign carriage and wearing a European military uniform. To depict him so openly and in foreign costume was very alien at the time. Can you spot other Western symbols of power combined with traditional elements to express Japanese national identity? Look at the French-style dragoons, bearing new Japanese *national* flags sporting the image of the rising sun.

Source 11 shows a similar juxtaposition of modern and traditional elements. It comes from a speech given in 1899 by Japan's first Western-style prime minister, Ito Hirobumi. Ito clearly takes pride in Japan's Western-style industrialization, but he views efforts to increase business activities and enhance national wealth first and foremost as ways to further the "imperial aim" for a stronger nation. Likewise, he credits constitutional government and popular freedoms to an imperial quest for national power and prestige rather than to the fulfillment of basic rights and claims that Japan's unique "national polity" make sovereignty "the prerogative of the emperor," not the people. Compare his view of the state with Bismarck's. Both rejected democracies in favor of strong monarchies on the grounds that monarchies offer the unity and stability necessary for rapid development. Do you find their positions justifiable?

[283]

Chapter 9

Industrializing

the Nation:

Germany

and Japan

(1860–1900)

In 1894 new industrial might allowed Japan to defeat China, traditionally the dominant power of East Asia, and then to make a bid for regional mastery by halting Russian expansion into the area in the Russo-Japanese War of 1905. The latter victory electrified nationalists throughout Asia, as well as Japan, for it demonstrated that an industrializing non-Western nation could successfully stand up to the West. But to less nationalistic eyes, the costs of development seemed disproportionately borne. Source 12, a cartoon, depicts all the benefits derived from victory in the Russo-Japanese War: imperial advisers, members of the Diet, local officials, government suppliers, and others in positions of advantage enjoy their rewards. But the only reward presented to the average citizen is a heavy burden labeled "taxes." Look carefully at the dress of the different groups. Who appears Western and who not? What does the cartoon suggest about the cultural and social associations of modernization in Japan?

Lack of unions and labor movements in Japan until well after the turn of the century left Japanese industrial workers especially vulnerable to exploitation, but women suffered the most. Like textile mills elsewhere, the silk mills that formed the mainstay of Japan's private industry preferred to hire women. Typically recruited as teenagers from rural areas, most lived in company dormitories under strict regulation that allowed little personal freedom, much less opportunities to organize.

A woodblock print (Source 13) shows the Spartan atmosphere of early silk factories. But far worse than the starkness of mill workers' lives was their insecurity. In Source 14, workers recall the harsh lot of rural women who crossed the local mountains through Nomugi Pass to find work in the mills of Okaya near the turn of the century. "Crossing Nomugi Pass" meant more than just traversing a geographic boundary. What was life like for these Japanese working women? What explains their willingness to accept such conditions? Even after the passage of the 1911 Factory Act to reform conditions, Japanese women continued to labor in circumstances that were among the harshest in the industrial world. Moreover, the Meiji regime created no government welfare programs like Germany's regarding such care as the obligation of the family, not the state. But who helped these women in their need?

EPILOGUE

Germany's entry into World War I in 1914 proved disastrous to its industrial growth. Social tensions, intensified by wartime strains, brought a revolution in 1918 that toppled the monarchy and forced acceptance of a humiliating peace. Liberals attempted to construct a democracy out of the ruins of the empire, but the Weimar Republic they created failed to restore Germany's former prosperity and prestige. Nearly bankrupted by war indemnities and the deteriorating postwar international economy, Germany suffered a lack of capital during the 1920s that hindered industrial growth and unleashed damaging inflation. When the Great Depression of the early 1930s brought massive unemployment and new social unrest, the demoralized nation repudiated liberal leadership, turning instead to Adolf Hitler whose Nazi Party advocated drastic reform under a fascist dictatorship. Hitler's militaristic policies, however, turned a brief industrial recovery into an even greater debacle, for he led Germany to a defeat in World War II marked by total industrial collapse and partition. Not until the 1950s did the divided postwar parts of West and East Germany begin to recover a measure of their former industrial prosperity.

Unlike Germany, Japan profited from World War I. As first European and then American industry turned to war production, Japan found new markets for its own manufactures, particularly in Asia. Having sided with the Allies, Japan was able to seize most of Germany's Asian and Pacific possessions. While the war thus weakened European nations, it left Japan wealthier and stronger than ever. With confidence born of this success, its leaders allowed a shift to true parliamentary rule following the death of the Meiji emperor in 1912. By the 1920s, competing liberal parties began to democratize the country. But social conflict at home and worsening conditions in the world led critics, especially in the army, to discredit them. When the worldwide Depression intensified social turmoil, army officers began to undermine civilian rule. In the name of preserving domestic harmony and fending off a revival of Western power in Asia, they slowly took control of the government, disbanding the Diet in 1941 and instituting a formal military dictatorship. Hopes of destroying Anglo-American power in Asia led them to ally with Germany in World War II, and like Germany, Japan experienced defeat and economic collapse in 1945. Ruled and rebuilt under American military occupation from 1945 to 1952, Japan, too, was only able to restore its shattered industries by the 1950s.

Despite great initial gains, then, neither nation unequivocally benefited from industrialization. The very development that initially made them so successful may actually have weakened them. Their governments, though claiming to manage economic change in the interest of the nation as a whole, failed to protect many citizens from the effects of that change, leaving them vulnerable and afraid. In the end, that failure left them open to assault from the left and right. Thus modern Germany and Japan may have ultimately foundered upon the kind of power struggles Weber warned would arise from such economic development. Was this the fault of industrialization itself—or their inability to deal effectively with the divisions and tensions it created?

CHAPTER TEN

WORLD WAR I: GLOBAL WAR

(1914–1918)

Readers of the *New York Times* who followed news developments from 1914 to 1917 could easily have concluded the hostilities they observed from afar were simply a European affair. Descriptions of battles in Belgium, France, and Greece, as well as confrontations between European ships at sea, dominated the *Times* headlines. Just about every other American newspaper conveyed a similar impression. One conspicuous exception was the African-American press, whose readers were very interested in military developments affecting Africa, where European colonies were drawn into the conflict. Little was written elsewhere about those events unfolding in Africa, although the *Times* itself, in a rare editorial on the subject, acknowledged that

some day great nations that are now colonies will trace through the history of 1914 the now unnoticed battles in Africa, . . . Historians will search

through the publications of today for comment on these battles and record their inability to find it with the same amusement as that which now they hunt for European comment on the American contests that decided the future of another continent [during the French and Indian War]. . . .[1]

That wider impact of what we now call the First World War was unclear to many at the time, and its proportions remain ill-appreciated even today. Of course, as soldiers from the United States joined in the efforts "over there" after 1917, awareness grew that the war was not confined to Europe alone. With Asian, African, and Caribbean soldiers also fighting on Europe's western front, the world-wide implications of the conflict should have been even clearer. But the extensive campaigns in Arabia, Africa, and Mesopotamia, as well as small conflicts elsewhere, were largely forgotten or simply ignored, at least in the popular press.

1. "Making History in the Dark," *New York Times,* May 28, 1915.

[286]

With so many different peoples involved, from both inside and outside Europe, was this really a global experience as well as a world war? To answer that question you need to know more than where the soldiers fought and in what numbers. Much more important is understanding the nature of their wartime experiences and the ways in which they viewed them. What were their motives for fighting? Were the conditions under which they campaigned different from place to place? And were the attitudes they formed as a result of their wartime service shaped more by their individual differences or by their participation in a worldwide conflict?

In this chapter you will read the accounts of soldiers and war workers from many places. Some recorded their thoughts almost immediately in letters and diaries; others only later recalled what they experienced, either on their own initiative or when asked about their recollections of World War I. The sources also include period song lyrics and photographs of soldiers and battlefield conditions.

The diversity of the evidence is striking. From intimate letters intended only for family to full historical accounts, and from personal as well as national propaganda to oral interviews years after the fact, all the sources make clear the importance of the conflict to these men and women. You will no doubt be struck as well as by the divergent cultures and nations from which these people were drawn into the fray. Keep those ideas in mind as you consider the central problem posed in this chapter. Were these men and women part of a truly global experience? If so, what were its common elements? And if it was not, what accounts for the differences in the ways they experienced this most memorable of wars?

BACKGROUND

In the popular language of the time, World War I was "The Great War for Civilization," at least to those in the English-speaking world. Even medals awarded by the British government to African soldiers for their participation in the "sideshow" campaigns in Africa bore that engraved message. But the conflict had not started that way. When hostilities began in August 1914, almost everyone expected a short war. The European wars of the preceding century had usually been brief, were fought by relatively small numbers of generally professional soldiers, and had never involved all of the continent's great powers. In fact, more than forty years had passed since any of the major states had battled, in the Franco-Prussian War of 1870–1871. During the intervening years, European nations had taken a variety of steps to avoid further bloodshed between their armies.

Foremost among these safeguards was a complex alliance system, linking in one way or another all the countries of Europe with treaties that pledged each to defend its allies should they be attacked. Economic and political demands for expansion were nonetheless great, but much of that energy was deflected for a time into colonial enterprises. Even in that arena, major agreements among most of the nations of Europe (and the United States) clearly spelled out how the search for new colonies might proceed so as to avoid direct confrontations between the parties.

The colonial expansions of the late nineteenth century did provide a major testing ground for war. Virtually every European nation fought against African, or sometimes, Asian peoples. In all but a handful of cases, European armies overwhelmed their opponents, frequently using new military technologies such as the machine gun and more deadly artillery. Most of those technologies were designed for defense against the kind of open confrontations between massed formations of soldiers that had characterized nineteenth-century warfare, at least until 1870. In the colonial setting this arsenal proved spectacularly successful in meeting the challenges of similar massed formations of local, less-well-equipped armies.

These new weapons shifted the balance of military power everywhere from attackers to defenders. The sheer destructive capacity of the new weapons forced soldiers into more secure defensive positions and limited their opportunities to face their adversaries directly. When they did—as in the European turmoil after August 1914—the results were likely to be extremely high casualties and only modest success in capturing ground. Exhausted after such attacks, armies created new defensive positions and plunged into the cycle again. This was the situation in western Europe. What most had expected to be a short war became instead a war of stalemate and attrition.

Across Europe, the lines of battle were formed and reformed in this manner. Armies were arrayed against each other in complex systems of earthen dugouts—trenches—which provided not only defensive fortifications but also an unpleasant network of domiciles for most of the soldiers on active duty. Between the trenches were desolate stretches of ground, frequently shelled until bare of vegetation and often criss-crossed with rolls of barbed wire. Such was the "no man's land" that came to symbolize the futility of this new kind of war. There soldiers entered at their peril, especially in the occasional massive attacks on the trenches opposite. Such assaults took an awful toll in human lives.

For those soldiers, their families and nations, as well as most neutral observers, campaigns in this new warfare exceeded in length and scope and intensity any they had known before. Of course, for some in the United States, this European war did not measure up to the ferocity of their own Civil War. Yet in many ways the cause for which men now fought seemed even greater. "Civilization itself seeming to be in the balance," President Woodrow Wilson noted when he asked Congress in 1917 for a declaration of war drawing the United States into the conflict. "The world," he concluded, "must be made safe for democracy."[2]

2. Woodrow Wilson, "War Message," 65th Congress, 1st Session, Senate Document No. 5.

The European war thus took on a universal character. With both the German invasion of Russia and the entry of the United States, the Great War had indeed extended beyond Europe. But well before Russians rose in revolution and American troops reached France, both in 1917, the peoples of Africa, Asia, and the Middle East were engaged in combat. In fact, within days of the first shots fired in August 1914, many colonial soldiers were hurriedly pressed into service, defending their homelands in the name of the European colonial powers that had come to rule over them. Others were cajoled, conscripted, even coerced into service as laborers to transport food and war materiel in lands where there were few, if any, motor roads and rail lines.

Indeed, the longest campaign of the First World War was fought in East Africa. There, hostilities began the day after the first fighting in Europe and did not stop until November 14, 1918, three days after an armistice silenced the guns in Europe. In Southwest Africa, in Cameroon, along the Tigris and Euphrates Rivers, in Arabia, Greece, and Egypt, other major campaigns were fought—each with many, if not most, of the participants from outside of Europe itself, all fighting on behalf of one or another of the European belligerents. Small campaigns, in the Chinese port city of Hangchow and the territory of Togo in west Africa,

for example, carried the conflict to far-flung reaches of the globe.

Perhaps even more surprising were the armies in Europe drawn from virtually all the other continents. West Indian regiments met Australian, Indian, and New Zealand soldiers in fighting alongside their British counterparts. Vietnamese, Malagasy, and Senegalese contingents fought both in and with French armies; indeed, at the end of the war just over half of all the soldiers still fighting for Frence were from her colonies. Laborers as well, drawn from the indigenous peoples of China, South Africa, and even the South Pacific island of Fiji came to Europe in support of the troops. By all accounts, the last to join the fray were American soldiers marshaled into effective combat not until 1918.

The widespread reach of the war revealed, if nothing else, the seriousness with which most nations viewed the conflict and the intensity of their efforts to ensure their own success and that of their allies. That scope alone, however, did not make this conflict a world war. The major belligerents remained European nations. It was across their lands that the most horrific battles were fought. And those continental nations suffered by far the greatest casualties. If the Great War did have a global impact, it might best be measured in the ways in which its diverse individual participants viewed their wartime roles.

THE METHOD

In this chapter you will examine several kinds of sources that give the perspective of common soldiers and other ordinary participants in the war. For the most part you will read the words of those people themselves. In a few cases you will read accounts written by officers which nonetheless reflect perspectives generally shared by the soldiers they commanded. Though we include a few photographs of such soldiers, most of the sources are written. Some, such as letters, were usually written down while their authors were engaged at the front. The song lyrics were sung during the war but may have actually been written down later.

Other sources were recorded after the participants left the field of battle, in some cases long after the war was over. Among these are oral testimonies recorded much later, when people were interviewed about their memories of the war years. The results of those interviews are presented here as printed transcripts of the original, frequently tape-recorded, conversations. Similar to the interviews are reminiscences of soldiers and others. These are accounts that were committed to writing by the participants, generally within a few years of their experiences. Most often these were free-flowing, general narratives of what happened to them during the war. Other accounts, also written after the participants had at least a short time to reflect on what had happened, take on the character of memoirs. These far more deliberate pieces usually attempt to place

wartime experiences within a larger historical context.

Source 1 is such a memoir, written by the famous French historian Marc Bloch. Although Bloch actually wrote his memoir during breaks in his service on the western front, he consciously structured it while consulting the daily journal he had kept even in combat. Already an experienced historian, his approach was to chronicle his experiences while at the same time placing them in the larger context of comparative history. A very well-educated man, he nonetheless knew the experiences of ordinary French soldiers, serving among them as an infantry sergeant during the earliest days of the war. Nearly one-third of his companions—and of all French soldiers—were killed or wounded in the first five months of the war. Source 2, a letter from Jean Chatanay to his wife, clearly illustrates their awareness of, and resignation to, that fatal reality. The poignant appeal of his letter led to its being published in many newspapers around the world during the winter of 1915–1916.

Following those French accounts are two letters of ordinary German soldiers who had been students when the war began: Franz Blumenfeld and Martin Drescher (Sources 3 and 4). Their letters are representative of a large number of similar accounts sent home by German student-soldiers during their wartime service. Do these German accounts bear any similarity to those of their French adversaries? Or were their experiences, in different armies and opposite sides of no man's land, in some way unique?

Next you will find an exceptional letter (Source 5) written by a young Italian lieutenant, Giosuè Borsi, to his mother. His letter, filled with confidence drawn from his faith, is selected from a collection of Borsi's wartime writings. Not exactly diary entries, these were really meditations, "confidences with God" others called them, written while he awaited the beginning of what he termed "the great ordeal." None of his work was intended for public consumption, but its contemplative nature earned it a wide reading following the war, especially in Italy and the United States. How do Borsi's ideas and experiences compare to those of other European soldiers?

Sources 6, 7, and 8 come from Russian soldiers. Two are from women, reflecting the lengths to which Russian leaders were prepared to go in defending their country. Source 6 is taken from a reporter's interview with Mary Goloubyova, an eighteen-year-old female soldier in what was popularly known as "The Legion of Death," the premier women's unit in the Russian Army. Source 8 is from a letter written by the commanding officer of a Cossack cavalry regiment, Colonel Alexandra Kokotseva; her "splendid Cossacks," as she describes them, were an unusual group, men and women serving together in combat. Between these two you will find part of a letter (Source 7) from an unidentified Russian male soldier, confused by the political change sweeping over his country and seeking solace in whatever quarter he might find it, even in the kindness of an English Red Cross nurse who had cared for him. Consider how the particular circumstances of their country, embroiled in both war and revolution, may have affected the outlook of these Russian soldiers.

Following these are two descriptions of wartime experiences from British soldiers. In Source 9, George F. Wear explains how he began service as a hospital corpsman and was then commissioned an infantry officer, serving on the western front for almost four years. Do you detect any change in him or his life over those four years? In Source 10 you will discover how indelible the war memories remained for British veterans as you read the testimony of Leonard Thompson, who was seventy-one years old when he was interviewed for a portrait of his village.

Of course, there is more to the picture of ordinary participants in World War I than just accounts of European soldiers fighting in European campaigns. To get a fuller understanding, you need to examine what soldiers from elsewhere had to say about their experiences. In Source 11 you will find portions of three letters written by T. E. Lawrence, better known as Lawrence of Arabia. A certifiable war hero, Lawrence served as a British liaison officer with the Arab forces in revolt against Ottoman Turks (Germany's allies) in Arabia. All three letters describe the same action, a raid on the Hejaz Railway near the small station of Harret Ammar. How does he evaluate his Arab allies? What differences, if any, do you observe in the impressions he conveys in each of the letters?

Some non-European participants in the war made their own statements about their experiences. Source 12 contains two of these, letters written from France to relatives at home by anonymous Indian soldiers serving in various units of Britain's Indian Army. These units had a long history of service to Britain, including combat roles outside India itself. But their assignments to a war in Europe were something entirely new, as their letters suggest. Both of these selections come from a collection of similar letters, all censored—and sometimes intercepted instead of being sent to their addresses—by British military authorities. Source 13 is also from a letter scrutinized by military censors, this one a confession of an African, Corporal Eleija Kimu of the King's African Rifles who fought in the East African campaign. Were only the letters of Indians and other non-Europeans censored?

Another way in which African experiences have been saved is through oral interviews. Private Fololiyani Longwe, whose testimony you will read in Source 14, also served in the King's African Rifles. How clear do his memories of that experience seem to be? Do they show similarities to any of the European accounts? Source 15, also the oral testimony of an African soldier, is quite different from Longwe's. Kande Kamara, from West Africa, served in the colonial forces of France. His military experiences were not in Africa, although many African soldiers of France served in those campaigns. Rather, he fought in France itself, one of many thousands of Africans who did so with the hope of being granted equality—or perhaps even French citizenship—in re-

turn for armed service on behalf of their colonial masters. Did such expectations effect Kande Kamara's memory of the war?

Africans and Indians were not the only colonial peoples to serve in the trenches of the First World War. Many Australians, New Zealanders, Canadians, and others constituted the British imperial forces fighting on the western front and elsewhere. Source 16 is from the reminiscences of a soldier in the Canadian Grenadier Guards. Surprisingly, Sergeant Alexander McClintock was an American, a Kentuckian who joined the Canadian Army late in 1915, well over a year before units from his native United States were committed to the war effort. His reminiscences, from which you will read an excerpt, described him as a "Fighting Kentuckian" when they were first published in the United States. But the Canadian edition of his book was quick to lay claim to his courage; in it he is referred to as a "Fighting Canadian"! Do you detect any particular differences in the account of Sergeant McClintock that might be explained by his multinational wartime experiences?

Next you will read the oral testimonies, recorded many years after the war, of two soldiers of the American Expeditionary Force that sailed to France following the nation's formal declaration of war in 1917 (Sources 17 and 18). Jesse Flowers and William Davis both responded to their nation's call to arms, though like many of their rural contemporaries, they knew little of the circumstances that made them soldiers. Do their accounts reflect this in any way? An African-American, Davis was aware of the controversy surrounding his participation in the war effort. How do his memories reveal that aspect of his war service?

Next you will find three photographs. Sources 19 and 20 are scenes associated with trench fighting. Both involve British units—the Northern Rhodesia Regiment and the Border Regiment—in various campaigns. Are there any similarities or differences in these scenes? What strikes you most about these photographs? Source 21 depicts a German soldier, an American prisoner of war. Can you associate him with any of the accounts you have previously read?

The lyrics of two World War I songs follow. Source 22 was recorded years after the war from the memories of African soldiers, many of whom remembered very similar versions of the lyric. The other (Source 23) was sung by American soldiers and later recorded by the well-known American poet, Carl Sandburg. What, if anything, do these song lyrics have in common? What might account for any similarities?

The final three sources are a little different in that they are not the accounts of soldiers. Rather they reflect the memories of noncombatants who were nonetheless involved quite directly in World War I. Although their roles differed greatly, there is one common element in their experiences: none of them fought or intended to fight; all three had other jobs to do. Source 24 is the reminiscence of Englishwoman M. I. Tatham, one of many nurses who served perilously close to the front lines. She was a volunteer

with Serbian forces fighting to defend their country from Austrian attacks. Max Yergen, author of Source 25, was an African-American who years later gained some prominence as a journalist. He was commissioned by the American Y.M.C.A. to provide recreational and religious activities for "colored" soldiers, first in India and later in East Africa.

Last of all, Source 26 is the story of a man known to us only as Nwose who was involuntarily recruited to serve as a carrier for British forces in the Cameroon campaign. His account, taken down by an English colonial official shortly after he returned home, is typical of that of literally hundreds of thousands of Africans who, often against their will, carried ammunition, food, and other war supplies—frequently balanced on their heads—to troops at the front. Were Nwose's experiences similar to those of the other noncombatants, or any of the soldiers whose stories you have read?

Indeed, do any common threads run through these sources? Do you notice any particularly striking differences? With so many different sources, these may seem to be nearly impossible questions. Yet it is from just such a variety of materials that historians normally work in trying to understand complex events—like wars—in the past. By making comparisons among the sources, either all at once or (more likely) within any of a number of classifications, you will find a fuller picture of their meaning. And you will be better able to respond to the central questions posed as the problem for this chapter.

Source 1 from Marc Bloch, Memoirs of War, 1914–1915, *trans. Carole Fink (Ithaca, N.Y., and London: Cornell University Press, 1980), pp. 89–93.*

THE EVIDENCE

1. From Sergeant Marc Bloch, 272d French Reserve Infantry Regiment, *Memoirs,* 1914

It is likely that as long as I live, at least if I do not become senile in my last days, I shall never forget the 10th of September, 1914. Even so, my recollections of that day are not altogether precise. Above all they are poorly articulated, a discontinuous series of images, vivid in themselves but badly arranged like a reel of movie film that showed here and there large gaps and the unintended reversal of certain scenes. On that day, under extremely violent fire from heavy artillery and machine guns, we advanced a few kilometers—at least three or four—from ten in the morning until six at night. Our losses were severe; my company alone, which was certainly not the worst hit, suffered almost one-third casualties. If my memory is correct, the time did not seem long; indeed, those dreadful hours must have passed fairly quickly. We advanced on an undulating field, at first dotted with clumps of trees, then completely bare. I recall that while crossing a hedge, I sharply questioned a man who had stopped. He answered, "I've been wounded." In fact, though he had not actually been hit, he had been stunned by the blast of a shell. He was the first to be hurt. Farther on I noticed the first body, a corporal who did not belong to our regiment. He lay on a slope all rigid with his face down, while around him were scattered some potatoes that had escaped from his camp kettle, which had opened as he fell. Machine gun bullets rustled through the branches like swarms of wasps. The heavy detonations of the shells shook the air, followed by the chorus of bursts that accompanied each explosion. . . . I hunched my head between my shoulders, awaiting the silence and perhaps the fatal blow.

. . . Then, on our lieutenant's order, we all rushed toward the right to reach a ridge behind which the next platoons had already taken cover. . . .

How long did we stay in that fold in the earth? How many minutes, or how many hours, I am not sure. We were crowded against each other and piled one on top of another.

. . . I was half lying on my neighbor to the left. I think I have never detested anyone so much as that individual, whom I had never seen before that day, never met again, and doubtless would not recognize if I ever should meet him in the future. He had cramps in his legs, on which I was lying, and he insisted that to relieve him I should raise myself, although this would have needlessly exposed me to death. I am still glad I refused, and I hope the self-centered clod suffers often from rheumatism.

. . . Some men near me were wounded. The day was nearly over. We prayed for the arrival of complete darkness, which would end the fighting. The German bombardment gradually slowed. . . .

It was there that we spent the night. From time to time a few bullets whistled by. About 10 P.M., I believe, the German machine guns resumed firing, without doing us any harm. They soon fell silent. We were famished. I had a can of sardines; I opened it, ate a few, and shared the rest. It was cold. . . . The smell of blood permeated the air. Yet despite this stale odor, despite the cries and the groans, despite our fears, I slept for a few hours, stretched out in a furrow.

Source 2 from "A Soldier's Letter to His Widow," The Literary Digest *51 (1915): 1109–1110.*

2. Jean Chatanay, Letter to His Wife, probably 1915

I write this letter because one never knows what may happen. If you get it, it will mean that France has wanted all I could give her. Don't mourn for me, for I shall have died happy. The only thing I worry about is the position you will be in with the children. But as for bringing up the girls I am not anxious. You will manage as well as I could have done. Kiss them for me, and tell them that their father has gone on a long journey, and did not forget them. . . . Promise not to bear any grudge to France if she takes me. I hope we shall meet again some day. My poor darling, I haven't even had time to think much about our love, great and strong tho it be.

Good-by, the long good-by. Be brave—

Sources 3 and 4 from A. F. Wedd, German Students' War Letters *(London: Methuen, 1929), pp. 9–10, 19–21.*

3. From Franz Blumenfeld, Letters to His Mother, 1914

I want to write to you about something else, which, judging from bits in your letters, you haven't quite understood: why I should have volunteered for the war? Of course it was not from any enthusiasm for war in general, nor because I thought it would be a fine thing to kill a great many people or otherwise distinguish myself. On the contrary, I think that war is a very, very evil thing, and I believe that even in this case it might have been averted by a more skillful diplomacy. But, now that it has been declared, I think it is a matter of course that one should feel oneself so much a member of the nation that one must unite one's fate as closely as possible with that of the whole. . . . For what counts is always the readiness to make a sacrifice, not the object for which the sacrifice is made.

This war seems to me, from all that I have heard, to be something so horrible, inhuman, mad, obsolete, and in every way depraving, that I have firmly resolved, if I do come back, to do everything in my power to prevent such a thing from ever happening again in the future. . . .

The sight of the slightly and dangerously wounded, the dead men and horses lying about, hurts, of course, but the pain of all that is not nearly so keen or lasting as one imagined it would be. Of course that is partly due to the fact that one knows one can't do anything to prevent it. But may it not at the same time be a beginning of a deplorable callousness, almost barbarity, or how is it possible that it gives me more pain to bear my own loneliness than to witness the sufferings of so many others? . . . What is the good of escaping all the bullets and shells, if my soul is injured?

4. Martin Drescher, Letter, 1914

It goes on from day to day: alternately awful marches and then a whole day's inactive vegetating; heat and cold; too much to eat and then a long spell of hunger. One talks about nothing but these material things and about the question of whether we shall be dead to-morrow or not. I have made up my mind to it pretty well. At first, of course, I trembled; the will to live is bound to be so strong; but the thought of immortality is a sublime compensation. And even though I do not hold the ordinary belief in personal immortality, yet last night I was cheered by the sight of the glittering stars and other remembrances and things I have noted in old days. . . . And I can now listen more calmly to the shells screaming overhead. I am firmly convinced that I, that is my soul has not lived just this one life, and that it will live over and over again—how I don't attempt to imagine, for that is useless. Thus I am calm and resigned.

Source 5 from Giosuè Borsi, A Soldier's Confidences with God, *trans. Pasquale Maltese (New York: P. J. Kenedy & Sons, 1919), pp. 337, 341, 350.*

5. Lieutenant Giosuè Borsi, Letter to His Mother, October 21, 1915

This letter, which you will receive only in case that I should fall in battle, I am writing in an advanced trench, where I have been since last night, with my soldiers, in expectation of the order to cross the river and move to the attack. . . .

I am calm, perfectly serene, and firmly resolved to do my duty in full to the last, like a brave and good soldier, confident to the utmost of our final unfailing victory; although I am not equally sure that I will live to see it. But this uncertainty does not trouble me in the least, nor has it any terror for me. I am happy in offering my life to my country; I am proud to spend it for so noble a purpose, and I know not how to thank Divine Providence for the opportunity—which I deem an honor—afforded me . . . to fight in this holy war for liberty and justice. . . .

Love and freedom for all, this is the ideal for which it is a pleasure to offer one's life. May God cause our sacrifice to be fruitful; may He take pity upon mankind, forgive and forget their offenses, and give them peace. Then, oh! dear mother, we shall not have died in vain. Just one more tender kiss.

Source 6 from " 'The Legion of Death'—Women Soldiers on the Firing-Line," in True Stories of the Great War, *ed. Francis Trevelyan Miller (New York: Review of Reviews, 1917), vol. 2, pp. 248–249.*

6. Mary Goloubyova, Reminiscence, probably 1916

We went into action a fortnight after our arrival at the front under heavy German cannon fire. Given the order to advance, we rushed out of our trench. Feeling no sense of danger, we dashed toward the enemy in the wood. The machine guns began knocking over my companions. We were ordered to lie down. I noticed those at the front with me were all women. The men were further back.

I began shooting, the gun kicking my shoulder so hard that it is still blue and stiff. I was glad when we were ordered to charge the machine guns in the woods. We paid dearly, but we held on, and by night our scouts discovered the machine gunners and we shelled them out.

After the first attack I was attached to a machine gun, carrying ammunition to an advanced position under the fire of hidden German machine guns. We were advancing and constantly in danger of capture by the Germans. On one trip over newly captured ground I saw what I considered a wounded German officer lying on the ground. I went to help him with my gun in my right hand and the machine-gun ammunition in my left.

Seeing this, he jumped to his knees and pulled out his revolver, but before he could shoot I dropped the ammunition and killed him. How did I feel on taking a human life? I had no sensation except to rid my country of an enemy. There was no sentimentality. We were trying to kill them and they were trying to kill us—that is all. Any Russian girl or any American girl in the same position would have the same feeling.

Source 7 from "The Bewilderment of the Russian Soldier," The Literary Digest *56, no. 10 (March 9, 1918): 62.*

7. A Russian Soldier's Letter to His Nurse, 1917

Here with us the light has gone out of everything. We are hungry, drest in rags, and barefooted, the food is very bad, we have very little bread, the only meat we get is horse-flesh, and that is not fresh. We have got a horse of our own, but have nothing to feed it with, so are thinking of eating it ourselves. There is no help for us anywhere. It is our fate to be thrown aside and forgotten by the world and to die of cold and hunger.

. . . While I write I wonder whether you will read my letter, for I am a soldier, and now every soldier is considered a traitor and is blamed for all that has happened. But . . . wherein is the soldier to blame? He is the same soldier he was in 1914. In most cases he has been wounded several times, has been poisoned by gas, has suffered, and is still suffering all the horrors of war, and yet—he is to blame for everything. And why? Because our whole Government are traitors.

Source 8 from "The Russian 'Joan of Arc's' Own Story," in True Stories of the Great War, *ed. Francis Trevelyan Miller (New York: Review of Reviews, 1917), vol. 6, pp. 352, 354.*

8. Colonel Alexandra Kokotseva, 6th Ural Cossacks, Letter to Friends, probably 1915

My splendid Cossacks![3] Who would have thought that they would consent to be commanded by a woman? Often have I told you of their superior attitude toward women. They expect their women to work for them, to serve them and be always submissive. Evidently my fierce little ones consider me as a sort of Superwoman. Or, perhaps they do not consider me a woman at all—except now that I am wounded and in the hospital—and respect merely my colonel's

---

3. **Cossacks:** cavalry organized by the tsarist government, largely recruited from the frontiers of southern Russia.

uniform. . . . At any rate they obey my slightest wish, perform the most reckless deeds, gayly court death, to win my approval. . . .

Do you say to yourself that "this terrible war" has robbed me of all my estimable "woman's weaknesses"? Do you picture me brazenly calloused to scenes of human agony and violent deaths for thousands in a single engagement which probably has no effect upon the final outcome?

You would be wrong. It is simply that if you are a soldier it is your duty to kill, and perhaps to be killed, in defense of your country. No matter how dreadful the things that happen, they are inseparable from war and you must get used to them. Gradually you do get used to them. If you did not your services to your country would be of no value. You would not be a true soldier, who must be able always to shrug his shoulders and say to himself, "Well, such things happen," and then go on faithfully with his soldier's work.

But believe me, these duties performed as well as I am able to perform them, promotions, honors—afterward they will be as nothing compared with what is dear to me as a woman. Through all this violence and carnage and misery I know that I shall have gained in all that becomes a woman—in faithfulness, tenderness, pity for the poor and unfortunate, and in charity.

Source 9 from George F. Wear, "17–24," in Everyman at War, *ed. C. B. Purdom (New York: Dutton, 1930), pp. 98–99, 101–102, 104, 106.*

9. From Lieutenant George Wear, Royal Field Artillery, Reminiscences, 1914–1918

I landed in France with a medical unit attached to the 7th Division in November 1914.

I was a boy just turned seventeen, straight from school, and all the thrill of romance and adventure was on me. The story-books were coming true, and by an extraordinary piece of luck I was privileged to be a participator. How enviously my school friends had written to me when they heard that we were definitely under orders to proceed, after a bare three months' training, on active service. . . .

At Poperinghe and other places we were soon hard at work with the wounded from Ypres. . . . Sights that made older men sick with horror served only to harden my determination, and, though often terrified and worn out by the unaccustomed heavy labour, I grew more and more anxious to play my part.

As the fighting died down, and our work grew less, a group of us, similar in age and station, gradually became dissatisfied with what we thought our inglorious share in the War. We felt we were not soldiering. The glamour was wearing off. . . . Several of us applied for commissions, and we counted the days till they came through, and, one by one, the lucky ones of us returned to England in the early summer of 1915.

I joined a Territorial reserve brigade of R.F.A. just being formed, and before my eighteenth birthday appeared at home resplendent in a second lieutenant's uniform. . . .

It was a mad merry time while it lasted, but the second winter of the War came on, and the time came near for going out again. The majority of us, I think, were anxious to go, though our reasons were no doubt selfish and vainglorious. . . .

It was a long time before I felt any fear. At first I had, like many others, been afraid of being afraid, but I soon learned there was no danger of that. The excitement and thrill of battle were on me. I was too young to think of anything else. . . .

The first time I was in action . . . we were at a quiet spot on the Front, and lived in a broken-down house a mile from the front line. One evening, just after supper, a 4.2 shell came through the wall into the room, bursting at once. We were thrown on the ground, the candles extinguished, and bits of plaster and falling brick showered on us. The door and window of the room, frames and all, were blown out, but, marvellously, no one was hurt. It was from this time that I began to experience what fear was. This sudden shock (I trembled for an hour afterwards) gave me a completely new outlook on life, life and war being, of course, synonymous terms. I crouched at the sound of a shell, found myself on a dark, quiet night in the trenches shivering with terror at what might happen. A distant machine-gun rattle would make me jump, and I often found it impossible to suppress such starts when not alone. I began to wonder if I was becoming a coward. . . .

Further periods of action followed in various places, but my diary entries for this time record little beyond the cold, frosty weather, an occasional casualty, a note of a trip to Amiens. For the rest, there was nothing but the deadly monotony of trench warfare. . . . Not that I personally had any longer any illusions about glory. In common with most others, I considered going up the line little more than a horrible necessity, the odd periods of rest in uncomfortable cold tents or huts surrounded by seas of mud a heavenly respite almost too good to be true. . . . I was one of the first to be hit, and, despite the pain of the wound and the terror that I should bleed to death before I was attended to, I kept on repeating to myself, "It's over now. It's over now."

And so it was, for me at any rate. When I came out of hospital many months later the Armistice had been signed. I was just twenty-one years of age, but I was an old man—cynical, irreligious, bitter, disillusioned. I have been trying to grow young ever since.

Source 10 from Ronald Blythe, Akenfield: Portrait of an English Village *(New York: Dell, 1969), p. 45.*

10. Leonard Thompson, Oral Testimony, 1960s

There is nobody can say that you have killed a man. I shot through so many because I was a machine-gunner. Did they all die?—I don't know. You got very frightened of the murdering and you did sometimes think, "What is all this about? What is it for?" But mostly you were thinking of how to stay alive. The more the killing, the more you thought about living. You felt brave and honoured that you should be fighting for England. You knew that all the people at home were for it. We believed we were fighting for a good cause and so, I expect, did the Turks. You didn't think personally. You can't get on with wars if you think personally. You can't say you *shot* a man, although you know you hit him, because there were so many guns going at the same time. But I should think that I killed several.

Source 11 from Malcolm Brown, ed., T. E. Lawrence: The Selected Letters *(New York: Norton, 1989), pp. 122–126.*

11. T. E. Lawrence, Letters, 1917

A. TO HIS MOTHER, SEPTEMBER 24

Writing to you isn't very hopeful, since it is clear that you never get any of my letters. . . .

By the way have any of my letters ever been opened by censor?

I'm now back in Akaba, after having had a little trip up country to the Railway, for the last fortnight. We met all sorts of difficulties, mostly political, but in the end bagged two locomotives and blew them up, after driving out the troops behind them. It was the usual Arab show, done at no cost to us, expensive for the Turks, but not decisive in any way, as it is a raid and not a sustained operation.

There are few people alive who have damaged railways as much as I have at any rate.

B. TO E. T. LEEDS,[4] SEPTEMBER 24

The last stunt has been a few days on the Hejaz Railway, in which I potted a train with two engines (oh, the Gods were kind) and we killed superior numbers, and I got a good Baluch prayer-rug and lost all my kit, and nearly my little self.

I'm not going to last out this game much longer: nerves going and temper wearing thin, and one wants an unlimited account of both. . . .

This letter isn't going to do you much good, for the amount of information it contains would go on a pin's head and roll about. However it's not a correspondence, but a discourse held with the only person to whom I have ever written regularly. . . .

I hope when the nightmare ends that I will wake up and become alive again. This killing and killing of Turks is horrible. When you charge in at the finish and find them all over the place in bits, and still alive many of them, and know that you have done hundreds in the same way before and must do hundreds more if you can.

C. TO MAJOR W. F. STERLING,[5] SEPTEMBER 25

I think people are prone to ascribe to me what the Arabs do (very efficiently, if oddly) on their own. . . .

Seriously, the Arabs put up a surprisingly good show. . . . The last stunt was the hold up of a train. It had two locomotives, and we gutted one with an electric mine. This rather jumbled up the trucks, which were full of Turks shooting at us. We had a Lewis, and flung bullets through the sides. So they hopped out and took cover behind the embankment, and shot at us between the wheels, at 50 yards. Then we tried a Stokes gun, and two beautiful shots dropped right in the middle of them. They couldn't stand that (12 died on the spot) and bolted away to the East across a 100 yard belt of open sand into some scrub. Unfortunately for them the Lewis covered the open stretch. The whole job took ten minutes, and they lost 70 killed, 30 wounded, 80 prisoners and about 25 got away. Of my hundred Howeitat and two British NCO's there was one (Arab) killed, and four (Arabs) wounded.

The Turks then nearly cut us off as we looted the train, and I lost some baggage, and nearly myself. My loot is a superfine red Baluch prayer-rug.

I hope this sounds the fun it is. The only pity is the sweat to work them up, and the wild scramble while it lasts. It's the most amateurish, Buffalo Billy sort of performance, and the only people who do it well are the Bedouin.

4. An Oxford friend and one of Lawrence's closest confidants.

5. A wartime colleague in Arabia.

Source 12 from "Letters Forwarded by the Censor, Indian Mails in France," printed portion of Censor's Report, India Office Library, London, L/MIL/5.

12. Indian Soldiers Serving in France, Undelivered Letters, 1915–1916

A. UNDELIVERED, AUGUST 1915

Here flying ships of various kinds are manoeuvering overhead and dropping bombs. Hundreds of kinds of guns are firing. Here maxim [machine] guns are being discharged, there bombs are being thrown by hand. . . . In some places the scoundrel Germans are loosing poisonous gas and liquid fire upon us. Everywhere the flying craft are fighting a battle among themselves.

B. UNDELIVERED, MARCH 1916

In India we have 50 religions, each of which claims that whatever God has created in the world is for it only; every one outside that particular sect is an unbeliever, . . . an heir of damnation. . . . But when you go out and see the world [as I now have] you realize how false is all this bragging. God is not the God of any particular religion, but He has the same regard for everyone.

Source 13 from Hector Duff, "Nyasaland and the World War, 1914–1918" (typescript, n.d.), Imperial War Museum Library, appendix I/B.

13. From Corporal Eleija Kimu, King's African Rifles, Undelivered Letter to His Wife, October 23, 1914

It is very sad but I may as well tell you that I killed one German [European] myself. I am not sleeping well. I am sleeping very badly. I am afraid because I killed him and I got my head muddled when I think of it. . . . I am a soldier and I delight in war. I have killed many black men and not felt like this, but that one white man I have killed has made me afraid—why I don't know. I am must telling you so that you will know how worried I am.

Source 14 from the Malawi oral history interview collection of Melvin E. Page.

14. Private Fololiyani Longwe, King's African Rifles, Oral Testimony Recorded August 23, 1973

The Sergeant Major told me that there was war. I told him that I would like to go to war as a soldier. . . . I was not interested in the fight itself, but in the salary it could give me. . . . They told me that if I died at the war, father and mother would be paid money. . . . It was terrible, a dangerous experience that was, but so long as I could survive and get money, it was okay.

War itself is bad, but going to the battlefield or where the war takes place is the worst. Think of lying on the ground where the hot sun is beating directly on your back. Think of yourself buried in a hole with only your head and hands outside, holding a gun. Imagine yourself facing this situation for seven days, no food, no water, yet you don't feel hungry; only death smelling all over the place. Listen to the sound from exploding bombs and machine guns, smoke all over and the vegetation burnt and, of course, deforested. Look at your friends getting killed, crying, and finally dead. These things we did, experienced, and saw.

I was wounded on the leg. I was taken to a dispensary in a trench; after having been treated with first aid, I was cured there. Ever since 1918 I was getting £1 a month [as a pension] . . . I also got two medals. I just keep them to remind me that I once joined the K.A.R. They are quite useless; I keep them for prestige.

Source 15 from Joe Harris Lunn, "Kande Kamara Speaks: An Oral History of the West African Experience in France, 1914–18," in Africa and the First World War, *ed. Melvin E. Page (London: Macmillan, 1987), pp. 40–41, 44–45, 48.*

15. Kande Kamara, Oral Testimony Recorded September 20–24, 1976

People would be dying and there [on the western front in France] were people who were frightened. . . . And some people, they behaved crazy and did absolutely mindless things because of the toughness of the war. . . . People would just collapse and pretend to have fainted, and the doctor would inspect them all over, and he would say, "I see no . . . symptoms of illness.". . . [Then the person] would pretend he was a dead man, and his left arm would fall down as if he were dead. And they made him stand up, he would scream in pain. And all these things happened just so people could return to their own country because they never wanted to fight in the war.

One of my younger brothers . . . was shot in the thigh . . . and he cried out . . . "Brother, they've shot me." But I didn't look at him—I didn't help him—because during wartime, even if your friend is shot dead, you would continue facing the enemy to save your own life. Because [officers] were watching you, and if you were afraid to shoot the enemy . . . your own people would shoot you down. . . . I didn't say anything; I kept quiet. I wasn't looking at him, but tears were running down my face.

Soon the doctor came with the ambulance to look in the gutters [trenches]. And they found my brother there, and . . . they picked him up, and my brother said, "I'm not going back in the vehicle." And he asked, "Why did I come here?" And they answered, "You came to fight." And he said, "I'm going to, just come tie my wound." And the doctor came and tied his leg and gave him some medicine. . . . Then my brother said, "Let me go . . . that's my brother down there, and wherever he dies, I will die there too." And that's when they said to him, "You have a really strong heart.". . . And because he wasn't going to stop fighting, and he was already wounded, and he was going to stay with me, he was promoted to sergeant for his bravery.

At the beginning, the white people were always in the front line. . . . But when we got to understand them . . . and when they started trusting us . . . that changed. . . . At the very end we were all mixed, because by then everyone knew that mind and their heart and no one was afraid of color except for innocents.

[When] you see a black sergeant . . . and a white corporal comes . . . and he doesn't salute the black sergeant, and the black sergeant would arrest him . . . [then you know you have] equality with the white man.

If we hadn't fought, if we—the black people—hadn't fought in western wars, and been taken overseas, and demonstrated some ability of human dignity, we wouldn't have been regarded today as anything.

Source 16 from Alexander McClintock, Best O' Luck: How a Fighting Kentuckian Won the Thanks of Britain's King *(New York: Grosset & Dunlap, 1917), pp. 114–115.*

16. From Sergeant Alexander McClintock, Canadian Grenadier Guards, Reminiscences, 1916

On the Somme, we were constantly preparing for a new advance, and we were only temporarily established on ground which we had but recently taken, after long drumming with big guns. The trenches were merely shell-holes connected by ditches, . . . only miserable "funk holes" [see Source 20], dug where it was possible to dig them without uncovering dead men. . . .

The communication trenches were all blown in and everything had to come to us overland, with the result that we never were quite sure when we should get ammunition, rations, or relief forces. The most awful thing was that the soil all about us was filled with freshly-buried men. If we undertook to cut a trench or enlarge a funk hole, our spades struck into human flesh, and the explosion of a big shell along our line sent decomposed and dismembered and sickening mementoes of an earlier fight showering amongst us. We lived in the muck and stench of "glorious" war; those of us who lived.

Sources 17 and 18 from the Forrest C. Pogue Oral History Institute collection, Murray State University.

17. Private Jesse P. Flowers, Oral Testimony Recorded June 30, 1983

Landed in Brest, France. We figured we'd get over there, they'd take us to some barracks and rest us up. Instead of that—the only time I ever fell out in my life—they unloaded us off the ship and everybody was weak and sick. I saw I wasn't going to make it, so I crawled in a roll of rope down on the riverfront. That night, they came by picking us up in a truck; soldiers were falling out, and they just picked you up and pitched you back in this truck. I thought they was taking us out to the barracks . . . but it wasn't nothing but open fields. We got out there, and there was two dead blacks laying out there under tents; their company had moved off and left them.

They took us out there and dumped us out there in a field, and I didn't know anybody, didn't know where my company was, or nothing else, so I just laid out in the field in the rain. A boy from Greenville, Kentucky, knew I had fallen out. He came looking for me and picked me up and they carried me over there and put me in half of his pup tent and my pup tent. Every time you reached up and touched the top of the tent the water would run down; you was wet all over anyway.

Next morning, they hauled me over to the infirmary and hauled me back, gave me a handful of pills. Second morning they hauled me over there again and hauled me back. And the third morning the captain standing over there said, "You take this man over there and leave him. That's my order. Don't you bring him back here anymore."

So finally . . . the third day, they took me over and put me in a hospital or something. Didn't have any doors or windows in it, but it was dry. The boy in number one bed died, and number two died. I was in the third bed, and I told the nurse, I said, "You move me!" She said, "No, you are going to make it. I'm going to leave you right where you are."

[*Indeed, Flowers recovered and joined his combat engineering unit, which was assigned to front line railroad support. He recounted one incident that occurred during the Argonne offensive, the last major campaign of the war.*]

One night when . . . I went up to the [railroad] yards about dark, I thought I saw somebody go into one of the buildings down there. So I eased up there, and I pulled out my gun and waltzed in. This little German boy, didn't look like he was more than fourteen or fifteen years old, held up his hands. I asked him what he was doing there, and he said, "I'm a French prisoner, and I got away from the prison camp." I said, "What do you expect, to get away home?" He said, "If you let me go, I'll be home by the morning.". . . He could talk pretty fair English.

I knew I would be subject to court martial if I let him go, but I said, "I'll tell you what I'm going to do. I'm going to walk down to the office, and I'll be back in a little while. I'm going to go down and see what they have to say." He said, "I sure would like to go home. I don't want to go back to that French prison camp. I got away from there, and they'll shoot me if they get me back there." I said, "I ain't taking any chance on your shooting. You stay here until I get back." Darn fool was still sitting up there when I got back!

Anyhow, I went back up there and give him a package of cigarettes. I said, "Now I'm going to walk down this way, and you start walking the other way. When I turn around, I don't want to see you anymore. I want you to be close to home." He said, "I'll be there in the morning, if you'll just let me go." I said, "I'm going this way, and you go this way. Now, I don't want to ever see you again." He said, "You won't," and I didn't. I walked about a hundred yards before I turned around, and he wasn't in sight.

18. Private William Davis, Oral Testimony Recorded September 25, 1979

I was drafted. This was in Louisville, Jefferson County, [Kentucky]. I went into a camp that they called Camp Taylor. . . . They gave us guns, but they took them away from us and gave us sticks and didn't allow us to have guns.

When I left Camp Taylor, I went to New Jersey and there . . . I was an orderly down at the officers' [mess] and the race riot started because black boys went into the canteen that was there, which every soldier was supposed to do. But the white boys didn't want them in there. They started a fight. And they began to fight with rocks, sticks, and everything. They called out to stop the fight the National Guard which was all white. . . . When they called them out, instead of waiting for the command to fire, there was one I remember, his hair, his hair was red. . . . And he fired the one shot and he killed a boy in the barracks, an innocent boy who didn't know anything about the fight. Killed a boy in the barracks.

[*Shortly thereafter Davis was sent to France, where he and his fellow African-Americans were assigned to a new unit.*]

We was placed with the 369th regiment of the Fighting Fifteenth of New York because we was sent over there as automatic replacements and we was to replace them. . . . When they sent us over there, the 369th was fighting, but . . . the white soldiers of the United States didn't want the black soldiers to fight. They wanted them to be [laborers only], wanted them to work. But the French—I want to make this clear; I hope I can because it was wrong—the French Army, the French commanders and the French theirselves said, "They came over here to fight and they are going to fight!" And they . . . signed us [into] the French army. I had all French equipment, I had a French [gas] mask, I didn't have a United States mask, I had a French rifle; all my equipment was French.

I wasn't trained even in combat; I was so-so. I wasn't trained enough that some of the French officers made a remark why they sent people over here to be killed. Because I wasn't trained properly enough.

Source 19 from the National Archives of Zimbabwe.

19. A Northern Rhodesia Regiment Dugout During the East African Campaign, probably 1917

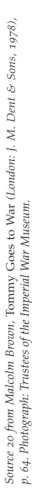

Source 20 from Malcolm Brown, Tommy Goes to War (London: J. M. Dent & Sons, 1978),
p. 64. Photograph: Trustees of the Imperial War Museum.

20. Funk Holes of the Border Regiment on the Somme, 1916

Source 21 from the National Archives.

21. German Boy Soldier, Captured October 15, 1918, by American Forces just Fourteen Days After Being Drafted into the Army

Source 22 from the Malawi oral history interview collection of Melvin E. Page.

22. King's African Rifles Marching Song

I am going, Mr. Captain,
You remain behind.
I am going Mr. Captain,
You remain behind

    Mr. Captain, do not come,
    Do not come.
    If I die, we will meet in Heaven.

I am going, Mr. Major,
You remain behind.
I am going, Mr. Major,
You remain behind.

    Mr. Major, do not come,
    Do not come.
    If I die, we will meet in Heaven.

I am going, Mr. Governor,
You remain behind.
I am going, Mr. Governor,
You remain behind.

    Mr. Governor, do not come,
    Do not come.
    If I die, we will meet in Heaven.

Source 23 from Carl Sandburg, comp., The American Songbag *(New York: Harcourt, Brace & World, 1927), pp. 442–443; words attributed to Harold Verner Johnson.*

23. "Where They Were," an American Soldiers' Song

If you want to know where the privates were,
   I'll tell you where they were,

I'll tell you where they were,
   Yes, I'll tell you where they were;
Oh, if you want to know where the privates were,
   I'll tell you where they were:
      Up to their necks in mud,
        I saw them, I saw them,
      Up to their necks in mud, I saw them
        Up to their necks in mud.

If you want to know where the captains were,
   I'll tell you where they were,
I'll tell you where they were,
   Yes, I'll tell you where they were;
Oh, if you want to know where the captains were,
   I'll tell you where they were:
      Drinking the privates' rum,
        I saw them, I saw them,
      Drinking the privates' rum, I saw them
        Drinking the privates' rum.

If you want to know where the officers were,
   I'll tell you where they were,
I'll tell you where they were,
   Yes, I'll tell you where they were;
Oh, if you want to know where the officers were,
   I'll tell you where they were:
      Down in their deep dugout,
        I saw them, I saw them,
      Down in their deep dugout, I saw them
        Down in their deep dugout.

And if you want to know where the generals were,
   I'll tell you where they were,
I'll tell you where they were,
   Yes, I'll tell you where they were;
Oh, if you want to know where the generals were,
   I'll tell you where they were:
      Back in gay Paree,
        I saw them, I saw them,
      Back in gay Paree, I saw them
        Back in gay Paree.

Source 24 from M. I. Tatham, "The Great Retreat in Serbia in 1915," in Everyman at War, *ed. C. B. Purdom (New York: Dutton, 1930), pp. 374–376, 378.*

24. Nurse M. I. Tatham, Stobart Field Hospital, Serbia, Reminiscences, 1915

The Bulgarians declared war early in October. Simultaneously the Austrians attacked on the north, and the field hospital had to retreat with the Army. We were in the town of Kraguyevatz, arsenal of Serbia, which had suffered the bombardment of Austrian aeroplanes for weeks before the evacuation, and was left an open city. Having sent off every man who had sound feet, and left those who were unable to move in charge of American doctors (who were then neutrals) the trek southwards began. It was southwards at first, for we had been told that, if we could reach Monastir, there was the possibility of transport to Salonika. The single railway line from Belgrade to Salonika had been cut the first day after the declaration of war by the Bulgarians; and there was the life-line, as it were, severed, for on that railway line all the stores, men, and ammunition were transported.

We started off with bullock-wagons with as much of the hospital equipment as we could carry, and for three weeks we trekked south—a long, slow procession of springless carts, each drawn by oxen, moving deliberately at the rate of two miles an hour—day or night was all one. Several times the unit halted, hoping that the retreat was stayed, for all the telephone wires were down, and no one knew exactly what was happening. . . .

The stream of the refugees grew daily greater—mothers, children, bedding, pots and pans, food and fodder, all packed into the jolting wagons; wounded soldiers, exhausted, starving, hopeless men, and (after the first few days) leaden skies and pitiless rain, and the awful, clinging, squelching mud. . . . The Serbians had at last realized that the enemy were out to finish her as a nation, and the only way to save herself was to run away. . . .

We had orders to go to a town called Rashka, and we trudged there in a jam of ox-wagons and soldiers, big guns and refugees, in the most appalling mud and pelting rain—and quite unquenchable good spirits. Until we were nearly there, when one of our number was shot through the lungs—an accidental shot, fired by an irate farmer after some flying refugees who were stealing his horses. The injured girl was taken to a Serbian dressing station about eight miles back along the road, with two doctors and a nurse; after which the rest of us tramped unhappily on, knowing that they would inevitably be taken prisoners, which they were two days later. They were well treated, however, by the Austrians, and when the girl who had been shot was sufficiently recovered to undertake the journey, they were all passed through Vienna and Switzerland, and so home to England. . . .

Then, two days before we would have reached Monastir, the Bulgarians took it. We had no choice now but to cross the mountains—the mountains of Albania and Montenegro, which we had been told were impassable for women in the winter. The three weeks' trek south had made us three weeks later in the beginning of the attempt, and the very first night we got to the narrow ways, the snow came. . . .

The worst night of the storm we sheltered in an Albanian hut. The fire smouldered in the middle of the mud floor, the smoke escaping through a hole in the roof—and round the fire squatted the family—unto the third and fourth generation! Around them again, the refugees, soldiers, and nurses, and the livestock of the little farm. (My neighbour on one side was a warm and comfortable calf!) Everything that could be sheltered was sheltered; those that had no shelter remained out on the mountain and died. . . . At the last, when the mountains were crossed, and the weary, muddy miles to the sea lay before us, nothing remained to most of us but what we carried ourselves. But we had our lives, and many had left theirs on those cruel heights. But for those exiles, literally bereft of everything that made life worth living—family, home, country—what use, after all, seemed even that?

Source 25 from Max Yergan, "A Y.M.C.A. Secretary in Africa," Southern Workman 47 (1918): 401–403.

25. Max Yergan, American Y.M.C.A. Field Secretary in East Africa, Reminiscences, 1916

We came at length to the training camp near Nairobi. There thousands of native African troops are brought from all parts of Africa . . . to this camp to be trained as fighting men for the British. One sees them sweeping into the camp, robed in blankets or in skins of the leopard or lion, and six months later they march out with the smartness of trained European soldiers. One scarcely knows what to think when one considers that those thousands of men are being trained to kill other men, with all of the force of the best-trained armies in the world. . . .

As they tramped down from that part of Africa to the coast, each man was given a handful of rice a day. They would soak the rice in water and then some would take it out and give it to the officers, saying, "We can perhaps live on the water a few days longer." Some fell out, as we marched down to the coast, with no complaint, simply accepting it as their lot—burning up with fever, dying from wounds they had received in battle, simply passing away with no complaint whatever. These are qualities which must mean something. . . .

I left Africa as an invalid on a hospital ship, after nine attacks of African fever. . . . These evidences of suffering make us cognizant of the necessity on our part of getting a vision of world affairs. We know not what to say. We simply realize that the hand of our great God is in this war.

Source 26 from E. M. Falk papers, Mss. Afr. S. 1808(6), Rhodes House Library, Oxford University.

26. Carrier Nwose, Nigeria
Carrier Corps, Oral Testimony
Recorded in 1916

We came back one night from our yam farm. The chief called us and handed us over to a Government messenger. I did not know where we were going to, but the chief and the messenger said that the white man had sent for us and so we must go. After three days we reached the white man's compound. Plenty of others had arrived from other villages far away. The white man wrote our names in a book, tied a brass number ticket around our necks and gave each man a blanket and food. Then he told us that we were going to the great war to help the King's soldiers who were preventing the Germans coming to our country and burning it. We left and marched far into the bush. . . .

After seven days we were given heavy loads to carry. There were biscuits inside them. Soldiers went in front, and then the carriers followed into the bush, far, very far.

One day shooting began in front. The white man told us to lie down and wait. The big guns came up and roared over the hills, and plenty of small ones helped. They fire cartridges like a string of beads as fast as a man can beat a drum. We lay and listened. The Germans fired, fired, fired, and then at last they ran away, but our second lieutenant was killed and the white sergeant major badly wounded.

Next day we came to a large town . . . full of soldiers. I fell down in the market place and lay for a long time under a tree. A white man had me carried to a house where there were other sick carriers. We were given medicine and food and water. My side hurt and I could not breathe. Abrome here had stomach complaint. I do not know how long it was that we stayed there. The white doctor said we must be sent home.

A white paymaster gave us each three pounds cash money. . . . We have walked home from station to station with our Government book [pay records] and the white men gave us guides to help us to reach home. Now that we have yams and palm oil to eat again we are happy. I am going to my farm. I will give the cash to the father of Alete, as I want to marry her.

QUESTIONS TO CONSIDER

To understand and analyze all these sources, and to compare them carefully and productively, it may help to think about them in groups. One way to do this would be to consider all the evidence from a particular country or area. Sources 16, 17, 18, 23, and 25, for example, are all American. Can you get beyond the obvious differences between them to discover what (if anything) they have in common? Such a grouping, however, poses some problems. Remember that the author of Source 16 was a United States citizen but fought in the Canadian Army! How did that choice shape his experiences? In what ways might his wartime memories have differed from those of his countrymen who served in U.S. units?

Other ways of grouping the materials might include combining those sources that describe fighting in particular campaigns or theaters. Sources 13, 14, 19, 22, and 25 concern the East African Campaign. Were there any ways in which experiences during this campaign were alike? Of course, you would also want to compare the sources concerning the fighting in both eastern and western Europe, at least, and perhaps elsewhere. Then you can compare the experiences in various theaters of war. Were there common elements, even major similarities? Or was the fighting different from place to place? You will also want to consider what might account for the similarities or differences.

Still another way to analyze these sources is to look for recurring topics or themes. Certainly you will want to consider the motivations of those who went to war. Were they primarily patriotic, fighting for their countries? And if they were, did they go willingly, even volunteering before troops were called to the colors? Were some conscripted into the war effort against their will? How did their attitudes toward war differ from those who volunteered? And which of these sources indicate an optimism toward their participation? Are any pessimistic? Can you find anything in the sources that would explain either attitude?

You might also group together those sources that provide images of actual fighting conditions. Can these be further broken down into subcategories such as waiting to engage in combat, being fired upon, and firing back? Do other sources explore attitudes of the soldiers toward killing, even toward death itself? What about the process of demobilization? Which of these accounts tell you about the experiences of coming home after the war? What other themes can you find that seemed important to these participants in the First World War?

As you group these soldiers' accounts, photographs, and song lyrics, some of the sources will likely fall into two, three, or even more of the categories you have identified. This should not surprise you. But to keep the ideas clear in your mind, you might make a series of lists, carefully noting which sources fall into what groups or themes, as well as what each contributes to your understanding of that theme. Once you have done that, you might also consider the similarities and differences of the accounts within each list. Always be prepared to go back and reexamine the sources in order to complete your lists. Your notes themselves will not provide all the answers to the questions posed, but they may help you organize the information you have read so that you can answer them.

Once you have read all the sources and attempted to organize their contents, stop for a moment to think about all of the evidence collectively. Consider what overall impression they convey about the nature of World War I. What, if anything, made it really a world war? Did most of the soldiers and others consider that they were fighting on a global stage? When did they express such views? Did soldiers in the heat of battle, or even shortly thereafter, think of the wider implications of what they were doing? Or did such realizations come

only much later? Why would this make a difference?

Also think about what impressions these men and women communicated to their loved ones or carried home with them about their war service. Were these based on what happened to them? Or did they derive more from individual expectations, either realized or unfulfilled? Were their national identities or personal experiences before the war more important? What do you think they might have felt had they known that another, similarly long and widespread international conflict would occur a generation later?

Finally, return to the problem questions posed at the beginning of the chapter. You should now be in position to offer answers to each of them. Did these common soldiers truly share in a global experience? If so, what were its common elements? And if it was not, what accounts for the differences in the ways they experienced this most memorable of wars?

EPILOGUE

There is no doubt that World War I transformed Europe. It also brought dramatic change to the United States and Russia. But its impact just as clearly shook the lives of millions of people in the farthest reaches of the world. If all the experiences of the preceding half-century had not done so, these four years of fighting changed the face of warfare forever, marrying increasingly destructive

technology with the quiet heroism of soldiers that had long characterized the practice of war. World War I also wrought a cataclysmic series of economic and political changes that proved even more important in both the long and short term.

Following the Treaty of Versailles (signed by all the major participants except the United States), international economic patterns were sharply altered. War debts troubled many nations, some seeking ways to pay them and others worrying that amounts owed would not be paid. Germany especially was burdened by reparations payments, demanded by some of her former enemies as compensation for the horrible costs of the conflict. These interlinking patterns of debts and payments were an ongoing source of international tensions and, ultimately, a contributing factor in the great worldwide economic depression of the 1930s.

Political changes in the aftermath of the First World War were even more profound. Everywhere nations faced expectations from their citizens for both rewards due their sufferings and greater popular participation in government decision making. The model of a demand economy and its accompanying (theoretical, at least) social equality in the new Soviet Union was popular in many quarters. Veterans were impatient with governments unresponsive to their needs and desires. Even among colonial peoples, expectations increased for changes in the ways they were governed. Few Africans or Asians were willing to accept, as many had done in the prewar years, continued colonial rule into the lifetimes of their children.

Such rising expectations were at least tacitly recognized by the international community as a whole. The League of Nations—proposed by U.S. President Woodrow Wilson, but with the United States ultimately absent from its member ranks—created a "mandate system" for German colonies and some of the old Ottoman Empire, which had been Germany's ally. Under this plan, the victors divided up those territories, each

to be governed under a mandate ensuring the advancement of the indigenous peoples toward eventual self-determination. The League was also intended to be a forum for international concerns and the peaceful resolution of disputes between nations. Although it was not exceptionally successful in such enterprises, the League of Nations did mark a departure in international affairs.

However important these changes were, they were frequently far removed from the experiences and concerns of the common soldiers for whom this had been "a war to end all wars." Their experiences shaped not only their own attitudes, but those of families, friends, and acquaintances for years to come. Many, feeling far removed from all the changes their efforts had brought, were increasingly alienated from civilian life. Their discontents with what the war had accomplished festered, despite the pride most felt in what they had done.

In Germany and Italy, Adolf Hitler and Benito Mussolini—themselves both veterans of World War I—took advantage of the frustrations of their fellow veterans, often enlisting their support for programs to regain what their nations had lost in war, especially power and prestige. Elsewhere, genuine fears that soldiers' sacrifices might not have prevented yet another war fed early efforts to appease both Hitler's demands in Europe and Mussolini's aggression in Ethiopia. The net result, however, was a second global conflict, a grim outcome the common soldiers of the first had so much hoped to avoid.

CHAPTER ELEVEN

THE DEMOCRATIZATION OF DESIRE:

DEPARTMENT STORES, ADVERTISING, AND

THE NEW CONSUMERISM[1] (1920s)

THE PROBLEM

The response to the death of American department store magnate John Wanamaker on December 12, 1922, was one normally reserved for important heads of state. In Wanamaker's native Philadelphia, public schools and the stock exchange were closed, the city council suspended its meetings, and thousands filed by the casket to pay their respects as Wanamaker's body lay in state in the Bethany Presbyterian Church. Condolences poured in from around the world and included expressions of sympathy from United States president Warren Harding and the secretary of state, Charles Evans Hughes. Graveside services were attended by inventor Thomas Edison, Chief Justice of the United States William Howard Taft, soup and ketchup king Howard Heinz, politician William Jennings Bryan, and a host of U.S. senators and governors. Indeed, John

Wanamaker was as honored in death as he had been powerful and influential in life.

Wanamaker and men like him throughout the world were products of the Industrial Revolution that swept through much of Europe, the Americas, and Japan in the nineteenth century. Mass production made a host of consumer goods available to the middle and skilled working classses for the first time at reasonable prices. In order to distribute these goods, the institution of the department store was born, the first one opening in Paris in 1852. By 1900, department stores were important in bringing consumer goods to the people in France, England, Germany, Japan, the United States, Canada, Brazil, Mexico, Australia, South Africa, New Zealand,

1. We are happy to attribute this chapter's title to William Leach, from his excellent book *Land of Desire: Merchants, Power, and the Rise of a New American Culture* (New York: Pantheon Books, 1993), p. 3.

Switzerland, Sweden, Norway, Belgium, and Denmark. Wherever they were founded, department stores bore remarkable similarities; from country to country they looked the same: a mammoth retail emporium selling a myriad of consumer items reasonably priced and grouped together in "departments."

Department store founders like John Wanamaker, however, could not simply open their establishments and expect masses of customers automatically to flock in. Wage earners had to be convinced that they actually *needed* these goods, that owning a felt fedora or a silk chemise would improve their status and happiness. Led by pioneer John Wanamaker, department store owners spent lavishly on newspaper advertising in order to *create* desire for the consumer goods they sold. As Wanamaker himself was fond of saying, "The time to advertise is all the time," and almost all department store owners did precisely that. So dependent did urban newspapers become on department store advertising that by 1904 one observer did not overstate the case when he remarked that the "newspaper of today is largely the creation of the department store." And, spurred by the spectacular success of depart-

ment store advertising, other businesses began to advertise their products and services as well, especially the manufacturers of what became "brand name" products.

In this chapter, you will be examining and analyzing a series of department store advertisements from six countries: the United States, Brazil, France, Canada, Australia, and the Union of South Africa. All of these promotions appeared in the 1920s, which was probably the height of the downtown department store phenomenon. Your task in this chapter is to determine the types of appeals department stores used to convince potential customers that they needed the goods the stores offered. What can these advertisements tell us about middle and skilled working classes' values, fears, aspirations, and visions of "the good life"? Keep in mind that each advertisement may have more than one appeal. Also be aware that appeals can be overt and obvious or may be quite subtle. Finally, note that various advertisements may be directed at particular demographic groups—middle-class women, for instance. In all, how did department store advertisements create what historian William Leach calls the "land of desire"?

BACKGROUND

Several interrelated factors were responsible for the rise of mass consumerism in the late nineteenth and early twentieth centuries in Europe, the Americas, Japan, and elsewhere.

To begin with, the Industrial Revolution and the evolution of the modern factory system made possible staggering increases in the production of manufactured goods. Traditional methods such as the "putting out system" and the apprenticeship system were fairly quickly replaced by

Chapter 11

The

Democratization

of Desire:

Department

Stores,

Advertising,

and the New

Consumerism

(1920s)

mechanized factories where, until the rise of the trade union movement, men, women, and children worked for slim wages with little hope of advancement or in a piece-work system that paid workers, not for their time, but for the amount of goods their machines produced. Beginning in the textile, clothing, shoe, and stick furniture industries, the factory system rapidly spread to most areas of production. Between 1890 and 1900 alone, the production of ready-to-wear clothing doubled; by 1914, factories were turning out almost four times the numbers of cheap glassware, lamps, and tableware as they had in 1890.

Several demographic trends also help to explain mass consumerism's advent. For one thing, Europe and the Americas both experienced rapid population increases between 1750 and 1900. Britain's population alone surged from approximately 8 million people in 1750 to over 40 million in 1900. The number of people in what became Germany in 1871 more than doubled between 1800 and 1900, and France's population growth, while somewhat less dramatic, was also impressive (from over 25 million in 1800 to around 39 million by 1900). Thanks to immigration and high natural increases, the Americas' population increases were even more incredible. At the same time, the birthrate in Europe actually was declining. Population increases, therefore, were largely the result of a higher survival rate, which can be explained primarily by greater food supplies and to a lesser extent by improvements in medicine. Life expectancy in France went from an av-

erage of around twenty-one years in 1660 to approximately thirty-eight years by 1832.

A growing number of these people made their livings in nonagricultural occupations, increasingly in urban factories. Manchester, England, once described by an observer as a "server of gold" because of the wealth its factories generated while many lived in horrible conditions, surged from 50,000 people in 1780 to 100,000 in 1801 to 400,000 by 1850. Most of these people had migrated from the countryside as part of a rural-to-urban population shift that took place throughout most of Europe and the Americas during the late eighteenth and nineteenth centuries. In Paris and London in 1850, over one-half of those cities' populations had not been born there. Without these demographic changes, it is questionable whether mass consumerism would have appeared where and when it did.

Finally, in spite of the fact that nineteenth-century writers and thinkers like Charles Dickens, Émile Zola, Karl Marx, Friedrich Engels, and others concentrated their attention on the seamier sides of the Industrial Revolution, for many people the factory system—and the accompanying agricultural and demographic changes—brought better and longer lives.[2] In England, real wages (that is, wages adjusted to take into account the cost of living) actually doubled between 1850 and 1906, and the average consumption of food and goods

2. Zola did call the department store the "cathedral of modern commerce."

in Great Britain increased per capita by 75 percent between 1780 and 1851. Other nations in Europe and the Americas could boast of equally impressive gains. Therefore, while the new industrial age meant frightful working and living conditions for many, on the whole the standard of living actually improved during the nineteenth century wherever industrialism had triumphed.

Thus the Industrial Revolution increased the ability to produce goods and, at the same time, increased people's ability to consume them. But how were these products to be distributed (sold) and how would the middle and skilled working classes come to perceive that they actually needed them? Small specialty stores that sold only one type of product (like shoes, for example) and street vendors would be insufficient, and mail-order distribution was far better suited to rural regions than to cities. It was at that point that department stores arose to bridge the chasm between producers and potential consumers.

Most of the nineteenth-century department store barons (including John Wanamaker himself) credited Frenchman Aristide Boucicaut with originating the department store concept. In 1852 in Paris, Boucicaut opened Bon Marché, a huge building that contained several merchandise departments. Markups from the wholesale prices were small, meaning that Bon Marché could sell items from 15 to 20 percent cheaper than single-line specialty shops. All items had fixed, marked prices, something of a revolution in retail trade: before

then no goods were labeled and prices were negotiated through individual bargaining. Boucicaut opened his doors to everyone and began the practice of free returns and exchanges, equally revolutionary for their time. In 1852 (the year it opened), Bon Marché sold 500,000 francs worth of goods. By 1860 it was selling over 5 million francs annually (20 million by 1870) and the modern department store was born. Bon Marché was soon followed by Galeries Lafayette and Le Printemps in Paris; Whiteley's, Harrod's, and Selfridges in London; Wertheim in Berlin; Magasin du Nord in Copenhagen; Steen and Strom in Oslo; Magazine zum Globus in Zurich; Nordiska Kompaniet in Stockholm; Mitsukoshi in Tokyo; Stuttafords in South Africa; A. T. Stewart in New York; and John Wanamaker's in Philadelphia. Aided by architectural innovations (the escalator, of which there were twenty-seven in New York's Gimbel's when that department store opened in 1927) and by technological improvements (electric lighting in 1878, cash registers in the 1880s, the pneumatic tube by the 1890s), department stores became retailing palaces that (as Wanamaker manager Robert Ogden once observed) "added to the sum of human happiness by increasing the power of money to supply the comforts of life."

To entice customers, department stores spent millions on newspaper advertising. In the United States alone, the total spent on newspaper advertising mushroomed from $40 million in 1880 to over $140 million in 1904. John Wanamaker, the bricklayer's son become merchant, opened

Chapter 11

The

Democratization

of Desire:

Department

Stores,

Advertising,

and the New

Consumerism

(1920s)

his first department store in 1877 and is generally credited with being the first to appreciate the value of mass advertising. Wanamaker quickly recognized that mass-circulation newspapers reached tens of thousands of his potential customers every day, and he immediately capitalized on that opportunity. Technological improvements like photoengraving made large "display" advertisements with pictures not only inexpensive but eye-catching. Largely because of his advertising, over 70,000 people swarmed into Wanamaker's Philadelphia department store on its opening day in 1877. As L. Frank Baum (an advertising pioneer who abandoned that field when his enor-

mously popular *The Wonderful Wizard of Oz* was published in 1900) remarked, "Without advertising, the modern merchant sinks into oblivion." Wanamaker and his fellow retail giants recognized the wisdom of Baum's pithy observation. At his death in 1922, Wanamaker's wealth was estimated at well over $25 million.

What appeals did Wanamaker and other department store owners make to their potential middle- and working-class customers? How did their newspaper advertisements create a "land of desire"? What do those advertisements reveal about popular values, fears, aspirations, and visions of "the good life"?

THE METHOD

No historian would suggest that newspaper advertisements of the past (or today's ads, for that matter) simply announce the availability of particular goods for sale. In addition to such announcements, advertisements are created with the intention of making people want to buy those products. Therefore, advertisements contain messages telling consumers why these purchases are desirable. Some of these messages are blatant, whereas others are remarkably subtle—so subtle that readers may not even recognize that a powerful message is being communicated. Yet even though the potential consumers of the past may have been oblivious to their advertising vulnerability, his-

torians can analyze those same advertisements in order to detect those underlying appeals.

Messages communicated in advertisements can be divided into the two general categories: *positive* messages and *negative* ones. Positive advertisements show the benefits—direct or indirect, explicit or implicit—that would come from purchasing the advertised product. For example, a *direct* benefit of owning a hat would be to keep rain or excessive sunlight off the head; an *indirect* benefit would be that wearing such a hat would communicate to others that the hat's owner was chic, fashionable, modern, or even affluent. At the same time, negative advertisements demonstrate the disastrous consequences of *not* purchasing the advertised product. And, like positive messages, negative messages can be direct or indirect. Returning to our advertisement for hats, a direct negative consequence would be a wet head (cold, flu, ruined coiffure) or a sunburned head. An indirect negative consequence would be to be thought of as unfashionable, frumpy, or even poor. Most effective advertisements combine positive and negative approaches, thereby evoking strong emotional responses that almost compel consumers to purchase the products being advertised.

By 1900, manufacturers, advertising agencies (an infant industry), and department store owners had developed a number of extremely sophisticated and effective appeals that were used in newspaper and magazine advertisements. As you examine and analyze department store advertisements from the United States, Brazil, France, Canada, Australia, and South Africa, make a list of the ways in which department stores appealed to potential customers. Keep in mind that each advertisement can contain several types of appeals, or messages. Also remember that neither the very rich nor the very poor did their shopping in department stores. Department stores were for the urban middle and working classes, and all advertising appeals would have targeted them.

In addition, it might be interesting to compare and contrast advertisements from different nations. Were the appeals to the urban middle and working classes in the United States, Brazil, France, Canada, Australia, and South Africa similar or different? How would you explain your findings?

Finally, what comparisons can be made between the advertisements of the early twentieth century included here and the advertisements that fill today's newspapers and magazines? If the appeals are similar, how would you explain this consistency? If they are different, does that signify a change in popular values, fears, aspirations, and visions of "the good life"?

The twelve advertisements in the Evidence section of this chapter are fairly representative of department store advertisements during the 1920s. Sources 1 and 2 are from the United States—Strawbridge & Clothier and Bonwit Teller, respectively. The majority of all department store advertisements emphasized women's clothing, with children's clothing and toys ranking next in advertising space expended. Why do you think this was so?

Sources 3 and 4 are advertisements from the Mappin Stores, Brazil's largest department store chain (they even sold major appliances, like refrigerators). Source 3 concentrates exclusively on men's clothing, whereas Source 4 reveals the very popular market for women of silks and fabrics—for those who made their own clothes. Are appeals to men and women different or similar?

Sources 5 and 6 are from France, the former promoting Bon Marché, generally believed to have been the world's first department store (*bon marché* can be translated as "good deal"). These two advertisements do not contain as much written copy as the advertisements from other nations. Therefore, you will have to

Chapter 11

The

Democratization

of Desire:

Department

Stores,

Advertising,

and the New

Consumerism

(1920s)

interpret from the artwork (as the original viewers of these advertisements had to do) what messages are being communicated. For a clue to the message, look closely at how the figures are drawn.

Sources 7 and 8 are from the Hudson's Bay Company of Canada. Chartered as a fur trading company by King Charles II of England on May 2, 1670, it is perhaps the oldest still extant company in the Western Hemisphere. Are the Hudson's Bay Company's appeals different from or similar to the advertisements you have analyzed so far?

Sources 9 and 10 are from Australia and Sources 11 and 12 are from Garlick's Department Store in Capetown, South Africa. Garlick's was founded in 1875 and by the 1920s it contained over fifty "departments." What special appeals did these department stores make to customers who clearly felt they were far removed geographically from the latest trends and fashions?

THE EVIDENCE

Source 1 from the Philadelphia Inquirer, *December 1, 1922. Courtesy of the Center for Research Libraries.*

1. Strawbridge & Clothier, Philadelphia, 1922

This Great Store is Gloriously Ready to Take Care of School and College Girls To-day

Daughter home from college and little sister with an extra holiday to enjoy, usually, we have discovered, plan this day for the greatest pleasure they can think of —selecting new clothes: A great coat or a darling of a fur neck scarf for that next big sports event; a dance frock to take back to college, or one of the new costume suits to wear on the return trip, or one of the new mannish sweaters—"all the girls are wearing them, mother, indeed they are—they're all the fashion." Oh! They'll all be here to-day, and we are gloriously ready for them.

Chapter 11

The

Democratization

of Desire:

Department

Stores,

Advertising,

and the New

Consumerism

(1920s)

Source 2 from the Philadelphia Bulletin, *November 14, 1923. Courtesy of the Atwater Kent Museum.*

2. Bonwit Teller & Co., Philadelphia, 1923

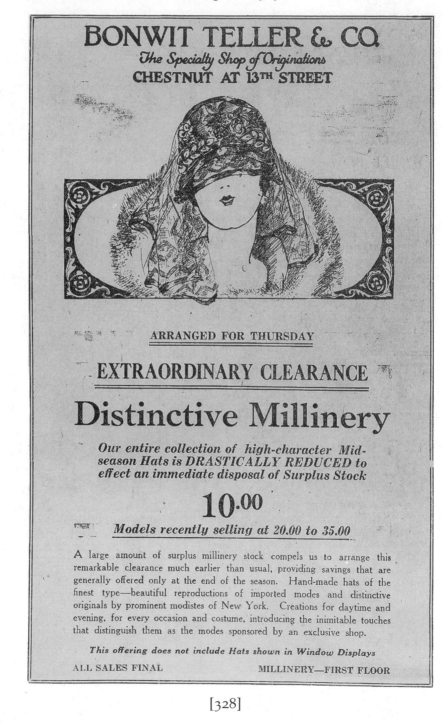

Source 3: Courtesy of Zuleika Alvim/Grifo.

3. Mappin Stores, Brazil

"Mappin" Tailors

TAILOR-MADE SUITS

Latest models

The WOOLS AND THREADS we use are directly imported.

Source 4: Courtesy of Zuleika Alvim/Grifo.

4. Mappin Stores, Brazil

Silks ←

The finest products from Lyon, Como and Milan ←

MAPPIN STORES

Sedas

SEDAS

As melhores producções de Lyon, Como e Milano

MOUSELINE CHIFFON qualidade superior, em 12 cores novas. Largura 1,10. Metro . . 22$000

RADIUM finissimo artigo em pura seda, 30 cores de plena voga. Largura 1,10. Metro 24$ e 29$000

SETIM MACAU de magnifica qualidade para almofadas e outros trabalhos. Todas as cores. Lagura 0,60 cms. Metro . . . . . . 15$000

TAFFETA «SYLPHIDE» tecido superior em cerca de 15 cores delicadas. Largura 100 cm. Metro 24$000

TUSSOR DE SEDA em bellissimas cores lisas rosa, fraise, verde, vermelho, natier, lilas, bois-de rose e branco. Largura 0,95 cm. Metro . 30$000

FOULARD «ZURICK» desenhos pintalgados e em listas sobre fundos de cor. Larg. 0,95 cm. Metro 32$000 28$000

GEORGETTE — Crepe de suave transparencia, cores unidas de rosa, lilas, beije, cinza, verde, marron, esmeralda, canario, ouro, bois-de-rose, grenat, vermelho, bordeaux, roxo, taupe, tabaco, champagne, gris, pervanche, marinho, branco e preto. Largura 100 cm. Metro . . . . 32$000

CREPE «CELES» — Tecido «souple» em lindas cores lisas ou listadas garantidas ás lavagens. Largura 0,85 cm. Metro . . . . . 38$000

RADIUM DE LYON, optima qualidade para vestidos, em mais de 30 cores lisas de grande moda. Largura 100 cm. Metro . . . . 38$000

RADIUM FANTASIA — Sortimento completamente novo, pequenos desenhos de alta novidade. Largura 100 cm. Metro . . . . . 45$000

VELLUDO CHIFFON, artigo francez, ultimas tonalidades do momento. Largura 100 cm. Metro 48$000 e . . . 55$000

Sedas pretas, marinho e branco

Possuimos, em qualquer data, a maior collecção, as melhores qualidades, pelos preços mais moderados da capital.

ALGODOES
de MANCHESTER

Typos de nossa especialidade, de uma preferenoia vasta e crescente

CRIMPS «NANKIN» — Esplendido tecido para peignoirs e vestidos caseiros, desenhos chinezes e japonezes. Larg. 0,80 Metro 5$500 e 4$500

TOBRALCO FANTASIA — Conhecido artigo inglez, desenhos de flores, listas e xadrez, absolutamente fixas. Larg. 100 cm. Metro . 8$500

TOBRALCO «TOATAL» — Fabricado com o melhor algodão, 30 côres garantidas. Larg. 100 cm. Metro . . . . 7$800

VOILE INGLEZ — Finissimo para vestidos em todos os nuances. Larg. 100 cm. Metro . 6$800

ORGANDY SUISSO — Esplendido organdy cristal em 15 côres. Largura 115 cm. Metro . 8$500

TRICOLINE legitima de Mitchell, tendo gravado na ourela, de 2 em 2 metros, o nome registrado «Tricoline»; 40 côres garantidas contra o sol e a agua. Largura 100 cm. Metro . . 9$800

TRICOLINE do mesmo fabricante, desenhos novos em listas largas ou estreitas. Largura 100 cm. Metro . . . . 11$500

GINGHAN — Artigo genuinamente escocez, cerca de 30 padrões modernos. Largura 0,90 Metro . . . . . . 9$800

FLANELLA CLYDELLA — Mistura de lã e algodão, 20 cores listadas garantidas contra a acção da agua e do sol. Larg. 0,85 Metro . 10$800

LINHOS

LINHO «HARRIS» — Para vestidos. Novas cores. Largura 100 cm. Metro . . . 9$800

LINHO BELGA — Para vestidos de campo sport e passeio. Largura 120 cm. Metro . . 12$500

CAMBRAIA IRLANDEZA — De puro linho para lingerie e vestidos. Largura 100 cm. Metro 12$500

Pecam amostras dos nossos tecidos

— 48 —

[330]

Source 5 from Kharbine/Tapabor, Paris.

5. Bon Marché, Paris, 1923

Outfits of the Summer

Chapter 11

The

Democratization

of Desire:

Department

Stores,

Advertising,

and the New

Consumerism

(1920s)

Source 6 from Kharbine/Tapabor, Paris.

6. Galeries Lafayette, Paris, 1924

General Display OF THE
NOVELTIES OF THE SEASON ◀

Sources 7 and 8 from the Manitoba Free Press, April 3, 1926; April 19, 1926. Legislative Library of Manitoba. Prints courtesy of Hudson's Bay Company Archives, Provincial Archives of Manitoba.

7. Hudson's Bay Company, Canada, 1926

"Lavender Line" Undies

Daintiness, Beauty and Simplicity are the Outstanding Features of These Newest Creations

—"Lavender Line" Underwear is tailored more carefully and finished more daintily than is usual, and the fabrics used are the finest of their kind. It is produced in shades of pink, peach, white, orchid, malmaison, chantilly, Versailles, Marie Antoinette and black. Prices are—

For Vests ....$1.95   For Bloomers $3.25

Simplicity

A Figure That's Lithe and Graceful

Achieve it With a "Compact"

—They're the ideal one-piece garments for she who would possess the softly moulded lines of the new mode.

—Compacts of firm cotton brocade, with Kendrick elastic, at _____ **$10.50**

—The finer silk brocades and satin treco, with hand-made elastic, at from _____ **$13.95** to **$25.00**

—Ask our expert corsetiers to give you a trial fitting.

Francette Foundation Garments

—In finest silk stripe treco, featuring the snug fitting under arm section required by the new silhouette.

Floor Two, H.B.C.

Sources 9 and 10: Courtesy of the Coles Myer Archives.

9. Myer's, Australia, 1929

For the forthcoming *Race and River Carnivals!*

RACE CARNIVAL MODES AT
THE MYER EMPORIUM LTD.!

The Spring Race Toilettes that await your selection at The Myer Emporium. These clever new creations are the most entrancing, the most fascinating fashions imaginable . . . you must come in and see for yourself how ravishing the colors, beautiful the new fabrics, which master-couturiers have transformed into the most engaging garments for race and reception occasions!

English, American and Continental Original Models—at Myer's!

Displayed in the Model and Misses' Salons, 2nd and 3rd Floors, Main Store—where the exclusive models from abroad present a collection of indescribable elegance for dinner, dance, daytime and sport occasions.

Hats and Accessories!

The very newest silhouettes in "face-framing" hats of straw, summer felt and fabric to be found on the Fourth Floor. Many are exclusive French and American models featuring lengthened backs, widened sides—in small, medium and large shapes. Shoes, Hose, Gloves, Bags, Sunshades, Scarves, Costume Jewellery and other chic accessories will be found in magnificent assortment—Ground Floor, Main Store.

Chapter 11

The

Democratization

of Desire:

Department

Stores,

Advertising,

and the New

Consumerism

(1920s)

10. Myer's, Australia, 1922

Sources 11 and 12 from the Capetown (South Africa) Cape Times, *November 4, 1926; December 1, 1926. Courtesy of the Center for Research Libraries.*

11. Garlick's, South Africa, 1926

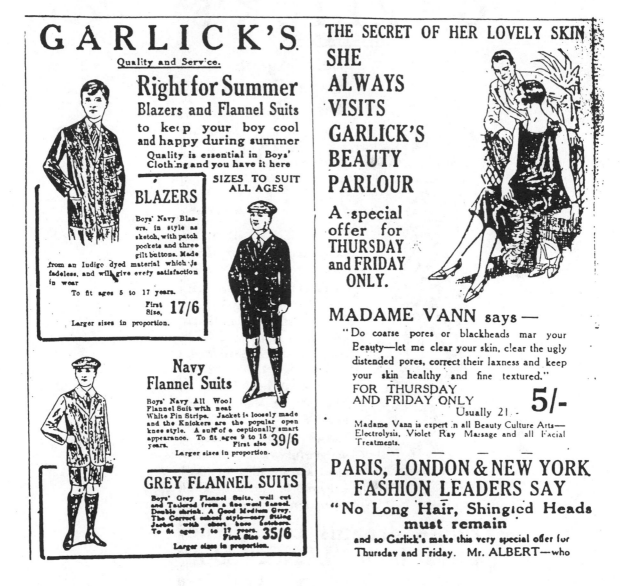

Chapter 11
The
Democratization
of Desire:
Department
Stores,
Advertising,
and the New
Consumerism
(1920s)

12. Garlick's, South Africa, 1926

ONLY 20 MORE SHOPPING DAYS TO XMAS.

GARLICK'S
Quality and Service.

Sole Agents in
Cape Town for
the Wonderful

"LENCI" DOLLS

Each "LENCI" Doll is
exclusively dressed and
specially designed.
"LENCI" Dolls are all
washable & unbreakable.
Each "LENCI" Doll is
artistically made: the hair
is real and can be combed,
in fact, the "LENCI" Doll
is the most beautiful and
best looking Doll on the
market.

XMAS finds us with a
wonderful variety in all
sizes and at all prices, all
colours in dresses and
costumes.

Make dreams come true
Let it be a "LENCI" Doll

Prices from **22/6**

TOY DEPT.————————————2nd FLOOR

GARLICK'S

QUESTIONS TO CONSIDER

Your task in this chapter is to analyze department store advertisements of the early twentieth century to determine what types of appeals these advertisements utilized and what those appeals reveal about popular values, fears, aspirations, and visions of "the good life."

As you examine the twelve advertisements presented as Evidence, keep in mind that department stores catered to the middle and working classes. Elite men and women did not patronize these establishments, in fact would have been horrified to have been seen in them. In London, most upper-class men and women went to tailoring establishments where their clothes were specially fitted—some had their measurements "on file" at exclusive shops. Similarly, the very poor did not shop in department stores either, mainly because even prices this low were beyond their means.

As you examine each advertisement, you will find it helpful to make notes. First, try to determine the *message* of each advertisement. To what emotions is the advertisement appealing?

As late as the seventeenth century, it was illegal in much of Europe and in some of the English colonies in North America for people to "dress above their station"—that is, to wear clothes normally worn by the elite. People were fined for wearing lace at their wrists and necks! By the nineteenth century, democratic revolutions in Europe and America had done away with such distinctions, and many people purposely tried to imitate their "betters" in dress. How do the advertisements from various countries subtly (or not so subtly) exploit that temptation to dress and appear like the elite? See especially Source 1, the "home from college" advertisement. The vast majority of young women and their mothers who read this advertisement had never been to college nor intended to go. How did the advertisement attempt to persuade noncollege women (and their mothers) to purchase these goods? See also Bonwit Teller's advertisement (Source 2), along with Sources 3, 4, 7, 8, 9, 10, and 11.

In the eighteenth and nineteenth centuries American elite women ordered dolls from London and Paris, dressed in the latest fashions, and then took the dolls' garments to their custom dressmakers to copy. This is a clear sign that upscale women regarded London and Paris as the centers—the *nes plus ultra*—of fashion. How do the advertisements from Brazil, Canada, Australia, and South Africa show that even middle-class shoppers wanted the latest "continental" fashions? See especially Sources 2, 3, 4, 7, 9 (Australia obviously regards "America" as a style center, too), and 11. It seems that the farther a department store was from Paris, New York, or London, the more the advertisements sought to emphasize that they had goods (or reproductions) from these fashion meccas. Source 10 makes it clear that the Melbourne buyer traveled all the way to Switzerland to secure these goods.

Chapter 11

The

Democratization

of Desire:

Department

Stores,

Advertising,

and the New

Consumerism

(1920s)

But above all, the middle-class shoppers were interested in value. In addition to the positive messages (be stylish) and the negative messages (don't be ordinary), middle-class shoppers above all were concerned with price. How did the advertisements emphasize savings (Sources 2, 4, 7, 8, 10, and 11)?

Many middle-class shoppers deferred buying things for themselves, choosing to help their children leapfrog over humble parents into the upper-middle class. How do these

advertisements (especially Sources 11 and 12) demonstrate this? How does this fit in with middle-class assumptions of "the good life"?

What is remarkable about these advertisements (from the United States, Brazil, France, Canada, Australia, and South Africa) is not how different they were but how similar. Indeed, the "democratization of desire" had conquered the world. The Industrial Revolution had embraced the world's middle class.

EPILOGUE

At their peak in the 1920s, urban department stores were important institutions in the industrialized world. To begin with, and as noted above, the department store served as a major way to distribute the goods that industrialism's factories continued to churn out. But in order to perform this function, department stores needed to convince a new generation of consumers, many of whom had been used to making their own clothing, tools, furniture, and toys, that it actually *needed* the goods that department stores offered for sale. This they did by newspaper advertising, using appeals to the middle and working classes to be smart, up-to-date, and stylish, to be generous parents—and all of this at affordable prices and in giant consumer palaces in which they were treated like royalty.

As you can see by the advertisements from these six countries, mass

production and mass consumption through the department store led to a homogenization of dress, furniture, and other goods. Accounting for climate, the middle and working classes in the industrial nations (as well as those in other nations who could afford imported goods) began to dress alike, something they had not done previously when they made most of their own clothes and accessories. Regional variations began to fade as department stores constantly urged the up-and-coming to buy the latest goods from Paris, London, or New York.

The department store was a major factor in the return of middle-class women to the center city, a place they had abandoned in the period from the 1830s to the 1850s as dirty, dangerous, and dominated by males. But department stores, realizing that middle-class women often controlled the homes' purse strings, made every effort to draw middle-class women back downtown. To assist these women with their purchases, department stores offered employment to female salesclerks, albeit at wages considerably lower than those of their male counterparts. By 1907, Germany boasted of approximately 200 department stores, where 80 percent of the clerks were women. In the United States, department stores in 1920 gave employment to 350,000 women salesclerks. A few women rose from salesclerks to buyers, positions considerably elevated in both pay and status. On the other hand, the proliferation of women shoppers also led to an increase in female shoplifters who could operate more boldly amid the new thousands of women shoppers and staff. Thus department stores added employment opportunities—both legal and illegal—for women in industrialized nations.[3]

Although no one could have predicted it, John Wanamaker's death in 1922 came at about the peak of the center-city department store. The Great Depression of the 1930s and World War II (in Europe 1939–1945) severely curtailed consumption, although American journalist James Rorty maintains that the "advanced system of dream-manufacture" survived these periods of cutbacks in the manufacture of civilian consumer goods. At war's end, led by the United States, the industrialized world experienced the profound demographic shift known as *suburbaniza-*

tion, in which people from the cities and the rural areas took up residence in the rimlands surrounding the urban centers. In the United States, in 1900 a bare 5.8 percent of Americans lived in suburbs. By 1990 that figure had exploded to 46.2 percent, and fourteen of the nation's most populous states had suburban populations over 50 percent.

In the United States and elsewhere, suburbanites often did not return to the city center to shop. By 1978, the United States had over 117 million registered automobiles, which would have created massive congestion and parking problems had shoppers wished to do so. Increasingly suburbanites made their purchases at massive shopping malls, which offered convenience, ample parking, and a variety of retail stores. In the United States in 1945, only eight shopping malls existed; by 1960, almost 4,000 catered to consumers. Suburbanization proceeded at slower paces in other nations, but the demographic shifts were nonetheless significant. Within a half-century of the department store's peak in the 1920s, the massive downtown palaces of consumer desire were either closed or on the wane. Their own branch establishments in the shopping malls were pale imitations of the center-city retail jewels.

Nevertheless, in its comparatively brief lifetime the department store performed a number of important economic and social functions for the industrialized world. Perhaps most important was its impact on the value systems of the industrialized nations. As middle and skilled work-

3. On women shoplifters in the United States, see Elaine B. Abelson, *When Ladies Go A-Thieving: Middle-Class Shoplifters in the Victorian Department Store* (New York: Oxford University Press, 1989).

Chapter 11

The

Democratization

of Desire:

Department

Stores,

Advertising,

and the New

Consumerism

(1920s)

ing-class people began to shift their self-definition and their definitions of others from who we (they) *are* to what we (they) *own*, a major upheaval in world-views was taking place, both in the industrialized nations and elsewhere.[4] People might continue to tell themselves that money does not buy happiness, but judging by their actions, a decreasing number of men and women actually believed it.

4. According to *The New York Times* (Dec. 27, 1991, and Aug. 15, 1992), the Nike Corporation, manufacturers of athletic shoes and sportswear, recorded a 1991 profit of $3 billion, while paying its Indonesian sneaker-makers $1.03 a day.

CHAPTER TWELVE

THE INDUSTRIAL CRISIS AND THE

CENTRALIZATION OF GOVERNMENT

(1924–1939)

On August 7, 1931, Britain's Chancellor of the Exchequer Philip Snowden wrote an alarming letter to Prime Minister Ramsay MacDonald; in part, it read,

> I have been thinking seriously and constantly about the whole situation these last few days, and the more I think the more I am convinced of the terrible gravity of it. . . . We cannot allow matters to drift into utter chaos, and we are perilously near that.[1]

The complete letter makes it clear that Snowden was referring to the Great Depression, the economic catastrophe that struck Europe, the Americas, and portions of Africa, Asia, the Middle East, and Oceania in

the late 1920s and 1930s. By 1931 it had become evident that recovery was not in the immediate future. Rather, the situation was growing increasingly grave. Prices of both industrial and agricultural products had collapsed, with world crop prices (which still represented 40 percent of all world trade) only 38.9 percent of what they had been in 1923–1925. Unemployment in the industrialized nations was staggering: over 2 million in Great Britain by 1932 (approximately 17.6 percent of the work force), 5.6 million in Germany (30.1 percent) and over 12 million in the United States (24 percent). The failure of the Austrian State Bank (Credit Anstalt) in May 1931 was acting to drag other banks in Germany and central Europe down with it. The government of Great Britain contemplated a 1931 deficit of £170 million and was in the process of defaulting on its annual £35 million debt payment to the United States. Indeed,

1. Snowden to MacDonald, August 7, 1931, quoted in David Marquand, *Ramsay MacDonald* (London: Jonathan Cape, 1977), p. 613.

Chapter 12

The Industrial

Crisis and the

Centralization

of Government

(1924–1939)

Snowden did not exaggerate the bleakness of the economic situation.

Equally ominous, the economic collapse created tremors in the political arena as well. In Germany, the September 1930 elections increased the number of Reichstag seats held by Adolf Hitler's National Socialist (Nazi) Party from 12 to 107. In Japan, parliamentary government found the military to be increasingly out of control. In Great Britain, the Labour Party government was near extinction and would be succeeded at the end of 1931 by a National Coalition government. And in the United States, the Democratic Party made healthy gains in the 1930 off-year elections and appeared poised to chase President Herbert Hoover and the Republicans from the White House in 1932. And where there was not political instability, there were other grim repercussions: harsh authoritarian governments in Portugal, Austria, and Spain; the Great Purge in the Soviet Union in 1936–1937; and a rise in militarism in Italy under Benito Mussolini.

Whether unstable or not, all of these governments would have to devise methods to respond to the economic catastrophe, the longest and deepest industrial depression the world ever had seen.

Your tasks in this chapter are twofold. First, you must analyze two very different types of evidence: sets of statistics that quantify the dismal global economy of the Depression years; and selections from period speeches by four government leaders: Ramsey MacDonald (prime minister of Great Britain, 1924, 1929–1935), Franklin Roosevelt (president of the United States, 1933–1945), Adolf Hitler (chancellor of Germany, 1933–1945), and Hashimoto Kingoro (prominent Japanese army officer, expansionist, and politician). Then, after examining and analyzing those statistics and speeches, you should be able to (1) describe the characteristics and effects of the Great Depression, and (2) explain how the leaders of different nations chose to respond to this crisis.

BACKGROUND

In order to understand the gravity of the worldwide depression of the 1930s, we should begin by examining the long-term structural changes in the world economy. For most of the nineteenth century, Great Britain had been the world's industrial leader and as such had played a crucial role in the international economy. As the birthplace of the Industrial Revolution in the late 1700s, Britain had taken an early lead in the manufacturing of textiles, clothing, and iron products, all of which were exported to Britain's empire and elsewhere. Profits from manufacturing, shipping, and insurance services had made London a world financial center that directed the extraction and importation of raw materials, the production of finished goods from those raw materials, and the shipment of manufactured products throughout the world.

The gradual spread of the Industrial Revolution not only challenged Great Britain's economic and financial dominance but also resulted in profound dislocations of the international economy. By the end of the nineteenth century, both Germany and the United States equalled Britain's industrial capacity, Japan was offering aggressive rivalry for Asian markets, and France, Italy, Russia, and nations in Latin America were industrializing as well, albeit more slowly. This industrial proliferation resulted in intense competition between nations for raw materials, fuel, and (most importantly) markets for manufactured goods. The imperialistic scramble for colonies that gripped the West in the late nineteenth century was a direct product of that competition. Some historians believe the outbreak of war in Europe in 1914 was another.

At the same time that widespread industrialization was altering the traditional structure of the world economy, the industrial nations were faced with a major agricultural crisis. World overproduction drove agricultural prices down until farmers and agricultural workers no longer could afford to buy the manufactured goods pouring off world assembly lines. Faced with ruin, farmers abandoned rural regions for the cities, hoping to find jobs in factories. In Japan alone, urban population went from 12 percent in 1895 to over 45 percent by 1935. And in the United States, the 1920 federal census revealed for the first time over 50 percent of Americans living in cities and towns. But factories, forced to compete with their counterparts throughout the world, could not sell all they were able to produce and therefore could not even hope to employ the horde of rural-to-urban migrants.

Thus even before the Great War erupted in Europe in 1914, the world economy was undergoing some fundamental structural changes that hinted at some rather frightening consequences. Increased international industrial competition, the collapse of world agricultural prices, and the rural-to-urban migration into already troubled industrial cities all spelled difficulties ahead.

The Great War (World War I, 1914–1918) brought further dislocations and world economic instability. The chief beneficiary of the conflict was the United States, already the world's most potent industrial nation before the outbreak of war.[2] Emerging from the war virtually unscathed, the United States immediately became the world's creditor, with billions of dollars of wartime and postwar reconstruction loans owed by the other participants.[3] Almost overnight, New York replaced London as the world's financial center (by 1930 the U.S. Federal Reserve held over half of the world's stock of gold) and American manufacturing, stimulated by massive production and consumption of automobiles, steel, rubber, electrical products (radios, vacuum cleaners, refrigerators, and the

2. By 1913, the United States produced one-third of the world's manufactured goods.

3. Even the majority of wartime and postwar relief deliveries by the United States were not gifts but loans (63%), as opposed to cash sales (29%) and outright gifts (only 8%).

Chapter 12

The Industrial

Crisis and the

Centralization

of Government

(1924–1939)

like), and housing construction, experienced a sustained boom almost unmatched in the history of the Industrial Revolution.

The postwar world was not so pleasant for other nations. After a brief postwar recovery, Great Britain slumped into a sustained recession for most of the 1920s, with never fewer than a million workers unemployed after March 1921. To combat hard times, British leaders were forced to keep wages down (this made exports cheaper, but precipitated the General Strike of 1926) and to raise interest rates (this restored value to the British pound, but choked off borrowing). Once the world's industrial leader, Great Britain in the 1920s was slipping rapidly.

In Germany, the situation was even more distressing. Led by a vengeful France, the victorious nations of World War I demanded that Germany pay huge reparations to compensate for wartime damages it had inflicted. Outraged by German nonpayment, in 1923 French and Belgian forces marched into the Ruhr (Germany's industrial heartland) to force payments or, failing that, to seize anything of value. The Germans responded with passive resistance and printed money to assist the Ruhr's residents. The German currency, already seriously inflated, simply became worthless and the entire economy collapsed, only to be propped up later by continued loans from the United States.[4] By the late 1920s, Germany was borrowing money from

the United States in order to make reparation payments to France, Britain, and Belgium, which in turn were repaying their own loans to the United States. These practices were extremely dangerous, since the whole system rested on the wellspring of funding by the United States. Moreover, the cry for reparations left a feeling of extreme bitterness in Germany. Even the French recognized this, as General Ferdinand Foch remarked of the Treaty of Versailles, "This is not a Peace. It is an Armistice for twenty years." Foch's dire prediction was off the mark by only two months.[5]

Japan had profited immensely from World War I, as it had been able to gain access to markets in Asia traditionally controlled by Europe and the United States. Between 1914 and 1919, the Japanese merchant fleet doubled in size, and some corporations experienced such enormous windfalls that they declared dividends of 100 percent on par value of their stock. But at the close of World War I Europe and the United States returned to Asia and shoved the Japanese out of their recently won markets. The Japanese economy collapsed in 1920 and many banks were forced to close. In addition, rapid population growth (from 44 million people in 1900 to 73 million by 1940) meant that for the first time Japan would have to become an importer of

4. Germany's wholesale price index (1913 = 100) was 245 in 1918, 800 in 1919, 1,400 in 1920, and had reached 126 *trillion* by December 1923.

5. Germany was forced to sign the Treaty of Versailles ending World War I on June 28, 1919; in response to Hitler's invasion of Poland, Britain and France declared war on Germany on September 3, 1939, thus beginning World War II.

food rather than an exporter. Partial recovery came with a drop in the value of the yen in 1924, thus making Japanese exports somewhat more attractive. But Japan still faced massive problems: how was the nation to secure access to raw materials for its industries (especially oil to fuel the factories) and markets for its manufactured goods?

The New York stock market crash of October 1929 was the push that toppled the whole unstable mechanism. Forced to pay for massive losses because banks had been speculating in the market, American banks and investors cut off loans to Europe and tried to call back money they already had loaned. In an effort to keep out foreign manufactured goods and thereby protect its own industries, the United States also raised tariffs, thereby setting off a wave of retaliatory increases in other nations. It was as if each nation was trying to seal itself up, like a watertight compartment, so as to solve its own economic troubles—an isolationist policy that was both shortsighted and ultimately disastrous.[6]

Great Britain's economy, already paralyzed, sickened even more, with unemployment gradually climbing to 2,725,000 by December 1930. Prime Minister Ramsay MacDonald mourned, "Is the sun of my country sinking?" Dependent on foreign loans, Germany's economy simply fell apart. The government tried to cut the budget, the result being that

by the beginning of 1932 one-third of Germany's work force was unemployed and another third was working only part-time. By late 1932, 25 percent of U.S. workers were unemployed and banks were totally closed or only partially operating in forty-seven of the nation's forty-eight states. In Japan, as elsewhere, production and prices both plummeted, while unemployment crept up. Of those who had jobs, wages were but 69 percent of what they had been in 1926 (rural cash incomes were only 33 percent) and exports by 1931 had dropped 50 percent.

The worldwide economic collapse had serious political ramifications in virtually every industrial nation. In Britain and the United States, the party in power when the Depression finally struck saw its power dramatically erode. In Great Britain, MacDonald (of the Labour Party) was able to stay on as prime minister, but he was forced to preside over a National Coalition government of Conservatives, Labourites, and Liberals. In the United States, Republican Hoover was ousted from the presidency by Democrat Franklin Roosevelt who offered the vague promise of a "new deal" to the American people. In Germany, voters turned to the National Socialists and Adolf Hitler, who preached a message of recovery, national pride, attacks on the struggling Weimar government, and a virulent anti-Semitism. In January 1933, backed by his own party as well as by powerful non-Nazi right-wing politicians and businessmen, Hitler was named chancellor of the German Republic. In Japan, the military increas-

6. Over 30 nations had formally protested to U.S. President Herbert Hoover about the tariff, and 1,000 economists had urged him not to sign the bill.

ingly appeared to be the best hope to lead the rapidly industrializing nation out of its economic doldrums as well as to counteract what many Japanese saw as an unhealthy embrace of Western culture (films, clothing, cigarette smoking, Western alcoholic beverages, Western dancing, and more) by middle-class young people.[7]

Each nation ultimately devised a plan for rescuing itself. By examining and analyzing the speeches of four prominent leaders of Great Britain, the United States, Germany, and Japan respectively, you will be able to determine how the leaders of each of the major industrialized powers proposed to battle the Great Depression.

[7]. The 1920s saw the advent in Japan of that nation's version of the "flaming youth" of the West. In the United States, women of this group were nicknamed flappers and in Japan such a woman was referred to as a *modan garu*, a Japanese variation of the English words "modern girl"; a male was called a *modan boi*.

THE METHOD

Before you discover how national leaders responded to the Great Depression, you need to appreciate the economic problems that each nation actually faced. To understand both the nature and severity of those problems, it will be necessary to employ statistical evidence, the same evidence that the governments themselves used in making economic choices and decisions. For this chapter, the statistical evidence has been arranged in statistical *sets* based on what is being measured (production or unemployment, for example).

As you examine each set of statistics, ask three questions: (1) What variable is being measured in this set? (2) How does this variable change over time? (3) How does this set relate to the other sets *and* to the economic picture as a whole? Think of each set as a piece of a picture puzzle; by answering question 3 for each set, you will be able to see where that set fits in the overall picture. For example, look at the index of industrial production for Germany between 1929 and 1938 (Source 1).[8] How does Germany's industrial production change over time? How can you account for that change? One way to increase industrial production is to expand exports (Source 2). Was Germany able to do that? Another method for increasing industrial production is to raise prices (Source 3), thereby boosting industry profits. Was Germany able to raise prices? And yet, Germany's industrial production did rise significantly (more than doubling between 1933 and 1938) and unemployment did fall (Source 5), to around 2.0 percent by 1938. How was Germany able to accomplish this impressive feat?

[8]. An index number is a statistical measure designed to show changes in a variable (such as industrial production, wages, or prices) over time. A base year is selected and given the value of 100. The index for other years is then expressed as a percentage of the base year level.

As you can see, each of the statistical sets is related to all the others. Taking one nation-state at a time, link the sets together like links in a chain. In this way, you will be able to assess the economic problems that each nation faced *and* to observe how each nation attempted to overcome its economic difficulties. Note that we do not have all the statistical evidence we would like to have—historians rarely do. Let's use Germany again as an example. If you look at the expenditures of the German government from 1924 on, you will notice that no statistics are available after 1934; can you guess why? By looking at the government's revenues, however, you can see that from 1924 to 1934 the German government's expenditures almost always exceeded revenues (1933 was the lone exception). Since we do have revenue figures after 1934, and since expenditures in documented years almost always exceeded those revenues, it is reasonable for us to suppose that the German government's expenditures after 1934 were roughly equal to (or more than) revenues. With this kind of logic, historians can "fill in some of the blanks" where statistics are missing.

After you have examined the statistics to get a clear picture of the nature and severity of the Great Depression, then move on to the four speeches excerpted in the Evidence section. Keep in mind that the *purpose* of a speech most often is *not* to present an objective picture of the topic at hand, in this case how to deal with economic disaster. Rather, the purpose of a speech is to convince, to exhort, to "sell" a particular idea or program. Thus these speeches are better classified as *propaganda*, than as objective analyses of a situation.

So how can we use speeches? To begin with, in this chapter each speaker advocates a particular approach to his nation's economic problems, an approach that must be presented with clarity and conviction if his listeners are to understand and agree—and act. What does each speaker propose as a general approach to his nation's problems? Be careful to read between the lines for more subtle messages. For example, in his speech to the Nazi *Parteitag* (party convention) on September 10, 1936, Hitler brags of the "roaring and hammering of the machines of the German resurrection" of the Krupp factories. What did Krupp manufacture primarily? Make notes as you go along.

Chapter 12
The Industrial
Crisis and the
Centralization
of Government
(1924–1939)

THE EVIDENCE

Sources 1 through 6 from League of Nations, Monthly Bulletin of Statistics *(Geneva: League of Nations, 1939), vol. 20, p. 12; pp. 20–25; pp. 29–30; p. 63; pp. 51–52; pp. 31–32.*

1. Index of Industrial Production, 1929–1938 (1929 = 100)

Year	Germany	Japan	Great Britain	United States
1929	100.0	100.0	100.0	100.0
1930	85.9	94.8	92.3	80.7
1931	67.6	91.6	83.8	68.1
1932	53.3	97.8	83.5	53.8
1933	60.7	113.2	88.2	63.9
1934	79.8	128.7	98.8	66.4
1935	94.0	141.8	105.8	75.6
1936	106.3	151.1	115.9	88.1
1937	117.2	170.8	123.7	92.2
1938 (May)	127.0	174.8	113.4	72.3

2. Imports and Exports in National Currencies, 1929–1938 (in millions)

Year	Germany (reichsmark)		Japan (yen)	
	Imports	*Exports*	*Imports*	*Exports*
1929	1,120.6	1,055.3	180.7	175.1
1930	866.1	944.0	125.6	119.2
1931	560.6	767.2	100.5	93.1
1932	388.9	473.1	115.3	113.5
1933	350.3	405.9	156.9	152.3
1934	370.9	347.2	187.0	177.8
1935	346.6	355.8	202.2	204.5
1936	351.1	397.3	225.2	219.3
1937	455.7	492.6	311.0	260.4
1938 (May)	456.8	427.1	251.1	209.6

Year	Great Britain (pound)		United States (dollar)	
	Imports	*Exports*	*Imports*	*Exports*
1929	92.59	60.78	361.6	429.8
1930	79.76	47.56	259.5	315.1
1931	66.45	32.55	174.0	198.2
1932	54.22	30.42	110.4	131.4
1933	52.16	30.66	119.4	137.3
1934	56.68	33.00	136.3	175.0
1935	58.39	35.49	169.9	186.9
1936	65.58	36.72	202.0	201.6
1937	79.39	43.45	250.8	274.9
1938 (May)	71.57	39.24	147.1	253.6

Chapter 12
The Industrial
Crisis and the
Centralization
of Government
(1924–1939)

3. Index of Wholesale Prices, 1928–1938 (1929 = 100)

Year	Germany	Japan	Great Britain	United States
1928	102.0	102.8	102.8	101.5
1929	100.0	100.0	100.0	100.0
1930	90.8	82.4	87.5	90.7
1931	80.8	69.6	76.8	76.6
1932	70.3	73.3	74.9	68.0
1933	68.0	81.6	75.0	69.2
1934	71.7	80.8	77.1	78.6
1935	74.2	84.4	77.9	83.9
1936	75.9	89.9	82.7	84.8
1937	77.2	108.4	95.2	90.6
1938 (Nov.)	77.1	115.5	88.9	82.5

4. Number of Bankruptcies, 1929–1938[9]

Year	Germany	Great Britain	United States
1929	821	345	1992
1930	945	369	2196
1931	1133	389	2357
1932	717	415	2652
1933	326	367	1692
1934	226	326	1008
1935	243	300	1020
1936	215	290	801
1937	189	280	791
1938	164	277	1070

9. Bankruptcy statistics for Japan are not available.

5. Unemployment (Numbers Out of Work and Percentage of Civilian Labor Force), 1930–1938

Year	Germany		Japan	
	Number	*Percentage*	*Number*	*Percentage*
1930	3,075,580	—	369,408	5.3%
1931	4,519,704	23.7%	422,755	6.1
1932	5,575,492	30.1	485,681	6.8
1933	4,804,428	25.8	408,710	5.6
1934	2,718,309	14.5	372,941	5.0
1935	2,151,039	11.6	356,044	4.6
1936	1,592,655	8.1	338,365	4.3
1937	912,312	4.5	295,443	3.7
1938 (June)	429,475	2.0	230,262	2.9

Year	Great Britain		United States[10]	
	Number	*Percentage*	*Number*	*Percentage*
1930	1,464,347	11.8%	4,340,000	8.7%
1931	2,129,359	16.7	8,020,000	15.9
1932	2,254,857	17.6	12,060,000	23.6
1933	2,110,090	16.4	12,830,000	24.9
1934	1,801,913	13.9	11,340,000	21.7
1935	1,714,844	13.1	10,610,000	20.1
1936	1,497,587	11.2	9,030,000	16.9
1937	1,277,928	9.4	7,700,000	14.3
1938 (Nov.)	1,529,133	10.8	10,390,000	19.0

10. United States statistics are from U.S. Department of Commerce, Bureau of the Census, *Historical Statistics of the United States* (Washington: Government Printing Office, 1975), vol. 2, p. 135.

Chapter 12
The Industrial
Crisis and the
Centralization
of Government
(1924–1939)

6. Cost of Living Index,
1928–1938 (1929 = 100)

Year	Germany	Japan	Great Britain	United States
1928	98.5	101.5	101.2	100.0
1929	100.0	100.0	100.0	100.0
1930	96.2	85.5	96.3	97.5
1931	88.4	74.7	89.6	89.0
1932	78.3	75.4	87.8	80.2
1933	76.6	80.3	85.4	76.2
1934	78.6	82.0	86.0	79.0
1935	80.0	83.6	87.2	81.1
1936	80.8	87.8	89.6	82.0
1937	81.2	96.1	93.9	84.7
1938	82.3	110.1	95.1	86.4

Source 7 from U.S. Department of Commerce, Bureau of the Census, Historical Statistics of the United States *(Washington: Government Printing Office, 1975), vol. 2, p. 225.*

7. Per Capita Personal
Income, United States,
1929–1940

Year	Average Annual Income
1929	$705
1930	625
1931	531
1932	401
1933	374
1934	427
1935	474
1936	535
1937	575
1938	526
1939	555
1940	593

Source 8 from B. R. Mitchell, European Historical Statistics, 1750–1970 *(New York: Columbia University Press, 1978), pp. 376–385, and* Historical Statistics of the United States, *vol. 2, p. 1104.*

8. Central Government Revenues and Expenditures in National Currencies, 1924–1940 (in millions)

	Germany (mark)				Great Britain (pound)		
Year	*Revenue*	*Expenditures*	*Surplus or Deficit*		*Revenue*	*Expenditures*	*Surplus or Deficit*
1924	4,650	5,027	−377		799	751	48
1925	4,731	5,683	−952		812	776	36
1926	5,313	6,616	−1,303		806	782	24
1927	6,357	7,168	−811		843	774	69
1928	6,568	8,517	−1,949		836	761	75
1929	6,741	8,187	−1,446		815	782	33
1930	6,634	8,392	−1,758		858	814	44
1931	5,704	6,995	−1,291		851	819	32
1932	4,994	5,965	−971		827	833	−6
1933	6,850	6,270	580		809	770	39
1934	8,220	8,221	−1		805	785	20
1935	9,650	Not available	—		845	829	16
1936	11,492	N/A	—		897	889	8
1937	13,964	N/A	—		949	909	40
1938	17,712	N/A	—		1,006	1,006	0
1939	23,575	N/A	—		1,132	1,401	−269

(continues on next page)

Chapter 12
The Industrial
Crisis and the
Centralization
of Government
(1924–1939)

Year	United States (dollar)		
	Revenue	Expenditures	Surplus or Deficit
1924	$3,871,214	$2,907,847	$963,367
1925	3,640,805	2,923,762	717,043
1926	3,795,108	2,929,964	865,144
1927	4,012,794	2,857,429	1,155,365
1928	3,900,329	2,961,245	939,083
1929	3,861,589	3,127,199	734,391
1930	4,057,884	3,320,211	737,673
1931	3,115,557	3,577,434	−461,877
1932	1,923,892	4,659,182	−2,735,290
1933	1,996,844	4,598,496	−2,601,652
1934	3,014,970	6,644,602	−3,629,632
1935	3,705,956	6,497,008	−2,791,052
1936	3,997,059	8,421,608	−4,424,549
1937	4,955,613	7,733,033	−2,777,421
1938	5,588,012	6,764,628	−1,176,617
1939	4,979,066	8,841,224	−3,862,158

Source 9 from Parliamentary Debates: House of Commons, *Fifth Series (London: H.M. Stationery Office, 1931), vol. 248 HC, pp. 646–660.*

9. Prime Minister Ramsay MacDonald, February 12, 1931

[*On February 12, 1931, a motion was introduced in the House of Commons calling for the government to "formulate and to present to Parliament an extensive policy" to provide work for the unemployed on public works projects, to be funded by borrowing. The prime minister rose to respond to that motion.*]

There is nothing the country can do with greater wisdom at this moment than to develop its resources, and make them effective as the soil from which our people are going to draw their life-blood, and to find capital for that development.

That is all the truer because the unemployment which we are now facing is not ordinary unemployment. It is not the unemployment we had to face two, three, or four years ago. . . . That was unemployment from day to day, from month to month, from season to season, unemployment of a normally operating capitalist system. The unemployment which we are facing to-day is partly that, undoubtedly. It was that when we came in. But now we are undergoing an industrial revolution. Economic conditions are changing. For instance, in order to face the extraordinarily increased severity of competition which this country has now to meet in the markets of the world, we have to economise our economic and our material power in the shape of machinery and in the shape of works. By that economy we cheapen production. But at the same time we are discharging men and women. In order to increase our efficiency, we are reducing employment, at any rate, for the time being.

But, after all, the men and women who live to-day have to face the problem to-day. They cannot be consoled by the fact that perhaps 10 or 12 years after this, owing to the expansion made possible by the cheapening of production, their sons or daughters will be absorbed in the expanded industry. That is not good enough for the men and women who are living to-day. Therefore, on account of the increasing efficiency, and on account of the reconditioning of our industry which is going on, thousands of men and women are being turned out of employment with a very, very small percentage of chance of ever being called upon again to engage in that industry. . . .

These are very important considerations. You are dealing with a body of unemployment which is not merely temporary. Between 2,500,000 and 2,750,000 of people now ranked as unemployed are not people who are out because there has been a breakdown of machinery in some factory, nor because there has been a seasonal change, nor because there has been a fluctuation in fashion, nor because there is a temporary cessation of the free flow of exchange; they are out on account of the reconditioning of the economic world, and, whoever faces the problem of unemployment now, has to face, not only the problem of public works to give temporary relief, but the problem of how to bring back people into contact with the raw material from which they were making their living. . . . The biggest part of the responsibility is not mentioned in this Motion at all, and that is, direct industrial stimulation so that labour may be absorbed not into work provided because of this unemployment, but that labour may be absorbed into normal industry.

We are asked if we can afford money for the relief of the unemployed. I say we can, but I am much more concerned with what, I think, is the more apposite question—Can we afford to have so many unemployed in existence? We cannot. That is the problem we really have to face. As regards public work, we have, first of all, to provide temporary work. Do remember that it is temporary. When the right hon. Gentleman makes an observation about the millions that have been spent on insurance having produced nothing, I disagree with him. If you had not spent a pound of that money, you would have found that you would have had to spend it on something else. If the money had been spent on public works, how many people would have been put to employment? By now these people would have been out of work because the work

Chapter 12

The Industrial

Crisis and the

Centralization

of Government

(1924–1939)

would have been finished. What struck me most in producing these schemes was how very limited and temporary that kind of work is bound to be. That is the first thing that has to be done. We have to provide it. I am not condemning it at all. I am only trying to impart to the House the kind of problem we are up against when we sit down, not to take part in a Debate in this House, but when we sit down in a committee-room facing the actual details of the problem, and struggling to meet and overcome the whole lot of them.

The second thing that has to be done is, by using neglected resources, the putting of men into permanent ways of earning a living. . . .

[*MacDonald goes on to remind Parliament of the "lag time" that exists between the appropriation and the actual spending of public funds. He then speaks of programs for slum clearance and new industrial cities and new industries, and of the necessity of the government maintaining a good credit rating.*]

The problem to be tackled is the provision of public works of a temporary character, the opening up of the land to the people of the country, giving them rights upon the soil and, finally, giving to industry vigilance, activity and adventure to enable it to carry on its production and back up this production by marketing. That is the problem we have to face, and that is the spirit and energy in which the Government are facing it and carrying it through. I appeal for a great national effort to enable us to carry on this work, to increase the programme of public works, to enable us to put more and more men upon them, to put more and more work in hand. I appeal to the country to stop the sort of pessimism to which a great contribution was made by the right hon. Gentleman who opened the Debate yesterday, and which I see is already being used with considerable effect. I appeal to the whole country to see that the prospects of this country are good, that we still have resources, that we still have the command of capital, that we still have the power of production and the energy that has made this country so great and powerful and splendid, and that by mobilising it, and only by mobilising it, to carry out the programme of the Government with energy and resource this problem will solve itself. This problem will be solved, a new source of power and wealth will be created in this nation, and we shall go on facing the world with its new problems even more successfully, on account of the experience of social organisation and the application of Socialist ideas, than has been possible in past generations.

Source 10 from B. D. Zevin, ed., Nothing to Fear: The Selected Addresses of Franklin Delano Roosevelt, 1932–1945 *(Boston: Houghton Mifflin Co., 1946), pp. 132–143.*

10. President Franklin Roosevelt, April 14, 1938[11]

Five years ago we faced a very serious problem of economic and social recovery. For four and a half years that recovery proceeded apace. It is only in the past seven months that it has received a visible setback.

And it is only within the past two months, as we have waited patiently to see whether the forces of business itself would counteract it, that it has become apparent that government itself can no longer safely fail to take aggressive government steps to meet it.

This recession has not returned us to the disasters and suffering of the beginning of 1933. Your money in the bank is safe; farmers are no longer in deep distress and have greater purchasing power; dangers of security speculation have been minimized; national income is almost 50 per cent higher than in 1932; and government has an established and accepted responsibility for relief.

But I know that many of you have lost your jobs or have seen your friends or members of your families lose their jobs, and I do not propose that the government shall pretend not to see these things. I know that the effect of our present difficulties has been uneven; that they have affected some groups and some localities seriously, but that they have been scarcely felt in others. But I conceive the first duty of government is to protect the economic welfare of all the people in all sections and in all groups. I said in my message opening the last session of Congress that if private enterprise did not provide jobs this spring, government would take up the slack—that I would not let the people down. We have all learned the lesson that government cannot afford to wait until it has lost the power to act.

Therefore, I have sent a message of far-reaching importance to the Congress. I want to read to you tonight certain passages from that message, and to talk with you about them. . . .

11. The April 14, 1938, address was delivered "live" over the radio, one of President Roosevelt's so-called Fireside Chats. In early 1937, Roosevelt had tried to remove government supports of the economy, but unable to stand without those supports, the economy began to deteriorate once again. This selection is from the printed release of the speech. Roosevelt deviated slightly from the printed text as he spoke to his radio audience. See Russell D. Buhite and David W. Levy, *FDR's Fireside Chats* (Norman: University of Oklahoma, 1992), pp. 111–123.

Chapter 12
The Industrial
Crisis and the
Centralization
of Government
(1924–1939)

[*Here Roosevelt explains what he believes
were the causes of the collapse of 1929—
chief among them, the underconsumption
of manufactured goods.*]

I then said this to the Congress:

"But the very vigor of the recovery in both durable goods and consumers' goods brought into the picture early in 1937 certain highly undesirable practices, which were in large part responsible for the economic decline which began in the later months of that year. Again production outran the ability to buy.

"There were many reasons for this overproduction. One was fear—fear of war abroad, fear of inflation, fear of nationwide strikes. None of these fears has been borne out.

". . . Production in many important lines of goods outran the ability of the public to purchase them. For example, through the winter and spring of 1937 cotton factories in hundreds of cases were running on a three-shift basis, piling up cotton goods in the factory and in the hands of middle men and retailers. For example, also, automobile manufacturers not only turned out a normal increase of finished cars, but encouraged the normal increase to run into abnormal figures, using every known method to push their sales. This meant, of course, that the steel mills of the Nation ran on a twenty-four hour basis, and the tire companies and cotton factories speeded up to meet the same type of abnormally stimulated demand. The buying power of the Nation lagged behind.

"Thus by the autumn of 1937 the Nation again had stocks on hand which the consuming public could not buy because the purchasing power of the consuming public had not kept pace with the production. . . ."

I went on to point out to the Senate and the House of Representatives that all the energies of government and business must be directed to increasing the national income, to putting more people into private jobs, to giving security and a feeling of security to all people in all walks of life.

I am constantly thinking of all our people—unemployed and employed alike—of their human problems of food and clothing and homes and education and health and old age. You and I agree that security is our greatest need; the chance to work, the opportunity of making a reasonable profit in our business—whether it be a very small business or a larger one—the possibility of selling our farm products for enough money for our families to live on decently. I know these are the things that decide the well-being of all our people.

Therefore, I am determined to do all in my power to help you attain that security, and because I know that the people themselves have a deep conviction that secure prosperity of that kind cannot be a lasting one except on a basis of business fair dealing and a basis where all from top to bottom share in prosperity, I repeated to the Congress today that neither it nor the Chief Executive can afford "to weaken or destroy great reforms which, during the past five years, have been effected on behalf of the American people. In our rehabilitation of the banking structure and of agriculture, in our provisions for adequate and cheaper credit for all types of business, in our acceptance of national responsibility for unemployment relief, in our strengthening of the credit of State and local government, in our encouragement of housing, slum clearance and home ownership, in our supervision of stock exchanges and public utility holding companies and the issuance of new securities, in our provision for social security, the electorate of America wants no backward steps taken. . . .

I came to the conclusion that the present-day problem calls for action both by the Government and by the people, that we suffer primarily from a failure of consumer demand because of lack of buying power. It is up to us to create an economic upturn.

"How and where can and should the Government help to start an upward spiral?"

I went on to propose three groups of measures and I will summarize the recommendations.

First, I asked for certain appropriations which are intended to keep the Government expenditures for work relief and similar purposes during the coming fiscal year at the same rate of expenditures as at present. That includes additional money for the Works Progress Administration; additional funds for the Farm Security Administration; additional allotments for the National Youth Administration, and more money for the Civilian Conservation Corps, in order that it can maintain the existing number of camps now in operation.

These appropriations, made necessary by increased unemployment, will cost about a billion and a quarter more than the estimates which I sent to the Congress on the third of January.

Second, I told the Congress that the Administration proposes to make additional bank reserves available for the credit needs of the country. About one billion four hundred million dollars of gold now in the Treasury will be used to pay these additional expenses of the Government, and three-quarters of a billion dollars of additional credit will be made available to the banks by reducing the reserves now required by the Federal Reserve Board.

These two steps, taking care of relief needs and adding to bank credits, are in our judgment insufficient by themselves to start the Nation on a sustained upward movement.

Therefore, I came to the third kind of Government action which I consider to be vital. I said to the Congress:

"You and I cannot afford to equip ourselves with two rounds of ammunition where three rounds are necessary. If we stop at relief and credit, we may find ourselves without ammunition before the enemy is routed. If we are fully equipped with the third round of ammunition, we stand to win the battle against adversity."

[361]

Chapter 12
*The Industrial
Crisis and the
Centralization
of Government
(1924–1939)*

The third proposal is to make definite additions to the purchasing power of the Nation by providing new work over and above the continuing of the old work.

First, to enable the United States Housing Authority to undertake the immediate construction of about three hundred million dollars of additional slum clearance projects.

Second, to renew a public works program by starting as quickly as possible about one billion dollars worth of needed permanent public improvements in states, counties and cities.

Third, to add one hundred million dollars to the estimate for federal aid highways in excess of the amount I recommended in January.

Fourth, to add thirty-seven million dollars over and above the former estimate of sixty-three million dollars for flood control and reclamation.

Fifth, to add twenty-five million dollars additional for federal buildings in various parts of the country.

In recommending this program I am thinking not only of the immediate economic needs of the people of the Nation, but also of their personal liberties—the most precious possession of all Americans. I am thinking of our democracy and of the recent trend in other parts of the world away from the democratic ideal.

Democracy has disappeared in several other great nations—not because the people of those nations disliked democracy, but because they had grown tired of unemployment and insecurity, of seeing their children hungry while they sat helpless in the face of government confusion and government weakness through lack of leadership in government. Finally, in desperation, they chose to sacrifice liberty in the hope of getting something to eat. We in America know that our own democratic institutions can be preserved and made to work. But in order to preserve them we need to act together, to meet the problems of the Nation boldly, and to prove that the practical operation of democratic government is equal to the task of protecting the security of the people.

Not only our future economic soundness but the very soundness of our democratic institutions depends on the determination of our Government to give employment to idle men. The people of America are in agreement in defending their liberties at any cost, and the first line of that defense lies in the protection of economic security. Your Government, seeking to protect democracy, must prove that Government is stronger than the forces of business depression.

History proves that dictatorships do not grow out of strong and successful governments, but out of weak and helpless ones. If by democratic methods people get a government strong enough to protect them from fear and starvation, their democracy succeeds; but if they do not, they grow impatient. Therefore, the only sure bulwark of continuing liberty is a government strong enough to protect the interests of the people, and a people strong enough and well enough informed to maintain its sovereign control over its government. . . .

What I said to the Congress in the close of my message I repeat to you.

"Let us unanimously recognize the fact that the Federal debt, whether it be twenty-five billions or forty billions, can only be paid if the Nation obtains a vastly increased citizen income. I repeat that if this citizen income can be raised to eighty billion dollars a year the national Government and the overwhelming majority of State and local governments will be 'out of the red.' The higher the national income goes the faster shall we be able to reduce the total of Federal and state and local debts. Viewed from every angle, today's purchasing power—the citizens' income of today—is not sufficient to drive the economic system at higher speed. Responsibility of Government requires us at this time to supplement the normal processes and in so supplementing them to make sure that the addition is adequate. We must start again on a long steady upward incline in national income.

". . . And in that process, which I believe is ready to start, let us avoid the pitfalls of the past—the overproduction, the overspeculation, and indeed all the extremes which we did not succeed in avoiding in 1929. In all of this, Government cannot and should not act alone. Business must help. I am sure business will help.

"We need more than the materials of recovery. We need a united national will. . . ."

Source 11 from Norman H. Baynes, ed., The Speeches of Adolf Hitler, April 1922–August 1939 *(London: Oxford University Press, 1942), vol. 1, pp. 650–654.*

11. Chancellor Adolf Hitler, September 10, 1936[12]

In all spheres of our national life there has been since four years ago an immense advance. The tempo and the scale of the political advance are unique, and above all the inner consolidation of the German nation is unique in history. . . .

On the evening of 30 January 1933 I made known to the German people in a short Proclamation the aims which we had set before us in our battle. I then asked that I might be granted four years: at the end of that time I wished to render account to the German people of the fulfilment or non-fulfilment of that promise.

12. Hitler's speech was intended to answer the question "What has National Socialism made out of Germany in the last four years?"

Chapter 12

The Industrial

Crisis and the

Centralization

of Government

(1924–1939)

Our foes were convinced that we should never have an opportunity to ask the nation for such a judgement, for the longest period that they were prepared to allow our Government was barely six to twelve weeks.

And what has National Socialism in these four years made of Germany? Who from amongst our foes would to-day have the effrontery to step forward as our accuser?

What appeared to them then fantastic and incapable of realization in my Proclamation seems to-day the most modest announcement of an achievement which towers above the promises then made. Our opponents thought that we could not carry out the programme of 1933 which now seems to us so small an affair. But what would they have said if I had propounded to them *that* programme which the National Socialist Government has as a matter of fact realized in not quite four years? How they would have jeered if on the 30th of January 1933 I had declared that within four years Germany would have reduced its six million unemployed to one million!

That the enforced expropriation of the German peasantry would have been brought to an end.

That the receipts from German agriculture would be higher than in any previous year in time of peace.

That the total national income would be raised from 41 milliards annually to over 56 milliards.[13]

That the German middle classes and German artisans would enjoy a new prosperity.

That trade would once more recover.

That German ports would no more resemble ship grave-yards.

That in 1936 on German wharves alone over 640,000 tons of shipping would be under construction.

That countless manufactories would not merely double but treble and quadruple the number of their workmen. And that in less than four years innumerable others would be rebuilt.

That a Krupp factory would vibrate once again with the roaring and the hammering of the machines of the German resurrection and that over all of these undertakings men would recognize as the supreme law of their effort not the unscrupulous profit of the individual but the service of the nation.

That the silent motor-works would not only spring into life but would be enlarged on an unheard of scale.

That the production of motor-cars would rise from 45,000 in the year 1932 to some quarter of a million.

That in four years the deficits of our States and cities would be wiped out.

That the Reich would gain from taxation an annual increase of nearly five milliards.

---

13. **milliard:** one billion (marks, in this case).

That the German Imperial Railway would at length recover, and that its trains would be the quickest in the world.

That to the German Reich would be given roads such that since the beginnings of human civilization they have never had their match for size and beauty: and that of the first 7,000 kilometres which were planned already after not quite four years 1,000 kilometres would be in use and over 4,000 kilometres would be in course of construction.

That enormous new settlements with hundreds of thousands of houses would come into being, while in ancient cities of the Reich mighty new buildings would arise which may be said to be the greatest in the world.

That hundreds upon hundreds of gigantic bridges would be thrown over gorges and valleys.

That German "Kultur" in these and similar new achievements would confirm its eternal value.

That German theatres and concerts of our German music would celebrate their resurrection.

That with all this the German people would take an active share in this revolutionary renewal of the spirit, while not a single Jew would make an appearance in this intellectual leadership of the German people.

If I had prophesied then that in four years the whole German Press would be filled with a new "ethos" and would be in the service of German aims, that for German business life (*Wirtschaft*) the law of a new professional honour would be proclaimed, so that in every sphere the German experiences a renewal of his personality and his action.

If I had at that time foretold that after these four years there would be only one single German people, that no Social Democracy, no Communism, no Centrum, not even a *bourgeois* party would any longer be able to sin against the life of Germany, that no trade union would any longer be able to incite the workers, and no employers' association to ruin the employers, that after these four years no German State would have its separate government, that in Germany there would no longer be any State-parliaments (*Landtage*), that the sixteen flags and the sixteen different traditions which they represented would have ceased to exist and have been brought together as one, and that the whole nation—from the workman to the soldier—would in the future march only in support of a single confession of faith and a single flag.

What would they have said if I had prophesied to them that Germany in these four years would have freed itself from the slave-fetters of Versailles, that the Reich would regain general compulsory military service, that every German, as before the War, would serve two years for the freedom of the country, that a new fleet would be under construction to protect our coasts and our trade, that a mighty new air arm would guarantee the security of our towns, our factories and works, that the Rhineland would be brought under the supremacy of the German nation, and that thereby the sovereignty of the Reich would be restored over the whole of its territory?

Chapter 12

The Industrial

Crisis and the

Centralization

of Government

(1924–1939)

What would they have said to my prophecy that the people, at that time so divided, before four years were past would—99 per cent of it—go to the polls and that 99 per cent would say "Yes" in support of the National Socialist policy of reconstruction, of national honour and freedom?

If four years ago I had prophesied this and much else I should have been branded as a madman and the whole world would have laughed at me. But all this is now accomplished fact, and this is the achievement of not quite four years. . . . The National Socialist political leadership of Germany in this short time has wrought a miracle.

Source 12 from Ryusaku Tsunoda, et al., comp., Sources of Japanese Tradition *(New York: Columbia University Press, 1958), vol. 2, pp. 289–291.*

12. Hashimoto Kingoro, Address to Young Men, 1930s

We have already said that there are only three ways left to Japan to escape from the pressure of surplus population. We are like a great crowd of people packed into a small and narrow room, and there are only three doors through which we might escape, namely emigration, advance into world markets, and expansion of territory. The first door, emigration, has been barred to us by the anti-Japanese immigration policies of other countries. The second door, advance into world markets, is being pushed shut by tariff barriers and the abrogation of commercial treaties. What should Japan do when two of the three doors have been closed against her?

It is quite natural that Japan should rush upon the last remaining door.

It may sound dangerous when we speak of territorial expansion, but the territorial expansion of which we speak does not in any sense of the word involve the occupation of the possessions of other countries, the planting of the Japanese flag thereon, and the declaration of their annexation to Japan. It is just that since the Powers [United States, Britain, France] have suppressed the circulation of Japanese materials and merchandise abroad, we are looking for some place overseas where Japanese capital, Japanese skills and Japanese labor can have free play, free from the oppression of the white race.

We would be satisfied with just this much. What moral right do the world powers who have themselves closed to us the two doors of emigration and advance into world markets have to criticize Japan's attempt to rush out of the third and last door?

If they do not approve of this, they should open the doors which they have closed against us and permit the free movement overseas of Japanese emigrants and merchandise. . . .

At the time of the Manchurian incident [1931], the entire world joined in criticism of Japan. They said that Japan was an untrustworthy nation. They said that she had recklessly brought cannon and machine guns into Manchuria, which was the territory of another country, flown airplanes over it, and finally occupied it. But the military action taken by Japan was not in the least a selfish one. Moreover, we do not recall ever having taken so much as an inch of territory belonging to another nation. The result of this incident was the establishment of the splendid new nation of Manchuria. The Powers are still discussing whether or not to recognize this new nation, but regardless of whether or not other nations recognize her, the Manchurian empire has already been established, and now, seven years after its creation, the empire is further consolidating its foundations with the aid of its friend, Japan.

And if it is still protested that our actions in Manchuria were excessively violent, we may wish to ask the white race just which country it was that sent warships and troops to India, South Africa, and Australia and slaughtered innocent natives, bound their hands and feet with iron chains, lashed their backs with iron whips, proclaimed these territories as their own, and still continues to hold them to this very day?

They will invariably reply, these were all lands inhabited by untamed savages. These people did not know how to develop the abundant resources of their land for the benefit of mankind. Therefore it was the wish of God, who created heaven and earth for mankind, for us to develop these undeveloped lands and to promote the happiness of mankind in their stead. God wills it.

This is quite a convenient argument for them. Let us take it at face value. Then there is another question that we must ask them.

Suppose that there is still on this earth land endowed with abundant natural resources that have not been developed at all by the white race. Would it not then be God's will and the will of Providence that Japan go there and develop those resources for the benefit of mankind?

And there still remain many such lands on this earth. . . .

QUESTIONS TO CONSIDER

Begin by examining the statistical tables (Sources 1 through 8). Some of the dimensions of this, the deepest and longest industrial depression in world history, are revealed in Source 1, the indexes of industrial production for Germany, Japan, Great Britain, and the United States—four major industrialized nations that were affected in somewhat different ways and at somewhat different times. Note that Japan and Great Britain did not experience the collapse of production in the 1930s in the same manner as Germany and the United States. How would you explain this? Also, both Germany and the United States "hit bottom" in the same year, 1932, and then began

Chapter 12

The Industrial

Crisis and the

Centralization

of Government

(1924–1939)

slowly to recover. Can any of the other statistical evidence help you understand why this was so? For example, if the domestic markets for industrial goods are glutted, then efforts to cut unemployment and increase wages (so that those workers once again can become consumers) would increase domestic demand. Is this what happened (see Sources 5 and 7)? But how would such efforts be paid for *if the stimulus was undertaken by the government?* (See Source 8.) In Source 8, note especially Great Britain's "different path." How would you explain this?

Another way to stimulate industrial production is to increase *exports* of industrial goods to other nations. How successful were these four industrial nations in increasing exports? How would you explain the comparative success or failure of each nation? (For example, why do you think German exports fell off in 1934 and 1935 even though industrial production was increasing rapidly?) Examine all of the statistical sets in this way, asking questions of each set and attempting to link them together. From the numbers, can you summarize the impact of the Depression on industrial production, employment, government revenues and expenditures, and so on, in each of the four nations under consideration?

Once you have pieced together a general background using the statistics, you are ready to move on to the speeches (Sources 9–12). Before you read each national leader's address, review the notes you made as you analyzed the statistics for his nation.

Ramsay MacDonald's speech in Parliament is a defense of his approach toward combating unemployment in Great Britain. MacDonald begins by explaining what *he* believes were the causes of the Great Depression in Britain. What factors does he cite? Note that the prime minister does *not* see the economic downturn as temporary in Britain. Therefore, his remedy is twofold, the first consisting of *temporary* work for the unemployed but the second involving a *permanent* restructuring of the British economy. How does MacDonald propose to accomplish phase two? What should government's role be? What should government's role *not* be?

Franklin Roosevelt's Fireside Chat details his strategies and principles for mobilizing the federal government to deal with the sudden economic downturn of 1937–1938 (see statistics in Sources 1 through 5, 7 and 8). Like MacDonald, Roosevelt also begins with his own analysis of the causes of the Depression, although this time in the United States. How does Roosevelt's analysis differ from MacDonald's? Note that Roosevelt believed the 1937–1938 downturn was a repeat of what had occurred in 1929–1932. Contrast Roosevelt's suggested solutions with those of MacDonald. How is the role of the central government different? How does each leader approach the notion of "deficit spending" (in which expenditures exceed revenues, the difference to be made up through borrowing, as in government bonds)? Roosevelt concludes his radio address by insisting that "business must help." What would MacDonald's reaction be to such a statement?

On the surface, Adolf Hitler's speech at the opening of the Nazi Party's 1936 convention is a simple listing of what Germany has accomplished since he became chancellor in January 1933. Faintly visible beneath the gloating, however, is an obscure outline of Hitler's plan to end the Depression in Germany (see the Epilogue section for a brief explanation of that plan).

Hitler begins by boasting of Germany's significant reduction in unemployment since the Nazi rise to power (from 6 million to 1 million). Do the statistics (Source 5) confirm his claim (by September 1936 the 1 million figure probably was an accurate one)? The main question is, *how* were the National Socialists able to bring this about? Hitler gives broad hints when he refers to the Krupp industries, the "silent motor-works," the revival of vehicle production, compulsory military service, the requirement of two years of service "for the freedom of the country" (see Epilogue for an explanation), the production of ships and airplanes, and the freedom "from the slave-fetters of Versailles." He also mentions the Rhineland being "brought under the supremacy of the German nation," a reference to the military occupation of that region in 1936 by Germany's revived half-million-man army. The other world powers did nothing, thereby encouraging Hitler's later aggressions. Finally, look at Hitler's comment regarding labor unions ("that no trade union would any longer be able to incite the workers"). What does Hitler really mean by that (see Epilogue)?

Hashimoto's address is as clear as Hitler's is vague. To Hashimoto, Japan's central problem is overpopulation, and he envisions only three possible resolutions. What were those three potential options? Why, in Hashimoto's opinion, were two of the three not possible? How would territorial expansion, in his view, solve Japan's economic problems? What would that expansion bring to Japan economically? Finally, how many of Japan's economic obstacles does Hashimoto attribute to anti-Japanese attitudes (racism?) of other nations? Explain.

Once you have analyzed the speeches to discern how each national leader proposed to deal with the Great Depression, it would be appropriate to compare and contrast the approaches urged upon Great Britain, the United States, Germany, and Japan. How were these approaches different? In what ways were they similar? For example, how would each nation deal with unemployment? Were Germany and Japan similar in their approaches? Was the United States similar to or different from Germany and Japan, and in what ways? What about Great Britain? How did each nation propose to involve government in ending the Depression?

Chapter 12
The Industrial
Crisis and the
Centralization
of Government
(1924–1939)

EPILOGUE

In some ways, the Great Depression of the 1930s was one of the eventual results of the Industrial Revolution. As industrialization expanded into nations and regions that previously had been consumers of the manufactures of others, international markets diminished and the scramble for remaining markets became fierce. In addition, in order to keep exported manufactures as inexpensive as possible (to make them more competitive in world markets), industrial wages had to be kept low, thus making it difficult for domestic workers to increase their own consumption of manufactured goods. In some ways, then, the Industrial Revolution was undermined by its own snowballing success.

As noted earlier, the Depression shook the industrialized nations' political foundations as profoundly as it did their economic ones. Japan suffered a wave of political assassinations and attempted coups (at least two of which were masterminded by Hashimoto) until the military finally emerged as the controlling force in that nation's politics, a position in part strengthened by the military's uneasy alliance with Japan's giant corporations (*zaibatsu*).[14] In Germany, the National Socialists had garnered 14.5 million votes in the 1932 election, in part a response to Hitler's promise of economic recovery. When prominent industrialists and army officers fell into step, German president Hindenburg was persuaded to name Hitler Germany's chancellor, on January 30, 1933. Within a year, the Nazi leader had turned Germany into a totalitarian state.

Political reactions in Great Britain and the United States were less extreme. In Britain, MacDonald was forced to accept a coalition government but was able to retain his post as prime minister. In the United States, in spite of some dire warnings that capitalism was near death, in 1932 voters elected moderate Democrat Franklin Roosevelt, and government changed hands peacefully in March 1933.

As you might expect after reading the speeches in this chapter, each of the major industrial powers sought to loosen the grip of the Depression in its own way; any international or cooperative efforts were abandoned following the collapse of the World Economic Conference of sixty-six nations in 1933. In some ways, Great Britain was the most fortunate. High interest rates and the economic slump of the 1920s had created pent-up demand for manufactured products. When Britain abandoned the gold standard[15] in 1931, prices fell and a

14. A *zaibatsu* resembles an American holding company, which manufactured several types of products and provided many services as well. In the 1920s, Mitsui was Japan's largest zaibatsu, having assets representing approximately 15 percent of all Japanese business firms.

15. **gold standard:** an international system in which each nation's currency was equal in value to and exchangeable for a specified amount of gold. The system provided monetary stability. Great Britain abandoned the gold standard in order to let the value of the pound fall, thereby instigating an inflationary trend.

natural "boomlet" was created. Unemployment remained high, however, and was not eradicated until Britain entered World War II in September 1939. But Britain did not need the massive infusions of government money into the economy that was necessary in other industrialized nations (see Source 8). This was indeed fortunate because the British government could ill afford the deficit financing that Germany and the United States utilized.

Germany's approach to the Depression was considerably more severe. Hitler instituted the compulsory National Labor Service to man public works projects, tried to drive women out of the work force (to make room for unemployed males), smashed labor unions, and increased government revenues for investment in fresh industrial production. Ominously, much of that industrial production was military goods, a policy that eventually would drive that nation into war (that, along with Hitler's megalomania).

As President Franklin Roosevelt's New Deal gradually took shape, its general philosophy seems to have been to stimulate domestic consumption in a variety of ways. Consumer demand, New Dealers reasoned, would bring people back to work to fill that demand. Hence the federal government engaged in deficit financing to put money in the hands of farmers (Agricultural Adjustment Act), the unemployed (Works Progress Administration), the elderly (Social Security), unemployed youth (Civilian Conservation Corps), and other groups. Yet unemployment in

the United States remained high (over 10 million in 1938, 19 percent of the civilian labor force) until the nation's entrance into World War II in 1941.

After 1931, recovery in Japan was comparatively rapid. Unemployment dropped steadily and real wages increased. This was partly the result of military expansion into Manchuria, but even more, Japan was able to orchestrate an enviable economic marriage of Western industrial technology and low Asian wages, a union that made Japan's manufactured goods more competitive in Asian markets.

Taken as a whole, the industrial world's varied responses to the Great Depression raises a number of questions. To begin with, we are almost compelled to question whether *any* actions of a central government can *cure* the ills of a depression. Doubtless governments may *alleviate* the worst effects of an economic collapse, but whether they can engineer national economic recovery is more debatable. In Great Britain, a natural economic upturn did more to move that nation toward recovery than all the government's nostrums. In the United States, it appears that the New Deal, although it gave Americans a tremendous psychological lift, had rather anemic results when it came to stimulating permanent recovery, perhaps because (as some economists claim) the extent of government intervention in the United States was too limited to stimulate total restoration. Neither nation experienced full employment until the war. And, of course, it was precisely

Chapter 12

The Industrial

Crisis and the

Centralization

of Government

(1924–1939)

that military build-up that allowed Germany and Japan to experience comparatively rapid turnarounds. Did it, therefore, take the horrific slaughter of World War II to bring the Depression to an end? What in fact had been the roles of governments and their policies and programs to battle the economic crisis? Were they effective, apart from the war?

Finally, the national responses to the Great Depression show that the refusal of nations to work together can have disastrous consequences. Speaking of the relationship between the crisis in Britain and the world situation, British government official Sir John Anderson wrote in 1930, "You cannot drain a bog while the surrounding country is still under water." In the nineteenth century, Britain had provided a kind of world leadership that benefited other nations as well as itself. When the world's economic center of gravity shifted to the United States about the time of World War I, that nation lacked the vision and experience to exercise a similar style of world leadership. Instead, the United States started the round of tariff increases in 1930, refused to participate in the World Economic Conference of 1933 (and actually was a major contributor to the summit's collapse), and followed a path toward recovery that (if it worked) would benefit no one but itself. And yet the United States was hardly alone in pursuing self-serving policies. Indeed, it is likely that the wisdom of King Solomon himself could not have persuaded the industrialized nations to work together.

Overworked and sick, Ramsay MacDonald resigned as prime minister in 1935 and died soon after, in 1937. Franklin Roosevelt won unprecedented third and fourth presidential elections (in 1940 and 1944), but did not live to see Allied victories over Germany and Japan in World War II. He died on April 12, 1945.

Adolf Hitler, driven by his own dark dreams and hatreds, committed suicide in his fortified bunker underneath a decimated Berlin just eighteen days after Roosevelt's death. Of the four speakers excerpted in this chapter, only Hashimoto Kingoro survived the war. Tried as a war criminal by the Americans, he was sentenced to life imprisonment but was released in 1955. He died in 1957.

CHAPTER THIRTEEN

THE CONGO CRISIS: INTERNATIONAL

PEACEKEEPING AFTER WORLD WAR II

(1960–1963)

Following World War II, the international community of nations, dreading a repeat of the two disastrous conflicts that already scarred the century, determined to find a means of peacefully resolving the problems of the postwar world. To many, the best hope seemed to be the United Nations. Yet the limitations of that UN role were recognized by Dag Hammarskjold as early as 1953, just one year after he became its Secretary General. "It may be said of the United Nations," he told a gathering of the World Council of Churches, "that what is required from the governments and peoples [of the world] is a renewed faith . . . expressed in a never abandoned, every day newly initiated, responsible action for peace."[1]

Of course, achieving such commitment and inspiring such action proved to be much more difficult than realizing their necessity. The longing for peace—an important aspect of the human condition for thousands of years—always seemed to take second place to the friction of differences, their escalation into conflict, and all too often, the outbreak of hostilities. This was no less true after 1945 than it had been for centuries before. It was not surprising, therefore, that the first peacekeeping efforts of the UN were beset with difficulties, including a less-than-commanding involvement as the umbrella organization for what was overwhelmingly United States action in the Korean War.

Throughout the 1950s, increasing demands by Asian and African peoples living under colonialism that they be given opportunities to govern themselves threatened to lead toward further conflicts. By the end of the decade, the growing numbers of newly independent countries, especially in

1. In T. S. Settle, ed., *The Light and the Rock: The Vision of Dag Hammarskjold* (New York: Dutton, 1966), p. 128.

Chapter 13
The Congo
Crisis:
International
Peacekeeping
after World
War II
(1960–1963)

Africa, presented the UN with even more complicated challenges to its peacekeeping mission. Perhaps the most demanding was the case of the former Belgian Congo, where the UN began its peacemaking role only days after the Republic of the Congo was granted its formal independence from Belgium in 1960.

Initially, a United Nations force of 3,500 troops from four African countries was sent to keep the peace and preserve the new nation. Known as ONUC (the acronym of its French title, "Organisation des Nations Unies au Congo"), the force eventually grew to 19,000 men from more than thirty countries before the UN withdrew more than three years later. In this chapter you will read official documents and statements by participants concerning the first year of United Nations peacekeeping efforts in the Congo; despite the limited time period, the materials you will see represent only a few of the most important documents available.

The types of evidence in this chapter present special problems for historians. Official documents—laws, resolutions, and diplomatic correspondence, for example, do not always tell the whole story; moreover, speeches and reminiscences by the participants usually give only one side of an issue. Yet historians must try to infer from such evidence a balanced picture of the past. They do this by comparing the differing accounts, by using third-party observations, and by using their own knowledge (even of the present) to fill in the gaps left by the sources. Historians work in all these ways, trying both to make sense of the past and to interpret what it may mean in the present and future; that is what you will be doing in this chapter.

Kwame Nkrumah, then president of Ghana, observed that the first year of ONUC operations revealed a "failure of the United Nations to deal effectively with the Congo situation."[2] Based on the evidence presented in this chapter, you will need to evaluate President Nkrumah's conclusion. Did the United Nations make any achievements in peacekeeping during its first year in the Congo? What issues concerning effective international peacekeeping did the ONUC operation raise in that first year? And did UN involvement offer any lessons for other similar actions over the next thirty years and beyond?

2. Kwame Nkrumah, *Challenge of the Congo* (New York: International Publishers, 1967), p. 105.

BACKGROUND

The region of central Africa that comprises the vast watershed of the great Congo River and its tributaries has been home to a variety of African peoples for thousands of years. Portugal claimed the territory after its seamen landed on the region's Atlantic coast in the fifteenth century. For centuries, apart from trading activities, this claim was little more than a legalistic fiction. But as other

European nations became interested in the Congo basin in the nineteenth century, the Portuguese wanted to defend their claims.

It was an American reporter and adventurer, Henry Morton Stanley, who helped bring about the greatest interest in the region. In 1877, following a journey from the Indian Ocean to the Atlantic through the Congo watershed, Stanley found an especially interested ear for his stories of wealth and opportunity in the person of King Leopold II of Belgium. Realizing his small nation would have little success in making a colonial claim to the area, Leopold created a private concern—the International African Association—for the purpose of controlling and exploiting the Congo. He employed Stanley to return to Africa and make treaties with indigenous rulers in order to legitimize IAA claims.

For much of the next century, the Congo was involved in a variety of experimental endeavors in what might be termed international peacekeeping. Certainly King Leopold believed his private, international approach would serve to reduce conflict over claims to the region, although initially that was not the case. Fearing it might lose its previous hold on the Congo, Portugal sought a powerful partner to help defend its interests. An 1884 treaty with Great Britain recognizing Portuguese claims served that purpose but also raised the ire of other European countries.

The issue was resolved at the Berlin Conference of 1884, called by Chancellor Bismarck of Germany, specifically to find a peaceful resolution of the Congo disputes. All the parties agreed that King Leopold, in his private capacity, should maintain control of what would be called the Congo Free State; its trade would be open to all the nations participating in the Berlin Conference without any restrictions or fees. Thus Leopold became the sole political authority over the entire Congo, an area equal in size to all of Europe (except Russia).

As an absentee ruler, however, Leopold was unable to exercise much direction or control over the state even if he had wanted to. In less than two decades, merchants from many lands—including those of the Free State itself—established patterns of trade that horribly exploited the African population. Again there was a political outcry over the Congo and calls resounded for international intervention. In 1907, the Belgian government intervened, taking national control of the Congo to avoid any international conflict that might embroil its king.

Following World War I, under the League of Nations mandate system for former German colonies, Belgium added the small territories of Rwanda and Burundi to its administration of the Belgian Congo. As part of its intended function of international peacekeeper, the League of Nations made annual reviews of the various mandated territories, including those of Belgium. And because of the close administrative association of her two adjacent mandates with Belgium's much larger colony, the Congo was once again, although indirectly, linked to an attempt to avert international conflict.

Chapter 13

The Congo

Crisis:

International

Peacekeeping

after World

War II

(1960–1963)

As an experiment in peacekeeping, however, the League of Nations was not a success. With no power to take any substantive actions of its own, the League could do little. Even its reviews of the mandated territories were insufficient to bring changes to the practices of colonial rule, which for Belgium meant little more than a veneer of paternalism over many of the same practices of exploitation that had ravaged the Congo Free State. Other colonial powers, such as Great Britain and France, were unwilling to see Belgian colonial administration challenged lest their own colonial regimes come under more careful scrutiny.

Of far more serious consequence to keeping the peace was the manifest failure of the League to take any action over Italy's invasion of Ethiopia in 1936. That debacle made clear that the League had no muscle to stem international aggression, and the world war that followed shortly after sealed its fate. Yet the victorious allies in that conflict were determined to create a stronger mechanism to preserve peace, and in 1945 the United Nations was created. Unlike the League of Nations, the UN was committed not only to its member states, but also to the human rights of individuals within those states. This gave the organization additional standing when it came to considering issues related to the end of imperialism in the postwar years.

The United Nations welcomed virtually all the new nations born in the postwar wave of decolonialization. The new standing of India, Israel, the Philippines, Tunisia, and others as (nearly) equal partners in the UN "family of nations" was part of the force that propelled nationalist sentiment throughout the crumbling colonial empires. Yet not every colony seemed equally able to meet the challenges of independence. Among those least able to do so was the Belgian Congo.

The effects of World War II were disastrous for Belgium, leaving it very little capacity—financial or human—to devote to its colony. Bankruptcy at home coupled with the paternalistic attitudes of Belgian colonial administrators resulted in escalating demands that the resources of the Congo be even more fully exploited for Belgium itself. There was little concern for the development of the colony or its people. For example, educational opportunities for the Congolese were minimal. Precious few Africans who managed to enter primary school completed that course of study. Fewer still received any secondary education. Those who did found a racial ceiling in employment; arbitrary limits were placed on their advancement.

In the *Force Publique*, the Belgian Congo's army and national police force, Congolese soldiers with fifteen or more years of service were never promoted beyond the rank of sergeant; yet they found that many of their superior officers had much less service and often, less education. Throughout both the government apparatus and private industry, similar barriers prevailed. Belgian officials found such arrangements to be not only comfortable, but also the "natural" order of things. And while this was not unheard of in other European colonies on the continent, the Belgians had little experience in dealing with Africans of considerable ability and achievement, in contrast to the growing numbers of such individuals in the British and French territories.

When confronted with growing aspirations for advancement and nationalist rhetoric among the Congolese, the Belgians found themselves unable to make any positive responses. Instead they quickly began to pursue a strategy to minimize their responsibilities to meet those demands and at the same time continue to exploit the resources on which they had come to rely. In that spirit, unenthusiastically yet pragmatically—with a sense of inevitability as well—the Belgian government moved in early 1960 toward granting independence to its only colony.

THE METHOD

In this chapter you will read a number of official, primarily United Nations, documents. You will find diplomatic correspondence and statements made to the UN General Assembly and Security Council, as well as to other audiences. Informal correspondence and memoirs, both by participants in some of the events, are also included. Each of these presents only a limited view of the situation. Read each one carefully, keeping in mind that some items of information may be referred to only in passing, and others you may need to infer from the available information.

The first three sources set the stage for the Congo crisis. The sections of the United Nations Charter in Source 1 will help you understand the UN peacekeeping role envisioned by its founders. Source 2, written in 1957 but not published until after his death, gives an indication of how the most dynamic and popular of Congolese nationalists, Patrice Lumumba, viewed the cause for which he was struggling. What do you think was his highest priority? Source 3 consists of just one of the 259 articles of the Basic Law establishing the Republic of the Congo. This was to be, in effect, the constitution of the new nation; its provisions had the formal approval of the Belgian parliament and the informal acceptance of most Congolese nationalists.

The subsequent evidence will help you understand what happened in the days and weeks that followed the proclamation of the Congo's independence on June 30, 1960. In Source 4, Andrée Blouin, the new nation's first diplomatic chief of protocol,[3] describes her view of the situation in the very first days of independence. Source 5 is from the pen of the UN Undersecretary General Ralph Bunche, a distinguished African-American diplomat, who was in the Congo capital

3. **chief of protocol:** an official who arranges and manages the visits and contacts between her government and those of other countries (and international organizations).

Chapter 13

The Congo

Crisis:

International

Peacekeeping

after World

War II

(1960–1963)

of Leopoldville during and shortly after independence ceremonies. How do his experiences compare with the descriptions of Blouin?

The unusual document that constitutes Source 6 is a part of the declaration of independence issued by local officials in the Congolese province of Katanga. In the extreme south of the country, Katanga is a mineral-rich region with extraordinary deposits of copper and other minerals, which at the time were being exploited by Belgian companies. What reasons for independence are expressed in the proclamation? Can you think of any reasons other than those explicitly stated?

The proclamation of the Katanga authorities was of obvious concern to the national government, as was Belgium's ongoing military presence throughout the country. In Source 7 Blouin returns to give some insight into the decision-making process that led to a formal request from the Republic of the Congo to the United Nations (Source 8), an organization to which it did not yet formally belong! The official responses from the UN came in the form of Security Council resolutions authorizing the body to take action. Three of these resolutions, all adopted within a month of the Congo government's request, make up Source 9. In what ways do the resolutions differ? What might account for those differences? Also note the votes of Security Council member states on each resolution. Do you note any significance in the votes?

Source 10 conveys news of the deployment of United Nations forces to the people of the Congo. What seems to be Undersecretary General Bunche's principal intent in this broadcast? Now read Source 11, Blouin's observations on the efforts of UN troops and the aftermath of their early service. What is her chief criticism of the UN force? How does she relate the activities of the peacekeepers to problems within the Congo government? What relationships do you see between her views and Dr. Bunche's address (in Source 10)?

Source 12 reveals some of the same frustrations as those expressed by Blouin, only on a slightly different subject. Do you find Lumumba's point to be an important one? Does it justify his conclusions? Hammarskjold's response, also clearly arising from frustration, was made before the General Assembly (Source 13). Do you think his major point is supported by the evidence he cites?

The continuing contentious problems in the Congo also were aired at UN headquarters in New York. Criticisms of the Secretary General, similar to the charges by Blouin, were voiced in the General Assembly, especially by the Soviet Union. The result was a resolution passed by the General Assembly in an Emergency Session called specifically to consider the Congo crisis (Source 14). What significance do you see in this resolution? The views of Secretary General Dag Hammarskjold on the resolution are obvious in Source 15, a private note to his Special Representative in the Congo, the Indian diplomat Rajeshwar Dayal. How important do you think Hammarskjold's observations may be? Regardless of the merits of the arguments, what might you conclude from these last four documents?

Now read Sources 16 and 17, both written several years after the events. The first presents a view of the situation by Thomas Kanza, minister in charge of United Nations affairs in Prime Minister Lumumba's government; the second considers the same issue from the perspective of Rajeshwar Dayal, Secretary General Hammarskjold's primary eyes and ears in the Congo. To what extent do they agree in their assessments? Why? Do their views benefit from the years the authors had to reflect on the subject? Do these two sources allow you to infer anything more about the disagreements regarding ONUC activities in the Congo?

As events continued to unfold in the Congo, Hammarskjold was criticized further in the General Assembly, with many delegations chafing at his interpretation of his role as well as his policies and decisions. In a revealing response to his critics (Source 18), he attempted to broaden the issues, to see them in terms of principles rather than personalities. Do you think he was correct in this approach?

In the Congo itself the situation deteriorated. President Kasavubu and Prime Minister Lumumba remained at odds; their disputes escalated beyond hope of reconciliation. At that point, Lumumba was put under arrest by Kasavubu's government, escaped, and was arrested again. He wrote to his wife from prison (Source 19) reflecting on his situation and that of his country. Then, as his circumstances worsened, he appealed to Mr. Dayal (Source 20). What do these two sources suggest about his attitude toward the United Nations

and its efforts in his country? Before any UN action could be taken on his appeal, Lumumba and two of his colleagues were transferred into the hands of his opponents in Katanga and shortly afterward killed.

Source 21 records the Security Council's response to the new circumstances; Hammarskjold's reactions are related in Source 22. What changes in the Congo situation, and in the United Nations efforts, do you detect following the death of Lumumba? Do the assertions of Secretary General Hammarskjold in Source 23 offer any insights into his view of the UN mission in the Congo? Had his views changed? Can you infer any reasons why President Kasavubu (and others) might have continued to disagree with Hammarskjold's interpretation of the UN mandate?

Does Source 24, another General Assembly resolution, suggest the development of any further disagreements about the role of the United Nations, or of its officials, in the Congo? If so, what are they? Also read Source 25, the observations of the Secretary General's newly appointed Special Representative in Katanga, Conor Cruise O'Brien of Ireland. Do his reflections conform to your reading of Resolution 1600 (XV)? Might his comments provide any insights that would support your inferences? And do the two "irreconcilable courses of action" O'Brien identifies offer any insight for future peacekeeping efforts?

Source 26 contains some of the conclusions arrived at by a senior United Nations official who served in the Congo, Rajeshwar Dayal. Do his gen-

Chapter 13

The Congo

Crisis:

International

Peacekeeping

after World

War II

(1960–1963)

eral conclusions suggest any specific steps that might be taken to ensure the success of peacekeeping endeavors?

The last two sources should redirect you to a consideration of the central problems posed in this chapter. Did the United Nations make any achievements in peacemaking during its first year in the Congo? What issues concerning international peacekeeping did the ONUC operation raise during that time? And did UN involvement in the new republic provide any lessons for other similar actions over the next thirty years and beyond?

THE EVIDENCE

Source 1 from Charter of the United Nations and the Statute of the International Court of Justice *(New York: United Nations, 1946).*

1. From the *Charter of the United Nations,* 1945

Chapter I: Purposes and Principles

ARTICLE 2

4. All Members shall refrain in their international relations from the threat or use of force against the territorial integrity or political independence of any state, or in any other manner inconsistent with the Purposes of the United Nations.

7. Nothing contained in the present Charter shall authorize the United Nations to intervene in matters which are essentially within the domestic jurisdiction of any state or shall require the Members to submit such matters to settlement under the present Charter; but this principle shall not prejudice the application of enforcement measures under Chapter VII.

Chapter VI: Pacific Settlement of Disputes

ARTICLE 34

The Security Council may investigate any dispute, or any situation which might lead to international friction or give rise to a dispute, in order to determine whether the continuance of the dispute or situation is likely to endanger the maintenance of international peace and security.

Chapter VII: Action With Respect to Threats to the Peace, Breaches of the Peace, and Acts of Aggression

ARTICLE 39

The Security Council shall determine the existence of any threat to the peace, breach of the peace, or act of aggression and shall make recommendations, or decide what measures shall be taken in accordance with Articles 41 and 42, to maintain or restore international peace and security.

ARTICLE 41

The Security Council may decide what measures not involving the use of armed force are to be employed to give effect to its decisions, and it may call upon the Members of the United Nations to apply such measures. These may include complete or partial interruption of economic relations and of rail, sea, air, postal, telegraphic, radio, and other means of communication, and the severance of diplomatic relations.

ARTICLE 42

Should the Security Council consider that measures provided for in Article 41 would be inadequate or have proved to be inadequate, it may take such action by air, sea, or land forces as may be necessary to maintain or restore international peace and security. Such action may include demonstrations, blockade, and other operations by air, sea, or land forces of Members of the United Nations.

Chapter XVI: Miscellaneous Provisions

ARTICLE 104

The Organization shall enjoy in the territory of each of its Members such legal capacity as may be necessary for the exercise of its functions and the fulfillment of its purposes.

Chapter 13

The Congo

Crisis:

International

Peacekeeping

after World

War II

(1960–1963)

Source 2 from Patrice Lumumba, Congo, My Country, *trans. Graham Heath (London and New York: Praeger, 1962), pp. 145–146.*

2. From Patrice Lumumba, *Congo, My Country*, 1957

What should be our attitude towards the complex and agonising problems which confront us and which involve the future of our country? It must be one of calm, level-headedness, correct behaviour, impartiality, objectivity, justice, patience, perseverance, constant faith and continuity of effort and action. We must not give way to discouragement if we are to complete our difficult journey with its many hazards, disappointments and rebuffs. . . . Our concern must be not to satisfy personal ambitions but to achieve the harmonious development of all Africans. We must give up any activities which may cause cleavages within our society.

Our success depends above all on our unity. . . .

The reforms which we are seeking must be achieved in a spirit of agreement and harmony. Anyone who plans rebellion or conspiracy will endanger the country and bring it into disrepute.

Source 3 from Kwame Nkrumah, Challenge of the Congo *(New York: International Publishers, 1967), p. 18.*

3. From *La Loi Fundamentale sur les Structures de Congo*, approved May 11, 1960

ARTICLE 6

The Congo constitutes, within its present boundaries, an indivisible and democratic state.

Source 4 from Andrée Blouin, in collaboration with Jean MacKellar, My Country, Africa *(New York: Praeger, 1983), pp. 253–254.*

4. From Andrée Blouin, "The Congo Catastrophe," 1961

In Leopoldville, on the eve of independence, out of a population of 350,000, there were at least 100,000 unemployed. This number was to swell "miraculously" at the proclamation of independence, and the people demanded "work and a good salary, at once." How was the new government to wave a magic wand and, within two days after the proclamation, find a solution for the catastrophe that the Belgians had been preparing for 80 years?

Before June 30th the Congo was already mortally wounded. First there had been the divisive personal and political rivalries, then the tribal conflicts, and then the demonstrations of the unemployed. Finally, on July 5th, it was the army's turn to add to the country's calamities. The Congolese soldiers refused to obey any longer the commands of their Belgian officers. They mutinied. . . .

The ship of state was listing dangerously as bad news continued to pile up everywhere.

Source 5 from Peggy Mann, Ralph Bunche, UN Peacemaker *(New York: Coward, McCann & Geoghegan, 1975), pp. 295–296.*

5. Ralph Bunche, "Chaos in Léopoldville," July 8, 1960

Chaos reigned in Léopoldville, with the police in hiding and the mutinous Congolese roaming all over the town on foot and in jeeps, with no officers and many of them with a large bottle of Polar beer in one hand and a sub-machine gun cradled under the other arm.

My suite was on the fourth floor of the Stanley Hotel. On this morning . . . there came a banging on my door and two Congolese soldiers came in and two remained at the door, all four carrying sub-machine guns. The two who came in were obviously under the influence of excessive beer.

They spoke no French and of course I understood nothing of what they were saying in their native tongue. They were quickly irritated at my failure to respond to whatever they said to me so they began to poke me in the ribs and back with the muzzles of their guns, and finally, at gun point, forced me out of the room and down the four flights of steps, jabbing me as we went. When I got down to the lobby, I found that other members of my staff were already down and we were herded together in the lobby, apparently until our captors had abandoned or forgotten the idea that we were all Belgian paratroopers or until the hotel bar's supply of beer had been exhausted. Then they just walked out and left us. . . . We were better off than some in similar situations in other parts of the city.

Chapter 13

The Congo

Crisis:

International

Peacekeeping

after World

War II

(1960–1963)

Source 6 from Jules Gérard-Libois, trans. Rebecca Young, Katanga Secession *(Madison: University of Wisconsin Press, 1966), pp. 328–329.*

6. Proclamation of Independence of Katanga, July 11, 1960

The independence of the Congo is an established fact since June 30, 1960.

What do we behold at present?

Throughout the Congo and particularly in Katanga and in Leopoldville province, we see a tactic of disorganization and terror at work, a tactic which we have seen applied in numerous instances and in how many countries now under Communist dictatorship.

After improper elections in certain provinces, which gave the majority to a single party, a number of electors being unable to cast their votes, a central government with an extremist majority was constituted.

Hardly was it constituted, before this government, setting at naught the stipulations of the *Loi Fondamentale,* attempted to meddle in affairs which properly belonged solely within the competent jurisdiction of the provincial governments. . . .

Katanga cannot bow to such proceedings. The Katangan government was elected by a provincial assembly, itself elected on the basis of a program for order and peace.

Under these circumstances, and before the dangers we would bring down upon us by prolonging our submission to the arbitrary will and Communistic intentions of the central government, the Katangan government has decided to proclaim the independence of Katanga.

This INDEPENDENCE is TOTAL. However, aware of the imperative necessity for economic cooperation with Belgium, the Katangan government, to which Belgium has just granted the assistance of its own troops to protect human life, calls upon Belgium to join with Katanga in close economic community.

Katanga calls upon Belgium to continue its technical, financial, and military support.

Source 7 from Andrée Blouin, in collaboration with Jean MacKellar, My Country, Africa *(New York: Praeger, 1983), p. 258.*

7. From Andrée Blouin, "The Congo Catastrophe," 1961

On my suggestion, Lumumba wired the U.S. government for cooperation in asking the Belgian government to remove its troops from Congolese soil. He knew the request would be refused. But making it would give him elbow room for maneuvering and it would also make clear, at last, the U.S. government's intentions with regard to the Congo.

The U.S. ambassador's answer did not even take a normal, diplomatic form. It was given the status of "not having been received."

It was then that Lumumba asked the United Nations for help.

Source 8 from United Nations, Security Council Official Records, Fifteenth Year, Supplement for July, August, and September 1960, document 4382.

8. Telegram to the Secretary General, July 12, 1960

The Government of the Republic of the Congo requests urgent dispatch by the United Nations of military assistance. This request is justified by the dispatch to the Congo of metropolitan Belgian troops in violation of the treaty of friendship signed between Belgium and the Republic of the Congo on June 29, 1960. Under the terms of that treaty, Belgian troops may only intervene on the express request of the Congolese government. No such request was ever made by the Government of the Republic of the Congo and we therefore regard the unsolicited Belgian action as an act of aggression against our country.

The real cause of most of the disturbances can be found in colonialist machinations. We accuse the Belgian government of having carefully prepared the secession of Katanga with a view to maintaining a hold on our country. The government, supported by the Congolese people, refuses to accept a *fait accompli* resulting from a conspiracy between Belgian imperialists and a small group of Katanga leaders. The overwhelming majority of the Katanga population is opposed to secession, which means the disguised perpetuation of the colonialist régime. The essential purpose of the requested military aid is to protect the national territory of the Congo against the present external aggression which is a threat to international peace. We strongly stress the extremely urgent need for the dispatch of United Nations troops to the Congo.

Joseph Kasavubu
*President of the Republic of the Congo and
Supreme Commander of the National Army*

Patrice Lumumba
Prime Minister and Minister of National Defence

Chapter 13

The Congo

Crisis:

International

Peacekeeping

after World

War II

(1960–1963)

Source 9 from United Nations, Security Council Official Records, Fifteenth Year; 873rd, 877th, and 885th meetings.

9. United Nations Security Council Resolutions on the Congo, 1960

A. RESOLUTION S/4387, JULY 14

The Security Council,

   Considering the report of the Secretary-General on a request for United Nations action in relation to the Republic of the Congo,

   Considering the request for military assistance addressed to the Secretary-General by the President and the Prime Minister of the Republic of the Congo,

   1. *Calls upon* the Government of Belgium to withdraw their troops from the territory of the Republic of the Congo;

   2. *Decides* to authorize the Secretary-General to take the necessary steps, in consultation with the Government of the Republic of the Congo, to provide the Government with such military assistance, as may be necessary, until, through the efforts of the Congolese Government with the technical assistance of the United Nations, the national security forces may be able, in the opinion of the Government, to meet fully their tasks;

   3. *Requests* the Secretary-General to report to the Security Council as appropriate.

   This resolution was adopted by eight votes (Argentina, Ceylon, Ecuador, Italy, Poland, Tunisia, USSR, and United States) to nil, with three abstentions (China, France, and the United Kingdom).

B. RESOLUTION S/4405, JULY 22

The Security Council,

   Having considered the first report by the Secretary-General on the implementation of Security Council resolution S/4387 of July 14th, 1960, . . .

   Considering that the complete restoration of law and order in the Republic of the Congo would effectively contribute to the maintenance of international peace and security, . . .

   2. *Requests* all States to refrain from any action which might tend to impede the restoration of law and order and the exercise by the Government of Congo of its authority and also to refrain from any action which might undermine

the territorial integrity and the political independence of the Republic of the Congo; . . .

This resolution was adopted unanimously.

C. RESOLUTION S/4426, AUGUST 9

The Security Council, . . .

Noting with satisfaction the progress made by the United Nations in carrying out the Security Council resolutions in respect of the territory of the Republic of the Congo other than the Province of Katanga,

Noting however that the United Nations had been prevented from implementing the aforesaid resolutions in the Province of Katanga although it was ready, and in fact attempted, to do so.

Recognizing that the withdrawal of Belgian troops from the Province of Katanga will be a positive contribution to and essential for the proper implementation of the Security Council resolutions, . . .

2. *Calls upon* the Government of Belgium to withdraw immediately its troops from the Province of Katanga under speedy modalities determined by the Secretary-General and to assist in every possible way the implementation of the Council's resolutions;

3. *Declares* that the entry of the United Nations force into the Province of Katanga is necessary for the full implementation of this resolution;

4. *Reaffirms* that the United Nations force in the Congo, will not be a party to or in any way intervene in or be used to influence the outcome of any internal conflict, constitutional or otherwise; . . .

This resolution was adopted by nine votes to nil, with two abstentions (France and Italy).

Source 10 from Thomas Kanza, Conflict in the Congo *(Harmondsworth, England: Penguin Books, 1972), p. 335.*

10. Ralph Bunche, Broadcast Message on the Arrival of UN Troops in the Congo, July 16, 1960

The first troops from the UN arrived at Njili airport last night, Friday. They were Tunisian. The first contingents of Ghanaians came by air this morning.

Chapter 13

The Congo

Crisis:

International

Peacekeeping

after World

War II

(1960–1963)

A lot more troops will be following in the next few days; they will be drawn from the armies of Ethiopia, Ghana, Morocco and Tunisia. . . .

The UN forces in the Congo are forces for peace. They will do everything they can to help restore calm, harmony, and safety for all, whites as well as blacks, in this troubled land. They will function exclusively under the control and command of the UN. . . .

I would like to ask you all not to expect miracles. The UN has gone into action very quickly, for it was only last Tuesday that I received the appeals addressed to the UN by the Congolese government [Source 8]. . . . I hope that everyone—both government and people—will give evidence of patience and moderation in the next few days. This alone can save your marvellous country from disaster.

Source 11 from Andrée Blouin, in collaboration with Jean MacKellar, My Country, Africa *(New York: Praeger, 1983), pp. 259, 264.*

11. From Andrée Blouin, "The *casques bleus*,"[4] 1961

Soon after July 14th, when Patrice Lumumba asked the United Nations to assist in stabilizing his new state, the *casques bleus,* or blue helmets, as they were known, arrived. Twenty-thousand of them. . . .

Since the United Nations' general secretary had not, with his *casques bleus,* made any real effort to end the Katanga secession, Lumumba, sick at heart, sent in Congolese troops. These troops were close to victory when Hammarskjöld saw that their success would open his own lack of efforts to charges of complicity. He had to act, and swiftly. He asked Kasavubu to stop immediately the advance of the Congolese troops. Kasavubu obeyed. . . .

On September 5th, President Kasavubu discharged the prime minister, and asked Ileo, president of the senate, to form a new cabinet. Sirens broke the heavy silence that weighed on Leopoldville.

Lumumba made immediate reply. He, in turn, discharged Kasavubu. The door opened on a gulf and the Congo plunged into the abyss.

---

4. *casques bleus:* blue helmets; in contrast to most modern military organizations, United Nations forces had adopted, well before the ONUC operation, blue helmets and berets for soldiers under its command precisely because it would distinguish them from other units.

Source 12 from Lumumba Speaks: The Speeches and Writings of Patrice Lumumba, *1958–1961, ed. Jean Van Lierde and trans. Helen R. Lane (Boston: Little, Brown, 1972), pp. 332–333.*

12. Patrice Lumumba, Letter to the Secretary General, August 15, 1960

Before leaving New York for the Congo, the Congolese delegations . . . insisted that you contact my government as soon as you arrived in Leopoldville before going on to Katanga, in accordance with the Security Council's resolution of July 14, 1960. I personally insisted on this in the letter I sent you on August 12, through the intermediary of your special representative, Mr. Ralph Bunche. But you completely ignored the legal government of the republic and sent a telegram from New York to Mr. Tshombe, the leader of the Katangese rebellion and an agent of the Belgian government. . . .

In view of all the foregoing, the government and the people of the Congo have lost their confidence in the secretary-general of the United Nations. As a consequence, we request as of this date that the Security Council immediately send to the Congo a group of neutral observers representing the following countries: Morocco, Tunisia, Ethiopia, Ghana, Guinea, the United Arab Republic, Sudan, Ceylon, Liberia, Mali, Burma, India, Afghanistan, and Lebanon. The mission of these observers will be to assure the immediate and total application of the resolutions of the Security Council of July 14 and 22 and August 9, 1960 [Source 9].

Source 13 from United Nations, General Assembly Official Records, Fourth Emergency Special Session, 859th plenary meeting.

13. Dag Hammarskjold, Statement During General Assembly Debate, September 18, 1960

It has been said that the breakthrough in Katanga and what I did personally in that context was done without consultation with the central government. I have told the Security Council that before going to Katanga I consulted the delegation here in New York. And the Assembly will remember that that delegation included the vice-prime minister, the foreign minister, the minister for United Nations affairs and two other members of the Cabinet. But obviously consultation with the central government means consultation with Mr. Lumumba. In all other cases about which I know, consultation with responsible,

Chapter 13

The Congo

Crisis:

International

Peacekeeping

after World

War II

(1960–1963)

constitutionally responsible members of the Cabinet concerning a certain question covers the whole need for consultation with the government.

Source 14 from United Nations, General Assembly Official Records, Fourth Emergency Special Session.

14. United Nations General Assembly Resolution 1471 (ES-IV), September 20, 1960

The General Assembly,

Having considered the situation in the Republic of the Congo,

Taking note of the resolutions of July 14th and 22nd, and of August 9th, 1960 of the Security Council,

Taking into account the unsatisfactory economic and political conditions that continue in the Republic of the Congo,

Considering that, with a view to preserving the unity, territorial integrity and political independence of the Congo, to protecting and advancing the welfare of its people, and to safeguarding international peace, it is essential for the United Nations to continue to assist the Central Government of the Congo,

1. *Fully supports* the resolutions of July 14th and 22nd, and of August 9th of the Security Council;

2. *Requests* the Secretary-General to continue to take vigorous action in accordance with the terms of the aforesaid resolutions and to assist the Central Government of the Congo in the restoration and maintenance of law and order throughout the territory of the Republic of the Congo and to safeguard its unity, territorial integrity and political independence in the interests of international peace and security;

3. *Appeals* to all Congolese within the Republic of the Congo to seek a speedy solution by peaceful means of all their internal conflicts for the unity and integrity of the Congo, with the assistance, as appropriate, of Asian and African representatives appointed by the Advisory Committee on the Congo, in consultation with the Secretary-General, for the purpose of conciliation; . . .

Source 15 from Rajeshwar Dayal, Mission for Hammarskjold: The Congo Crisis *(Princeton, N.J.: Princeton University Press, 1976), p. 84.*

15. Dag Hammarskjold,
Cable to Rajeshwar Dayal,
September 20, 1960

The real significance of today's result [of the vote on resolution 1471] in the General Assembly is on [the] general political level more than on yours or ours. It means that a certain big power [i.e., the Soviet Union] had shown its hand so badly, especially in [its] attack on [the U.N.] Secretariat and Command as [a] stumbling block for certain ambitions, and that in fact the United Afro-Asians in [the] demonstration vote [on resolution 1471] had to tell them [i.e., the Soviet Union] off. This situation, in turn, was registered [i.e., understood] by the big power beforehand and all [the members of the U.N.] got definite proof that if the Afro-Asians stick together, or if only the Africans stick together, they represent a new big power to which certain others have to bow. You know [this is] the theory on which I have worked now for two months. Today it was fully vindicated and I regard the fact that the Afro-Asian group in this way stood up to the test, found its own strength and a new cohesion, is more important than any other result.

Source 16 from Thomas Kanza, Conflict in the Congo *(Harmondsworth, England: Penguin Books, 1972), pp. 219–220, 238, 243.*

16. From Thomas Kanza,
"Lumumba and
Hammarskjold," 1972

The survival of Lumumba seemed to depend on his sincerely collaborating with the UN, and above all with Hammarskjöld. It seemed that their fates were linked for the future. Would they help one another, or destroy one another? . . .

In 1960 Hammarskjöld manifestly believed that the West had a sacred mission towards Africa in general, and especially the Congo; but he could at times be blinded by his determination to become a world hero of peace. . . .

As for Lumumba, he made the fatal mistake of underestimating both the influence of the USA in the United Nations and the powerful means that Hammarskjöld himself had at his disposal, together with the skilful and effective use that Hammarskjöld could make of his relationships with and prestige among the various member states. Lumumba simply did not grasp the nature of Hammarskjöld's secret ambition. . . .

Chapter 13

The Congo

Crisis:

International

Peacekeeping

after World

War II

(1960–1963)

Lumumba's stay in New York [July 24–26, 1960] was not a success in its main purpose. His meetings with Hammarskjöld were not as relaxed and friendly as we had hoped. Almost immediately after the normal courtesies had been exchanged there arose a series of misunderstandings and disagreements, . . . a real conflict of personalities, and one which could have serious results on the whole future relationship between the central Congolese government and the UN. The two principals were equally determined to get their point of view across, and each persistently underestimated the other.

Lumumba remained extremely demanding and impatient, while Hammarskjöld simply noted down his suggestions and continued to promise continued assistance to the Congo and its government.

I knew that Hammarskjöld was committed to "assisting the Congo and the central government"; but contrary to all my hopes, he gave no hint of any intention to collaborate with Lumumba as an individual. . . .

Lumumba had become convinced that Hammarskjöld was working mainly for Western interests, and that he could not be trusted even as a man, because of his preconceived ideas about the means by which the Congo's integral security was to be preserved. Tragic though it may seem, Hammarskjöld, too, had similarly judged Lumumba; he no longer gave him the benefit of the doubt as he had before they met. To him Lumumba did not deserve . . . trust. . . .

Source 17 from Rajeshwar Dayal, Mission for Hammarskjold: The Congo Crisis *(Princeton, N.J.: Princeton University Press, 1976), pp. 307–309.*

17. Rajeshwar Dayal, "Hammarskjold and Lumumba," 1976

In the 1950s, the cold war was an accepted but uneasy condition of international life. The United Nations was divided between the Western and Eastern groups of powers, with the middle and smaller powers oscillating uneasily between the two poles. . . .

Hammarskjold implicitly believed that the moral force of the Organization far surpassed the strength of its arms. That conviction later underlay his reluctance to use force in the Congo, where his principles and convictions were put to their severest test. He was convinced that right means had to be employed to attain right ends: a unity brought about by force would be no unity at all. . . .

Hammarskjold was generally meticulously correct in his dealings with United Nations delegations, keeping close personal or indirect contact through his associates with those whose interests or views were of particular consequence. Yet, . . . Hammarskjold could not pardon Lumumba's inadequacies and crudeness. They were both deeply sensitive people, Hammarskjold's sensitivity expressing itself in an utter refinement of spirit and behaviour, Lumumba's in dark suspicion and blind anger. Hammarskjold, who always tried to rise from the particular to the impersonal, was pitted against Lumumba, in whom impersonal love of country was metamorphosed into a sense of personal dignity. While Hammarskjold believed that one should see the other objectively, but at the same time view his difficulty subjectively, he in fact judged Lumumba from his own elevated standpoint, not from that of the rough-hewn African's.

Source 18 from United Nations, General Assembly Official Records, Fifteenth Session, 871st plenary meeting.

18. Dag Hammarskjold, Statement During General Assembly Debate, September 26, 1960

The question before the General Assembly is no longer one of certain actions but one of the principles guiding them. Time and again the United Nations has had to face situations in which a wrong move might have tended to throw the weight of the Organization over in favour of this or that specific party in a conflict of a primarily domestic character. To permit that to happen is indeed to intervene in domestic affairs contrary to the letter and the spirit of the Charter.

To avoid doing so is to be true to the letter and spirit of the Charter, whatever disappointment it might cause those who might have thought that they could add to their political weight by drawing the United Nations over to their side.

This is, of course, the basic reason for the principle spelled out at the very first stage of the Congo operation, and approved by the Security Council, to the effect that the United Nations Force is not under the orders of a government requesting its assistance and cannot be permitted to become a party to any internal conflict, be it one in which the government is engaged or not. It is common experience that nothing, in the heat of emotion, is regarded as more partial by one who takes himself the position of a party than strict impartiality.

Further, as I have said, this is a question not of a man but of an institution. Use whatever words you like, independence, impartiality, objectivity—they all describe essential aspects of what, without exception, must be the attitude of the Secretary-General.

Chapter 13

The Congo

Crisis:

International

Peacekeeping

after World

War II

(1960–1963)

Sources 19 and 20 from Lumumba Speaks: The Speeches and Writings of Patrice Lumumba, 1958–1961, *ed. Jean Van Lierde and trans. Helen R. Lane (Boston: Little, Brown, 1972), pp. 421–425.*

19. Patrice Lumumba, Letter to His Wife, December 1960

My beloved companion,

I write you these words not knowing whether you will receive them, when you will receive them, and whether I will still be alive when you read them. Throughout my struggle for the independence of my country, I have never doubted for a single instant that the sacred cause to which my comrades and I have dedicated our entire lives would triumph in the end. . . . It is not my person that is important. What is important is the Congo, our poor people whose independence has been turned into a cage, with people looking at us from outside the bars, sometimes with charitable compassion, sometimes with glee and delight. . . .

Do not weep for me, my companion, I know that my country, now suffering so much, will be able to defend its independence and its freedom. Long live the Congo! Long live Africa!

20. Patrice Lumumba, Letter to Rajeshwar Dayal, January 4, 1961

On December 27 of last year, I was pleased to receive a visit from the Red Cross, which has concerned itself with my situation as well as that of the other members of Parliament who are being held here. I reported the inhuman conditions we have been forced to endure to the Red Cross. . . .

In a word, we are living amid absolutely impossible conditions; moreover, they are against the law. . . .

The provisions of the law regarding preliminary hearings have not been respected.

The provisions of the penal code have not been respected either. This is a purely arbitrary detention; moreover, we should have been granted parliamentary immunity.

That is the situation, and I beg you to pass word of it on to the secretary-general of the United Nations, with my thanks for his intervention on my behalf.

Sources 21 and 22 from United Nations, Security Council Official Records, Sixteenth Year, 942nd meeting.

21. Security Council Resolution S/4741, February 21, 1961

The Security Council,

  Having considered the situation in the Congo,

  Having learned with deep regret the announcement of the killing of the Congolese leaders, Mr Patrice Lumumba, Mr Maurice Mpolo and Mr Joseph Okito,

  Deeply concerned at the grave repercussions of these crimes and the danger of widespread civil war and bloodshed in the Congo and the threat to international peace and security, . . .

  1. *Urges* that the United Nations take immediately all appropriate measures to prevent the occurrence of civil war in the Congo, including arrangements for cease-fires, the halting of all military operations, the prevention of clashes and the use of force, if necessary, in the last resort; . . .

  5. *Reaffirms* the Security Council resolutions of July 14th, July 22nd and August 9th, 1960, and the General Assembly resolution 1474 (ES-IV) of September 20th, 1960, and reminds all States of their obligation under these resolutions.

22. Dag Hammarskjold, Statement to the Security Council, February 21, 1961

I strongly welcome the first three-power resolution [S/4741] adopted today by the Council as giving a stronger and clearer framework for United Nations action although, as so often before, it does not provide a wider legal basis or new means for implementation.

  I note the reaffirmation of previous resolutions which entrusted the Secretary-General with execution of the decisions of the Security Council in the Congo affairs. . . .

  Some have found it proper to label me the "organizer of the murder of Mr. Lumumba." Regarding the long series of developments finally leading to the tragedy, may I first refer to the fact that Mr. Lumumba, on November 7, made a statement in which, in unequivocal terms, he expressed his appreciation for the assistance of the United Nations and his confidence in the Secretary-General. With respect to later events, the arrest and detention and, subsequently,

Chapter 13
The Congo
Crisis:
International
Peacekeeping
after World
War II
(1960–1963)

the transfer to Katanga, it does appear necessary for me to draw attention to certain facts which have been ignored.

The accusations addressed to me suggest that the action I took upon learning of Mr. Lumumba's arrest was inadequate. In fact, what must be implied is that I should have ordered the United Nations Force in the Congo to take military initiative in order to liberate Mr. Lumumba from the custody of the Armée nationale congolaise at Thysville. But could there be any question that the use of such military force against the authorities in Thysville would have constituted a clear departure from the mandate and its clear Charter framework? What I should like to recall here is that this conclusion represents not merely my judgement but conforms to the views of most Member states.

Source 23 from United Nations, Security Council Official Records, Supplement for January, February, and March 1961, documents S/4775, section IV.

23. Dag Hammarskjold, Letter to Joseph Kasavubu, March 12, 1961

I have read your message of March 11 with concern, because it seems to me to reflect some continued misunderstanding of the principles which must apply to the United Nations operation. You should not doubt our sincerity when I say that the United Nations is animated solely by the interest to assist the Congolese people but realizes that that must be done in such a way as to safeguard not only the Congo, but Africa and the world, against the present threat to peace and security, while fully protecting the independence and integrity of the country. Part of the difficulty in the present situation derives from the fact that, in these conditions, assistance to the Congo cannot be detached from the much wider international problem of peace, which may sometimes seem to lead to reactions on the United Nations side running counter to Congolese views; naturally, there is not, and there cannot be, any such conflict of interest as the primary concern of the Congolese people also must be the maintenance of peace around the Congo and the prevention of possible military intervention on the part of foreign powers.

Source 24 from United Nations, General Assembly Official Records, Fifteenth Session, 983rd plenary session.

24. General Assembly Resolution 1600 (XV), April 15, 1961

The General Assembly,
   Having considered the situation in the Republic of the Congo,
   Gravely concerned at the danger of civil war and foreign intervention and at the threat to international peace and security, . . .

   3. *Considers it essential* that necessary and effective measures be taken by the Secretary-General immediately to prevent the introduction of arms, military equipment, and supplies into the Congo, except in conformity with the resolutions of the United Nations; . . .

Source 25 from Conor Cruise O'Brien, To Katanga and Back: A UN Case History *(New York: Grosset & Dunlap, 1962), pp. 45–46.*

25. Conor Cruise O'Brien, "Mr. Hammarskjold's Confidence," 1962

At his Press conference [May 29, 1961], Mr Hammarskjold radiated serenity and confidence . . . [which] was connected not with the Congo news . . . but with his recent triumph at the resumed Fifteenth Session of the General Assembly. The Assembly, including most of the neutrals, had, by clear implication, voted 83–11 in favour of the proposition that there *were* neutral men and that he was one of them.[5] . . . The idea of the United Nations, and of his own office, which he had defended so staunchly and so ingeniously, seemed about to prevail.

   . . . [I]t had not yet prevailed, and there remained great barriers, not yet fully known, to be surmounted before success would be assured. For that massive vote of confidence had been equivocal; it was, at bottom, a vote of

5. O'Brien refers to the vote of the General Assembly to retain the words "by the Secretary-General" in clause 3 of Resolution 1600 (XV); see Source 24. Hammarskjold did see himself as a neutral man, an international civil servant capable of making sound, independent judgments free from national bias. He laid out this attitude in an important lecture delivered at Oxford University on May 30, 1961: "The International Civil Servant in Law and in Fact."

Chapter 13

The Congo

Crisis:

International

Peacekeeping

after World

War II

(1960–1963)

confidence in his capacity and intention *to follow two different and possibly irreconcilable courses of action.* . . .

For the Afro-Asian supporters of the resolutions—and of the vote of confidence—the resolutions implied that the secessionist régime in Katanga would be brought down by the immediate evacuation of the foreign officers and political advisers on which the régime was generally believed to depend for its continued existence . . . that Mr Hammarskjold would see to it that this task was carried out, using, in the words of the resolution, "force, if necessary, in the last resort." . . . [B]ut the British delegation [representing the views of other Western powers] made it clear what the resolution, in its opinion, did *not* mean: it did not mean what its framers thought it meant—power to use force if necessary against Mr Tshombe's mercenary-led army. The "confidence" of these Western countries hinged on what they assumed to be [Hammarskjold's] intention never to do what the "confidence" of the Afro-Asians expected him to do *if necessary.*

Source 26 from Rajeshwar Dayal, Mission for Hammarskjold: The Congo Crisis *(Princeton, N.J.: Princeton University Press, 1976), p. 310.*

26. Rajeshwar Dayal, "The Congo Operation," 1976

The Congo Operation seriously over-taxed the limited strength of the United Nations. Assuredly, the Secretary-General had on many previous occasions stretched the functions of the Organization—but never to breaking-point—and had successfully demonstrated its capabilities. After all, the Organization derived its power not so much from the Charter as from what the member states, and especially the great powers, were prepared to endow it with. In the case of the Congo, there was increasing reluctance to provide the required degree of support—moral, political, and financial—that the needs of the situation demanded.

QUESTIONS TO CONSIDER

The evidence presented in this chapter requires that you take at least two intermediate steps before you can answer the central questions. First, use the evidence to construct—at least in your mind—a narrative of the events. What was going on in the Congo? at the United Nations? How were the two related? What were the principal directions of the interplay between both centers of action? Is the sequence of events important? You may wish to sketch a simple time line to guide your narrative.

In this step you will also need to identify all of the major characters and institutions involved. (If you cannot pronounce all their names, at least try to visualize their spelling; that may help you remember them.) What positions did each of them hold? Was that fact important to their observations? What were the relationships between them? Do some seem more reliable than others? Why? Again, writing down a list may help, noting the key points after each name; it may be helpful to use this list to better evaluate each piece of the evidence. With your time line and list of players completed, try to formulate a clear narrative of what happened.

Once you have the narrative of events in mind, then you will need to analyze and synthesize the evidence; this is where your powers of inference will come into play. You will need to apply what general knowledge you have of events, circumstances, and people, as well as your awareness of history, to your reading of the evidence. Your aim in doing this will be to create a more complete picture of the events, to reach the most plausible answers possible to the central questions posed in this chapter.

You will need, as well, to apply your powers of inference to some preliminary questions about the evidence itself. For example, what, if anything, does each source tell you about the objectives and/or the constraints on the ONUC operation? Are there other issues—about the Congo, international relations, the United Nations, or peacekeeping, for example—that each source can help you better understand? The narrative you have constructed, as well as your general knowledge, may also help you infer answers to these and other questions, which you can use to analyze each piece of evidence.

The evidence in this chapter also poses a particular problem that historians sometimes face in analyzing situations such as international peacekeeping in the Congo. To what extent do the decisions of institutions—in this case the resolutions passed by the United Nations General Assembly and Security Council—provide evidence of what those institutions do? Is that evidence best found in **how** and **why** they reach a particular decision? Or is it more important to understand **what** the institutions decide to do? Can the institutional decision be better understood by viewing the ideas and actions of its separate parts? Or, to put it in terms of this

Chapter 13

The Congo

Crisis:

International

Peacekeeping

after World

War II

(1960–1963)

topic, are national and individual ideas and decisions more important than the nations and organizations that they represent? Again, you may find it necessary to infer some of the answers since the sources themselves may not speak directly to these questions.

EPILOGUE

On September 18, 1961, Dag Hammarskjold died when his plane crashed while attempting to land at Ndola, in northern Zambia, just south of Katanga. The Secretary General had gone to the Congo a few days before to deal with what was a worsening political and military situation, hoping that his presence might help push the parties toward a more peaceful solution to the problems. ONUC troops had previously attacked Katangese forces, attempting to enforce UN resolutions by removing a number of foreign mercenary troops employed by the Katanga government. Hammarskjold, unable to resolve the problems from Leopoldville, determined to go to Katanga himself. It was the last decision he made as Secretary General.

After Hammarskjold's death the ONUC operations were thrown into a shambles from which they did not recover for many months. Even after the UN operation ended, the political situation in the Congo remained fluid, with several attempts to establish stable governments. Until a military coup in November 1965 led by General Joseph Mobutu (later known as Mobutu Sese-Seku), none were successful; he remains in power into the 1990s. But in maintaining his government over that time, Mobutu has discarded almost all vestiges of democracy and relies on the military to enforce his will.

Thus, UN troops, withdrawn on the fourth anniversary of Congolese independence, seem not to have left any substantial legacy of peace. The troubled efforts of the United Nations in this case bore little fruit. In fact, the former UN special representative in the Congo, Rajeshwar Dayal, concluded that "one consequence of Congo [operations of the UN] has been the atrophying of the peacekeeping functions of the United Nations."[6] Although that was almost certainly true in 1976 when Dayal made that assessment, the last two decades have seen some more successful UN peacekeeping operations, for example that in Cambodia, and other international efforts to accomplish similar goals, such as NATO efforts in Bosnia.

Nonetheless, the president of the United States was probably correct when he observed in an address at the Fiftieth Anniversary Celebration of the United Nations, "Peacekeeping can only succeed," he said, "when the parties to a conflict understand that they cannot profit from war." He

6. Dayal, *Mission for Hammarskjold*, p. 311.

also echoed Dayal's view (see Source 26) but no doubt with more recent examples than 1960–1961 in mind, "We have too often asked our peacekeepers to work miracles while denying them the military and political support required."[7] At the very least, that was the legacy of the United Nations in the Congo.

7. William J. Clinton, "Remarks by the President at UN50 Charter Ceremony," June 26, 1995; ⟨http://library.whitehouse.gov⟩.

CHAPTER FOURTEEN

FEMINISM AND THE

PEACE MOVEMENT (1910–1990)

Beginning in the 1820s in Britain, women throughout the world formed organizations that worked for demilitarization, pacifism, and, following the invention of the atomic bomb, an end to nuclear weapons. These organizations were particularly active in two periods: the pre– and post–World War I years, when they protested the military build-up that led to that war and then worked with other groups after Versailles to prevent future military conflicts; and the decades of the 1960s–1980s, when they protested the mushrooming nuclear arsenals that chilled the Cold War between the United States and the Soviet Union. Women's peace organizations, because they were often international or had international connections, promoted dialogue among women from diverse cultures, as well as working toward change in the policies of specific governments. Women who were peace activists varied widely in age, level of education, and social background. Some of them were also involved in groups pressing for womens' rights; others joined groups that included both female and male members and worked in other areas of social concern, such as civil rights or labor organizing.

Many of the women who belonged to women's peace groups were also active in peace organizations for both women and men that were forming at the same time. Those involved in women's groups, however, had to confront an issue that did not face those involved in mixed-sex groups—why was it important that there be separate groups for women working for peace? This was a tricky issue for many, for they were often also advocates of women's equality or greater political rights, and to stress the ways in which men and women *differed* might be counterproductive. Many women activists have left a record of the way in which they addressed this issue, both in the formal position papers of the groups they founded or were involved in, and in oral interviews conducted later. In this chapter you will be using both position papers and interviews, along with posters and drawings made by women peace activists, to answer the following questions:

How did twentieth-century women involved in women's peace groups view the relationship between their being women and their advocacy of peace? How did they translate their ideas into actions, and how did their ideas shape the types of actions they regarded as appropriate to achieving their aims?

BACKGROUND

Though the peace movement in the United States and Europe was probably most visible during the 1960s and 1970s in protests against the Vietnam War, calls for peace and disarmament have a long history. In 1793, Dr. Benjamin Rush, a signer of the Declaration of Independence, and Benjamin Bannecker, an African-American mathematician and architect, called for the establishment of a department of peace to go along with the recently established War Department. (In 1949, this branch of the government was reorganized and given the title Department of Defense; it is the largest federal department and, since its inception, has received the major portion of the federal budget.) After the Napoleonic Wars in 1816, English Quakers formed the London Peace Society, which quickly established branches in many other English towns. Women participated in these societies, and in the 1820s a few of them set up Female Auxiliary Peace Societies, the first organized women's peace groups. Swedish author Fredrika Bremer continued these

efforts in continental Europe, forming the Women's Peace Union in 1854 and writing against war during the Crimean War (1854–1856).

In the United States, the Civil War acted as a catalyst for peace groups in the way that the Napoleonic and Crimean Wars had sparked them in Europe. The American Civil War is often regarded as the first modern "total war," fought not only against a government or armed forces but against an opponent's economic means of existence and civilian population. It was clear to many people that future wars would bring similar devastation, and in the mid-nineteenth century a series of international peace congresses was held in Europe; these conferences called for the establishment of a congress of nations and international court of arbitration, the end of military education, and the control of arms sales. In the Western Hemisphere, the first Pan-American Congress met in 1889–90, and in 1899 one of the aims of these congresses became a reality with the establishment of the Permanent Court of Arbitration at The Hague in the Netherlands. (With the founding of the League of Nations after World

War I this body became the World Court, and, with the founding of the United Nations after World War II, the International Court of Justice; its permanent seat is still in The Hague.)

The peace movement of the nineteenth century was one of many movements of social reform whose agendas and aims were linked, and in which women played major roles. Individuals and groups advocating the abolition of slavery or the restriction of alcohol often linked their goals with those of the peace movement; the largest U.S. temperance group, for example, the Women's Christian Temperance Union, believing that the violence at home caused by alcohol was connected to the international violence of war, had a department of peace. The connections between the women's rights movement and the peace movement were even stronger. The major women's suffrage organizations, the International Council of Women and the International Woman Suffrage Alliance, had platforms that supported peace and arbitration, viewing their own international cooperation as a model that nations could follow. Not all peace organizations allowed women to be full members, inspiring some women to step up their call for equal rights in the same way that the abolition movement's exclusion of women had led female abolitionists to become stronger advocates of women's suffrage.

Despite all efforts for the peaceful arbitration of international disputes, the late nineteenth and early twentieth century saw a military build-up throughout Europe that, combined with intense nationalism and impe-

rialistic rivalries, led to the outbreak of World War I in 1914. Though the war caused a break in the workings of the Permanent Court of Arbitration and other international bodies, it served as a spur for women's peace activities. In 1915 Aletta Jacobs, a physician from the Netherlands, and Chrystal Macmillan, a lawyer from Scotland, organized an international women's peace conference. This was held at The Hague, with over one thousand delegates from twelve nations, though the British, French, and Russian delegates were forbidden by their governments to attend. The U.S. delegation of forty-seven women included many involved with the newly formed Women's Peace Party (WPP), including its chair, the social reformer Jane Addams. The meeting sent delegations to the leaders of many countries to lobby for an end to the war, and linked peace and women's rights explicitly in its closing statement:

> The International Congress of Women is convinced that one of the strongest forces for the prevention of war will be the combined influence of the women of all countries. . . . But as women can only make their influence effective if they have equal political rights with men, this Congress declares that it is the duty of the women of all countries to work with all their force for their political enfranchisement.[1]

1. "Program from the International Women's Congress, April 28, 29, 30, 1915," quoted in Harriet Hyman Alonso, *Peace as a Women's Issue: A History of the U.S. Movement for World Peace and Women's Rights* (Syracuse: Syracuse University Press, 1930), p. 68.

In the United States, the two aims of the International Congress for Women—world peace and political rights for women—came into conflict. Carrie Chapman Catt, one of the founders of the Women's Peace Party and the president of the National American Woman Suffrage Association, decided to offer President Wilson the assistance of suffragists as the United States entered the war, in 1917, in return for his support of women's suffrage. This move angered Addams and other leaders of the WPP (such as Crystal Eastman), who felt that the group's pacifism should never be compromised. The split, combined with government surveillance of antiwar groups and legal restrictions on their publication or dissemination of materials, meant that the WPP was not very active during the rest of the war. Immediately afterward, both sides gained victories: women were granted the vote in 1920, and the WPP, still alive, reorganized as the U.S. branch of the Women's International League for Peace and Freedom (WILPF). With women's suffrage achieved, Catt returned to peace organizing, founding the National Committee on the Cause and Cure of War (NCCW), a coalition of moderate women's groups such as the YWCA, National Council of Jewish Women, Women's Christian Temperance Union, the American Association of University Women, and several women's missionary groups. (World War I caused a similar split within British suffrage groups between those who decided to support the war effort and those who opposed the war.)

Government harassment of peace activists did not end when the war ended, for the WILPF offices in Chicago were frequently raided, and Emily Green Balch, the group's secretary-treasurer, lost her position on the faculty of Wellesley College because of her peace work. Women were often charged with being Communists because of their international interests and connections; the most notorious example was the "Spider Web" conspiracy chart, which from the early 1920s linked peace groups and Communist organizations. This chart was distributed by the War Department and often included the poem: "Miss Bolshevicki has come to town/With a Russian cap and German Gown/In Women's clubs she's sure to be found/For she's come to disarm AMERICA."[2] Balch's reputation was somewhat redeemed when she received the Nobel Peace Prize in 1946; Jane Addams received it in 1931, making them the only two U.S. women ever so honored.

During the 1920s and 1930s the major international peace efforts centered around establishing legislative or negotiated alternatives to war. The League of Nations was established by the peace treaties that ended World War I and was successful in preventing a number of conflicts during the 1920s. In 1928 many nations signed the Kellogg-Briand Pact calling for the use of peaceful means of resolving conflicts and condemning war as an instrument of national pol-

2. Quoted in Nancy Cott, *The Grounding of Modern Feminism* (New Haven: Yale University Press, 1987), p. 94.

icy, though the lack of any measures of enforcement meant that the pact would not have much actual effect. Both WILPF and NCCW supported these moves, although some more radical women's peace groups, such as the Women's Peace Union, felt they did not go far enough, and worked for a constitutional amendment to outlaw war completely. In their efforts to achieve world peace, all of the women's groups used tactics they had developed in the suffrage campaign—parades, letter-writing campaigns, petitions, direct lobbying—and in some cases they also used tactics of nonviolent resistance developed by Gandhi in the campaign for Indian independence from the British. During this period they often worked on Latin American issues, calling, for example, for the removal of U.S. troops from Haiti, where they were stationed from 1915 to 1937.

The rise of Nazism in Germany brought an end to the League of Nations, a renewal of war, and a crisis of conscience for peace groups. Most groups and individuals eventually gave up their absolute pacifist stance and opposed fascism, while continuing to oppose government policies that restricted freedom at home. For example, WILPF members in the United States supported conscientious objectors and opposed the internment of Japanese-Americans in camps, while those in Denmark and Norway were active in the resistance against the Nazis. After the war, WILPF was made an official nongovernmental organization affiliated with the United Nations, and it pushed for the establishment of UNICEF and the UN High Commission for Refugees.

The atomic bombs that ended World War II created a new issue for peace groups—nuclear disarmament. WILPF combined with mixed-sex groups such as the National Committee for a Sane Nuclear Policy (SANE) to protest nuclear testing. In 1961, five women in Washington who were members of SANE formed Women Strike for Peace (WSP) to organize one-day actions protesting American and Soviet nuclear policies. They galvanized thousands of women who had not been active before, particularly around the issue of the contamination of milk by strontium 90, a radioactive isotope that is the chief immediate hazard in the fallout from above-ground nuclear tests. WSP was intentionally nonhierarchical with no dues or official membership; most of the women who took part in its one-day strikes across the country were white, middle-class mothers who wore white gloves and brought photographs of their children along on demonstrations. Their ladylike demeanor and middle-class status did not protect them from government investigations in this virulently anticommunist period, and in 1962 members of WSP testified before the House Un-American Activities Committee. Their testimony made the committee look ridiculous, a point captured in a Herblock cartoon in the *Washington Post* in which one congressman is shown asking another: "I came in late; which was it that was un-American—women or peace?"[3] WSP actions influenced the passage of the 1963 Test-Ban Treaty, which banned testing of atomic weapons in the atmosphere, outer space, and below water.

From 1962 to 1975, the overriding issue for U.S. peace groups was the Vietnam War, and women's groups combined with many other peace groups in actions ranging from literature distribution to nonviolent protests to mass demonstrations such as the 1969 Vietnam Moratorium. Protests against the war took place not only in the United States but throughout the world, often organized by student groups as part of the international student movement. At the same time, the civil rights movement in the United States used similar tactics and often involved the same people as the antiwar movement, in the same way that the abolitionist and peace movements of the nineteenth century had been linked. Like those in the nineteenth century, these twentieth-century movements for social change also led to a reinvigoration of the women's rights movement. Though they had the right to vote and were working for social justice, women activists discovered that they were still excluded from leadership positions and that their opinions were not taken seriously. This twentieth-century women's rights movement is usually termed the *women's liberation movement*, and it eventually led to sweeping changes in women's

3. *Washington Post*, December 11, 1962.

legal rights, employment opportunities, and political power.

For women's peace organizations, this renewal of feminism often led to their making explicit connections again between the violence of war and violence against women. This became a more prominent part of women's peace activities after the end of the Vietnam War, when the attention of peace organizations in the United States and Europe was focused on the build-up of nuclear arsenals and an increase in military spending that was accompanied by cuts in social programs. New groups were formed, such as Women's Action for Nuclear Disarmament (WAND), Babies Against the Bomb, Women Opposed to the Nuclear Threat (WONT), and Women Against Military Madness (WAMM). New types of strategies were adopted, such as the establishment of permanent peace camps at missile and military production sites in Europe, the United States, Canada, and Australia, the theatrical action of thousands of women encircling the Pentagon in the Women's Pentagon Actions of 1980 and 1981. Older strategies, such as marches, petition campaigns, and civil disobedience, continued as women pressured their governments to begin nuclear disarmament. In 1985 an international group of women formed Women for a Meaningful Summit and visited the diplomats involved in the disarmament talks between the United States and the Soviet Union. (There were, however, no women present as negotiators.)

The decade 1975–1985 was designated by the United Nations as the Decade for Women, bringing worldwide organizing around issues involving women's economic, political, and social roles. The decade was highlighted by three international conferences: Mexico City in 1975, Copenhagen in 1980, and Nairobi in 1985. WILPF members tried to get disarmament language into the official statements at the Mexico City conference, but they were not successful; UN organizers regarded disarmament and peace issues as "too political" and not truly "women's issues." By the Copenhagen conference, however, this attitude had changed, and by 1985 the whole conference in Nairobi was titled "Equality, Development, and Peace." Alongside the official UN conference, nongovernmental organizations had their own much larger conference that brought together over 14,000 women from around the world. Statements emerging from this conference clearly defined peace as a primary women's issue, and also pointed to the environmental and economic costs of the arms race. In the decade since Nairobi, women's peace groups have addressed issues of racism and uneven worldwide development more directly, as their idea of "peace" has broadened from a focus on disarmament to include many issues of social justice.

THE METHOD

Traditionally, political history was thought of as the history of politics, with governmental and military leaders as the main actors, and laws, decrees, parliamentary debates, and other official documents as its primary records. These are still important, but today political history is being seen in a broader sense as the history not only of politics but of all relations involving power, and a wider range of sources is now being used to understand the power relationships in past societies and the ways in which individuals and groups who are not officially part of the government have shaped political decisions. This has meant relying on the documents produced by such individuals and groups, as well as interviews and discussions with a wide range of people. Political historians now use techniques of *oral history* first developed by anthropologists and social historians, which combine interviews with the exploration of written sources to arrive at a fuller picture of political changes and events.

Historians interested in women's lives in the recent past have also found oral history to be a valuable tool. Women's experiences and opinions are much less likely to make it into official records, both because women have been excluded from positions of political power until very recently and because groups that did include women often assumed that their views would be the same as those of the men in the group and so did not record them. Women's groups were much less likely than men's to keep formal records of their discussions, and their actions and roles have often been downplayed in newspaper and other published accounts. Thus interviews with participants are one of the few ways we can reconstruct women's involvement in groups that worked for political and social change and get some idea of their motivations and goals.

Because it allows you to come into direct contact with the history makers you wish to study, oral history is a very appealing research method, but it is most useful when written records are available for verification. Memories are not always accurate, and people may have reasons to vary their stories from what actually happened. For example, Margaret Hope Bacon discovered while writing a biography of Mildred Scott Olmsted, who held various national offices with WILPF from 1922 to 1966, that Olmsted "had forgotten the very existence of men and women who opposed her. Even when I would show her in writing the evidence of such opposition, she continued not to remember it."[4]

Your sources for this chapter include selections from the written documents and speeches of women involved in the peace movement, position papers and posters of several peace groups, and selections from oral interviews with several women activists. They have been arranged in

chronological order because it is important to keep the historical context in mind as you are reading and evaluating them. The documents come from the two key periods of the women's peace movement: the World War I era and the 1960s to the 1980s. These two periods were chosen because (1) women's peace groups were most active during these periods, and (2) these were periods of strong women's rights movements. Thus, women who were active in the peace movement during these times often felt compelled to address our first question directly, to comment about how they viewed the relationship between their being women and their advocating peace.

As you use the sources to answer the first question, you will be addressing an issue not only in political and women's history, but also in a very new area of historical investigation: *gender*. Only very recently have historians begun to study how past societies fashioned their notions of what it means to be male or female. They stress the fact that gender is not simply biological, but socially constructed and historically variable, for norms of feminine and masculine behavior change. Women peace activists were one of the few groups forced to confront the social construction of gender directly in what they were doing and thinking, as they addressed such questions as whether men were naturally more warlike than women or whether being mothers or prospective mothers made women more inclined to peace. As you read and look at the sources in

---

4. Margaret Hope Bacon, *One Woman's Passion for Peace and Freedom: The Life of Mildred Scott Olmsted* (Syracuse: Syracuse University Press, 1993), p. xvii.

this chapter, note whether they view women as somehow more peaceful than men. If they do, to what do the authors ascribe these differences: biology? education? social pressures? Do they think this inclination can or should be changed? Do they view women's peacefulness in a completely positive manner, or do they also see it as reflecting passivity? How do sources that do *not* view women as more peaceful than men explain why they feel there should be separate women's peace groups and why wars have traditionally been fought by male combatants?

Whatever their opinions about gender differences with regard to war and peace, women's peace groups carried out various actions to attempt to change government policies. Your sources discuss some of these actions. The second question in this chapter asks you to examine how these groups turned their ideas into actions, and how their ideas about gender differences shaped the types of actions they regarded as appropriate. As you read and look at the sources, note the types of actions that are discussed. Which of these appear to be shaped, either implicitly or explicitly, by the

fact that these are *women's* peace groups? What special problems and opportunities do the women involved in these groups see as arising from their being women or from their training about acceptable female norms of behavior? Do they see any tensions between their ideas and actions, and how do they resolve these?

Along with thinking about the content of your sources for this chapter, you also need to keep in mind differences between the type of sources that you are using, as would anyone using oral interviews. How might ideas expressed in the official position papers and speeches differ from those conveyed in interviews conducted later? All of the interviews published here were conducted by women sympathetic to the peace movement. How might this have shaped their content? As you answer the questions in this chapter, you should also think about the appropriateness of each type of source. What do the oral interviews add that could not be gained from other sources? What does the information gained from all these sources add to our picture of political developments in the twentieth century?

Source 1 from Olive Schreiner, Woman and Labor *(New York: Frederick A. Stokes, 1911), pp. 175, 176, 178–179, 180, 185.*

1. From Olive Schreiner, *Woman and Labor,* 1911

[*Olive Schreiner (1855–1920) was a
South African writer and women's
rights advocate.*]

There is, perhaps, no woman, whether she have borne children, or be merely potentially a child-bearer, who could look down upon a battlefield covered with slain, but the thought would rise in her, "So many mothers' sons! So many young bodies brought into the world to lie there! So many months of weariness and pain while bones and muscles were shaped within! So many hours of anguish and struggle that breath might be! So many baby mouths drawing life at women's breasts;—all this, that men might lie with glazed eyeballs, and swollen faces, and fixed, blue, unclosed mouths, and great limbs tossed. . . .

On that day when the woman takes her place beside the man in the governance and arrangement of external affairs of her race will also be that day that heralds the death of war as a means of arranging human differences. . . .

It is not because of woman's cowardice, incapacity, nor, above all, because of her general superior virtue, that she will end war when her voice is fully and clearly heard in the governance of states—it is because, on this one point, and on this point almost alone, the knowledge of woman, simply as woman, is superior to that of man; she knows the history of human flesh; she knows its cost; he does not. . . .

Men's bodies are our woman's works of art. Given to us power to control, we will never carelessly throw them in to fill up the gaps in human relationships made by international ambitions and greeds. The thought would never come to us as women, "Cast in men's bodies; settle the thing so!" . . .

War will pass when intellectual culture and activity have made possible to the female an equal share in the control and governance of modern national life; it will probably not pass away much sooner; its extinction will not be delayed much longer.

It is especially in the domain of war that we, the bearers of men's bodies, who supply its most valuable munition, who, not amid the clamor and ardor of battle, but singly, and alone, with a three-in-the-morning courage, shed our blood and face death that the battlefield might have its food, a food more precious to us than our heart's blood; it is we especially who, in the domain of war, have our word to say, a word no man can say for us. It is our intention to enter into the domain of war and to labor there till in the course of generations we have extinguished it.

Source 2 from Maude Royden, "War and the Women's Movement," in C. R. Buxton and G. L. Dickinson, Towards a Lasting Settlement *(London: Allen and Unwin, 1915), p. 106.*

2. Maude Royden on Women and War, 1915

[*A. Maude Royden (1876–1956) was a British writer and strong supporter of women's suffrage. She edited a suffragist newspaper and became the first woman to hold a regular preaching position in the Anglican Church.*]

The belief that women are innately more pacific than men has been severely shaken, if not altogether destroyed. It is now very evident that they can be as virulently militarist, as blindly partisan, not as the soldier, for in him such qualities are generally absent, but as the male non-combatant, for whom the same cannot always be said. Among women, as among men, there are extremists for war and for peace; pacifists and militarists; women who are as passionately convinced as Bernhardi[5] that war is a good thing, women who accept it as a terrible necessity, women who repudiate it altogether. All these views they share with men. There appears to be no cleavage of opinion along sex lines.

5. Friedrich von Bernhardi (1849–1930) was a German general and military writer known for his strong expression of German ambitions.

Source 3 from Jane Addams, "Account of Her Interview with the Foreign Ministers of Europe," speech published in The Survey, *New York, July 17, 1915. Quoted in Cambridge Women's Peace Collective,* My Country Is the Whole World: An Anthology of Women's Work on Peace and War *(London: Pandora Press, 1984), pp. 86–87.*

3. Jane Addams on Women and War, Carnegie Hall, New York, 1915

[Jane Addams (1860–1935), the American social reformer and founder of Hull House (a settlement house for immigrants in Chicago), was the first president of WILPF and, in 1931, was awarded the Nobel Peace Prize.]

Let me say just a word about the women in the various countries. The belief that a woman is against war simply and only because she is a woman and not a man, does not, of course, hold. In every country there are many, many women who believe that the War is inevitable and righteous, and that the highest possible service is being performed by their sons who go into the Army; just as there are thousands of men believing that in every country; the majority of women and men doubtless believe that.

But the women do have a sort of pang about it. Let us take the case of an artist, an artist who is in an artillery corps, let us say, and is commanded to fire upon a wonderful thing, say St Mark's at Venice, or the Duomo at Florence, or any other great architectural and beautiful thing. I am sure he would have just a little more compunction than the man who had never given himself to creating beauty and did not know the cost of it. There is certainly that deterrent on the part of the women, who have nurtured these soldiers from the time they were little things, who brought them into the world and brought them up to the age of fighting, and now see them destroyed. That curious revolt comes out again and again, even in the women who are most patriotic and who say: "I have five sons and a son-in-law in the trenches. I wish I had more sons to give." Even those women, when they are taken off their guard, give a certain protest, a certain plaint against the whole situation which very few men I think are able to formulate.

Now, what is it that these women do in the hospitals? They nurse the men back to health and send them to the trenches, and the soldiers say to them: "You are so good to us when we are wounded, you do everything in the world to make life possible and to restore us; why do you not have a little pity for us when we are in the trenches? Why do you not put forth a little of this same effort and this same tenderness to see what might be done to pull us out of those miserable places?"

That testimony came to us, not from the nurses of one country, and not from the nurses who were taking care of the soldiers on one side, but from those who were taking care of them upon every side.

And it seems to make it quite clear that whether we are able to recognize it or not, there has grown up a generation in Europe, as there has doubtless grown up a generation in America, who have revolted against war. It is a god they know not of, that they are not willing to serve; because all of their sensibilities and their training upon which their highest ideals depend, revolt against the whole situation.

Source 4 from Crystal Eastman, "A Program for Voting Women," pamphlet of Women's Peace Party of New York, March 1918, quoted in Blanche Wiesen Cook, Crystal Eastman on Women and Revolution *(New York: Oxford University Press, 1978), pp. 266–267.*

4. Crystal Eastman on the Women's Peace Movement, 1919

[*Crystal Eastman (1881–1928) was an American feminist, socialist, and labor lawyer. She was one of the founders of the Woman's Peace Party and the American Civil Liberties Union, which was originally set up to defend conscientious objectors.*]

Why a *Woman's* Peace Party?, I am often asked. Is peace any more a concern of women than of men? Is it not of universal human concern? For a feminist—one who believes in breaking down sex barriers so that women and men can work and play and build the world together—it is not an easy question to answer. Yet the answer, when I finally worked it out in my own mind, convinced me that we should be proud and glad, even as feminists, to work for the Woman's Peace Party.

To begin with, there is a great and unique tradition behind our movement which would be lost if we merged our Woman's Peace Party in the general revolutionary international movement of the time. Do not forget that it was women who gathered at The Hague, a thousand strong, in the early months of the war, women from all the great belligerent and neutral countries, who conferred there together in friendship and sorrow and sanity while the mad war raged around them. Their great conference, despite its soundness and constructive statesmanship, failed of its purpose, failed of its hope. But from the beginning of the war down to the Russo–German armistice there was no world step of such daring and directness, nor of such honest, unfaltering international spirit and purpose, as the organization of the International Committee of Women for Permanent Peace at The Hague in April, 1915. This Committee has branches in twenty-two countries. The Woman's Peace Party is the American section of the Committee, and our party, organized February 1 and 2, is the New York State Branch.

When the great peace conference comes, a Congress of Women made up of groups from these twenty-two countries will meet in the same city to demand that the deliberate intelligent organization of the world for lasting peace shall be the outcome of that conference.

These established international connections make it important to keep this a woman's movement.

But there is an added reason. We women of New York State, politically speaking, have just been born. We have been born into a world at war and this fact cannot fail to color greatly the whole field of our political thinking and to determine largely the emphasis of our political action. What we hope, then, to accomplish by keeping our movement distinct is to bring thousands upon thousands of women—women of the international mind—to dedicate their new political power, not to local reforms or personal ambitions, not to discovering the difference between the Democratic and Republican parties, but to *ridding the world of war.*

Source 5 from Käthe Kollwitz, The Sacrifice (Das Opfer), Rosenwald Collection, © 1996 Board of Trustees, National Gallery of Art, Washington, 1922/23. Woodcut in black, reworked with white gouache, on japan paper. Plate 1 from "War" (Klipstein 1955 177.ii/vii (trial proof). Image: .372 × .402 cm. ($14\frac{5}{8}$" × $15\frac{13}{16}$"); sheet: .415 × 437 cm. ($16\frac{5}{16}$" × $17\frac{3}{16}$").

5. Käthe Kollwitz, *The Sacrifice,* 1922

[*Käthe Kollwitz (1867–1945) was a German artist and sculptor whose works were ordered removed from public view by Adolf Hitler in the 1930s because of their political and social content.*]

[416]

Source 6 and 7 from Judith Porter Adams, Peacework: Oral Histories of Women Peace Activists *(Boston: Twayne Publishers, 1991), pp. 194–198.*

6. An Oral Interview with Dagmar Wilson, 1991

[Dagmar Wilson (b. 1916) is a graphic designer and children's book illustrator who was one of the founders of Women Strike for Peace.]

Thirty years ago I was responsible for an action that resulted in a national peace movement which is still going strong. Women Strike for Peace. I'm not really a "political" person, although I was brought up as a pacifist. As a child growing up in the years following the "war to end wars"—World War I—I believed that nations would work out their conflicts rather than fight. Other wonderful things were happening too. Women had been liberated—my mother was a voter. I went to a progressive school for boys and girls, which in Europe, where I grew up, was not common. Socialism seemed like a wonderful experiment. I really believed that the world was moving forward in many areas, all favorable to mankind.

However, after World War II, I realized that there was something happening that was beyond politics and that affected all human beings. I felt that the question of survival on earth was not a matter of politics, nor a matter of power between governments, but was a matter of deeper concerns common to all humanity.

Many things moved me to become active step by step, but the last straw was the arrest of Bertrand Russell in 1961 in London's Trafalgar Square. He sat down with others to block traffic as a protest. He let it be known that having tried through normal channels to alert the world to the extreme danger that we were in, pitting ourselves against each other with these destructive new weapons, he felt it necessary to make a gesture. I was impressed by that. One night soon after his arrest, I was talking about his protest to some English friends who were visiting my husband and me here in the United States. They were turning me off with jokes and making cynical wisecracks. They were intelligent people distinguished in their professions, and I was distressed by their response. This was also the time of the Berlin Wall. The media had said it might mean war, and of course, war would mean nuclear war. Our administration was telling us to build fallout shelters to protect our families. I felt indignant, more than indignant. I felt insulted as a human being that responsible people, governments, were asking us to do anything so stupid, as ineffectual as this, instead of coming to grips with the problems that were causing the tensions we were facing. My husband, who knew me well enough to realize that I was getting quite tense, said, "Well, women are

very good at getting their way when they make up their minds to do something."

That phrase stayed with me. The next day I called a friend at the Committee
for a Sane Nuclear Policy in Washington, D.C., to ask if SANE was going to
respond to the Committee of 100 in support of Russell's actions. I said, "I feel
like chartering a plane and filling it with women to picket the jail." This guy
said, "Well, that's an idea for your women's movement." I said, "Women's
movement? What do you mean?" I hadn't mentioned anything of that kind; I
hadn't even thought about it. Anyway, he gave me an idea.

I stayed by the phone and thought, and thought, and thought. I said to myself, "Well, what about a women's movement?" I picked up the telephone and
started calling all my women friends from my phone book and Christmas
card list. I wanted to see what they thought. I have always been very tele-
phone-shy, so this was an unusual thing for me to do. It turned out that everybody that I spoke with had been worrying about this problem. We women
thought that the fallout shelter idea was an inane, insane, and an unsuitable
response to the world situation and spelled disaster. The response I got was
really quite enlightening. Each woman had it in the front of her mind, including a lot of women who were really not politically active.

I soon gathered together in my own living room a small group of women
out of those whom I had called. Three days later we met at my house. Six days
later, at a big meeting planned by SANE, we announced an "action." This
marked the formation of Women Strike for Peace.

What we planned was a one-day event. The women would go on strike and
leave the men "holding the baby." We said: "Now what do you think would
happen if all the women went on strike?" The whole country would stand
still. We thought it was a good way to demonstrate our own power and show
that women were an essential part of our social structure and had a right to be
heard. Six weeks from that day, there were demonstrations in sixty cities in
the United States.

We were not part of the women's liberation movement. Ours was a peace
movement activated by women. And there is a difference. We were women
working for the good of humanity. One woman in our early group who was a
very good writer wrote a statement of purpose that was powerful. One of the
strengths of the movement was that it was cliché free. We were not political
activists who were used to the old phrases. We were speaking much more
out of our everyday experiences, but we were educated and literate. This was
our statement:

> We represent a resolute stand of women in the United States against the unprece-
> dented threat to life from nuclear holocaust. We're women of all races, creeds, and
> political persuasions who are dedicated to the achievement of general and complete
> disarmament under effective international control. We cherish the right and accept
> the responsibility of the individual in democratic society to act and influence the

course of government. We demand of governments that nuclear weapons tests be banned forever, that the arms race end, and that the world abolish all weapons of destruction under United Nations safeguards. We urge immediate planning at local, state and national levels for a peacetime economy with freedom and justice for all. We urge our government to anticipate world tensions and conflicts through constructive nonmilitary actions and through the United Nations. We join with women throughout the world to challenge the right of any nation or group of nations to hold the power of life or death over the world.

That really sums up my personal beliefs; I couldn't have stated it as well.

We saw women as a vehicle for a new peace action. There were already many peace groups and individuals, but the situation was still grave. These groups had become part of the peace establishment, and we didn't think they were as effective as they once were. We were able to do things that couldn't have happened in an already existing organization. I hoped that WSP would go on as long as it was effective, but I believed that in time it would be replaced by something else.

We had learned that nuclear testing was having hazardous effects on our environment, specifically on the open fields on which cows were grazing. This was contaminating the milk supply with strontium 90. This touched us very closely. We found out that strontium 90 was replacing calcium in children's bones. When we heard voices from Capitol Hill saying, "Well, well, it's too bad; this is just one of the hazards of the nuclear age," we really began to wonder about the sanity of our nation's leaders. Women Strike for Peace was an idea whose time had come. I was the lightning conductor; it just happened to be me. The time had come when either the people of the Earth would live together or die together.

In January of WSP's second year the New York women decided to come to the White House to stage a demonstration. They filled the longest train that had ever left Pennsylvania Station in the history of the railway, all with women. That day President Kennedy was scheduled for a press conference, and we thought no one would pay any attention to our demonstration. There was an enormous rain storm that soaked all the women who were coming off the train, ruining their hats—we always made a "respectable" appearance with hats and gloves. They walked through the rain to the White House and became soaked to the skin. At the president's press conference a well-known journalist representing the *New York Post* asked, "Do you think that demonstrations at this time have any influence on you and on the public and on the direction which we take in policy?" The president replied by saying that he had seen the large numbers of women out there in the rain and that we could understand that he agreed with our message and that our message had been received. We got wonderful publicity out of that, since the press conference was televised and broadcast nationally.

Soon after we began with one-day actions all over the country. We had permanent relationships with the sixty cities that had demonstrated on the first day. We had established a phone "tree" so that we could organize actions quickly. Eventually we realized that we had to have regular meetings and we had to have a national office, and so a national movement grew from our simple beginning with a one-day action. But we never had elected representatives; we preferred a movement rather than an organization. We continued to make decisions by consensus. So many people had been penalized in the past for left-wing activities. Our structure—or lack of it—meant that it would be very, very hard for anyone to be held accountable for the whole movement.

We soon had a program researching the effects of strontium 90. We took groups of people to government offices where we found everybody very willing to give us the facts. They were not reassuring. However, getting the word out was difficult. We took the press with us wherever we could. The publications that we issued were used in universities. We were respected; we weren't just a hysterical mob of women. People recognized that we had brains, and we were sensible.

We organized a delegation of one hundred women—fifty from the United States and fifty from European countries, including the Soviet Union—to visit the 1962 eighteen-nation disarmament conference in Geneva. We lobbied all the delegations and wanted to address the plenary session. We were informed that instead of addressing the plenary session, we could meet with the Soviet and United States cochairs. A young woman—she was a Quaker—volunteered to organize us for the meeting. I learned the power of Quaker silence from her. We marched through a light rain to where the sessions were held in the suburbs of Geneva. The rain seemed to be a good omen for us; we'd always succeeded in the rain. We walked in silence, which was quite a tour de force for us chatterboxes. We waited for an hour and forty-five minutes in total silence. Finally the Soviet and American cochairmen, Valaerian Zorin and Arthur Dean, came in with their translators, secretaries, and a few press. The important thing was that they walked into a room that was totally silent; the silence was palpable. Then I got up and spoke, which I did feeling rather like a schoolmistress. We wanted them to know that we held them responsible for the future of the human race and we thought it was time they got on with the business of ending the nuclear arms race. We presented them with mountains of petitions. The press coverage in Europe of our action was excellent. That was our first really international venture.

WSP played a critical role in the 1963 Partial Test Ban Treaty's passage, but our greatest triumph was our confrontation with the House Un-American Activities Committee. They pounced on us in 1962 by subpoenaing nine WSP women. We were advised by others who had a go-around with the Committee that we "should not make a big fuss." But one of our women said, "No, this is not the way we're going to do it. If they're subpoenaing Dagmar Wilson, we should all volunteer to testify." Now that was an absolutely brilliant idea. We sent telegrams through our network saying, "Volunteer to testify. Come if you can. Hospitality offered. Bring your baby." Hundreds of women volunteered to testify. This was a new twist—most people were tempted to run a mile when the Committee pointed its magic wand at them.

I was the last one to be subpoenaed. It was a great relief to me, to be able to have my say. I had the benefit of two days of hearings before my turn came. By that time I felt quite comfortable. My testimony was summed up best by someone who said that I treated the attorney for the Committee just as though he were a rather tiresome dinner partner.

Our WSP meetings were very informal, with no protocol; we ran them like we ran our carpools. Well, that was extremely baffling to these political gentlemen. And at one point one said, "I don't understand how you get anything done at all." I answered, "Well, it puzzles us sometimes too."

The Committee was trying to find out if there was Communist influence in the peace movement. WSP was concerned about war and peace; we didn't think the world was worth blowing up over political differences. We could see ourselves marching arm in arm with Soviet mothers for the sake of our children, so we were not intimidated by the Committee's strategies. I was asked at the end of my testimony whether we would examine our books to see if we had Communist women in our midst, and I said, "Certainly not"— we would not do anything of the kind. "In fact," I said, "unless the whole human race joins us in our quest for peace, God help us."

One of the funny things about our "inquisition" before the Committee was that we were asked, in a sinister tone, if we had a mimeograph machine. It's true that we were mimeographing materials to distribute among ourselves. You know, someone's baby was always around, and we kidded ourselves that the print might appear on a child's diaper. Anybody turning a baby over might find a description of where our next meeting was going to be. So much for the sinister implication of a mimeograph machine.

We got very good press. I think that everybody was thoroughly fed up with the Committee. Congress was embarrassed by it, and the press was bored with it.

7. An Oral Interview with Madeline Duckles, 1991

[Madeline Duckles (b. 1916) joined WILPF in the 1940s and was an organizer for Women Strike for Peace. During the Vietnam War, she helped organize a program to fly napalm-burned children to the United States for treatment.]

We've made progress in civil rights, environmental issues; we've progressed on every level except for peace. Here we are, armed to the teeth when Women Strike for Peace began protesting nuclear testing when strontium 90 was appearing in children's teeth. We wanted to do something quickly. So women all over the country called a "strike" and left their work and families to protest. At that time, we had exploded two bombs and now the world has about fifty thousand nuclear weapons. So we haven't made any progress at all!

And WILPF was working hard right after women's suffrage trying to get women more involved in the political process, trying to stop war toys and get the U.S. out of Central America in 1917 and we're still there now. The problems persist.

My political education began when I went to the University of California here at Berkeley. At that time the YWCA was where the action was. There were a few remarkable women in charge of it. There were discussions of race relations, the Spanish Civil War, and labor issues. I began at the University in 1933, and this was the year of the great longshoremen's strike in San Francisco. I had never been to a union meeting before. We were gathering canned goods for the strikers. It was for me a very exciting time. All kinds of political issues were discussed.

I don't remember rejecting the values of my family, which I suppose you would call redneck, but working for peace and justice issues seemed to me natural and right and proper. When people say to me, "How do you happen to be in the peace movement?" it always seems to me the most ridiculous question because we've reached the point where this *should* be the normal thing for people to do. But still, war and preparation for war is normal, and to be in the peace movement is abnormal.

Women bring to the peace movement the best feminist qualities, which are patience, tolerance, compassion, and a hell of a lot of intelligence. We're much more loath to make judgments. We have the courage to change our minds. We're not nearly so reticent about admitting mistakes and changing course when we do wrong. Of course, there are aggressive women, but they are not the "norm" for women.

The women's movement activated a great many women, and it activated them on the issues of equality for women in jobs and the Equal Rights Amendment more than it did on the peace issues. For a long time we were trying to get to NOW to set up a peace platform. I have a speech I give on any occasion that peace is a woman's issue. My current speech, in case you would like to hear it, is that foreign policy must become a community issue, when in an administration, foreign policy is military policy. Military policy means a loss of our community services and ultimately a loss of our lives. We're in double jeopardy: if the weapons they're making are used, we'll all be dead, and meanwhile, the arms race is killing us economically. I'll stop my speech there.

Source 8 from a leaflet distributed at the Women's Pentagon Action in 1980 and published by the Women's Pentagon Action Group, Washington, D.C.

8. Unity Statement, Women's Pentagon Action, 1980

These are the frightening facts, and the hopeful ideas and feelings that are bringing women together. We invite you to read them.

We are gathering at the Pentagon on November 16 because we fear for our lives. We fear for the life of this planet, our Earth, and the life of the children who are our human future.

We are women who come in most part from the northeastern region of our United States. We are city women who know the wreckage and fear of city streets, we are country women who grieve the loss of the small farm and have lived on the poisoned earth. We are young and older, we are married, single, lesbian. We live in different kinds of households, in groups, families, alone; some are single parents.

We work at a variety of jobs. We are students-teachers-factory workers-office workers-lawyers-farmers-doctors-builders-waitresses-weavers-poets-engineers-homeworkers-electricians-artists-blacksmiths. We are all daughters and sisters.

We have come here to mourn and rage and defy the Pentagon because it is the workplace of the imperial power which threatens us all. Every day while we work, study, love, the colonels and generals who are planning our annihilation walk calmly in and out the doors of its five sides. They have accumulated over 30,000 nuclear bombs at the rate of three to six bombs every day.

They are determined to produce the billion-dollar MX missile. They are creating a technology called Stealth—the invisible, unperceivable arsenal. They have revived the cruel old killer, nerve gas. They have proclaimed Directive 59 which asks for 'small nuclear wars, prolonged but limited.' The Soviet Union works hard to keep up with United States initiatives. We can destroy each other's cities, towns, schools, children many times over. The United States has sent 'advisors,' money and arms to El Salvador and Guatamala to enable those juntas to massacre their own people.

The very same men, the same legislative committees that offer trillions of dollars to the Pentagon have brutally cut day care, children's lunches, battered women's shelters. . . .

The President has just decided to produce the neutron bomb, which kills people but leaves property intact.

There is fear among the people, and that fear, created by the industrial militarists is used as an excuse to accelerate the arms race. "We will protect you . . ." they say, but we have never been so endangered, so close to the end of human time.

We women are gathering because life on the precipice is intolerable.

We want to know what anger in these men, what fear which can only be satisfied by destruction, what coldness of heart and ambition drives their days.

We want to know because we do not want that dominance which is exploitative and murderous in international relations, and so dangerous to women and children at home—we do not want that sickness transferred by the violent society through the fathers to the sons. . . .

We want an end to the arms race. No more bombs. No more amazing inventions for death.

Sources 9 and 10 from Lynne Jones, ed., Keeping the Peace: A Women's Peace Handbook
(London: The Women's Press, 1983), pp. 23, 24, 25–26; pp. 64–67.

9. Nottingham Women Oppose the Nuclear Threat (WONT) on Working as a Group, 1981

Nottingham WONT started as a women's group against nuclear power. . . .

As our group has evolved, another motive for meeting as women on the nuclear issue has become important—that is, the need to develop a specifically feminist analysis of nuclear threat, and to show the links between women's oppression and nuclear technology. We feel that feminism has a particular analysis of the structures and causes of all violence (not just the "women's issues" of sexual and domestic violence), and of the changes necessary to remove it. We identify the primary source of violence as gender structure in the individual, in families, in societies, and believe that while society remains deeply sexist, no peace movement can win long-term substantial victories.

We don't think that women have a special role in the peace movement because we are "naturally" more peaceful, more protective, or more vulnerable than men. Nor do we look to women as the "Earth Mothers" who will save the planet from male aggression. Rather, we believe that it is this very role division that makes the horrors of war possible. The so-called masculine, manly qualities of toughness, dominance, not showing emotion or admitting dependence, can be seen as the driving force behind war; but they depend on women playing the opposite (but not equal) role, in which the caring qualities are associated with inferiority and powerlessness. So women's role in peacemaking should not be conciliatory but assertive, breaking out of our role, forcing men to accept women's ideas and organisation, forcing them to do their own caring. Women have for too long provided the mirrors in which men see their aggression as an heroic quality, and themselves magnified larger than life. Nuclear technology is built on the arrogance and confidence of mastery (over nature as over women) which this has fed. . . .

WONT groups are specifically feminist, so they could not by themselves constitute a broad-based mass women's anti-nuclear movement. Most of the women involved in WONT are also involved in the women's movement, and many have an "alternative life-style," living in shared households, not having a 'straight' job, etc. However, we want to reach all kinds of women, and to do this, we have tried giving talks to women's groups, running workshops, doing street theatre, etc. Our aim is to help create a broad-based women's peace movement of which WONT would be an autonomous part. . . . Our approach to actions is close to that of the nonviolent direction action wing of the national movement, and we use street theatre, striking symbolic actions, and music, rather than mass demonstrations and rallies.

[424]

WONT is a decentralised organisation. Local groups are autonomous and very varied. WONT exists nationally through national gatherings once or twice a year, regional meetings, personal contacts and an occasional newsletter. There is a national contact address, and groups take turns at answering mail. We have a telephone tree for urgent messages. Nottingham WONT meets weekly, and we often see each other during the week as many of us live or work close to each other. (This creates problems for new women joining the group who are not in that particular community.) There are no "officers" but we take turns to facilitate. This means preparing an agenda, seeing that we stick to the point in discussions, are working reasonably efficiently, and that everyone gets a chance to contribute. It's an easy job in our group, for everyone is aware of these things; so the facilitator just had to be a bit more aware, to notice the time, to sense we are nearing a decision. We reach decisions by consensus. If we cannot reach a decision, it is usually because we are all unsure, rather than because different women hold irreconcilable views. We usually approach decisions by a general discussion, and then let each woman say what she thinks to see if there is general agreement. If one woman disagrees with a generally held view, then we try to see if any accommodation can be made to satisfy her as well. We will postpone a decision to another meeting if the discussion goes on a long time without getting anywhere.

10. Tamar Swade on Nuclear Weapons, 1983

[*Tamar Swade was an English antinuclear
activist and the founder of
Babies Against the Bomb.*]

Being pregnant and in the anti-nuclear movement happened at the same time for me. I joined a study group with five other women and we gave talks on nuclear power. This led to our writing the booklet, *Nuclear Resisters*.

By then my baby had been born and the effort of demand-feeding it at the same time as researching and writing my share of the booklet was enormous. The group was wonderfully supportive, but I felt that the pressures of coping with a newborn baby—the lack of sleep, exhaustion and lack of time—clashed with the needs of an ordinary group. I wasn't free to run off and collect things or proofread as the others were, and I could no longer get out easily in the evenings when the usual anti-nuclear/peace meetings take place.

I'd suddenly become a different kind of social being and I realised I needed to start a group where everybody understood my position because they were in it too, where it was fine to go "brrm-brrm" or "whoopsy!" to a child in the middle of a sentence if necessary, or change a nappy.

I found that I had joined a separate species of two-legged, four-wheeled creatures who carry their young in push-chair pouches, who emerge from their homes during the day to swarm the parks, forage in the super-markets and disappear without trace at nightfall. Occasionally some converged for a "coffee morning" or a mother-and-baby group run by the National Childbirth Trust. Here there was much discussion about nappy rash, (not) sleeping and other problems pertaining to the day-to-day survival of mother and infant.

If only these thousands of women could inform and organise themselves, what an untapped force for peace! Why not start a mother-and-baby group whose discussions included *long-term* survival?

At first, therefore, we were called "Mother and baby anti-nuclear group." As this was rather a mouthful, we were somehow gradually shortened to "Babies against the Bomb," which stayed with us. We meet during the day, with our babies or young children. Meetings are friendly and informal and we campaign wherever and however we feel we can be most effective.

Several women who have enquired about the group have never been involved in any campaigning at all, but the fact of having a child has made them think differently about the future. Those of us who had been involved before often feel an added urgency to our desire for peace after having a child.

There are some feminists who frown upon this attitude and I would like to answer them.

There is something utterly vulnerable and loveable about a newborn baby, something wholly fascinating about this creature whose every impulse is towards survival but who is so dependent for it upon others. Its cries wrench the heart and it is agonising to think of someone so little and blameless being hurt.

I am responsible for its existence—and no amount of word-juggling can get away from this. It is my responsibility and my urgent desire to ensure its survival, to speak for its rights since it can't do so for itself.

And it's not only for my child I feel this. The same feeling now extends to all children. Through my child the immorality of this world where people needlessly starve to death, has become intolerable. With pain I could not have known before, I grieve for those women in the Third World who hear their children crying for food but who can't feed them or themselves.

I know hundreds of women who feel this. Each of them in turn probably knows hundreds of others who feel the same. Some are feminists through and through, others don't know what "feminism" means. One woman told me that the mention of nuclear war conjures up the waking nightmare of her children burning. Another pictures kissing her children goodbye for the last time. A third said her particular nightmare was that the four-minute warning would come while she was at work and she wouldn't be able to cross town in time to get to them. . . .

In fact, it seems that millions of women in numerous cultures throughout history have had similar experiences in relation to their children. Should we all feel ashamed of this deep gut-feeling? For me, feminism is about choice, about every woman's freedom to feel and act and be valued. Does it make me any less of a person if my immediate, instinctive reaction to nuclear war is in my capacity as a mother? Judging by my friends in the campaign who are mothers, certainly not! Does it mean that I suddenly care less about living myself? Rubbish! It's more that another dimension had been added to my caring.

Our priority is peace. What does it matter how we come to want it? Let's be tolerant, supportive, sisterly. This will make us stronger and more effective; we are less likely to succeed if we are divided. If *we* can't do it, what hope is there for the rest of the world?

Source 11 from Coretta Scott King, "The Judgement of History Will Show," speech given at the International Women's Conference for Peace and Nuclear Disarmament (1984), and published in the Newsletter of the Center for Defence Information, vol. 13, no. 8.

11. Coretta Scott King on Women and the Nuclear Arms Race, 1984

[*Coretta Scott King (b. 1927), the widow of Dr. Martin Luther King, Jr., is a civil rights activist and has been an active member of WILPF since 1960. She is president of the Martin Luther King, Jr., Center for Non-Violent Social Change.*]

You can't fight poverty and discrimination, you can't provide health, security and decent housing, and you can't have a clean environment in the lengthening shadow of nuclear arsenals. The nuclear arms race creates far-reaching social problems in a number of ways. The judgement of history will show that the massive economic insecurity and the psychological numbing and alienation caused by militarization of commerce and society have had a profound effect upon our lives. The proliferation of nuclear weapons is not only the major threat to the survival of humanity; it is also the primary cause of poverty and economic stagnation around the world. The arms race is a shameful theft of funds from programs that would enrich our planet. Here in America, the cost of one bomber could pay for two fully equipped hospitals. With a serious arms control program (not just shallow treaties for show which allow weapons to continue to proliferate less noticed by the public than before), the nations of the world could apply countless billions of dollars saved to advancing social and economic progress.

The supporters of the nuclear arms race claim that peace can only be achieved through strength. Apparently, they mean an ability to destroy the world an infinite number of times. We must ask just what it is that makes the nation safe and secure. If we ruin our economy to engage in an accelerated arms race, are we really any stronger? When we demoralize and polarize millions of jobless, homeless and impoverished Americans, it seems to me that we are dangerously weak at the very fabric of our society. In this sense, the nuclear arms race breeds insecurity, not strength.

Sources 12 and 13 from Lynne Jones, ed., Keeping the Peace: A Women's Peace Handbook (London: The Women's Press, 1983), p. 125; p. 19.

13. Poster for a Multigroup Demonstration in Amsterdam Against the Installation of Cruise Missiles, 1981[6]

12. Poster for Families Against the Bomb Rally, 1982

6. The main text reads "Against new atomic weapons in Europe."

Source 14 from Ann Snitow, "Holding the Line at Greenham Common: Being Joyously Political in Dangerous Times," Mother Jones, February/March 1985.

14. Ann Snitow on Women Against Military Buildups, 1985

[*Ann Snitow (b. 1943) is an American writer who also teaches literature and women's studies.*]

Back in 1981 when I first heard about the women's peace camp at Greenham Common, I was impressed but a little worried, too. Here was a stubborn little band of squatters obstructing business as usual at a huge military base. But the early media reports celebrated these women as orderly housewives and mothers who would never make this vulgar noise just for themselves but were naturally concerned about their children, innocent animals, and growing plants.

My feminist reaction was: not *again*. I had joined the women's liberation movement in 1970 to escape this very myth of the special altruism of women, our innate peacefulness, our handy patience for repetitive tasks, our peculiar endurance—no doubt perfect for sitting numbly in the Greenham mud, babies and arms outstretched, begging men to keep our children safe from nuclear war.

We feminists had argued back then that women's work had to be done by men, too: no more "women only" when it came to emotional generosity or trips to the launderette. We did form women-only groups—an autonomous women's movement—but this was to forge a necessary solidarity for resistance, not to cordon off a magic femaleness as distorted in its way as the old reverence for motherhood. Women have a long history of allowing their own goals to be eclipsed by others, and even feminist groups have often been subsumed by other movements. Given this suspiciously unselfish past, I was uneasy with women-only groups that did not concentrate on overcoming the specific oppression of women.

And why should demilitarization be women's special task? If there's one thing in this world that *won't* discriminate in men's favor, it's a nuclear explosion. Since the army is a dense locale of male symbols, actions, and forms of association, let men sit in the drizzle, I thought; let *them* worry about the children for a change.

But even before going to Greenham I should have known better than to have trusted its media image. If the women were such nice little home birds, what were they doing out in the wild, balking at male authority, refusing to shut up or go back home? I've been to Greenham twice now in the effort to understand why many thousands of women have passed through the camps, why thousands are organized in support groups all over Britain and beyond, why thousands more can be roused to help in emergencies or show up for big actions.

What I discovered has stirred my political imagination more than any activism since that first, intense feminist surge 15 years ago. Though I still have many critical questions about Greenham, I see it as a rich source of fresh thinking about how to be joyously, effectively political in a conservative, dangerous time. . . .

The Greenham women I talked to take great pains to point out that the purpose of Greenham is not to exclude men but to include women—at last. Though a few women there might still tell you women are biologically more peaceful than men, this view has been mostly replaced by a far more complex analysis of why women need to break with our old, private complicity with public male violence. No one at Greenham seems to be arguing that the always evolving Greenham value system is inevitably female. The women recognize their continuity with the Quakers, with Gandhi, with the entire pacifist tradition, and with the anarchist critique of the state. At the same time, women, the Greenham campers believe, may have a separate statement to make about violence because we have our own specific history in relation to it. . . .

A whole activist generation is being forged at Greenham, not of age but of shared experience. These women are disobedient, disloyal to civilization, experienced in taking direct action, advanced in their ability to make a wide range of political connections. The movable hearth is their schoolroom, where they piece together a stunning if raffish political patchwork.

Before visiting Greenham, I had feared that its politics would prove simpleminded, that those absolutes, life and death, would have cast more complex social questions in the shade. How, for instance, could the old question What do women want? survive when the subject is Mutual Assured Destruction (MAD, U.S. military slang for nuclear deterrence). . . .

I wonder if women are having to learn at Greenham—with a difference—what men learn too early and carry too far: the courage to dare, to test reaction, to define oneself *against* others. Nonviolent direct action takes great courage. The big men on their horses or machines are doing as ordered—which is comfortable for them. In contrast, it can be truly terrifying to refuse to do what an angry, pushing policeman tells you to do. For women particularly, such acts are fresh and new and this cutting across the grain of feminine socialization is a favorite, daring sport of the young at the fence. Such initiations give women a revolutionary taste of conflict, lived out fully, in our own persons, with gender no longer a reliable determinant of the rules

Certainly it is no use for women to turn self-righteous, as I had found myself doing—claiming a higher moral ground than men. On that ground we are admired but ignored. As Dorothy Dinnerstein has argued in *The Mermaid and the Minotaur,* emotional women have traditionally been treated like court jesters that the king keeps around to express his own anxieties—and thus vent them harmlessly. A woman's body lying down in a road in front of a missile

[430]

launcher has a very different symbolic resonance for everyone from that of a male body in the same position. Greenham's radical feminist critics wonder just what kind of peace a female lying down can bring. Won't men simply allow women to lie in the mud forever because the demonstrators themselves only underline men's concept of what is female (passivity, protest, peace) and what is male (aggression, action, war)?

Before I came to Greenham, I shared these worries. But at Greenham at its best, women's nonviolent direct action becomes not another face of female passivity but a difficult political practice with its own unique discipline. The trick—a hard one—is to skew the dynamics of the old male-female relationships toward new meanings, to interrupt the old conversation between overconfident kings and hysterical, powerless jesters. This will surely include an acknowledgment of our past complicity with men and war making and a dramatization of our new refusal to aid and assist. (I think of a delicious young woman I heard singing out to a group of also very young soldiers: "We don't find you sexy anymore, you know, with your little musket, fife, and drum.")

Perhaps some of the new meanings we need will be found buried in the old ones. If women feel powerless, we can try to share this feeling, to make individual men see that they, too, are relatively powerless in the face of a wildly escalating arms race. Naturally, this is a message men resist, but the women at Greenham are endlessly clever at dramatizing how the army shares their impotence: The army cannot prevent them from getting inside the fence or shaking it down. It cannot prevent them from blockading the gates. It cannot prevent them from returning after each eviction.

Or, rather, it could prevent all this, but only by becoming a visibly brutal force, and this would be another kind of defeat, since the British armed services and police want to maintain their image of patriarchal protectors; they do not want to appear to be batterers of nonviolent women. Greenham women expose the contradictions of gender: by being women they dramatize powerlessness but they also disarm the powerful. . . .

QUESTIONS TO CONSIDER

As you read and look at the sources, you need to keep in mind the historical context in which the women were writing, and think how this influenced their ideas and plans for action. Source 1 was written in 1911, before women in most U.S. states or any European country (except Finland) had the vote and before the outbreak of World War I. How might these factors have affected Olive Schreiner's views of what would happen when women gained a political voice? To what does she attribute gender differences in attitudes toward war?

Sources 2 and 3 both date from 1915. The outbreak of World War I was accompanied by intense nationalistic and anti-German rhetoric and demonstrations, first in England and later in the United States. How might this have shaped Maude Royden's and Jane Addams's views about whether women were "naturally" more peaceful? Both Schreiner and Addams comment on a woman's role as a mother to explain the source of women's dislike of war; what differences do you see in the two authors on this point?

Source 4 dates from 1919, just after the end of World War I and as women in the United States and England were being given the right to vote. What does Crystal Eastman hope will be the focus of women's political activities? Why does she feel the Women's Peace conference at The Hague was important? What makes the women's peace movement distinctive in her opinion? How does this differ from the ideas of Schreiner and Addams about why women are particularly interested in peace?

Source 5 is the first visual source for this chapter, a woodcut created by the German artist Käthe Kollwitz shortly after World War I. Kollwitz lost her son in that war, and though she had been a supporter of German aims at the beginning of the war, by its end she was joining antiwar demonstrations and promoting pacifism. She produced numerous images in the 1920s and 1930s that were later used by various peace groups on posters and pamphlets, including this one, entitled *The Sacrifice*. How does this fit with the ideas expressed in the written sources about mothers' response to war?

With Sources 6 and 7, we jump ahead to the 1960s and the beginnings of the women's antinuclear movement. These sources come from oral interviews with two of the women who started Women Strike for Peace, Dagmar Wilson and Madeline Duckles. Unlike Sources 1 through 4, which are speeches and position papers, Sources 6 and 7 are oral histories produced long after the events they describe. What drew these women into working for peace? What do they see as distinctive about women's involvement in peace groups? These sources refer explicitly to the types of actions WSP was involved in; how were these shaped by the fact that this was a women's peace group? How was the response these actions generated on the part of political officials shaped by the gender of those who took part? By their status as middle-class women and mothers? How do the organizational structures and methods of making decisions in WSP make it different from other political groups? How is this—at least in Wilson's eyes—related to the fact that this is a women's group? What aspects of these interviews might have been shaped by the fact that they were recorded thirty years after WSP was founded?

Sources 8 through 11 are again statements of individuals or groups, written in the early 1980s to describe their motivations, aims, and methods of action. Source 8 is the "Unity Statement" for the Women's Pentagon Action, written in 1980 by Grace Paley in consultation with many others. What does it say has motivated women to action? Though its views on the relationship between women and peace are not expressed as explicitly as they have been in some of the other sources you have read, what implicit connection does the credo make? What connection does it make between the arms race and other economic issues, and how does it connect these to women? How does this compare to the way in which this was done in the oral interview with Madeline Duckles (Source 7)? Source 9 is the official statement of Women Opposed to the Nuclear Threat in Nottingham, England. What does it view as the reason for women's special role in the peace movement? What other issues does it link with a control of the arms race? What actions does Nottingham WONT undertake, and how does it view these as shaped by the gender of its members? How does its organizational structure and decision-making process compare to that of WSP? To other organizations with which you are familiar?

Source 10 is a statement from Tamar Swade, the founder of Babies Against the Bomb. How would you compare her motivation and the way this group was founded with that of Dagmar Wilson and WSP? How would you compare her views about motherhood as a motivation for peace work with those of Olive Schreiner in Source 1? Why do you feel these views led to her being criticized, and what is her answer to this criticism?

Source 11 comes from a speech given by Coretta Scott King at an International Women's Conference for Peace and Nuclear Disarmament. In this, as in the Unity Statement in Source 8, King is implicit rather than explicit in her connection between the arms race and what have traditionally been considered "women's concerns." How does she link these? Her audience for this speech is predominantly women; how might her argument have been shaped by this?

Sources 12 and 13 are posters from two demonstrations organized by women's peace groups against the installation of the Cruise and Pershing II missiles in Europe, scheduled for 1983. How do the images in the posters differ in their depiction of women responding to the nuclear threat? How do they fit with the ideas you have read of the various individuals and groups?

Source 14 is in some ways oral history in the making; that is, it is a discussion by a woman interested in peace issues about her encounter with other women involved in actions protesting military build-ups. It can thus be the raw material for an oral history of the *author's* development as a peace activist, or for a history of the women's encampment at Greenham Common in England based on oral interviews. Therefore, you will need to pay attention to a variety of things at once as you read this: the actions that the women activists undertake; the reasons they give for these actions; the way in which they see these actions as shaped by the fact that they are women; the way in which the author explains the women's motivations; the interplay between the author and the women she is speaking with. As you would when evaluating any oral history (or actually any history at all), you need to think about how the author's preconceptions might have shaped her analysis. In this selection, the author is fairly explicit about her opinions, making this issue perhaps easier to address here than it is in many studies in which the authors do not reveal their preconceptions and point of view.

You have now read and looked at a great many sources stretched out

over seventy-five years, and can return to the central questions: How did twentieth-century women involved in women's peace groups view the relationship between their being women and their advocating peace? How did they translate their ideas into actions, and how did their ideas shape the types of actions they regarded as appropriate to achieving their aims?

EPILOGUE

The collapse of the Soviet Union and the end of the Cold War arms race marked another shift in focus for women's peace groups. Some of them ceased to be active, while others turned their attention to military spending worldwide and broader economic, social, and political concerns. WILPF, for example, at an international congress in 1986 adopted as its new program, "Toward a Nuclear-Weapon and Hunger-Free Twenty-first Century." This was not a completely new direction, of course, for we have seen the connection between military expenditures and economic hardship made in the writings of peace activists from earlier decades. Noting the continuing use of rape as a means of military coercion throughout the world, WILPF started an international campaign in 1990 to confront the issue of violence against women, not limiting this to rape but working against all forms of physical, economic, and political coercion. At the moment women's peace groups are not often the chief organizers of mass demonstrations or theatrical actions,

but they are part of many such actions such as those that opposed the Persian Gulf War in 1991 and those for victims of AIDS.

Other women involved in peace work have turned their attention to education, for example developing programs for kindergartners about how to resolve conflicts nonviolently and establishing peace studies programs at colleges and universities. More than two hundred campuses across the United States now have peace studies programs of some sort, and Syracuse University offers a Ph.D. in peace studies. A long-time peace activist with many groups, Rose Marciano Lucey, was one of the key forces in a citizens' lobby to establish a U.S. Peace Academy, approved by Congress in 1986. Should you wish to use this chapter as a springboard for further investigation, perhaps doing some oral history yourself, the peace studies program at your own or a nearby college or university would be a good place to start.

Just as women's peace groups are changing but still thriving, exploring gender differences in terms of peace and war remains a thriving industry. Public opinion polls have discovered what they have labeled the "gender gap" in terms of support for military involvement; with respect to every engagement or contemplated engagement, women are consistently more opposed to war than men. Particularly during national elections, this translates into votes for the candidate perceived to be less militarily aggressive, and, because more women than men vote, the gap in votes may be even wider than the gap in public opinion. This gap has not been wide enough, as Olive Schreiner hoped, to "herald the death of war as a means of arranging human differences," but it is something contemporary women peace activists note they will be looking to in the future. At the same time, some feminist groups and many individual women favor an increased role for women in combat, supporting Maude Royden's words that "the belief that women are innately more pacific than men has been severely shaken." The connection between feminism and pacifism continues to be a complex and debated issue.

CHAPTER FIFTEEN

GLOBALISM AND TRIBALISM:

CHALLENGES TO THE CONTEMPORARY

NATION-STATE (1980s–1990s)

The collapse of the Soviet Union in 1991 was greeted by most Western nations (especially the United States) with self-congratulatory jubilation. The resulting end of the Cold War, U.S. president George Bush hoped, would usher in a New World Order of peace, stability, and general prosperity. Some euphoric Western political leaders even spoke of a "peace dividend," in which funds previously spent for armaments could be redirected into social programs or used to reduce burdensome government deficits. Indeed, not since the end of World War II in 1945 had the West been so optimistic about the future.

And yet, the end of the Cold War appeared to leave the world not more stable but actually less so. No longer distracted by the Cold War's conflicts between the so-called Great Powers (the People's Republic of China, the Soviet Union, and the United States), political observers came to recognize two parallel trends that were undermining the West's hope for a New World Order and, at the same time, were weakening one of the West's most cherished—and exported—institutions: the political nation-state. On one hand, the New World Order and the nation-state were threatened by pan-national trends such as economic globalism, supranational religious movements, and other phenomena that transcended borders and boundaries. On the other hand, the New World Order and the nation-state were weakened by ethnic conflicts (some called it a "new tribalism"[1]) in which certain nation-states (Yugoslavia, Russia, Rwanda, Burundi, for instance) actually collapsed while others in both the developed and developing worlds (India,

1. Contemporary observers who use this term are referring to ethnic separatist movements within a nation-state.

the People's Republic of China, Kenya, France, Germany, England, the United States, to name but a few) witnessed a disturbing escalation of ethnic violence. Losses of life in these "tribal" clashes have been particularly severe. According to United Nations estimates, as of mid-1994 approximately 1 million deaths had occurred in the civil war in Rwanda, 200,000 in the "ethnic cleansing" in Bosnia, and over 2.4 million refugees in Rwanda and Somalia alone. As some surveyed the disorderly and dangerous situations throughout the world, a few even became nostalgic for the Cold War, in which the superpowers had exercised a degree of control over their own minorities as well as over their own satellites.

Although historians cannot (and should not) predict how these two trends will affect the political institution of the nation-state—and indeed the future of the world's peoples—historians can tentatively examine and analyze the *causes* of this apparent erosion or fragmentation of the nation-state in both the developed and developing regions. To what extent did the end of the Cold War result in both pan-national surges and subnational insurrections that the superpowers previously had been willing and able to control? Or were these trends present throughout the Cold War period but merely ignored by Western and non-Western analysts who chose to concentrate their attention on the interplay of the major powers? To what extent did demographic, economic, and environmental factors create or heighten pan-national and subnational tensions? Conversely, have Western observers always overexaggerated the success of the nation-state in resisting pan-national movements or in homogenizing the various peoples under its political wing?

Your task in this chapter is to identify and interview at least one person who has been (or is now) in a position to offer you insight into the apparent weakening of the nation-state in both the West and the non-West. Then, using your interview, along with those of your classmates and those provided in the Evidence section of this chapter, state what you believe are the causes of the two parallel trends described above. Many nations retain historians in their state departments or foreign ministries to provide important historical background to the officials who determine foreign policy. Your assignment in this chapter is somewhat similar to the work expected of such historians.

BACKGROUND

Whenever today's Western students look at a globe of the earth, they almost reflexively assume that the entire world is composed of Western-style nation-states. Indeed, nearly all Westerners think of the nation-state as the normal state of affairs and simultaneously as the highest form of political evolution.

Chapter 15

Globalism and

Tribalism:

Challenges to the

Contemporary

Nation-State

(1980s–1990s)

And yet, the modern Western-style nation-state is a comparatively recent creation, dating back probably no further than the French Revolution (1789) and nationalistic reactions against the empire building of Napoleon Bonaparte (early 1800s). One could argue that the United States did not become a modern nation-state until the defeat of the Confederacy in the American Civil War, which ended in 1865. Canada did not formally become a nation until 1867; Italy and Germany did not come into existence as we know them until 1870 and 1871, respectively. Indeed, it could even be said that the *modern* nation-state (in which people of various ethnic, racial, and religious groups[2] pledge loyalty to their nation over their fealty to their own particular group) did not occur until even later than that, aided by the development in the late nineteenth century of national symbols, monuments (the Eiffel Tower in France, the Washington Monument in the United States, the monument to William I of Germany), liturgy (pledges to the nation or the flag), national heroes and "holy" days commemorated on coins, postage stamps, and holidays, national athletic competitions (the Davis Cup in tennis in 1900; the revival of the Olympic Games in 1896), all of which were intended to "invent" an overarching unity among peoples governed by the nation-state.[3]

Western imperialism of the late nineteenth century gave the Western nations the opportunity to export the institution of the nation-state to Africa, the Middle East, and parts of Asia. As a result, many so-called national boundaries were drawn by the imperial powers themselves with little or no participation by the indigenous peoples and with little attention paid to tribal lands, divisions, or rivalries. Sub-Saharan Africa, for example, was carved into nations at the 1884 Conference of Berlin, and the nations of the Middle East divided on a drawing board by European powers in 1916.

This is not to say that the host populations unanimously opposed the institution of the nation-state. Many members of the Westernized urban elites viewed that political institution as preferable to smaller ethnic enclaves, territories of feudalistic warlords, or traditionalist religious dominions. These elites saw the adoption of the Western political model as a way to bring about Western-style modernization through efficient bureaucracies, improved transportation, and the attraction of Western capital as well as technological and administrative expertise.

The independence movements following World War II appeared to

---

2. Until very recently, almost no ethnically homogeneous nation-state existed, the exceptions being Japan, Finland, and Albania. The People's Republic of China, for example, is composed of fifty-five officially recognized ethnic groups.

3. The dictionary of the Royal Spanish Academy did not contain the modern definition of nationalism until 1884. See E. J. Hobsbawn, *Nations and Nationalism Since 1780: Programme, Myth, Reality* (Cambridge: Cambridge University Press, 1990), p. 14.

leave these Western-style nation-states intact and in the hands of Westernized elites (Jawaharlal Nehru in India, Gamal Abdel Nasser in Egypt, and Riza Shah Pahlavi in Iran, to name but a few). As their Western counterparts had done nearly a century before, these leaders created symbols of national unity (flags, holidays, heroes, and monuments) to weld their respective states together into secular, multiethnic national wholes. As India's Nehru watched the outbreak of Hindu-Muslim conflict in his newly independent nation, he spoke disparagingly of his countrymen who possessed "that narrowing religious outlook."

At the same time that these independence movements were taking shape, most of the attention of the developed nations was centered on the postwar collapse of the Grand Alliance that had defeated Germany and Japan and the advent of the Cold War, whose principal adversaries were the United States, the Soviet Union, and (after 1949) the People's Republic of China. Each of these superpowers maneuvered for position geopolitically. The United States attempted to control the rimlands surrounding the Soviet Union by placing military bases in Western Europe, Turkey, Japan, the Philippines, and Southeast Asia. For its part, the Soviet Union concentrated on protecting its western borders by controlling the nations of Eastern Europe, while simultaneously trying to gain some advantages in the Middle East (for oil and access to the Mediterranean) and Africa. Another world war was

avoided, although "brushfire wars" did erupt in Korea, Vietnam, and elsewhere. The developing nations either allied themselves with one of the superpowers or tried to remain outside of any of the superpowers' spheres while accepting foreign aid from all of them (Egypt, for example, accepted funds from both the Soviet Union and the United States to build the enormous Aswan Dam). While most world leaders publicly decried the continuation of the Cold War (especially the tremendously costly arms race), privately many came to see the Cold War as bringing some stability and order, as long as each of the superpowers could control its satellites. For the developing nations, some of which held precious raw materials and resources that the superpowers desperately needed, the Cold War was not totally unwelcome, for it allowed some developing nations to reap fortunes of foreign aid.

But beneath the Cold War's fragile stability, demographic, economic, environmental, and ideological forces were eroding the power and unity of the nation-state, especially—although not solely—in the developing nations (many of which had been former colonies of the Western powers). Their preoccupation with the Cold War had caused many observers to ignore these forces, although more perceptive analysts warned of the potential danger. When the Cold War came to an end in the early 1990s, many people were stunned by the presence and potency of these forces as well as by outbreaks of violence in Yugoslavia, Liberia, Chechnya,

Chapter 15

Globalism and

Tribalism:

Challenges to the

Contemporary

Nation-State

(1980s–1990s)

Rwanda, Burundi, Somalia, and else-where. They naturally assumed that the end of the Cold War was the *cause* of this instability, although many of these eruptions had been more than simmering long before the end of the Cold War (religious violence in India between Hindus and Muslims, for example, claimed approximately 600,000 lives in 1947).

The most serious threat to the developing nation has been population growth. In 1900, the world's population was estimated at 1.6 billion. By 1990, it had reached 5.3 billion, and the most modest projections estimate that the world's population will reach 7.6 billion by 2025. Most of this demographic explosion has come in the developing nations. In 1947, the population of Bangladesh (then West Pakistan) was 32 million. By 1994, it had reached 117 million and, driven by a birthrate of 43 per 1,000, may be twice that by 2024. India, with 350 million people in 1947, by 1994 had reached 911.4 million and is projected to double that number by 2030. Birth control has been almost a complete failure, as only 31 percent of Bangladesh's married women use contraception (in the United States the percentage is 69.1 percent).[4] Such population increases have placed enormous strains on the governments of these nations and may well be responsible for some of the other destabilizing forces.

4. Under an ambitious program to control population in the People's Republic of China (1.192 billion people in 1991), the government reports that 80.9 percent of married women use contraception.

A more serious demographic problem is migration. In recent years, approximately 110 million people in the People's Republic of China have abandoned the rural regions for the cities, making this the greatest mass migration in modern history. By the year 2010, it is estimated that over one-half of the world's population will live in increasingly immense and overcrowded cities. By 2000, the population of Mexico City is projected to reach 26 million; Sao Paulo, 20 million; Bombay and Calcutta, 16 million each; and Jakarta, Tehran, Seoul, Shanghai, and Belli, 13 million each. Experts almost shudder when they contemplate the potential for epidemics, starvation, violence, and political collapse. To what extent has this massive migration undermined the nation-state in the developing world?

As if population growth, migration, and "tribal" violence were not enough to weaken the nation-state in the developing world (many of which had not had the time to achieve stability after colonialism), global transnational trends threaten this political institution as well. The developed nations (principally the United States, Western Europe, and Japan) have drained natural resources out of these regions. For example, the United States, with 5 percent of the world's population, consumes over 25 percent of the world's natural resources, thus further impoverishing the developing nations and making it even more difficult for them to deal with population and migration problems. In 1989, the per capita gross national product of the United States, Canada, the Soviet Union, Australia, most of Western Europe, Japan, and New Zealand exceeded $6,000. No nation in Africa could come close to that figure, most of them having a per capita GNP below $1,000. Indeed, in the rest of the world, only Turkey, Saudi Arabia, and Kuwait surpassed the $6,000 figure. Multinational corporations, some with assets greater than those of many developing nations, continued to undermine the power of the incipient nation-state. In a world in which markets are more important than missiles, developing nations remain at a distinct disadvantage. As a member of Nepal's commission to draft a democratic constitution in 1990, Daman Dhugane reported on his poll of what the people wanted in their new constitution. "All they say is 'airplanes.' Everyone wants an airfield and an airplane, plus seeds and fertilizer. How can we write that into the constitution?"[5]

This kind of economic colonialism has been thought to have been responsible for the rise of pan-national anti-Western movements, such as Islamic fundamentalism. In Iran in 1979, Muslim fundamentalists overthrew the government of the Shah, who was seen (correctly) as trying to Westernize his nation-state. During that coup, Islamic fundamentalists referred to United States president Jimmy Carter as *yazid*, an agent of Satan. Later, Hamas, the Palestinian Islamic movement, attacked President George Bush as "the chief of the false gods." Throughout the Middle East and North Africa, national leaders have taken strong measures to preserve their nation-states against this transnational upsurge. In June of 1995, Egyptian President Hosni Mubarak narrowly escaped an assassination attempt while attending the opening summit of the Organization of African Unity in Ethiopia; Egyptian fundamentalists were the chief suspects.

In all, a number of trends seem to threaten the authority and even the existence of the nation-state in the developing world. Moreover, attempts by the industrialized nations to preserve these nations (in Iran in the 1970s, in Somalia, Rwanda, and Bosnia in the 1990s) have proven to have been anemic and in general ineffective. Speaking of Somalia, British historian E. J. Hobsbawm asserted that "the USA and the rest of the UN forces of occupation of several tens of thousands withdrew ignominiously when confronted with the option of an indefinite occupation. . . ."[6]

Yet it would be a mistake to believe that the weakening of the nation-state is a phenomenon unique to the developing world. Developed nations too have been victims of transnational trends (multinational corporations, environmental catastrophes, international terrorism) as well as of increased racial and ethnic violence. Are the causes of these phemonena the same as in the developing nations?

5. Robin Wright and Doyle McManus, *Flashpoints: Promise and Peril in a New World* (New York: Alfred A. Knopf, 1991), p. 88.

6. E. J. Hobsbawm, *The Age of Extremes: A History of the World, 1914–1991* (New York: Pantheon Books, 1994), p. 562.

Chapter 15

Globalism and

Tribalism:

Challenges to the

Contemporary

Nation-State

(1980s–1990s)

In terms of population control and density, no developed nation faces the specters that haunt the nation-state in the developing world. And yet the urban crises that confront leaders in the developing world also challenge their more affluent counterparts. Moreover, the importation of people to do what economist John Kenneth Galbraith calls the "unpleasant" jobs (North Africans in France; Africans, Pakistanis, and Indians in England; Hispanics in the United States) appears to have increased tensions in these already multiethnic nations.[7] This rise in ethnic tensions has led to calls for immigration restrictions in all the Western nations, simultaneous with the emergence of radical nativist groups (skinheads in the United States, Britain, and Germany; neo-Nazis in Germany). More recently, the interest in French author Jean Raispaul's nativist novel *Camp of the Saints* (published originally in 1973 but considerably more popular now than then) seems to show an increase in nativist ideology.

Morever, the West's conversion to a postindustrial economy has not been without pain; witness the erosion of industrial jobs and the corresponding mounting pressure on government-financed social programs. Yet with

deficits running high in many of these nations, the impulse has not been to increase government funding for social programs but rather to pare it down. Adding to this problem has been the increasingly unequal distribution of wealth in the developed nations, widening the chasm between rich and poor and increasing tensions and violence. Thus developed nations, most of which are older and clearly more affluent than the developing nations, also have seen their share of nation-state erosion, although the causes of that erosion may not be the same.

How, then, are we to explain the undermining of the nation-state in both the developing and developed worlds? Are any causal factors common to both regions? How much of the current situation can we attribute to the end of the Cold War? Is the multiethnic nation-state no more than a temporary historical phenomenon, to be supplanted in the future by other political institutions? Almost every day, newspapers report stories that directly or indirectly touch on these questions. But it would be invaluable to be able to speak with a person who possesses more direct knowledge of the trends noted above (as examples, an elected representative, a person working in a consular or diplomatic office, a recent arrival from one of the many "trouble spots," or a person working with a nonprofit relief agency). We could then use that interview evidence, along with what we learn from the news media, to gain insights into the causes of the present world situation.

7. The United States is the best—but not the only—example of a multiethnic nation-state. The 1990 federal census reported that approximately 70 percent of Americans were of northern and western European origins comprising sixteen separate ethnic groups. In Russia, approximately 82 percent of the residents are Russians. On the importation of labor, see John Kenneth Galbraith, *The Culture of Contentment* (Boston: Houghton Mifflin Co., 1991), pp. 30–41.

THE METHOD

Historians often wish they could ask specific questions of the participants in a historical event—questions that surviving diaries, yellowed letters, and other archival documents do not answer. Moreover, many people—especially the poor, the unschooled, the members of minority groups—did not leave written records and thus are often overlooked by historians.

But when historians are dealing with the comparatively recent past, they do have an opportunity to ask questions by using a technique called oral history. Oral history—interviewing famous and not-so-famous people about their lives and the events they observed or participated in—can greatly enrich our knowledge of the past. It can help the historian capture the "spirit of an age" as seen through the eyes of average citizens, and it often bridges the gap between impersonal forces (wars, epidemics, depressions) and personal, individual responses to them. Furthermore, oral history allows the unique to emerge from the total picture: the conscientious objector who would not serve in the army, the woman who did not marry and devote herself to raising a family, and so forth.

Oral history is both fascinating and challenging. On the surface, it seems easy to do, but it is really rather difficult to do well. There is always the danger that the student may "lead" the interview by imposing his or her ideas on the subject. Equally possible, the student may be led away from the subject by the person being interviewed.

Still other problems complicate the process: the student may miss the subtleties in what is being said or may assume that an exceptional person is representative of many people. Some older men and women like to tell only the "smiling side" of their personal history—that is, they prefer to talk about the good things that happened to them, not the bad things. Others have forgotten what actually happened or are influenced by reading or television. Some older people cannot resist sending a message to younger people by recounting how hard it was in the past, how few luxuries they had when they were young, how far they had to walk to school, and so on. Yet oral history, when used carefully and judiciously along with other sources, is an invaluable tool for recreating a sense of the past.

Recently, much attention had been paid—and rightly so—to protecting the rights and privacy of human subjects. For this reason, the federal government requires that the interviewee consent to the interview and be fully aware of how the interview is to be used. The interviewer thus must explain the purpose of the interview, and the person being interviewed must sign a release form (for samples, see Sources 1 through 3). Although these requirements are intended to apply mostly to psychologists and sociologists, historians who use oral history are bound as well.

Because interviewees inevitably hold certain points of view and

Chapter 15

Globalism and

Tribalism:

Challenges to the

Contemporary

Nation-State

(1980s–1990s)

because their memories are not always reliable, historians avoid using oral history as their only source of evidence. Before any interview takes place, the historian does a great deal of background reading in newspapers, published memoirs, and government reports. These sources provide basic factual information as well as points of view other than that of the interviewee. *The New York Times* and *The London Times* both publish indexes that can be used to find reports and articles on selected topics, and microfilm copies of weekly newsmagazines (like *Time* and *Newsweek*) have indexes at the beginning of each microfilm reel. *InfoTrac* is an on-line index to periodicals, including academic, business, and general works. Major newspapers and newsmagazines can also be searched through the World Wide Web. Visit the reference room of your school library or in a nearby large public library. In addition, the archives at Vanderbilt University in Nashville, Tennessee, contain videotapes of all the major television networks' news programs since August 1968. *Never* conduct an interview without first doing a great deal of preparation. Adequate preparation will help you formulate pertinent questions, will keep you from leaving out any important subjects, and will prevent you from making glaring errors during the interview.

When selecting the person to interview, you should find out what particular expertise the potential interviewee possesses. Has he or she worked in a consular office or an embassy, the state department, or with one of the many nonprofit international relief agencies (the International Red Cross, to name but one)? Has the person lived in one of the world's developing nations and maintained friendships and correspondents there? Is the person a member of Congress who has studied the problems covered in the Background section of this chapter, or a professor who teaches in this area and has traveled abroad to gain additional, first-hand insights? Has the person served in the military in one of the "trouble spots" (like Bosnia, Somalia, or Kuwait)? At first, you may think that your community contains none of these people, but if you do a bit of digging, you will be surprised how many such people live and work nearby.

Instructions for Interviewers

1. Establish the date, time, and place of the interview well in advance. You may wish to call and remind the interviewee a few days before your appointment.

2. Clearly state the purpose of the interview at the outset. In other words, explain why the class is doing this project.

3. Prepare for the interview by carefully reading background information and by writing down and arranging in order the questions you will ask. This list is your interview guide.

4. It is usually a good idea to keep most of your major questions broad and general, so as to give the interviewee as much latitude as possible. Avoid questions that can be answered yes or no, or with simply a

word or two. And *listen.* An interviewee's answer may cause you to think of a specific question that can be asked for more detail.

5. Avoid loaded questions, such as "Everyone in the developing nation-states hates the U.S. government, don't they?" Instead, keep your questions as neutral as possible: "From your experiences, what do people in the developing nation-states think of the U.S. government?" The latter, called an open-ended question, allows the interviewee the full range of possibilities when giving you an answer.

6. Ask any questions involving controversial matters toward the end of the interview, when the interviewee is more comfortable with you.

7. Always be courteous, and be sure to give the person enough time to think, remember, and answer. Never argue, even if you strongly disagree with an answer or statement. Remember that the purpose of the interview is to find out what someone else thinks, not to tell what you think.

8. Always take notes, even if you are tape-recording the interview. Notes will help clarify unclear portions of the tape and will be essential if the recorder malfunctions or the tape is accidentally erased.

9. Many who use oral history believe that the release forms should be signed at the beginning of the interview; others insist that this often inhibits the person who is to be interviewed and therefore should not be done until the end of the session. Although students who are using the material only for a class exercise are not always held strictly to the federal requirements, it is still better to obtain a signed release. Without such a release, the tape cannot be heard and used by anyone else (or deposited in an oral history collection), and the information the tape contains cannot be published or made known outside the classroom.

10. Try to write up the results of your interview as soon as possible after completing the interview. Even in rough form, these notes will help you capture the sense of what was said as well as the actual information that was presented.

A Suggested Interview Plan

Remember that the person who has agreed to be interviewed by you is a *person,* with his or her own schedule, as well as feelings, sensitivities, and emotions. Be on time for your interview, and dress appropriately. If you intend to tape-record the interview, ask permission first. But if you believe that a tape recorder will inhibit the interviewee, leave it at home and plan to take thorough notes. *Do not* rely on your memory.

The following suggestions will help you get started. Begin by establishing the interviewee's credentials and particular area(s) of expertise. This will come in handy when you analyze the interview later. Be sure to get the following important data on the interviewee:

1. Name

2. Age

Chapter 15

Globalism and

Tribalism:

Challenges to the

Contemporary

Nation-State

(1980s–1990s)

3. Race

4. Sex

5. Occupation

6. U.S. citizen? Born abroad?

7. Educational background

8. Foreign travels/study/work

9. Particular area(s) of expertise (world politics, feeding the hungry, friends or relatives in developing world, international business, particular city or locale)

10. Sources for interviewee's remarks (study, travel, business, contacts abroad, military, and so forth)

Once you have established the interviewee's credentials, *do not* simply jump into meaty questions about the causes of nation-state difficulties. Instead, frame limited questions that concentrate on the interviewee's particular area or region of expertise. For example, if your interviewee's focus is the former nation-state of Yugoslavia, ask specific (and, remember, open) questions about the collapse of that nation and the subsequent conflicts that erupted in 1991 between the major contestants (Croats, Serbs, Bosnian Serbs, Bosnian Muslims, Macedonians).[8] Allow your interviewee to relate anecdotes or memorable experiences, or to tell of conversations with other observers or nationals.

Once you have exhausted that mine of information, try to get the

interviewee to connect his or her insights with situations in other regions. Is there some common denominator between the Yugoslav animosities and, for example, the ethnic violence in India, Somalia, Bosnia, Rwanda, or Russia? Here your background labors will come in handy. Don't push your interviewee to make connections, but offer some information and observe how your interviewee integrates and uses it.

Finally, again without pressing the interviewee, try to elicit some general comments about the *causes* of these events. What relationship (if any) does your interviewee see between these events and the end of the Cold War? How (if at all) do demographic, environmental, economic, and ideological factors play a role? As you can see, you have guided the interview through four stages, from personal credentials and background to the interviewee's views regarding a widening sphere of experiences, events, and forces or trends.

One of the most important skills that novice interviewers must learn is that of knowing when to ask follow-up questions. These questions, obviously, cannot be planned in advance, but they can be invaluable in clarifying an interviewee's statement on a particular subject. For example, an interviewee might remark that "global politics are more stable today than ever before," an assertion that the interviewer cannot allow to let pass without some clarification. In response to such a statement, an effective interviewer might say, "Why do you say that?" or, "When did global politics become so stable?" or even,

---

8. Actually twenty-four separate ethnic groups composed the former nation-state of Yugoslavia.

"How would you respond to those who say global politics today are *less* stable?" Keep in mind the basic rule of journalism: find the answers to the questions who/what/where/when/how/why. Before you conduct your own interview, you might want to practice on a fellow student or friend.

When the time comes to write up your interview, you will have two distinct choices on how to go about doing it. You will find an example of each of these choices in the Evidence section. The first option is the *transcribed interview* (Source 4), in which you write word-for-word the questions and the answers of the interview. This method allows the readers to recreate in their own minds exactly how the interview progressed. The second option is known as the *interpretive interview* (Source 5), in which

you, the interviewer, edit the material to remove unimportant details, "smooth out" the interview by writing transitional sentences, and add your own observations, say of body language or tone of voice, that would not be recorded in a transcribed interview. (For example: "Before she responded, she grimaced, and then said, 'I saw too much killing, too much,' as her voice grew so soft that it could barely be heard.") Remember, you are not allowed to alter what the interviewee actually has said, nor can you invent observations for dramatic flair. As you can readily see, both types of interviews have certain distinct advantages and disadvantages. If you are in doubt about which option to choose, consult your instructor (who may in fact tell the class which format to use).

Chapter 15

Globalism and

Tribalism:

Challenges to the

Contemporary

Nation-State

(1980s–1990s)

THE EVIDENCE

Sources 1 and 2 from Collum Davis, Kathryn Back, and Kay MacLean, Oral History: From Tape to Type *(Chicago: American Library Assn., 1977), pp. 14, 15.*

1. Sample Unconditional Release

<u>Tri-County Historical Society</u>

For and in consideration of the participation by <u>Tri-County Historical Society</u> in any programs involving the dissemination of tape-recorded memories and oral history material for publication, copyright, and other uses, I hereby release all right, title, or interest in and to all of my tape-recorded memoirs to <u>Tri-County Historical Society</u> and declare that they may be used without any restriction whatsoever and may be copyrighted and published by the said <u>Society,</u> which may also assign said copyright and publication rights to serious research scholars.

In addition to the rights and authority given to you under the preceding paragraph, I hereby authorize you to edit, publish, sell and/or license the use of my oral history memoir in any other manner which the <u>Society</u> considers to be desirable and I waive any claim to any payments which may be received as a consequence thereof by the <u>Society.</u>

PLACE   <u>Indianapolis,</u>

             <u>Indiana</u>

DATE   <u>July 14, 1975</u>

<u>Harold S. Johnson</u>

(Interviewee)

<u>Jane Rogers</u>

(for Tri-County Historical Society)

2. Sample Conditional Release

Tri-County Historical Society

I hereby release all right, title, or interest in and to all or any part of my tape-recorded memoirs to   Tri-County Historical Society,   subject to the following stipulations:

That my memoirs are to be *closed* until five years following my death.

PLACE   Indianapolis,

Indiana

DATE   July 14, 1975

Harold S. Johnson

(Interviewee)

Jane Rogers

(for Tri-County Historical Society)

Source 3 from the University of Tennessee.

3. Form Developed by a Large United States History Survey Class at the University of Tennessee, Knoxville, 1984

This form is to state that I have been interviewed by ———(Interviewer)——— on ———(date)——— on my recollections of the Vietnam War era. I understand that this interview will be used in a class project at the University of Tennessee, and that the results will be saved for future historians.

Signature

Date

Chapter 15

Globalism and

Tribalism:

Challenges to the

Contemporary

Nation-State

(1980s–1990s)

Sources 4 and 5 from interviews conducted by the authors in November 1995.

4. Dr. Robert J. Lieber

[*Robert Lieber is professor and chairman of
the Government Department at
Georgetown University. His special fields
of expertise are American foreign policy
and United States relations with Europe
and the Middle East. He is the author of
six books (the most recent of which is*
No Common Power: Understanding
International Relations, *published in
1995), numerous collections of essays, and
contributions to* The New York Times,
The Washington Post, The Christian
Science Monitor, *and others. He has
served as an adviser to several presidential
campaigns and has appeared on* Nightline,
This Week with David Brinkley,
Crossfire, Larry King Live, *and* Good
Morning, America.]

QUESTION: Let me ask you this, Dr. Lieber. If you were a physician and the nation-states of the world were your patients, how would you rate their general health?

LIEBER: I'm not sure that's a question that can be answered because you are applying a metaphor, an organic metaphor, to the situation of states, and I don't really think that's the best way of getting a handle on the situation. I would frame the question somewhat differently: Has the age of the nation-state passed? Is the world at the end of the twentieth century a world in which nation-states are completely outmoded? My answer to that is that the nation-state still has a good deal of life in it. A lot has changed in the twentieth century but I think in the aftermath of the end of the Cold War, and with all the incredible international economic activity going on now, a lot of people have been writing the epitaph or the death warrant for the state, and that is grossly premature.

It is certainly true that an enormous amount of international activity takes place across state boundaries and without regard to the preferences and policies of the governments of the individual countries of the world, but it is well worth remembering that international economic relationships—trade, investments, and so on—have often played a huge role in international relations. Indeed, on the eve of World War I, there was an enormous amount of trade back and forth among the countries of Europe—the Great Powers—and because of the impact of that war, the Depression of the 1930s, and World War II, the level of trade among the countries of Western Europe did not recover to its 1914 level until the mid-1970s. So, my reply to this question about the health of the state is that, yes, there is a lot that goes on across state boundaries among states and peoples, particularly economical, but at the same time, that trade and economic activity and the media are no substitute for the state. People remain organized politically in states. Sovereignty is on the basis of states. Only the state has the capacity to effectively organize its people for action, whether it is through things like education, taxation, or even monetary affairs, and the state will be with us for a long time to come.

QUESTION: Putting the question a different way, events recently in Bosnia, in Somalia, and most recently, Canada, seem to show an increase in ethnic awareness among people and even hostility and some violence. Is it correct that this is a recent phenomenon? And, if so, how would you explain it?

LIEBER: There are two simultaneous and competing tendencies taking place at the same time. At one level, there is the tendency toward fragmentation. Ethnic groups in countries like the former Yugoslavia, or Canada, as well as in Eastern Europe, and the former Soviet Union, have been seeking to break off and form their own independent states, and regional and ethnic pressures exist in plenty of other places as well. At the same time, there are many things going on that are increasingly global—communications, the new technologies, the Internet, satellite communications, cellular phones, culture, movies, software, diseases, environmental questions, religious movements, trade, investment, and the like. There are things that challenge the state from above, whereas ethnic separatism challenges the state from below. To some extent, these are competing phenomena. I think the explanation for why ethnic separatism has increased in recent years is probably twofold. One, the end of the Cold War has unleashed a series of tendencies toward fragmentation which were previously suppressed by this almost worldwide confrontation between East and West. Two, some of these things that go on are reactions to modernity, that is the collapse of traditional society which has been a process that has been going on over three or four centuries, has proceeded at different paces in different areas, and people frequently seek some form of identity in a modern world where many of the traditional underpinnings are disappearing. People look for new forms of meaning, and one of those unfortunately is sometimes in the form of ethnic nationalism. I also think it is something that is often whipped up by politicians in ways which are very dangerous.

QUESTION: On the second, the reaction to modernity and the collapse of the traditional society, would Iran be a good example of that phenomenon, one in which the Shah had attempted to modernize that nation and I suppose even to Westernize it?

LIEBER: The Iranian case is rather more specific. After all, it happened more than fifteen years ago, and it had as much to do with the incompetent, sometimes brutal, and increasingly isolated regime of the Shah and the fact that he

Chapter 15

Globalism and

Tribalism:

Challenges to the

Contemporary

Nation-State

(1980s–1990s)

simultaneously managed to alienate so many groups in the society. And so I doubt that you can generalize from important aspects of Iran more widely. On the other hand, the phenomenon of radical extreme fundamentalist Islam has been evidenced elsewhere in the region—for example, in Sudan and in movements seeking to oppose the Arab-Israeli peace process or impose an Islamic dictatorship in Algeria. To some extent, those movements are born in part out of frustration with the difficulties of modernization, the impact of the modern economy, people's search for meaning. On the other hand, and certainly in the region, it is a kind of inauthentic response to the problems that face people in those areas. The fact is that Islamic fundamentalist regimes do not have any answers for the problems of poverty, or education, or unemployment, or the economy and, in a sense, they don't really offer their people a genuine way to address the very real problems many of them face.

QUESTION: Another example: Prior to the Quebec vote on October 30, 1995, one separatist leader said that Canada really wasn't a nation at all. He said it was, and I'm quoting, "an artificial thing." Would you agree with that statement?

LIEBER: No, not at all. There are, I guess, two separate questions here. One about Canada: Canada has been a state for a lot longer than probably three-quarters of the members of the United Nations. It is a multiethnic, multilingual state, but the temptations of independence for Quebec have perhaps a lot more to do with nationalist ambitions of politicians than they do with the realities of Canada. The Canadian people both inside Quebec and outside are better off if they hang together than if they fragment.

QUESTION: The United States is a multiethnic nation, and some observers have seen what they say is an increase in ethnic tensions in the United States as well. Is this part of this phenomenon or is this something else, something different?

LIEBER: Well, let's take that one step at a time. I mentioned that with Canada there were two separate issues. One was what the basis is for separatism for Quebec. The other is what it takes to have a successful multiethnic country. There are very few successful examples of multiethnic states being coherent and stable. There is Switzerland, which is one admirable example. But I think the most successful example in many ways is the United States. But it's worth knowing that the reason the United States is so successful is that all of us, with the exception of Native Americans, have come to the United States from someplace else. And we have acculturated to a common language, a common set of political institutions, and a common set of political values. In effect, the U.S. is multiethnic by ancestry but we have a shared and common culture, language, and so forth. I think it is very important that we not lose sight of that. If you create a situation which fosters the permanent fragmentation of the country into different language groups—the printing of ballots, for instance, in different languages—I think is ultimately damaging to any effort at national coherence. The experience of all the different immigrant groups to

[452]

the United States, and again everybody has come to the U.S. from someplace else except the Native Americans, was that successive generations learned the common language—English—went to school in the United States, normally in public schools, and came to feel part of a common country with its values, Constitution, and procedures. As long as a culturation process continues for immigrant groups, the U.S. is likely to remain a stable, coherent, and successful state which embraces people of many, many faiths, races, ethnicities, and so forth.

QUESTION: Isn't there an increasing voice among some people in the United States for multilingual education, for ballots printed in other languages?

LIEBER: That's a good question. I think those steps are disastrous and exceptionally shortsighted. The U.S. is a robust, durable country, but the examples of the former Yugoslavia and of Lebanon—each of which have been shattered by ethnic fratricide—suggest the perils of encouraging linguistic fragmentation. I think it does an incredible disservice to immigrant groups not to educate the children in English, which was the common experience of all previous immigrant groups. It does not prepare them to succeed in American economic and public life, and it perpetuates a fragmentation which is harmful to these people. Moreover, I think there is no case for printing ballots in foreign languages. Now, let me say, this is a very different question from people having elements of ethnic camaraderie or newspapers or publications or civic groups which preserve some of the old traditions of people's ancestors once they have come.

QUESTION: One of your fields of specialization is international politics in natural resources, most specifically, oil. What role does that increasing competition for decreasing resources play in this multiethnic nation-state?

LIEBER: That's an easy question to answer. By and large, there is not a problem of diminishing resources. There are areas in which resource scarcity is a problem, but in many other realms, resources are ultimately defined as much in economic terms as in physical terms. For example, the supply of oil is in large measure a question of technology and geography, as much as it is physically what is out there. There are other common resources that are fragile and can be used up. There is pollution—pollution of the seas, pollution of water supplies—and clearly this is an area in which the interests of one group may be damaging to those of another. And in some regions, such as those with acute overpopulation, problems of water and arable land are very real. But when we think of natural resources in terms of minerals like iron ore or gold or bauxite or aluminum or oil or coal or natural gas just to cite a few, by and large there is not a problem of physical shortfalls of these things, and many modern technologies and manufacturing processes use, relatively speaking, far fewer quantities of these natural resources than was the case half a century or a century ago.

QUESTION: There has been a feeling among some people that the major superpowers—the former Soviet Union, People's Republic of China, and the

Chapter 15

Globalism and

Tribalism:

Challenges to the

Contemporary

Nation-State

(1980s–1990s)

United States—were basically able to keep their satellites in line and keep these ethnic tensions tamped down. Have you heard in your position anyone who is nostalgic for the Cold War, who would like to go back to that kind of stability?

LIEBER: Well, there is a difference between identifying something that existed and being nostalgic for it. There are good reasons for not being nostalgic about the Cold War. The imposition of Soviet domination in Eastern Europe and elsewhere was often a brutal business and led to a great deal of suffering for many of the people who were victimized by it. So there is no reason for nostalgia. Moreover, there was the constant threat of regional and world war because of the military confrontation between the two blocs driven basically by the nature of the Soviet system. At the same time, it is quite true that the Cold War tended to damp down ethnic fragmentation. You have a parallel for it early in the twentieth century and that is the breakup of the Austro-Hungarian Empire, the empire of the Hapsburgs. At the end of World War I in 1918, there was a great fragmentation in Eastern Europe. That empire in a perilous and fragile way had nonetheless kept together many different ethnic groups. And with the collapse of that empire together with three other empires (the Ottoman Empire of the Turks, the Empire of the Russian Czars, and the Empire of the Germans), this led to an incredible amount of ethnic fragmentation in Eastern Europe and had tragic consequences in the end. Most of the new states created by the peace of Versailles were unstable (with the exception of cases like Czechoslovakia) and many of them after a short period of time became dictatorships. Ultimately the instability in the region coupled with the rise of fascism led to World War II.

QUESTION: You are in a position to talk with people who are policymakers. They must ask you formally or informally, first of all, if the United States can do anything to bring about an end to these ethnic tensions or if the United States' efforts (whether they be in Somalia or elsewhere) would be pretty anemic. What did you tell people like that?

LIEBER: First, if the U.S. does not provide leadership, the problem is that there are very, very few circumstances in which somebody else can or will. By and large, there are very few cases in which some other country or group of countries or organization, for example the European Union or the United Nations, has the will or the capacity to provide international leadership and to resolve conflict. We saw that, I think, with the fragmentation of Yugoslavia beginning in 1991, and because both the Bush administration and the Clinton administration initially sought to let the Europeans provide the lead. The situation deteriorated and led to a horrendous conflict in which as many as 200,000 or more people have perished. The efforts to deal with the Bosnian conflict and the break-up of Yugoslavia have increasingly involved a greater U.S. role and again it tends to reflect the fact that the U.S. is able to provide leadership in collaboration with other actors. However, without the Cold War, it's a lot harder to mobilize Americans to pay the costs of foreign involvement, whether financial or otherwise. And that has been evident in the reluctance of

[454]

Congress and the American public to support foreign aid and a lot of hesitation about involvement of American troops overseas, and so forth. And so, in a post–Cold War world it is a lot harder for any government led by a person of whatever party in the United States, to operate than was the case during the Cold War.

QUESTION: Is part of that the experience in Vietnam?

LIEBER: The Vietnam experience is a large part of this, but this is also the first time in approximately sixty years in which the U.S. has not faced some great foreign threat. In the mid-to-late 1930s, it was fascism. Then it was World War II from 1941 to 1945. Then, after a brief pause, it was the Cold War and the Soviet threat. However one assesses these threats, there was always some overarching foreign peril around which American foreign policy and grand strategy had to focus. Threats of comparable magnitude—at least for now—no longer exist and, not surprisingly, it is simply harder to conceive and carry out coherent foreign policies.

QUESTION: Of course, looking across the future, which is an unfair question, what nations do you think have the best chance of existing in the next fifty to one hundred years? What nations do you think have the least best chances?

LIEBER: Well, let me clarify something in terminology that's very important, and often terminology is misused by people who should know better. The term *nation* means "a people." Often they share language or tradition or history or ethnicity or religion. But a nation is not the same thing as a state. A state is a political and legal institution in a specific geographical area, with particular responsibility for the enforcement of order there. On occasion, you will find a nation and a state closely coincide. For example, almost all Swedes live in Sweden. Another clear case of the nation would be Japan. But there are many instances in which people of a given nation or nationality or ethnicity live outside the boundaries. For example, we've talked about Canada. The French-Canadians in Quebec don't live in France, they live in Canada. That's just one illustration. Some states, many states, have peoples within their boundaries who are not part of the dominant ethnicity. So you have to be very careful about terms like "nation," "state," "country," "government," and so forth.

QUESTION: Let me then use the correct terminology. Which states do you think have the best chance of survival, and which states have the worst chance?

LIEBER: The only states whose survival seems imperiled are those states who are in conditions of utter and abject poverty and despair or who are currently wrecked by ferocious deadly civil wars. So one thinks of countries like Rwanda and Burundi, maybe Liberia, potentially Nigeria, one thinks of some of the pieces of the former Soviet Union, Chechnya, which is still part of Russia, or one thinks of the situation in the Balkans, including not only the pieces of the former Yugoslavia but some of its neighbors. Having said that, I think it's a reasonably sound prospect that the countries and states which are household names will be around for a long time to come.

Chapter 15

Globalism and

Tribalism:

Challenges to the

Contemporary

Nation-State

(1980s–1990s)

5. Dr. Natalia Lakiza-Sachuk

[*Natalia Lakiza-Sachuk is the principal consultant to the National Institute for Strategic Studies of the Council of National Security of Ukraine. A demographer by training, she is the author of over 150 scientific publications on the sociodemographic development of Ukraine and other post-communist countries. As the head of the Department of Demographic Policy and Strategic Research of the Committee on Problems of Women, Children and the Family, she reports directly to the President of Ukraine.*]

In her office on an uncharacteristically warm November day, Natalia Lakiza-Sachuk removed her stylish topcoat and sat comfortably in a straight chair. Although her English was excellent, she held a small Ukrainian-English dictionary, to which she rarely needed to refer.

When she spoke of the period when Ukraine was part of the Soviet Union, her open, friendly face held a slight frown. "The Soviet authorities tried to repress all national movements in the Soviet republics, including Ukraine," she explained. She spoke with great emotion of what she called the "artificial famines" that Ukrainians suffered as a result of Soviet confiscation of their food. "We had great losses in our population due to the anti-national policy of the Soviet Union against the Ukraine," she said. Although Natalia Lakiza-Sachuk could not have remembered those "artificial famines" (which took place in the 1920s and 1930s), simply telling about them obviously was painful for her.

But the Soviet Union could not crush Ukrainian nationalism. "You know," she mused, "I think that nationalism not only has negative meanings but positive as well. [During the Soviet period] utilization of the Ukrainian language was limited because most literature, which was called Soviet literature, was in Russian, and our children were taught mostly in Russian." She spoke of the Ukrainian history that had been lost, as well as Ukrainian literature and culture. "There were very limited points where real Ukrainian culture was saved," she noted sadly. But, even so, Ukrainian national feelings were not extinguished.

It was a painful subject, but Dr. Lakiza-Sachuk was determined not to drop it. "In Ukraine today," she explained, "we are not only trying to renovate our Ukrainian culture but also to support the cultures of our ethnic minorities." With more than one hundred ethnic groups living in Ukraine, however, she admitted that the problem is "complex." "I think we are building a multinational state in Ukraine," she said, adding that she felt it unlikely that those ethnic minorities would themselves want to break away to form their own nation-states. "I think that it is impossible now, because to separate it is necessary to have conditions, circumstances, and I think that not one group in Ukraine has such conditions, including the Russian population." Confessing herself to be an optimist, she hoped that Ukraine would avoid the conflict that was taking place in Yugoslavia and further hoped that the Yugoslav difficulties could be solved by peaceful means as well.

"But I would like to explain," she added, "that most countries in the world are artificial, because they have been created by circumstances such as wars of unification and conquest, marriages of royal families, or treaties between leaders." Thus, the situation in many countries today is "dangerous" and unpredictable.

Dr. Lakiza-Sachuk had been in Washington, D.C., engaged in research. Therefore, the subject almost naturally arose of the United States as a multi-ethnic nation. Her son, nine years old, had been enrolled in an American school and in his class he was the only student of European descent. He had enjoyed the experience "very much." Speaking of the United States as a multi-ethnic country, she thought it was better to offer a range of educational choices to schoolchildren of different ethnic groups. "And I think it is a better way, to allow people to choose the programs for their children, to freely choose these programs, and I think that American schools have such possibilities."

On the other hand, Dr. Lakiza-Sachuk recognized that the United States was not without its own ethnic conflicts. "You have large problems between people from different nationalities," she said. "I am afraid to name this conflict, but I feel it."

Interviewer: "You think it may be racial conflicts?"

Lakiza-Sachuk frowned, "Yes."

On more familiar ground, she brought up the subject of Chechnya's efforts to break away from Russia. "I believe that every nation has the right to be independent or to have an independent way of development inside a larger country," she exclaimed. But oil in Chechnya combined with Russia's determination not to allow additional breakaways made the situation dangerous.

Another potential source of disorder, she believed, were pan-national movements. Ukraine, for instance, has a growing Islamic population and a relatively large-scale immigration of Muslims. "It is a demographic problem and perhaps even a security problem," she said, especially if that population became politically activated by a pan-Islamic movement or leader. Although she did not anticipate a strong urge to limit immigration (as there is in the United States), "we have to regulate it, and it is possible to control it."

Could she anticipate a time when the world's major military powers would simply intervene in various nation-states to put down or mediate these

Chapter 15

Globalism and

Tribalism:

Challenges to the

Contemporary

Nation-State

(1980s–1990s)

conflicts (as occurred in early 1996 in the former Yugoslavia)? Although she wouldn't rule that out, she maintained that military intervention should be the last step. "It is very dangerous," she warned, speaking softly but firmly. "We are at a point at which America simply cannot or will not solve any conflict over the world. So we have to look for new ways to solve international conflicts. We have to look for new diplomacy, new developments in international relations." But, she maintained, "if we will solve the economic and social problems, then we will not have any ethnic conflicts around the world."

Too optimistic, again? "Perhaps. But often the causes of this bloodshed [are] not actually ethnic, but economic or social. Sometimes a country can solve its problems by itself with its own policies. Sometimes it cannot, and will need economic help from outside. Or, as in Bosnia, even military intervention. But we must be extremely careful, because each conflict—whether in Bosnia or Canada or Ukraine or the United States—is a bit different."

Dr. Lakiza-Sachuk had to leave. She rose quickly, then took her overcoat. A smile, a firm handshake, and she was gone.

QUESTIONS TO CONSIDER

Having examined and analyzed the two interviews in the Evidence section, you no doubt recognize several shortcomings in the interview as a historical source. To begin with, no historian would *ever* consider basing his or her conclusion on only one interview. The person being interviewed (the interviewee) is offering only one perspective, an opinion that might be in direct conflict with the opinions of other potential interviewees. For example, note that, in Dr. Robert Lieber's opinion (Source 4), an opinion based on extensive research, "there is not a problem of diminishing [natural] resources." As you are aware, others have a very different opinion. Further, Dr. Natalia Lakiza-Sachuk (Source 5) believes that "if you solve the economic and social problems, then we will not have any ethnic conflicts around the world." Again, others disagree strongly. Thus, the historian (or journalist, anthropologist, political scientist, sociologist, whatever) cannot base a scholarly work on simply one interview. To be thorough, a researcher must interview several people in order to get a balanced picture. They usually combine interviews with other sources—newspaper reports and editorials, memoirs, letters, editorial cartoons, primary documents, and the like. When one historian was asked how many history books were in her school's library, she replied, "But you must understand: they're *all* history books!"

Not only did the limitations of the interview as evidence become apparent as you read Sources 4 and 5, but the stylistic differences that distinguish the transcribed interview from the interpretive interview also became obvious. What do you see as

[458]

the strengths and weaknesses of each form of reporting an interview? Which form would a historian who was *not* the interviewer prefer?

Dr. Robert Lieber of Georgetown University believes that the nation-state "still has a good deal of life in it." How does he support his opinion? Why does he believe the nation-state is not only extremely durable but also necessary? At the same time, Dr. Lieber enumerates several contemporary threats to the institution of the nation-state. What are they? How does he predict the nation-state will be able to withstand those challenges (in the Middle East, Canada, the United States)?

On the Cold War, how does Lieber use historical evidence to support his view that there are "good reasons for not being nostalgic about the Cold War"? What does he think the United States's foreign policy should be in the post–Cold War world? How does he support that opinion?

Dr. Natalia Lakiza-Sachuk, an academician employed by the Ukrainian government, has a different perspective from that of Dr. Lieber. What do you think accounts for that difference?

Dr. Lakiza-Sachuk, unlike Dr. Lieber, believes that the situation of the nation-state is "dangerous." Why? How does she think her own nation-state, Ukraine, will avoid these dangers? What evidence does she offer to support her opinion? How will her own nation-state cope with ethnic and pan-national movements? What is her opinion of the ethnic discord in the United States?

What does Dr. Lakiza-Sachuk think of military intervention by the so-called Great Powers? What does she see as the source of ethnic tensions? Finally, what is her hope for her own Ukraine? for the other nation-states of the world?

EPILOGUE

Historians cannot—and should not—predict the future, what is going to happen. Indeed, the more conservative historians do not believe that a historian should study any event that has occurred since his or her birthday. Why do those historians believe this?

And yet, although historians should not offer predictions *or* analyze recent events, historians still have an important role to play in today's policymaking and public arena. As governmental officials (including the president and the cabinet) undertake to steer the ship of state, they need the rudder of a sound historical perspective. Similarly, journalists, political appointees, and other academicians (especially political scientists, anthropologists, and sociologists) will desperately need historical background in order to frame their own work in correct perspective.

A good historian must be able to use all the evidence at his or her disposal. Not only must more traditional types of evidence be considered, but

Chapter 15

Globalism and

Tribalism:

Challenges to the

Contemporary

Nation-State

(1980s–1990s)

less orthodox sources (such as cartoons, films, demographic data, interviews, and so on) must also be examined and analyzed. Only by looking at *all* the evidence can a historian be effective and useful.

Therefore, this book is not just for those men and women who want to be historians—a noble profession, but not the only one. Those of you who seek to become journalists, business executives, government leaders, medical practitioners, academicians, clerics, or responsible citizens in your own respective communities will come to understand that this book has helped you a great deal. Indeed, the ability to examine and analyze evidence is the true mark of an educated person.

At the same time, we hope that this volume has convinced you that you will need a *world perspective* as you approach the twenty-first century. As global economics, pan-national movements, international migration, and world demographics increasingly affect all of our lives, we will need a world understanding of these historical trends and events. Toward that understanding on your part, we hope this volume has made a modest contribution.

TEXT CREDITS

Chapter 2   Page 39: From C. R. Boxer, ed., *The Tragic History of the Sea, 1589–1622: Narratives of the Shipwrecks of the Portuguese East Indiamen.* Copyright © 1959. Reprinted by permission of David Higham Associates. **Page 41:** From John Williams Blake (ed. and trans.), *Europeans in West Africa, 1450–1560,* Vol. I. Copyright © 1942. Reprinted by permission of David Higham Associates. **Page 42:** Reprinted by permission of Curtis Brown, Ltd. Copyright © 1964 by Basil Davidson. **Page 47:** From *The Broken Spears* by Miguel Leon-Portilla. Copyright © 1962, 1990 by Beacon Press. Reprinted by permission of Beacon Press, Boston. **Pages 52; 53:** Excerpted from George Elison, *Deus Destroyed: The Image of Christianity in Early Modern Japan* (1973). Reprinted by permission of the author.

Chapter 3   Pages 69; 77: Reprinted with the permission of The Free Press, a division of Simon & Schuster from *Chinese Civilization and Society: A Sourcebook* by Patricia Buckley Ebrey. Copyright © 1981 by The Free Press. **Page 78:** From *The Humanist Way in Ancient China* by Ch'u Chai and Winberg Chai, ed. and trans. Copyright © 1965 by Bantam Books, Inc. Used by permission of Bantam Books, a division of Bantam Doubleday Dell Publishing Group, Inc. **Page 80:** From *The Bonds of Matrimony/Hsing shih Yin yüan Chuan (volume one), A Seventeenth Century Chinese Novel,* translated by Eve Alison Nyren. Copyright © 1995. Reprinted by permission of Edwin Mellen Press. **Page 83:** From *The Columbia Book of Later Chinese Poetry,* translated and edited by Jonathan Chaves. Copyright © 1986 by Columbia University Press. Reprinted by permission of the publisher. **Page 85:** From *Sources of Chinese Tradition* by William Theodore de Bary. Copyright © 1964 by Columbia University Press. Reprinted with permission of the publisher.

Chapter 4   Page 100: From *The Lê Code: Law in Traditional Vietnam* by Nguyen Ngoc Huy and Ta Van Tai with cooperation of Tran Van Liem, 1987, pp. 110, 111, 203, 204, 205. Reprinted with the permission of The Ohio University Press, Athens, Ohio. **Page 102:** From M. C. Hoadley and M. B. Hooker, *An Introduction to Javanese Law: A Translation of and Commentary on the Agama,* notes by Barbara Watson Andaya. Reprinted by permission of The University of Arizona Press. **Page 108:** *Southern Vietnam under the Nguyen: Documents on the Economic History of Cochinchina (Dang Trong), 1602–1777,* edited by Li Tana and Anthony Reid (1993), pp. 17–19. Reproduced here with the kind permission of the publisher, Institute of Southeast Asian Studies, Singapore. **Page 110:** From *History of Sumatra* by William Mardsen. Copyright © 1966 by William Mardsen. Used by permission of Oxford University Press, Inc. **Page 120:** Reprinted, by permission, from Ratanbai, untitled poem [My spinning wheel is dear to me, my sister], translated by Nita Ramaiya, in *Women Writing in India: 600 B.C. to the Present,* volume 1, edited by Susie Tharu and K. Lalita (New York: The Feminist Press at The City University of New York, 1991), pp. 89–90. Copyright © 1991 by the Feminist Press at The City University of New York.

Chapter 5   Page 134: From *The Educational Writings of John Locke,* edited by James Axtell. Reprinted with permission of Cambridge University Press. **Page 136:** From *Diary of Cotton Mather,* Vol. I, 1681–1709. Reprinted with permission of Frederick Ungar/The Continuum Publishing Company. **Page 148:** Reproduced by permission of Louisiana State University Press from *Slave Testimony: Two Centuries of Letters, Speeches, Interviews, and Autobiographies,* edited by John W. Blassingame. Copyright © 1977 by Louisiana State University Press.

Chapter 6   Page 170: From Paul E. Lovejoy, "The Volume of the Atlantic Slave Trade: A Consensus," *Journal of African History* 22 (1982), p. 494. Reprinted with permission of Cambridge University Press. **Page 171:** From E. A. Wrigley, *Population and History.* Copyright © 1969. Reproduced with permission of The McGraw-Hill Companies. **Pages 173; 175:** From Patrick Manning, *Slavery and African Life.* Copyright © 1990 by permission of Cambridge University Press.

Chapter 8   Pages 231; 232: From *The Sword of Truth,* by Mervyn Hiskett. Copyright © 1973 by Mervyn Hiskett. Used by permission of Oxford University Press, Inc. **Page 233:** From R. A. Adeleye and I. Mukoshy, trans. and ed. *Research Bulletin,* Center of Arabic Documentation (Ibadan), 2, 1, January 1966. Copyright © 1966. Reprinted by permission of Ibadan University Press. **Page 234:** From Alhaji Hassan and Mallam Shuaibu Ha'ibi, *A Chronicle of Abuja,* translated by F. Heath. Copyright © 1952. Reprinted by permission of Ibadan University Press. **Pages 237; 239; 242:** From Mervyn Hiskett, ed. and trans., *Tazyin al-Waraqat of 'Abdullah ibn Muhammad.* Copyright © 1963. Reprinted by permission of Ibadan University Press. **Page 237:** From "The Wathiqat Ahl al-Sudan: A Manifesto of the Fulani jihad," translated by A. D. H. Bivar, *Journal of African History* 2, 1961, pp. 239–241. Reprinted with the permission of Cambridge University Press. **Page 241:** From Thomas Hodgkin, *Nigerian Perspectives,* Second Edition, translated by H. F. C. Smith, pp. 261–264. Copyright © 1975. Reprinted by permission of Oxford University Press.

Chapter 9   Page 260: From "Nineteenth Century Europe: Liberalism and Its Critics," translated by Paul Silverman in Boyer, *Readings in Western Civilization,* document 41, volume 8, 1979, pp. 438–46off. Reprinted by permission of the publisher, The University of Chicago Press. **Page 266:** From Susanne Miller and Heinrich Potthoff, *A History of German Social Democracy From 1848 to the Present,* Appendix 3, translated by J. A. Underwood. Reprinted by permission of Berg Publishers. **Page 269:** From Louis L. Synder, *The Blood and Iron Chancellor: A Documentary-Biography of Otto von Bismarck,* as item 73, pp. 280–283. Reprinted by permission of Wadsworth Publishing Co. **Page 272:** From David J. Lu, *Japan: A Documentary History* (Armonk, N.Y.: M. E. Sharpe, 1996) pp. 321–322. Reprinted by permission of the author. **Page 275:** From *Sources of Japanese Tradition* by William Theodore de Bary. Copyright © 1960 by Columbia University Press. Reprinted with permission of the publisher. **Page 279:** From *Peasants, Rebels, and Outcastes* by Mikiso Hane. Copyright © 1982 by Mikiso Hane. Reprinted by permission of Pantheon Books, a division of Random House, Inc.

Chapter 10   Pages 295; 296: From A. F. Wedd, *German Students' War Letters,* pp. 9–10, 19–21, 298. Copyright © 1929. Reprinted by permission of the publishers, Methuen & Co. **Page 301:** From *T. E. Lawrence: The Selected Letters* by Malcolm Brown, editor. Copyright © 1988 by Malcolm Brown. Reprinted by permission of W. W. Norton & Company, Inc., and J. M. Dent, Publisher. **Pages 304; 312:** From Melvin E. Page, *Malawian Oral History Collection.* Reprinted by permission. **Page 304:** From Joe Harris Lunn, "Kande Kamara Speaks: An Oral History of the West African Experience in France, 1914–18," in *Africa and the First World War,* edited by Melvin E. Page. Copyright © 1987 Melvin Page. Reprinted with permission of St. Martin's Press, Incorporated, and Macmillan Ltd. **Pages 306; 307:** Reprinted by permission of Forrest C. Pogue Oral History Institute, Murray State University. **Page 312:** Excerpt from "Where They Were" in *The American Songbag* by Carl Sandburg, copyright 1927 by Harcourt Brace & Company and renewed 1955 by Carl Sandburg, reprinted by permission of the publisher.

Chapter 12   Page 363: From Norman H. Baynes (ed.), *The Speeches of Adolf Hitler, April 1922– August 1939,* vol. I. Copyright © 1942. Published by Oxford University Press for the Royal Institute of International Affairs, London. Reprinted by permission of the Royal Institute of International Affairs. **Page 366:** From *Sources of Japanese Tradition* by William Theodore de Bary. Copyright © 1958 by Columbia University Press. Reprinted with permission of the publisher.

Chapter 13   Pages 382; 392; 398: From Andrée Blouin, in collaboration with Jean MacKellar, *My Country, Africa,* pp. 253–254, 258, 259, 264. Copyright © 1983. **Pages 389; 394:** From *Lumuma Speaks,* by Patrice Lumuma. Translation copyright © 1972 by Little, Brown and Company, Inc. By permission of Little, Brown and Company.

Chapter 14   Pages 417; 421: Excerpted with permission of Twayne Publishers, an imprint of Simon & Schuster Macmillan, from *Peacework: Oral Histories of Women Peace Activists* by Judith Porter Adams. Copyright © 1991 by G. K. Hall & Co. **Page 424:** From Lynne Jones (ed.), *Keeping the Peace: A Women's Peace Handbook,* pp. 23, 24, 25–26. Copyright © 1983. Reprinted by permission. **Page 425:** From Tamar Swade in Lynne Jones (ed.), *Keeping the Peace: A Women's Peace Handbook.* Copyright © 1983. Reprinted by permission of Tamar Swade. **Page 427:** Reprinted with the permission of the Center for Defense Information. **Page 429:** From Ann Snitow, "Holding the Line at

Greenham Common: Being Joyously Political in Dangerous Times," *Mother Jones,* Feb/March 1985. Reprinted with permission of *Mother Jones* magazine, © 1985. Foundation for National Progress.

Chapter 15   Pages 446; 447: From Collum Davis, Kathryn Back and Kay MacLean, *Oral History: From Tape to Type.* Copyright © 1977. Reprinted by permission of The American Library Association. **Page 448:** Interview used by permission of Robert J. Lieber. **Page 454:** Interview used by permission of Natalia Lakiza-Sachuk.